COMMUNITY CORRECTIONS

DISCARD

D1472892

COMMUNITY CORRECTIONS

STEPHEN E. DOEREN, Ph.D.
Wichita State University
Department of Administration of Justice

MARY J. HAGEMAN, Ph.D.
Virginia Commonwealth University
Department of Administration of Justice and Public Safety

Criminal Justice Studies
Anderson Publishing Co.
Cincinnati, Ohio

DISCARD

Pfeiffer College
Misenheimer, N. C. 28109

118022

Library of Congress Cataloging in Publication Data

Doeren, Stephen E.
    Community corrections.

    (Criminal justice studies)
    Includes bibliographical references and index.
    1. Community-based corrections—United States.
I. Hageman, Mary J.   II. Title.   III. Series.
HV9304.D63   364.6'8   82-4053
ISBN 0-87084-187-4   AACR2

The project editor for this book was Martin D. Schwartz, Ph.D.
Cover design by David Cambron

Table of Contents

Acknowledgments

Chapter

Acknowledgments

It is with a deep sense of gratitude and appreciation that the authors acknowledge the debt owed the many persons who have contributed in various ways to the completion of this book. We are particularly grateful to Steven J. Davies, former Deputy Director of the Kansas State Industrial Reformatory, Chuck Townsend, Executive Director of the Halfway House for Adults, Inc., Michael Lawson, Agency Administrator of Residential Homes for Boys, Inc., Marty Miller, Director of the Sedgwick County (Kansas) Pre-Trial Diversion Program and Bill Fox, Probation Officer, for consenting to interviews, supplying needed materials and/or arranging interviews with participants in community corrections programs for the "Up Close and Personal" sections of the book. Special thanks are extended to those participants in such community corrections programs as diversion, probation, parole, halfway houses, work release, study release and furloughs who were more than willing to share their experiences in such programs with the authors so that students would be aware of the advantages and shortcomings of these programs from an "insider's viewpoint."

Sincere thanks are also extended to Martin D. Schwartz for his insightful and critical comments of the manuscript. They have contributed to a better final version of the book.

Lastly, a very special thank you is expressed to our families who have endured our sacrifices and offered meaningful encouragement and emotional support throughout the period of this project. They, in no small way, contributed to the completion of this book.

S.E.D. and M.J.H.

Chapter 1
Introduction

Prisons and correctional institutions constitute the hard-core foundation of the American correctional system. Historically, the imprisonment of an offender in a correctional institution has served a variety of purposes, including incapacitation, retribution, deterrence and rehabilitation. These traditional objectives are defined as the following: *incapacitation*—to prevent offenders from committing further criminal acts and thereby protecting society by isolating them from the community; *retribution*—to serve as repayment to the victim and/or society for injuries incurred through the imposition of a deserving amount of punishment; and *deterrence*—to reduce the future incidence of criminal acts by offenders themselves and potential offenders in society through the punishment of those persons convicted of crime. By comparison, *rehabilitation*, another objective of imprisonment, is of relatively recent origin. The emphasis of rehabilitation is to change the offender so that he/she may become a law-abiding member of the community. This goal is to be achieved through the identification of those antecedent factors which contributed to the offender's criminal behavior and the subsequent provision of appropriate treatment programs, such as education, vocational training and counseling.

The objectives of the institution-based model of corrections, as cited above, have frequently been described as contradictory in nature. Furthermore, the institution-based model of corrections is a dynamic rather than static one. That is, the history of imprisonment has experienced periods in which one or more of the objectives of imprisonment have predominated while others have been de-emphasized and/or abandoned only later to have resurfaced and regained popularity.

The Effectiveness of Institutional Corrections

One of the primary concerns with the conventional institution-based corrections model is its relevance and effectiveness in achieving what, in the last analysis, according to many correctional authorities, must be considered the ultimate objective of the correctional system—changing offenders into non-offenders. Rehabilitation is, indeed, a commendable goal. However, the failure of institution-based corrections as an instrument

1

of rehabilitation has been attested to by research study after research study. The inability of the correctional system to rehabilitate those committed to their care and custody is borne out by the statistics compiled by such organizations, investigative bodies and commissions as the President's Commission on Law Enforcement and the Administration of Justice, the National Advisory Commission on Criminal Justice Standards and Goals (Corrections), the U.S. House of Representatives' Select Committee on Crime, the American Friends Service Committee, the Bureau of Criminal Statistics, State of California and the Bureau of Correctional Statistics, Washington, D.C.

Several researchers concerned with the direction and effectiveness of corrections have introduced empirical evidence which substantiates the failure of existing correctional programs in changing offenders into non-offenders. Bailey conducted a content analysis of 100 reports of empirical evaluations of correctional treatment. His analysis revealed that "on the basis of this sample of outcome reports with all of its limitations, evidence supporting the efficacy of correctional treatment is slight, inconsistent, and of questionable reliability."[1] A review of correctional research conducted by Hood led him to conclude that exposure to various correctional treatment methods made little or no difference in participating in subsequent criminal behavior.[2] Despite drawing some strong criticisms, a study conducted by Lipton, Martinson and Wilks has been viewed by many as the coup de grace on the ineffectiveness of the correctional system. After examining data on the results of 231 correctional programs, they concluded that "with few and isolated exceptions, the rehabilitative efforts that have been reported have had no appreciable effect on recidivism."[3]

Reviews of the correctional literature conducted by Skoler and Carlson have resulted in similar summary statements regarding the effectiveness of the correctional system as an instrument of rehabilitation. Although existing statistics in the correctional field are somewhat suspect and undependable, Skoler notes "... they appear nevertheless to repudiate the effectiveness of institutional treatment in the rehabilitation of both adult and juvenile offenders."[4] Carlson states "Rehabilitation is not dead yet, but the literature is littered with death warrants."[5]

Obstacles to Rehabilitation in Institutional Corrections

The late Nathan F. Leopold, Jr., himself a celebrated criminal, ex-con and strong advocate of penal reform, considered the failure of institution-based corrections as an instrument of rehabilitation to be an inevitable conclusion. Leopold states:

> Prisons simply do not rehabilitate. There are very few individuals I
> think who are rehabilitated in prison; never, I believe, are they

rehabilitated by prison. On the contrary, they are rehabilitated in spite of prison. The entire organization of most prisons is such that it puts positive obstacles in the way of rehabilitation.[6]

Veteran observers of institutional corrections, correctional practitioners, academicians and offenders themselves have identified several inherent features of the institutional corrections process which have contributed to its overall ineffectiveness in achieving its rehabilitative objective.

Institutional Violence

The contemporary correctional institution, or prison, is a violent place. Institutional violence expressed as riots, attacks by one inmate (or group of inmates) against another inmate, sexual victimization of inmates, staff mistreatment and brutality toward inmates and inmate assaults on correctional personnel, is a pervasive feature of imprisonment. Violence in correctional institutions creates an atmosphere perfectly designed to impede, if not totally defeat or destroy, any wholehearted rehabilitative program in the conventional prison. The preoccupation with personal safety on behalf of inmates and staff is not an environment which is conducive to the promotion of rehabilitation.

Episodes of intra-inmate violence are easily introduced through the presentation of specific examples. According to Toch, approximately four out of every 100 inmates confined in the California prison system were seriously injured in 1974.[7] Astrachan's study of the Louisiana State Penitentiary at Angola, Louisiana revealed that institutional violence was a problem of epidemic proportions. From 1969-1972, a total of 211 stabbings, including 11 fatal stabbings, were officially reported at that institution. During the first 11 months of 1973, a total of 137 stabbings, including nine fatal stabbings, were reported and in the following eighteen months there were 213 stabbings committed, including 20 fatal stabbings.[8] Serrill discovered an equally distressing situation at the Walpole Prison in Massachusetts. From early 1972 until January 1975, a total of 15 inmates were murdered and 100's were assaulted with pieces of pipe, stabbed and beaten by a small group of prisoners who wandered through the 500 inmate facility.[9] In a January, 1976, ruling regarding the Alabama prison system, U.S. District Court Judge Frank M. Johnson, Jr. stated, "Robbery, rape, extortion, theft and assault are everyday occurrences among the general inmate population. Rather than face this constant danger, some inmates voluntarily subject themselves to the inhuman conditions of prison isolation cells."[10] Toch's investigation also revealed that there was an average of 120-130 inmate deaths for the country as a whole in 1974-1975.[11]

Violent prison riots, attributed to such factors as racism, the institutional environment, antisocial characteristics of inmates, inadequate personnel, inadequate facilities, poor communication, insufficient funding, poor management, too rigid prison administration and inequities in the judicial system, have also complicated rehabilitative efforts. The following examples of institutional riots are illustrative of those which have occurred in U.S. prisons during the past few decades. In early February, 1980, one of the most savage prison riots in American history occurred at the New Mexico State Penitentiary at Santa Fe. This primitive episode of depravity and destruction resulted in 33 inmate deaths, 80 injuries and a pile of fragments, rubble and ashes where New Mexico's maximum-security prison used to be. Among those factors identified as contributing to the riot were: the practice of maintaining mentally ill inmates in the prison population, the mingling of serious offenders with offenders who should have been placed in medium- and minimum-security facilities, overcrowding, understaffing and lack of meaningful programs for work and recreation. Prior to the New Mexico State Penitentiary riot, it was Attica which had become the word synonymous with institutional violence for the contemporary American public.

The violent nature of the prison uprising at the Attica Correctional Center in New York State has earned this episode the characterization by some as one of the bloodiest one day encounters between Americans since the Civil War.[12] Commencing on September 9, 1971, and lasting four days, this episode of institutional violence involved approximately 1,000 inmates. During the riot a total of 33 guards were held hostage, $3 million of damage was inflicted, 32 inmates and ten guards were killed and 200 inmates were injured. Additional examples of prison riots are also easily recollected.

On February 13, 1971, a riot involving 600 inmates occurred at the Raiford State Prison in Florida. The reported causative factors of the riot included inmate demands for conjugal visits, better food, lockers and tables in cells, better vocational training, improved parole procedures, the right to have hobby supplies in cells, payment for prison work and more programs by outside entertainment. A total of 64 inmates received injuries during the riot. The demand for separate quarters for black and white inmates triggered a riot at the Cummins Prison Farm in Arkansas on November 23, 1970. Approximately 500 inmates were involved in this two day episode of institutional violence.[13] A riot involving 400 inmates occurred at Central Prison in North Carolina on April 18, 1968, which claimed the lives of five inmates. In addition, 78 inmates, two state police, and three guards were injured. The reported causes of the riot included the anger of powerful inmates regarding a drive to rid the prison of racketeering, homosexuality and extortion, and inmate grievances about more television, better food, longer visiting hours and overcrowded conditions.

Institutional violence is also expressed in the form of the sexual victimization of inmates. Although the lack of reliable statistics precludes an accurate assessment of prison homosexuality, Huffman's investigation of homosexuality within prison revealed that: "We cannot tell how frequent because we lack reliable statistics. It is, we think, so frequent that we may call it an 'occupational hazard' to being an inmate."[14] Buffum's more recent review of the various estimates of the incidence of prison homosexuality among males revealed that it generally ranges between 30 to 45 percent.[15] Jones' study of the Tennessee State Penitentiary led him to conclude that there was "the continuous commission of homosexual rapes" at that institution.[16]

One of the most publicized studies of prison homosexuality is Alan J. Davis' study entitled, "Sexual Assaults in the Philadelphia Prison System and Sheriff's Vans." Davis discovered that during a 26 month period, from June, 1966, to July, 1968, a total of 156 sexual assaults involving a minimum of 97 different victims and 176 aggressors occurred in the Philadelphia prison system.[17] These statistics reflected only those cases that could be documented and substantiated. According to Davis, these figures represented only the tip of the iceberg; in actuality, the situation was much worse.

The following passage suggests the enormity of the problem:

> In brief, we found that sexual assaults in the Philadelphia prison system are epidemic. As Superintendent Hendrick and three of the wardens admitted, virtually every slightly-built young man committed by the courts is sexually approached within a day or two after his admission to prison. Many of these young men are repeatedly raped by gangs of inmates. Others, because of the threat of gang rape, seek protection by entering into a homosexual relationship with an individual tormentor. Only the tougher and more hardened young men, and those few so obviously frail that they are immediately locked up for their own protection, escape homosexual rape.
>
> After a young man has been raped, he is marked as a sexual victim for the duration of this confinement. This mark follows him from institution to institution. Many of these young men return to their communities ashamed and full of hatred. This then, is the sexual system that exists in the Philadelphia prisons. It is a system that imposes a punishment that is not and could not be, included in the sentence of the court.[18]

Those inmates who have been the victims of homosexual encounters in prison are reluctant in many instances to confide this information to prison authorities. Inmates often have little, if any, confidence in the ability of correctional officers to protect them from retaliation if they should complain; inmates frequently want to avoid the shame and embarrassment they believe would follow a complaint. Inmates often believe that nothing will be done by prison officials anyhow, and inmates fear that if they complain they themselves will be punished by possibly being removed to another cellblock or by being denied parole.

The incidence of sexual victimization within prison vividly suggests that the prison can be a strange and often abnormally destructive environment for a human being. Although other researchers, such as John Irwin and Hans Toch, believe that the reported occurrence of sexual assaults in prison is exaggerated, it is difficult to deny that this situation creates an environment which can have serious psychological and demoralizing effects upon the inmate.

Competing Objectives: Custody and Control Versus Rehabilitation

The goals and objectives of correctional institutions have traditionally been set forth in hazy and ambiguous terms. The goals of imprisonment have usually centered upon punishment, custody and control and prisoner rehabilitation. Many authorities doubt, however, whether such goals as punishment, custody and control and rehabilitation can be mutually and simultaneously attained at satisfactory levels in the same institution. According to many penologists, this expectation of achieving such divergent goals has, in fact, contributed to the ineffectiveness of many correctional programs.

Most wardens and penal administrators, if candid, would probably acknowledge that custody and control of the inmate population is their first priority, rather than rehabilitation. Operationally, this means preventing escapes, reducing episodes of institutional violence, such as riots, major disturbances, stabbings, deaths and homosexual attacks, and minimizing and controlling the introduction of contraband, such as guns, knives and drugs, into the institution.

Custody and control of the inmate population is certainly an important and necessary objective at any correctional institution. Indeed, without such a foundation the prospects for rehabilitation are drastically reduced, if not eliminated. However, this preoccupation with security requires a substantial investment in terms of the institution's manpower, monetary appropriations and facilities. Regrettably, the rehabilitation component of the institution, as represented by treatment programs such as education, vocational training, counseling, self-improvement programs and clinical and mental health services, frequently suffers. The laudable goal of rehabilitation, consequently is only paid lip service.

This is borne out by the fact that on a nationwide basis it is estimated that only five percent of prison budgets go for those services the institutions label as treatment.[19] Furthermore, the resources allocated for treatment services amount to only about ten percent of the institutional staffs.[20] Seymour notes that only 20 percent of those people employed in correctional institutions have any connection with rehabilitation. He states that it is estimated that there is only one teacher for every 150 inmates, one social worker for every 300 inmates, one counselor for every 750 inmates, one psychiatrist for every 1,000 inmates and one vocational guidance counselor for every 2,000 inmates.[21]

These figures point to a glaring contradiction between perceived goals and the appropriate means to achieve these goals. If offenders are sent to prison for, among other things, rehabilitation, there appears to be little basis for providing them with such minimal, if any, treatment programs and treatment personnel. The failure of institutional corrections to rehabilitate offenders may be attributable to the inability of the institution to mobilize the appropriate and prerequisite resources, e.g., personnel, monetary appropriations and facilities, for rehabilitation.

Community Severance

The institutional setting of corrections isolates offenders from the community and prevents and interrupts their contact with normal social life, such as interaction with friends, relatives and family members, and participation in occupational and social life. Imprisonment, in essence, works against rehabilitation insofar as it maximizes community severance by making it difficult for inmates to maintain relationships with the "free" world to which most offenders will eventually be released and be expected to successfully readjust. The institution helps to destroy or sever positive relationships with family and friends by excessive restrictions on mail and visitation. Additionally, the remote locations of many prisons (they are often situated in rural areas far from urban centers where the majority of offenders reside) make visiting more difficult for families and friends of prisoners.

This aspect of institutionalization may, in the opinion of many authorities, destroy the offender's chances of successfully readjusting to society upon release. As noted by the President's Commission on Law Enforcement and the Administration of Justice:

> Institutions tend to isolate offenders from society, both physically and psychologically, cutting them off from schools, jobs, families and supportive influences and increases the probability that the label of criminal will be indelibly impressed upon them.[22]

With the severance of normal community contacts, offenders are often forced into undesirable substitute relationships. The offender's daily contacts are largely limited to relationsips with other prisoners. According to the National Advisory Commission on Criminal Justice Standards and Goals (Corrections):

> While severing positive relationships these restrictions have virtually forced the offender to develop strong ties with other committed offenders in substitute relationships.[23]

Nagel, a well known penologist, calls attention to the potential negative impact of such relationships in the following passage:

> ...the inmate community being distinctly antisocial, works against the goals of larger society and thereby against rehabilitative efforts. The status that inmates acquire is gauged by the intensity and consistency of their antiauthority reaction to the prison situation, and therefore the behavior of the convicts is determined by convicts themselves. Through assimilation and acculturation, prisoners take on the delinquent values, norms, customs, and general culture of the penitentiary. The prison represents—in fact is—the ultimate in social rejection, and its inmates develop increased antisocial values in order to "reject the rejectors."[24]

Even offenders themselves are cognizant of the potential deleterious effects of establishing relationships with other prisoners. As an inmate states in Sykes' *Society of Captives:*

> The worst thing about prison is that you have to live with other prisoners. One cannot reasonably expect those with whom one lives to abide by the rules of society.[25]

There is a considerable body of knowledge concerning the inmate society. Of primary importance is Clemmer's landmark study of prisons in which he identified a cohesive inmate subculture that put pressure on inmates to adopt the norms, values and culture of the inmate society. Clemmer referred to this process as "prisonization".[26]

In the institutional corrections environment in which relationships with the normal outside world are effectively severed and inmates are forced into substitute relationships with other inmates, i.e., persons who have been institutionalized because they have violated the norms of society, it would certainly not appear that the correctional environment is one in which it would be probable to change an offender into a non-offender. Insofar as the inmate social system has been defined by Cloward as one "of social relationships governed by norms that are largely at odds with those espoused by the officials and the conventional society,"[27] it is not surprising that prisons are referred to as "colleges of crime" rather than "colleges of law-abiding behavior."

Rigorous Regimentation of Inmates

Inmates are usually permitted little opportunity to engage in independent action or to exercise individual expression in prison. Their behavior is restricted and regulated by inflexible rules and regulations and a rigid schedule which dictates virtually their every activity. Practically everything an inmate does, including when and where to eat, sleep, shower, work, recreate, what to read, who to visit and what items can be possessed, is largely determined for the inmate by the prision staff rather than through a process of individual decisionmaking.[28] This situation often results in the acquisition by the inmate of a system of passive-dependent behaviors which are appropriate for institutional living but which, in many respects, are contrary to the requirements of community living. Leopold addresses the issue of the importance of inmate decisionmaking in the following manner:

> If a prison is to rehabilitate, among the things it must help to do is to buttress the individual's decision making faculty; it must help to mature the individual, to make him self-reliant. In fact, it does just the opposite: the inmate's every decision is made for him; he is permitted no latitude in making up his own mind.[29]

This message was echoed by the National Advisory Commission on Criminal Justice Standards and Goals (Corrections). It asserted that:

> The entire institutional stay should be oriented toward the offender's return to the community and the problems existing there. At present, both inmates and staff are preoccupied with problems of daily routine and the technical requirements.
>
> Closed institutions tend to close the minds of their captives... Institutionalization becomes an end in itself, reinforced by staff-sponsored values encouraging repressive and regimented behavior. This repression and regimentation is irrelevant and counter-productive to the offender's adoption of non-delinquent or non-criminalistic lifestyle in the community, where he must be able to make his own decisions.[30]

Lack of Individualized Treatment

According to Weston and Wells:

> Nothing less than an individual approach to the problems of each offender...in prison...can possibly eradicate the causative factors and maladjustments responsible for the individual's criminal behavior patterns and lead to his rehabilitation and reentry into the community. To have any broad objectives, each person must be considered a specific problem.[31]

Although the importance of classification and differential treatment of inmates are recognized by prison officials, the factors of inadequate treatment personnel, programs, budget and facilities, together with overcrowded conditions, often force prison administrators to deal with inmates on a "mass" rather than individual basis. In other words, it is difficult to consider each inmate a specific problem.

The problem of providing individualized treatment is compounded by the fact that offenders can be differentiated from one another on the basis of several salient variables which might suggest the necessity of differential processing if the goal of rehabilitation is to be achieved. Some of the more salient variables are:

1. Age
2. Socioeconomic status
3. Race
4. Marital status
5. Place of residence
6. Psychological health
7. Physiological health
8. Drug history
9. Type(s) of offense(s) for which committed, e.g., homicide, assault, rape, burglary, robbery, narcotics or dangerous drugs
10. Length of sentence
11. Offender class, i.e., the number of felonies the subject has been convicted of
12. Arrest record

The assumption needs to be made by penal administrators that some kinds of inmates benefit and others do not from exposure to certain kinds of programs as contrasted to others. This assumption is a sound one. However, the decision to place inmates in certain programs is often dictated by commonsense and tradition-bound policies rather than upon a comparison of the characteristics of inmates with their reactions to certain types of programs. All programs are not equally effective with all types of inmates. Penal administrators must initiate a purposive process within the correctional system in which they "match" offenders characterized by the appropriate background variables with those programs which have the greatest probability for rehabilitative success for them.

Overcrowding and Inadequate Facilities

Offenders are frequently confined in correctional institutions plagued by serious problems of overcrowding and depressing physical conditions. Such conditions represent a negative environment in which it is difficult to deal with inmates on a meaningful level to say nothing of the potential emotional and psychological impact upon the inmate population.

According to an American Correctional Association study, 56 of the 113 maximum security prisons still in operation were built prior to 1900 and six were constructed before 1830.[32] Characterized by a general state of neglect and disrepair, as evidenced by deteriorating conditions, peeling paint, corroded pipes and nonfunctional toilets and showers, as well as by small cells and multi-tiered cellhouses, some prisons have been described as cruel and unsuitable for human habitation.

The problem of prison overcrowding is evidenced by the fact that several states have recently been placed under court orders to reduce overcrowding in their state correctional institutions by restricting or prohibiting new admittances. Prisons have been overburdened by an excessive number of adult commitments without having the appropriate corresponding increase in correctional personnel, programs, facilities and monetary appropriations. This condition generates strain within the correctional system and retards the system's effectiveness in achieving its objectives.

Some institutions have been forced to take immediate steps to respond to the serious problem of overcrowding. At the Louisiana State Penitentiary at Angola, Louisiana, a facility designed for approximately 2,641 inmates but which prior to a recent court order housed approximately 4,000 inmates, four to five inmates were assigned quarters in cells measuring six feet by six feet.[33] South Carolina, a state whose prison population has been up to 60 percent over capacity, has also been forced to improvise in the area of quarter assignments to accommodate the excessive number of offenders committed by the criminal courts to the South Carolina Department of Corrections. At that state's Central Correctional Institution, approximately 550 to 600 inmates have been quartered in a century old cellblock which was originally designed to house 200 inmates. Small one person cells were occupied by two to three inmates.[34] Due to overcrowding, the Florida Department of Corrections prohibited the acceptance of new commitments on three separate occasions in 1974 and 1975. Four new prisons were opened in 1976 in response to the problem. However, the problem has continued to worsen. As a result, inmates have been quartered on a temporary basis in trailers, tents and warehouses as well as in cells.[35] Other noteworthy examples of overcrowding include the Pontiac Correctional Center in Illinois, which was constructed in 1871 to hold 600 prisoners and which houses about 2,000 inmates today, and the Georgia State Prison at Reidsville, which was built to hold 1,100 prisoners and which now holds nearly 2,500 inmates.

Although the average inmate population of most major prisons in the United States is approximately 2,000 prisoners, there are several correctional institutions which have held considerably more. For example, the State Prison of Southern Michigan has quartered over 6,500 inmates; San Quentin State Prison in California, the Louisiana State Penitentiary, the Ohio State Penitentiary and the Statesville Correctional Center in Illinois have each held more than 4,000 inmates; and the Florida State Prison at Raiford and the Missouri State Penitentiary at Jefferson City have each housed more than 3,000 inmates.

On October 4, 1981, the Bureau of Justice Statistics reported that the populations of prisons in the United States was at a record high. According to the report, there was a record 349,118 inmates in prison on June 30, 1981. The report referred to an unprecedented growth rate in the American prison population as evidenced by the increase of more than 20,000 inmates in state and federal prison populations in the first six months of 1981. This number exceeded the total number of inmates who were added in all of 1980. The report noted that several state prisons are now taxed to their limit by inmate populations and, in fact, some state prisons housed almost twice their rated capacity. The report mentioned that state prisons by necessity have resorted to housing inmates in tents, prefabricted buildings and abandoned military barracks. Extreme measures, such as double-bunking, have even been utilized by some states to cope with their excessive prison populations. Tougher sentencing legislation has been identified as one of the principal factors which has contributed to this startling increase. According to the report, in the past four years mandatory sentencing statutes have been passed in 37 states and determinate sentencing laws that send violent offenders to prison for a fixed number of years, without parole, have been passed in 15 states. Additionally, the states of Indiana, Illinois, Maine and New Mexico have passed laws that have done completely away with parole.[36]

Wolf, Phillips, and Fixsen offer some meaningful and insightful comments regarding the general failure of institutional treatment programs. They are of particular relevance for institution-based corrections. They state:

> If the goals of the treatment programs of our institutions are to teach a (person) to become a successful member of his community, then the treatment program must teach him to live in a bisexual world, to acquire the social skills necessary for family and community living, to achieve the vocational and academic requirements for employment, to learn to work for money, and to spend or save money for his needs. Almost none of these skills can be taught in a custodial institution. In an institution, the (person) is usually segregated on the basis of sex, taught dependency on a hospital-like routine, given little work that would transfer as a useful skill to the outside community, and taught to live on the 'welfare system' of the institution rather than to learn to be as responsible as possible for his own needs.[37]

The Need For Alternatives to Institutional Corrections

A search for alternatives to the correctional system has been inspired by the problems inherent in the institution-based corrections process, its great expense and primarily by its history of repeated failure as an instrument of rehabilitation. One of the principal events that has paramount significance for the future of corrections is the development of programs for offenders which substitute treatment in the community for institutionalization or imprisonment. Collectively, these programs constitute what is termed "community-based corrections."

The community-based corrections model, based upon a philosophy of reintegration, received great impetus from the President's Commission on Law Enforcement and the Administration of Justice. The Commission concluded that: "The goal of reintegration is likely to be furthered much more readily by working with offenders in the community than by incarceration."[38] In recommending the utilization of community-based corrections for all but the hard-core offenders, the Corrections Task Force of the President's Commission on Law Enforcement and the Administration of Justice stated:

> The task of corrections, therefore, includes building or rebuilding solid ties between the offender and the community, integrating or reintegrating the offender into community life-restoring family ties, obtaining employment and education, securing in the large sense a place for the offender in the routine functioning of society. This requires not only efforts directed towards changing the individual offender, which have been almost the exclusive focus of rehabilitation, but also mobilization and change of the community and its institutions.[39]

Nora Klapmuts of the National Council on Crime and Delinquency and Bennett J. Cooper, the former Director of the Ohio Department of Corrections, echoed the message of the President's Commission in calling attention to the inability of institutional corrections to successfully change the offender and the important implications this has for shifting to a community-based treatment strategy. Klapmuts states:

> The distinctive characteristic of the current reform effort is its emphasis in abolishing rather than in improving the prison... In the light of criminological theory of the past decades, which views crime and delinquency as symptoms of disorganization of the community as much as of individual personalities—or even as a product of an inadequate mesh between the two—imprisonment is coming to be viewed as hopelessly anachronistic. It is now widely believed that reintegration of the offender with the law-abiding community—the primary goal of the 'new' correction—cannot be accomplished by isolating the offender in an artificial custodial setting.[40]

In a similar vein, Cooper notes: "It's just impossible and illogical that you take persons away from normal society and put them in an abnormal society (a prison) and expect then to adjust to the community (when they are released from prison)."[41]

A Definition of Community-Based Corrections

Considerable confusion exists concerning the concept of community-based corrections. This is evidenced by the popularly held misconceptions that surround the concept. In an effort to clarify this concept, Coates has attempted to isolate these misconceptions and dispel them on the basis of their flaws in reasoning. Lastly, he suggests those features which meaningfully serve as a basis for making a determination as to whether or not a program is deserving of the community-based classification.

According to Coates, the following five statements consitute the leading misconceptions surrounding the concept of "community-based":

1. It is community-based because it is so labeled.
2. It is community-based because others are not.
3. If it is located in a community, then it is community-based.
4. Programs with minimal control or supervision are community-based.
5. Programs operated by private agencies rather than by the state are community-based.[42]

Coates has vehemently criticized each of the above methods as a means of defining "community-based" because whether taken singularly or collectively they fail to clarify the importance of focusing on *community relationships* as the key set of variables in determining the degree to which a program is community-based.

It is community-based because it is so labeled. Coates cautions that programs are often referred to or are defined as community-based solely on the basis of being labeled as such by administrators. When queried as to what is a community-based program, administrators frequently respond by saying "Program X is a community-based program." However, this labeling decision has usually not been based upon a program's correspondence or congruence with any universal set of criteria or guidelines that can be generalized from one social system to another. Consequently, a program identified as community-based in system A may not be regarded as community-based in system B. In essence, programs have frequently been identified as community-based on the basis of an unsatisfactory and unconscientious labeling process rather than upon their compliance with an operationalized definition of "community-based".

It is community-based because others are not. This frequently encountered misconception simply describes what a community-based program is not. It too, however, neglects to analyze and identify the specific characteristics of community-based programs. Administrators relying on this approach will often resort to describing those programs as community-based which are different from the traditional methods of treating the offender. However, no effort is introduced to identify those characteristics or criteria which would concretely establish a program as community-based.

If it is located in a community, then it is community-based. Coates notes that of all the criteria employed to distinguish between institution-based and community-based programs, location is the most frequently utilized.

However, it is also an unsatisfactory indicator of the degree to which a program is community-based. It should be remembered that many institutions are located in communities just as are programs such as halfway houses. The crucial point is that just because a program is located in a "community" is no assurance that it will develop and establish ties with that community. As Coates points out: "Too many programs are merely islands within the community—*small* institutions, but institutions nevertheless."[43] This faulty line of thinking is illustrative of what social scientists call the "geographic fallacy" which permeates much of our thinking about communities. People often have the tendency to think of a community as an area with rather easily identifiable geographic boundaries. It is true that any social unit, including a community, must occupy physical space. However, a community as a sociological concept must be perceived principally as occupying social rather than physical space. Consequently, a community is not an area but a social system. It is delineated in terms of role relationships, or community ties, and not simply location.

Programs with minimal control or supervision are community-based. According to Coates, many people mistakenly identify as community-based programs those which involve little supervision and, therefore, reduced community protection. Coates acknowledges that some community-based programs do entail little overt supervision but by the same token the same can be said for some institutional programs which have less restrictive components, such as study release and furloughs. Therefore, degrees of control and supervision do not discriminate sufficiently enough between institution-based and community-based programs.

Programs operated by private agencies rather than by the state are community-based. Whether a program is administered by the public or private sector is of little relevance in making a determination as to whether a program is community-based. Coates notes that programs operated by private agencies can be isolated from community groups and services to the same degree as state operated programs. The significant point is not whether the program is operated by the state or by private agencies but whether the program has been able to establish and maintain ties with community groups and services.

If labeling, location, degree of control and supervision, the nature of program administration (public or private) and variance from traditional treatment approaches do not provide an adequate basis by which to identify the degree to which a program is "community-based," the pertinent question becomes, "What, then, is the salient factor?" Coates provides the answer in the following passage:

> The idea of community is central to the conceptualization of community-based corrections... community (means) the smallest

local territory that incorporates a network of relationships
providing most of the goods and services required by persons living
within the boundaries of the territory. These services include
schools, employment, food distribution, banks, churches, and
sanitation services.

How should we now conceive of community-based corrections?
Specifically, how do we isolate those essential qualities that make
some programs more community based than others?

The words *community-based* focus attention on the nature of the
links between programs and the community. Key variables that
sharply focus on this notion of linkage and provide a basis for
differentiating among programs are the *extent* and *quality* of the
relationships among program staff, clients, and the community in
which the program is located...The nature of these client and staff
relationships with the community provides the underpinning for a
continuum of services ranging from the least to the most community
based...

The frequency and duration of community relationships are
important in this concept of community-based corrections, but the
quality of relationships is especially so...The relationships of
particular interest here are those that support the efforts of
offenders to become re-established and functioning in legitimate
roles. These include relationships that encourage clients and enable
them to appreciate their self-worth, that match community-
resources to client needs, and that advocate better community
resources and freer access to those resources.[44]

Therefore, it is the type and degree of effort involved in establishing
meaningful ties or relationships between the offender and the community
which provides a relevant basis for differentiation. Utilizing this factor as a
foundation, *community-based corrections may be defined as: any
correctional-related activity purposively aimed at directly assisting and
supporting the efforts of offenders to establish meaningful ties or
relationships with the community for the specific purpose of becoming
reestablished and functional in legitimate roles in the community.* Clearly
and unmistakably, then, the goal of community-based corrections is the
successful reintegration of the offender into the community.

Defined in this manner, there are a wide variety of programs which
could conceivably fall within the parameters of community-based
corrections, including diversion, probation, parole, work release, study
release, furloughs and halfway houses.

The Advantages of Community-Based Corrections

The proponents of community-based corrections have vigorously
encouraged its adoption as an alternative to imprisonment. Most advocates

have emphasized the practical values of community-based correctional programs; others have stressed their social values.

Coates has conveniently summarized the position of those advocating community-based corrections on the basis of their practical values and advantages:

1. Community-based settings will be more humane than the large, ware-housing, congregate, or cottage based institutions.
2. The further an individual is allowed to penetrate the formal criminal justice system the more difficult it is for him to be successfully retrieved and retained in the community. Providing services for individuals in localized community settings is supposed to minimize commitments and exposure to the more repressive institutions.
3. Community-based services are less costly than institutional services.
4. Community-based services, because staff and clients are closer to the community resources, will improve the probability of successful client reintegration.[45]

Austin MacCormick, a noted penologist, is considered to be one of the leading spokesmen advocating the adoption of community-based corrections on the merits of their social values. He states:

1. By practical demonstration [the community-based correctional program] confirms the validity of the correctional approach to the offender as opposed to the purely punitive approach. Thus it advances our social thinking and social philosophy another notch and pegs it fair. Social progress in general is the sum total, but it also stimulates progress in related fields. This is particularly true of the fields that are concerned with socially disapproved behavior.
2. It helps maintain the unity of society by holding families together. It strengthens the concept of individual responsibility by permitting and requiring the offender with a family to support it, and to carry out his other family responsibilities conscientiously.
3. It strengthens the concept of community responsibility to the individual by keeping the offender within the community instead of rejecting him from it and by bringing all the community's resources to bear on his problems. Conversely, it does not let him escape his responsibility to the community as a whole, not merely to his family, but requires him to function as a citizen and helps him to do so.
4. It increases the public's understanding and acceptance of crime and delinquency as social problems which must be viewed in the frame of the total social structure and not in the narrow frame of law enforcement.

5. It strengthens the concept of socialized justice by demonstrating that the interests of the individual and of society are not antithetical, not separate but inseparable.[46]

A Comparison of Institution-Based And Community-Based Corrections

The previous discussion indicates that there are some significant differences between the institution-based and community-based correctional models. Figure 1.1 compares the two models on the dimensions of monetary cost, environmental conditions, location, philosophical basis and effectiveness as an instrument of rehabilitation. (These dimensions will be treated on a more elaborate basis in later chapters.)

It should be noted that, on the basis of the information presently available on the success rates of traditional correctional institutions, it can be safely stated that they have not been effective. However, in recommending community-based corrections as a viable alternative to imprisonment, caution must be exercised not to defend this approach more vigorously than it deserves at this point in time. Although community-based corrections has certain obvious advantages over institution-based corrections, total reliance on community-based programs is unrealistic, impractical and inappropriate insofar as some offenders are extremely dangerous and require institutionalization. However, the employment of community-based alternatives is deserving of expansion insofar as a substantial number of offenders presently incarcerated are no more dangerous than many of those placed on probation. Restricting imprisonment to hard-core dangerous offenders and placing minor

Figure 1.1   A Comparison of Institution-Based and Community-Based Corrections.

CHARACTERISTIC	COMMUNITY-BASED	INSTITUTION-BASED
Monetary Cost	Less Costly	More Costly
Environmental Conditions	Natural: Promotes Normal Social and Community Relationships	Artificial: Promotes Abnormal Social Relationships
Location	Treatment is Based in the Community	Treatment is Based in an Institutional/Custodial Setting
Effectiveness as an Instrument of Rehabilitation	Questionable Effectiveness; At Least as Effective as Institution-Based Corrections	Clearly Not Effective
Philosophical Basis	Reintegration	Incapacitation/Retribution/Deterrence/Rehabilitation

offenders and non-violent offenders in some variant of community-based corrections program would seem to provide less expensive, more humane treatment, with at least an equal, if not a better, chance for success than imprisonment.

Community-based corrections is not, and should not, be viewed as a panacea for the massive problems presently being experienced by our correctional system. Rather, it should be perceived as one positive alternative to institution-based corrections that is deserving of experimentation since it offers definite advantages in terms of financial, social and human costs.

Notes

1. Walter C. Bailey, "Correctional Outcome: An Evaluation of 100 Reports," *Journal of Criminal Law, Criminology and Police Science*, Volume 57 (June, 1966), p. 157.

2. R.C. Hood, "Research on the Effectiveness of Punishments and Treatments," in *The Criminal in Confinement*, edited by Leon Radzinowicz and Marvin E. Wolfgang (New York: Basic Books, 1971), p. 159.

3. Robert Martinson, "What Works? - Questions and Answers about Prison Reform," *The Public Interest*, Volume 35 (Spring, 1974), p. 25.

4. D. Skoler, "Future Trends in Juvenile and Adult Community-Based Corrections," *Juvenile Court Judges Journal*, Volume 21 (1971), p. 98.

5. R. Carlson, *The Dilemma of Corrections* (Lexington, Massachusetts: Lexington Books, D.C. Heath and Company, 1976), p. 32.

6. Nathan F.Leopold, Jr., "Imprisonment Has No Future in a Free Society," *Key Issues: A Journal of Controversial Issues in Criminology*, Volume 2 (1965), p. 29.

7. H. Toch, *Police, Prisons, and the Problems of Violence* (Rockville, Maryland: National Institute of Mental Health Center for Studies of Crime and Delinquency, 1977), p. 52.

8. A. Astrachan, "Profile/Louisiana," *Corrections Magazine*, Volume 2 (September/October, 1975), p. 19.

9. M.S. Serrill, "Walpole Prison: After the Storm," *Corrections Magazine*, Volume 2 (November/December, 1975), pp. 49-50.

10. Toch, *Police, Prisons*, p. 52.

11. Ibid.

12. New York State Special Commission of Attica, *Attica (The Official Report of the New York State Special Commission on Attica)* (New York: Praeger Publishers, 1972), p. xi.

13. South Carolina Department of Corrections, *Collective Violence in Correctional Institutions: A Search for Causes* (Columbia, South Carolina: State Printing Company, 1973), p. 70.

14. A.V. Huffman, "Sex Deviation in a Prison Community," *Journal of Social Therapy*, Volume 6 (1960), p. 180.

15. P.C. Buffum, *Homosexuality in Prison* (Washington D.C.: U.S. Government Printing Office, 1972).

16. David A. Jones, *The Health Risks of Imprisonment* (Lexington, Massachusetts: D.C. Heath and Company, 1976), p. 156.

17. A.J. Davis, "Sexual Assaults in the Philadelphia Prison System and Sheriff's Vans," *Transaction* (December, 1968), pp. 8-16.

18. Ibid., p. 9.

19. Jessica Mitford, *Kind and Unusual Punishment: The Prison Business* (New York: Alfred A. Knopf, 1973), p. 97.

20. American Correctional Association, *Manual of Correctional Standards* (Washington, D.C.: American Correctional Association, 1966).

21. W.N. Seymour, *Why Justice Fails* (New York: William Morrow and Company, 1973).

22. President's Commission on Law Enforcement and Administration of Justice, *The Challenge of Crime in a Free Society* (Washington, D.C.: U.S. Government Printing Office, 1967), p. 165.

23. National Advisory Commission on Criminal Justice Standards and Goals, *Corrections* (Washington, D.C.: U.S. Government Printing Office, 1973), p. 364.

24. W.G. Nagel, "With Friends Like These Who Needs Enemies?", *Crime and Delinquency* (July, 1974), p. 231.

25. G. Sykes, *The Society of Captives* (Princeton, New Jersey: Princeton University Press, 1958), pp. 70-78.

26. D. Clemmer, *The Prison Community* (New York: Holt, Reinhart and Winston, 1940).

27. Richard A. Cloward, "Social Control in the Prison," in *Theoretical Studies in Social Organization of the Prision*, edited by Richard A. Cloward, Donald R. Cressey, George H. Grosser, Richard McCleery, Lloyd E. Ohlin, Gresham M. Sykes and Sheldon L. Messinger (New York: Social Science Research Council, 1960), p. 21.

28. Gresham M. Sykes, *Crime and Society* (New York: Random House, 1967), p. 179.

29. Leopold, "Imprisonment Has No Future," p. 29.

30. National Advisory Commission on Criminal Justice Standards and Goals, *Corrections*, p. 364.

31. P.B. Weston and K.M. Wells, *Criminal Justice* (Pacific Palisades, California: Goodyear Publishing Company, Inc., 1976), p. 10.

32. American Correctional Association, *1971 Directory of Institutions and Agencies of America, Canada and Great Britain* (College Park, Maryland: American Correctional Association, 1971).

33. Astrachan, "Profile/Louisiana," p. 302.

34. S. Gettinger, "U.S. Prison Population Hits All-Time High," *Corrections Magazine* Volume 2 (March, 1976), p. 12.

35. R. Wilson, "U.S. Prison Population Sets Another Record," *Corrections Magazine*, Volume 3 (March, 1977), pp. 15-16.

36. Washington Post Services, "Population of Prisons Hits Peak," *The Wichita Eagle-Beacon*, October 5, 1981, pp. 1A and 6A.

37. Montrose M. Wolf, Elery L. Phillips, and Dean L. Fixsen, "The Teaching Family: A New Model for the Treatment of Deviant Child Behavior in the Community," in *Behavior Modification*, edited by Sidney W. Byou and Emilio Ribes-Inesta (New York Academic Press, 1972), pp. 51-52.

38. President's Commission of Law Enforcement and Administration of Justice, *The Challenge of Crime in a Free Society*, p. 165.
39. Corrections Task Force of the President's Commission on Law Enforcement and the Administration of Justice, *Task Force Report: Corrections* (Washington, D.C.: U.S. Government Printing Office, 1967), p. 7.
40. N. Klapmust, "Community Alternatives to Prison," *Crime and Delinquency* (June, 1973), p. 305.
41. B.J. Cooper, Quoted in *Corrections in the Community*, edited by E.E. Miller and M.R. Montilla (Reston, Virginia: Reston Publishing Company, 1977), p. v.
42. R.J. Coates, "Community-Based Corrections: Concept, Impact, Dangers," in *Juvenile Correctional Reform in Massachusetts*, edited by L. E. Ohlin, A.D. Miller and R.J. Coates (Washinton, D.C.: U.S. Government Printing Office, 1976), p. 25.
43. Ibid.
44. Ibid., pp. 23-24.
45. Ibid., p. 29.
46. Austin MacCormick, "The Potential Value of Probation," *Federal Probation*, Volume 19 (March, 1955), pp. 4-5.

Chapter 2
Diversion

Diversion, as both a concept and a process, is not new, although it has recently been utilized to develop all kinds of different programs. As a concept, diversion usually is defined as a *formally acknowledged and organized program to remove an offender from the traditional processing* through the criminal or juvenile justice system.

Purpose

Due to the recommendations by the American Bar Association and the Corrections Task Force of the National Advisory Commission on Criminal Justice, diversion programs have been implemented in communities throughout the United States. Most of these diversion programs have been financed in their initial years by funds from the Law Enforcement Assistance Administration in the U.S. Department of Justice. In general, but not necessarily in all programs, the goals of diversion are:

1. To provide the criminal justice system with a more flexible approach than does the traditional process in order that the system (a) may be more responsive to the needs of defendants and society, and (b) may preserve its energies to effectively process cases that would be more appropriately handled through the adversary system.

2. To provide defendants with an opportunity to avoid the consequences of criminal processing, to avoid conviction and the consequences of criminal conviction.

3. To help in deterring and reducing criminal activities by offering to the defendant the necessary opportunities to affect such changes as are necessary; at a minimum to demonstrate whether such reduction took place.

4. To allocate available resources to keep the justice system running at an optimum level. (This may include decreasing jail and prison populations in institutions already overcrowded.)

5. To allow alleged offenders to maintain the responsibility and burdens of making decisions and managing one's own life.

6. To permit the individual to provide for himself/herself and family through employment.
7. To permit the individual to restitute to the victim.[1]

Based upon explicit criteria of eligibility, diversion programs generally seek to provide clients with counseling and other services in areas such as education, employment, finances, health, substance abuse and the like. Programs vary with respect to eligible offenses and operating procedures. Eligibility requires that the offender does not present a clear and present danger to society and that no constructive purpose would be served by conviction and sentence.

Diversion programs vary in philosophy and practice from one jurisdiction to another. Yet, theoretically the programs are to benefit the offender, the criminal justice system and society.

History

Diversion is not a new practice. One might consider John Augustus in Boston, 1841, as developing a diversion program when he practiced an alternative to jail called probation. John Augustus, the local cobbler, attended the police court in that city and decided to stand bail for a man charged with being a common drunkard. The court permitted the defendant to leave with Mr. Augustus, and he was ordered to appear for sentence in three weeks.

When that time came, the defendant appeared showing such convincing signs of reform that the judge waived the usual penalty— imprisonment in the House of Corrections. Instead, the judge imposed a nominal fine of one cent and court costs. Although the early cases handled by Augustus were adult males charged with common drunkenness, by the time he died (some eighteen years later) he had "bailed on probation some 2,000 persons including women, children and persons charged with a wide variety of offenses."[2]

The establishment of the Juvenile Court in Cook County, Illinois, in 1899, was another early diversion program. Prior to 1899, any person over the age of eight was processed through the criminal justice system. Some humane communities, like New York City in 1825, provided a separate "prison" for young people called the House of Refuge. The word "refuge" was a misnomer at best, for knowing about the treatment and conditions in those institutions gives additional understanding of the violence which periodically wracked the refuges. Knifings upon other children as well as guards, massive escapes and fires that devastated and destroyed parts of the refuges, caused many city fathers to question the use of these facilities. As the years progressed and more cities built separate facilities for children, the problem only intensified. In fact, in 1863, the state prison inspectors called the Boston House "too much of a prison, too little an institution of instruction, too much the residence of law and punishment, too little the home of grace and culture."[3]

The violent and exploitative nature of these early Houses of Refuge and reform schools raised concern and questions among the citizenry as to the ability of the state to reform young people. Such was the case in Chicago, when a group of women were influenced in a subtle manner by the entirely male Chicago Bar Association and Catholic philanthropic organization. These women, called "child-savers" by some, proposed to the state legislators a separate court for juveniles.[4] The proposed juvenile court would process only salvageable children and place them on probation as opposed to sending them to the 65 reformatories that had been established throughout the United States prior to 1900.[5]

Even today, only 28 states have exclusive, original jurisdiction over all children below a certain age. In the remaining 22 states, the juvenile court faces a host of restrictions on whom it can adjudicate. For example, in eight states, if a child has committed a homicide, the child never sees the officials in the juvenile court. The mandatory transfer for homicides or any other capital or life-term offenses means the child is tried in criminal court just as centuries before.[6]

Juvenile Diversion

The juvenile court as a social experiment came under attack from several directions in the 1960's. Social groups, parents' organizations, associations of judges and probation officers, to mention only a few, wrote *amicus curiae* briefs to the Supreme Court for the landmark decision *In re Gault* (1967). Yet, the real direction of the Court had been established in an earlier case, *Kent* v. *U.S.* (1966). Justice Fortas, writing for five members of the Court, expressed the fact in *Kent*, that there was evidence (lack of personnel, facilities and techniques to perform adequately as representatives of the state in a *parens patriae* capacity) for grounds of concern. As he saw it, the child received the worst of both worlds in that he received neither the protections accorded to adults nor the solicitous care and regeneration treatment postulated for children.[7]

Proponents of "radical nonintervention" in the 1960's - 1970's argued that children should be diverted from the exceedingly costly and corruptible training schools into less punitive methods that could be developed by community treatment programs under the auspices of youth service bureaus.[8] Some states, like New York, began to develop such bureaus. For example, in 1975, the juvenile judge in New York City had several options in which he could "sentence" a youngster, i.e., drug or alcohol program, state training school, mental health facility, state-run community residence, home or probation, private agency, state adult system or the New York City Division of Special Services for Children, including group home, foster home or private agency. Keep in mind that police and juvenile courts have been *informally* utilizing diversion for years. In fact, in 1975, police in New York City reported 17,000 felony cases involving juveniles. Yet, in that same year, only 1,800 children reached the last stage—sentencing.[9]

For a moment, let us amplify the point of distinction between informal and formal diversion. The literature is rich with both empirical studies and personal experiences which show that police may release offenders either with an informal caution or a formal caution.[10] This element of discretion on the part of the police officer is affected by the size of the community, the seriousness of the offense and "police perception of the function and effectiveness of the juvenile court."[11] Other factors include the "need to provide help or guidance—reflected, for example, in the criteria of family conditions and status; and the probability of offending in the future, reflected in the criteria of previous record, companions, work record, dress and demeanor."[12]

In addition, once a juvenile offender is referred by the police to the probation department of the juvenile court, the officials may release the offenders, refer them to court or place them on informal supervision. In short, throughout the criminal justice system, agents exercise their discretion to arrest or prosecute such that informal diversion occurs. Thus, a community may have many more individuals come into the juvenile justice system, but only a few actually reach the last stage of sentencing.

To handle this problem of informal and formal diversion, more *formalized* programs were developed to assist juveniles through the innovative and experimental programs developed by such states as New York. Some of the formalized diversion programs to be discussed modeled themselves around earlier, more tradtional approaches, like forestry camps and psychiatric treatment centers. A newer model of diversion is exhibited by Massachusetts, which, like New York, developed newer community-based services.

Forestry Camps

California established a short-lived probation camp in 1927 in Riverside County which terminated in 1931 because of lack of funds. Then, the state began a camp for transient boys. The Youth Authority Act of 1941, as amended in 1943, established state camps as part of the many alternatives developed as a division of the total program of state training facilities for delinquents. Various other states began experimenting with camps so that, by 1971, 24 states operated 67 camps. The camps were developed to deal with a small capacity of persons in simple structures so that through work-centered activities, a youth and his immediate supervisor (counselor) could develop a close relationship.[13]

Camp Brace, a minimum security camp operated by the New York State Division for Youth during the 1970's, had placement for about 45 youths. The camp was called an "opportunity camp." It was designed to serve the needs of pre-delinquent boys aged 15, 16 and 17 years who came to the camp on a voluntary basis. (Usually, someone in the court system would ask the youth if they would like to go.) The idea was to provide a home away from the environment in which the youth was experiencing difficulties, i.e., home, school, etc. Public officials knew that if the youth were allowed to continue in that present pattern in their home environment, it would lead to serious delinquent behavior.

As with most camps, Camp Brace did not accept youth with serious emotional problems or a history of violence. The therapeutic community in the camp utilized reality therapy (discussed in greater detail in Chapter Ten). Many of the young people appreciated having three meals a day, working and learning—activities that were not common in their lives. Yet, the program was a short term program—one year or less with the average stay about six months.

More recently, Camp Brace has been made into a moderately secure facility. The shift in the public attitude to get "tough" with youth has meant that the camp now accepts youth who have committed more serious offenses than misdemeanors and who have been placed there by the Family Court. In addition, gestalt therapy has been added to reality therapy as a program for behavioral change.

Psychiatric Training Centers

Another traditional attempt at diversion centered around the seriously maladjusted child. These children, as aggressive, unstable persons in training schools, were often punished into submission or placed in a dark isolation room for specific periods of time without modifying their behaviors. These emotionally disturbed youngsters were neither completely psychotic nor feebleminded. Redl and Wineman[14] called them "children who hate" and were instrumental in establishing a group home to help mitigate the early and severe parental rejection these children felt.

Another example is the Annex of State Training Schools for Boys, Goshen, New York, which, from 1947 to the present, has become a highly therapeutic community with carefully planned and supervised activities. Professional guidance for the staff and treatment of the boys comes from psychiatrists, psychologists and social workers. Through an atmosphere of warmth, understanding and controls, such as denial of privileges, the youth is led to a clear understanding of himself and the effect his behavior has on others so as to help the youth control his own behavior.[15]

Diversion in Massachusetts

Under the leadership of Dr. Jerome Miller (now in Illinois), Massachusetts closed all training schools and set up alternative programs for juveniles who came to the attention of the courts. Miller established 17 group homes scattered around the state to function as therapeutic communities with intensive counseling, group and family therapy and vocational and education programs. For the first- or second-time offenders he set up a four week intensive training program in survival techniques called the Homeward Bound Program on Cape Cod. The test of the course was the actual survival of a two week solo experience in the wilderness. This program, similar to ones established in our western states, has established that youths gain a greater confidence in their ability to provide for themselves as well as an understanding of who they are and how they fit into this universe. Miller also made full use of the more traditional alternatives including foster homes, neighborhood youth camps, independent placement and probation. For the children who truly needed intensive, secure treatment, units staffed with psychiatric and social workers were established in detention homes throughout the state.[16]

At the time, this so-called "radical" reorganization of the Department of Youth Services over a period of only a few years by Miller brought confusion and controversy. Today, these programs have become accepted and many of the problems have been worked out. Now this state serves as a model for others in developing such programs.

Adult Diversion

The application of diversion programs to adult offenders began early in the 1960's. Carter accounts for this emphasis on diversion with "three factors: (1) increasing recognition of deficiencies in the nonsystem of justice; (2) rediscovery of the ancient truth that the community significantly impacts upon behavior; and (3) growing demands of the citizenry to be active participants in the affairs of government."[17]

The criminal justice system always has employed, and probably always will employ the concept of discretion: pre-charge conferences, plea-bargaining and early dispositions without trial to relieve overburdened courts. Their flexibility and informality were adaptable to the individualized, rapid handling of cases. However, the merits of administrative conveniences had to be weighed against the lack of safeguards for the offender. In the absence of clear policy guidelines, dispositions that are too informal have a tendency to discount the decisionmaker's accountability, and undue leniency or coercion can result.[18] The President's Commission on Law Enforcement and Administration of Justice[19] was one of the first authoritative expressions of the desirability of diversion. Although that report noted that many offenders were in need of treatment or supervision rather than criminal sanctions, the report also noted that prosecutors lack legitimate alternatives to charging or dismissing. To answer this need for fairness, the American Bar Association developed standards and policy guidelines for pre-trial diversion and established a National Pre-Trial Diversion Service Center[20] with the express purpose of stimulating pre-trial diversion programs and acting as a clearinghouse for gathering data on the progress, problems and measures of success. At the end of 1973, the ABA listed 57 pre-trial intervention programs in 24 states. By June, 1975, there were six more states with legislation concerning pre-trial intervention and 117 other identifiable programs functioning in urban centers.[21]

Since diversion programs can and have been created by different groups to intervene at any of the stages in the prosecution of persons accused of criminal offenses, diversion programs are known by many different titles. To facilitate the discussion and to give a general understanding as to how they operate, diversion will be explained as pre-trial, pre-arrest, and post-trial.

Pre-Trial Diversion

One of the most common forms of pre-trial diversion has been the "release on own recognizance" (ROR)—the pre-trial release of an accused person without the necessity of a money bond. ROR programs, pioneered by the Vera Institute of Justice in an experiment called "The Manhattan Bail Project" which began in 1961, developed out of a growing recognition that the bail system often constituted an unsatisfactory pre-trial release procedure. The bail system is considered unsatisfactory for the following reasons: (1) it discriminates against the poor; (2) it contributes to the high costs of criminal justice system operations because the state must pay to detain those alleged offenders in jail who are unable to pay bail; (3) it is maintained by some authorities that those persons detained in jail and awaiting trial are more likely to receive subsequent convictions than those persons released on bail; and (4) those individuals who are unable to pay bail are subjected to the potentially dehumanizing and degrading effects of the detention process.

The Vera Institute's "Manhattan Bail Project" developed a release recommendation to provide alternatives to cash bail for indigents and others unable to raise the funds for release. Their release recommendation was based on an assessment of the offender's prior record, family and community ties, health, employment or school information and length of residence in the community. The verified information was scored by assigning numerical weights to each area, and, depending on the total score, was used in making a recommendation for release or detainment.

Through this method, the courts in New York City were able to increase the use of ROR without a subsequent increase in the rate of failure to appear in court.[22] This pioneering program not only laid the groundwork for adult pre-trial diversion programs; it also gave such programs visibility.

Several other events merit attention in the development of pre-trial diversion programs. For example, in 1965, the first formal deferred-prosecution program for adults was originated by Robert F. Leonard, the presecutor of Genesee County (Flint), Michigan. Two years later, in 1967, the U.S. Department of Labor funded two pilot court-based pre-trial intervention programs in New York City (Manhattan Court Employment Project) and Washington, D.C. (Project Crossroads). This triad of programs is often identified as comprising the deferred prosecution, now commonly called pre-trial intervention.[23]

Formal statements of endorsement representing the need for and expansion of diversionary programs were provided by such bodies as the President's Commission on Law Enforcement and Administration of Justice (1967), the American Correctional Association (1971) and the National Advisory Commission on Criminal Justice Standards and Goals (1973). Together with funding provided by the Law Enforcement Assistance Administration (LEAA) and the U.S. Department of Justice, this led to the proliferation of pre-trial diversion programs.

Also of significance in this movement toward the adoption of pre-trial diversion programs was the establishment of The National Pre-Trial Intervention Service Center in Washington, D.C., in 1971, by the American Bar Association. This organization has been instrumental in developing pre-trial intervention program standards and guidelines, and providing technical assistance and published materials to existent programs and agencies interested in beginning programs.

If the intervention occurs before the trial stage, the diversion program is called pre-trial intervention. This term means that the individual has been formally arrested and charges brought before the court by the prosecutor.

In the federal system and some states the process of pre-trial intervention is referred to as "deferred prosecution," while other states may refer to it as "probation without adjudication" or "accelerated rehabilitation disposition." Pre-trial diversion programs operate upon the assumptions that there are some individuals who would benefit more by not going completely through the criminal justice system and possibly to prison. When a "first-time" offender or someone acting under mitigating circumstances is viewed by the police, the prosecutor, the judge, the victim and other authorities as a "good risk" to remain in the community so as to receive the needed human services, the offender is placed under voluntary supervision. At the time of arraignment, eligible individuals are diverted from the process of criminal prosecution so as to participate in a supervised program, such as attending school or college, getting a job or arranging for futher job training. The suspension of the criminal prosecution for a specific period of time is to permit the offender either to complete successfully his/her program and/or to demonstrate a lawful lifestyle. Most pre-trial diversion programs are conditional in the sense that, if the offender fails to live up to the agreements or gets arrested for other acts, the offender is removed from the program and criminal prosecution is resumed for the first offense, as well as for the second offense.

It is interesting to note that *The Directory of Criminal Justice Diversion Programs for 1976* listed 148 active programs in 37 states. In addition, New Jersey and Pennsylvania have State Supreme Court rules authorizing pre-trial intervention on a statewide basis.[24]

Pre-trial diversions tend to share these characteristics: (a) a voluntary program—the choice of whether to accept the diversion option, once offered, is left to the potential client, i.e., the defendant or alleged offender; (b) program intervention occurs prior to adjudication; (c) services are provided to the client; and (d) program completion results in a dismissal or nonfiling of criminal charges.

Most of these programs focus on first-time offenders, and, in some cases, second offenders charged with less serious offenses. Thus, these programs divert offenders who would most likely receive probation if they were normally processed through the courts. Intervention, however, occurs much earlier with referrals to community resources. More importantly, successful participants are free from a record of criminal conviction and the courts are saved from the higher costs of prosecution.

Administration/Process

Criteria

Criteria for participation in a pre-trial diversion program can be established by the solicitation of input from several sources, i.e., community and other criminal justice agencies. Usually, to be eligible for participation, an individual has to be evaluated along the following criteria (which may vary depending upon the program and its geographic location):

1. The relative age of the alleged offender.
2. The nature of the alleged offense and its impact on the public sense of security and justice.
3. Drug addiction, alcoholism or mental stability of the alleged offender.
4. The willingness of the individual to participate in the project and the amenability of the individual to treatment.

5. The alleged offender's community reputation and the impact of criminal charges on persons other than the alleged offender.
6. The alleged offender's history of physical violence.
7. The alleged offender's involvement with organized crime.
8. The alleged offender's history of criminality.
9. The need to pursue criminal conviction.[25]

The target age is usually between 17 and 25. The diversion programs are usually limited to non-violent criminals and misdemeanants. Persons who have committed violent crimes or who possess an extensive criminal history usually are not eligible for the project. If the alleged offender demonstrates unstable behavior and/or addiction to drugs or alcoholism, he/she is usually referred for psychological or psychiatric assistance outside the jurisdiction of these projects. In short, diversion programs are completely voluntary and require the full desire, cooperation and consent of the alleged offender before participation. In addition, in some programs the arresting officer and the victim must concur with program participation. Any prior record of physical violence weighs heavily against the individual's chances to participate. Any suspected involvement with organized crime can also automatically disqualify the alleged offender. Some programs require restitution to the victim as part of the acceptance of moral responsibility for the alleged act by the participant.

After the screening process has taken place to determine the eligibility of the individual, the prospective client is then asked to consent to a waiver of his right to a speedy trial.

Operations

The pre-trial intervention staff determines whether the individual has made bond or is still in jail. In the event the alleged offender is still incarcerated, the staff person interviews the alleged offender as to eligibility for the program. At this stage, many diversion programs strongly propose that every prospective participant be represented and instructed by legal counsel regarding the more profound aspects of program participation. Basically, these aspects are:

1. The defendant remains under control of the criminal justice system, his community liberty being dependent upon conforming with the rules and program requirements of the pre-trial intervention program.
2. The defendant remains fully subject to prosecution and criminal sanctions (fines, probation, incarceration) for all alleged criminal conduct if he fails to meet the program requirements for successful termination.

3. The accused, in order to participate in the program, must waive or at least postpone assertion of certain constitutional protections available to those accused of a crime, e.g., the right to a speedy trial.

Pre-trial intervention is usually suggested only as an alternative in those cases where the probability of guilt is high and only when the alleged offender fully and knowingly consents to participation in such a program. If the individual does not want to participate in the program, or the arresting officer or the victim objects, the offender is returned to the prosecuting attorney's office for prosecution.

If an individual qualifies for the program, assistance is offered in an attempt to obtain a release. The staff person makes an assessment of each participant's educational, vocational and psychological needs. Programs emphasize educational training, vocational training, or, most often, employment. The staff person and the alleged offender, who may be represented by counsel, develop and negotiate a contract. Through this contract, specific plans and goals for the participant are usually enumerated. Each month thereafter, a monthly progress report is often written and progress on these goals or changes in treatment direction is noted. Referrals to existing community agencies are made whenever the need exists.

Also assessed in the first interview are the appropriate level and the type of assistance required by the different individuals. If the participant does not need extensive supervision and rehabilitative services and meets a number of other significant criteria relating to stability, offense, group participation, age, length of time in program, attitude, etc., he/she may be placed in a self-corrective category. These individuals are seen less frequently than are other program participants and telephone contact may be substituted for every other personal contact.

The participant is seen frequently in his/her natural situation, either at home, at school or at place of employment. The relaxed counseling environment is more revealing. If the participant resides at home, contact is usually established with the participant's parents or guardians. Interaction between the subject and his parents can be observed and problems in their relationship can be incorporated as an objective for therapeutic intervention. Cooperation and involvement of other significant persons in the participant's life (siblings, employer, guidance counselor, teacher, etc.) is encouraged in that it contributes additional support.

The period for program participation usually ranges from six to twelve months. When the staff person determines that a participant has met all the program requirements, is employed or in school and is not in need of additional counseling, a recommendation is usually made to terminate the subject from active participation.

The prosecuting attorney often has the discretionary authority to determine whether the alleged offender has adequately fulfilled the requirements of the contract, and thereby has full authority to reinstate prosecution prior to the completion date. However, the decision of the prosecuting attorney will be based primarily upon the recommendation of the program staff. In some programs, a short ceremony is held in the prosecuting attorney's office with the group of participants completing the program. After a short presentation by the prosecuting attorney, each participant is given a copy of "No Bill of Information Recommendation"* that will be placed in his/her file which is then closed.

The participant is then assigned to a follow-up program. During the year he is usually required to consult his counselor once every three months. Most of the counseling during this period is of a supportive nature. However, if needed, additional referrals and other counseling services can be utilized by the participant.

Termination

If an active participant violates the program's rules and regulations, the individual is given notice of the violation in writing. The Pre-Trial Intervention Program operated by the East Baton Rouge Parish (County), Louisiana District Attorney's Office has formulated the following procedures for appeal once a participant has been notified by letter of its intent to terminate him/her from the program and the individual requests a hearing to appeal that termination decision.

APPEAL HEARING PROCEDURE

   I. TYPE:
     A. Informal
  II. BOARD CONSISTS OF:
     A. Program director
     B. One counselor (who has no knowledge of the case)
     C. Two active participants
     D. One member-at-large
 III. NATURE:
     A. The hearing is informal, with the counselor presenting the reason for the termination and the appealing participant then presenting reasons why the termination should be withheld.

       The options open to the Appeal Board are to sustain the termination, sustain the appeal and retain the participant without conditions or to sustain the participant with conditions.

---

*The Bill of Information is similar to a grand jury's indictment. It is a method of indictment used by a prosecutor. The information document specifies the final criminal charges on which the defendant is arraigned, must plead and may face sentencing. In a no-bill, there is no bill of indictment.

Appeal hearings are a matter of rights for a participant who is terminated for any reason other than a rearrest or the discovery of the existence of a prior arrest record. In the latter instance, the decision to terminate is made by the Administrator and the participant is not advised of his rights to an appeal.

In the event a participant is retained in the program subsequent to an appeal hearing, and he is terminated once again, the foregoing procedure should be used and the participant does have a right to a second appeal hearing; however, the sole determination to be made by the board is as to whether or not the allegations for which the second termination was made, in fact occurred. If the board finds that the allegations are correct, it must terminate the participant and the board does not have the option of retaining the participant with further conditions. At the second appeal hearing, the only reason for retaining the participant would be a finding that the allegations or violations did not, in fact, occur.

IV. PROCEDURE:

A. At the outset of an appeal hearing, it is the responsibility of the Administrator sitting on the board to (1) explain the purpose of the hearing and the options available to the appeal board, (2) to introduce the respective board members, and (3) to state the procedure to be followed which involves first the counselor's presentation of reasons for the termination followed by an opportunity for the participant to state his position. Both the counselor and the participant may be questioned by board members and, following the presentation of the evidence, both the counselor and the participant will be asked to leave the room while the board reaches a decision.

B. The counselor should present the evidence in a professional manner and should not at any time engage in argument with the participant. The counselor should also present any documentation or witnesses that might be necessary to prove a particular violation.

C. Following the presentations by the counselor and the participant, both parties are to leave the room while the board deliberates and following deliberation, a vote shall be taken by written ballot and the majority decision shall prevail.

If the participant does not request a hearing he is terminated unsatisfactorily and his case is returned to the District Attorney's Office for prosecution.

An active participant who is rearrested is immediately terminated unsatisfactorily and his case returned to the District Attorney's Office for prosecution on the offense which he was originally in the program for as well as the offense of the second arrest.[26]

Pre-Arrest Diversion

While some communities are implementing pre-trial diversion programs, other communities are developing pre-arrest diversion programs. In the victim confrontation program established in Columbus, Ohio, the disputants are permitted to confront each other and work out the problem in a controlled setting. When this procedure fails, criminal affidavits can be filed and the complainants can pursue formal criminal action. Minor interpersonal disputes which result in assault and battery, menacing threats or larceny, are illustrative of the types of situations that are amenable to such a diversion program. Thus, a jilted boyfriend may take the $300 stereo he gave his fiancee; landlord and tenant may settle their disagreement; and friends may clarify their misunderstandings.[27]

Jurisdiction for this victim confrontation stems primarily from interpersonal disputes, in which there is a continuing relationship. The hope is that charges will not be drawn if victims can confront each other. Furthermore, these disputes do not occur in the presence of an officer, nor where a warrantless arrest is justified.

In the past few years, several pre-arrest or citizen dispute resolution programs have been set up throughout the United States. Programs like the one described for Columbus, Ohio, and others located in such communities as Orlando and Miami, Florida, are operated through the prosecuting attorney's office. Yet, all kinds of agencies within the criminal justice system can and do sponsor such programs, i.e., courts, bar associations and police. Some programs are conducted by large independent agencies like the Institute on Mediation and Conflict Resolution, along with the Vera Institute in Brooklyn. In general, these pre-arrest diversion programs are informal, voluntary and reconciliation-focused. If a person is dissatisfied with this program, the individual may still file an official complaint and proceed through the criminal justice system.

Post-Trial Diversion

Diversion from sentence to a state correctional agency has operated with adults mostly in diversionary alcohol and drug programs. Based upon the principle of diminishing capacity to commit crimes due to one's addiction, addicts convicted of misdemeanors and felonies were to be certified and committed (in a way similar to civil commitments to mental institutions) to a comprehensive agency that would treat addicts in their facilities and/or out-patient aftercare programs.

A nationwide program that refers drug addicts to community services is Treatment Alternatives to Street Crime (TASC). Although TASC only arranges for treatment in existing community agencies, its purpose is to monitor client performance and to keep the court, prosecutor's office or probation department advised of the offender's progress. Sometimes these programs try to win pre-trial release on the condition that they participate in drug treatment.[28]

Another example of post-trial diversion programs stem around victims in child abuse or incest cases. Recent surveys suggest that psychologists and health care professionals are using the court system, not as a last-resort punitive measure, but as a catalyst for change. Many sex offenders, including incestors, deny their actions and refuse treatment unless they are under the threat of civil or criminal prosecution. For example, Seattle's Sexual Assault Center (SAC) has developed such a program wherein offenders are convicted but receive treatment instead of a prison sentence. The SAC provides services such as medical care, gathering of forensic evidence, crisis intervention, legal counseling for parents and children and therapy for victims and offenders. The SAC also offers training for attorneys and law enforcement officials in child development and techniques for interviewing child victims/witnesses. With this approach and the cooperation of the victims and their families with the prosecution, 90 percent of the cases handled by the SAC have resulted in convictions. In 73 percent of the cases, the defendant pleaded guilty and no trial was necessary. With the guilty pleas, the sentence was replaced with psychological treatment at either the SAC or another facility.[29]

In this legal model of responsibility for incest offenders, criminal justicians argue that abusers need to be faced with the consequences of their behavior. An abuser may have a personality dysfunction similar to many of the other kinds of offenders that use the court service. However, having interpersonal difficulties is not an excusable reason or a defense to a crime. In this approach, then, an abuser is held responsible for one's behavior and treatment is recommended instead of a prison sentence— when and wherever possible.

Problems

Critics who fault diversion do so for several reasons. First, some critics argue that diversion widens the net of the criminal justice system. This means that the criminal justice system now has to handle more people formally whereas in the past, those individuals might have been informally handled. Secondly, some critics believe that as certainty of punishment increases, rates of criminal activity decrease. So, when criminal justice systems employ diversion programs they are diminishing the pain and power of punishment, causing recidivism to increase.

Another group of persons argue that since diversion programs fail to address the primary cause which brought the alleged offender to the attention of the legal authorities, the conditions of lawlessness may continue. When diversion programs operate to involve participants in more legal aspects of life without addressing the primary cause of the deviant behavior, the problem then will never be solved or resolved.[30]

Another concern expressed by Richard J. Lundman in his article "Will Diversion Reduce Recidivism?", is that more juvenile and adult offenders will be under the control of the state with individuals such as intake officers having more discretion. Without the constitutional procedural safeguards, intake workers might be more prone to base decisions on such variables as class, sex age, minority status and demeanor. According to Lundman, without the use of universalistic rather than particularistic criteria, diversion may magnify rather than alleviate existing abuse.[31]

Perhaps, one of the major problems with diversion is its foundation— the presumption of guilt. Even though an overwhelming majority of programs do not require an admission of guilt, there is presumption of guilt inherent in the system. This presumption of guilt causes alleged offenders to be placed in a probation type status under a contract which limits rights and individual freedoms. However admirable its goals and intentions, pre-trial intervention presents constitutional and moral weaknesses which must be resolved before any program can be completely credible. The constitutional violations that have been noticed in many programs have been due process, the right to counsel, confrontation and the presumption of guilt without a hearing or trial by jury.[32] Because of this concern, some programs insure the participants have legal counsel so that if the alleged offender does decide to use a diversion program, he/she will have more information regarding the advantages and disadvantages of that decision.

Furthermore, Mullen has noted that if alleged offenders fail on pre-trial supervision, they are returned for prosecution that may be more vigorous than what the original prosecution would have been. She argued that instead of fostering diversion programs that have "matured" without convincing evidence that they affect pre-trial criminal process problems, "we ought to deal with the problem of delay in disposing of court cases or moving release back to an earlier stage such as pre-arrest."[33]

Another area of criticism stems around the fact that diversion only creates another criminal justice agency: pre-trial intervention programs. When these new agencies are established, diversion programs mandate other social service agencies as well as the public as volunteers to interact in formal and informal ways. The boundaries between the various human services will have to disappear as they move to an "open system" of integration for a common goal. This "open system" model will not be easily facilitated, given the fact that the criminal justice system itself is a large, uncoordinated set of subsystems with large gaps in service, irrational resource allocation, inadequate information and a range of treatment modes that lack a consistent and workable rationale. Seeking and informing the concerned public in a community and creating an interdependent system will be no easy task. Minority groups without accurate and complete information about diversion programs may not encourage their members to apply for diversion programs. The "fear of the system" is often extended to these programs.

Lastly, some critics maintain that diversion programs can create some unfortunate problems for the efficient operation of the criminal justice system. In some instances the participation of an alleged offender in a diversion program may eventually jeopardize the successful prosecution of a case due to the potential loss of witnesses. For example, if an alleged offender who participated in a pre-trial intervention program failed to comply with program requirements and the prosecuting attorney decided to initiate prosecution, the probability of losing important witnesses during the period of diversion program participation would be increased. Consequently, the probability of successful prosecution would, in turn, diminish.

The proponents of diversion maintain that the merits of diversion more than offset the aforementioned problem areas. They justify diversion on the following grounds: (1) diversion represents a more economical manner of dealing with the problem of crime in society; (2) diversion reduces the prospects of stigmatization of offenders by enabling them to avoid a criminal record; (3) diversion, by reducing the total case load, relieves an already overtaxed and overburdened criminal justice system which, in turn, permits the system to devote its efforts and energies on more serious criminals; (4) diversion seeks to provide clients with needed services and resources and is a more humane way of dealing with offenders; and (5) diversion serves as a means of segregating less serious offenders, such as misdemeanants and minor offenders, from more serious offenders, such as habitual felony offenders, who are processed through the criminal justice system.

Cost

Compared with formal processing, diversion is significantly less expensive method of attempting to solve the problem of crime. Savings could be made by being able to limit the numbers of judges, prosecutors, and defense attorneys, as well as the number of jail cells needed to confine alleged offenders prior to trial and/or sentencing. Baron, Funey and Thornton have reported that diversion is only about one-tenth as expensive as regular intake.[34] Gemignani has estimated that by 1977, almost $1.5 billion could have been saved by the adoption of a national strategy of diversion.[35]

According to the Institute for Law and Social Research in Washington, D.C., the cost of a trial is $2.47 per minute for the midwest area, slightly higher on both coasts and lower in the south. For Wichita, when 114 cases were successfully diverted in the 18th Judicial District in 1978, the diversion coordinator estimated a $405,475.20 savings to the taxpayers.[36]

In the pre-arrest diversion program in Columbus, Ohio (the Night Prosecutor's Program) cases were handled involving interpersonal disputes in which law students as hearing officers diverted 3,992 cases during the fiscal year ending September 1, 1973. "Estimating the cost of processing one criminal case to be $200, a savings of $798,400 was realized—all for the initial cost of $60,000 federal funds and $20,000 city funds."[37]

The much publicized program in Genesee County, Michigan, the Citizen's Probation Authority, was able to minimize costs by using volunteers with social work and other related professional backgrounds.

The amount of money saved by the court system, thereby, may be utilized to support existing social service agencies. Indeed, the cost of rehabilitation may be the same amount. What differs is that the money is shared by other community agencies. Some communities may foolishly believe that they can continue to increase referrals to social agencies without increasing money for expansion of staff and services. High turnover rates among social workers in such agencies is just another immeasureable cost that surpasses the often insensitive taxpayers' attention. Evaluation of diversion programs should consider the implementation of community programs and the geographic area to be covered, number of individuals being served and training or skills of personnel to deal with some of the problems they are being asked to handle. Sometimes, new agencies may need to be developed to handle the job in offering services. Agencies which deal with volunteers and clientele may need to establish new guidelines or adapt different modes for handling the referrals of participants of diversion programs who may comply in behavior but lack the commitment for individual change.

Another hidden cost is the public information program to bring about citizen involvement and cooperation in these programs of diversion. The cost of insuring that the public is informed fully about these matters will be repaid many times over. People in a community usually do not want diversion programs to creep into their community unannounced and without their approval. A good information system will address the people's concerns for control and predictability of the offenders and the programs.

Diversion is generally considered to be far more humane than formal processing. Consequently, it is difficult to assess the cost factor of diversion programs solely in a monetary sense. There also needs to be a recognition of the potential psychological and sociological impact upon the alleged offender of both formal and diversionary processing. In addition, some researchers believe that the deeper an offender penetrates the criminal justice system, the more frequently he/she is recycled through it. The earlier this process begins, the greater is the probability that he/she will continue because of the stigmatizing consequences of the processing.

Effectiveness

Three factors make it extremely difficult to assess the overall effectiveness of diversion programs: (1) there is a wide variety of programs which are identified under the "diversionary" label; (2) generally, there is a low quality of program evaluation; and (3) mixed findings have been reported by those empirical studies which have been conducted of diversion programs. Some critics also suggest that successful diversion programs are much more likely to be evaluated and their results reported. These serious limitations need to be recognized. They suggest the difficulty of attempting to draw any general conclusions regarding the efficacy of diversion programs.

The following diversion programs are introduced as examples of programs which have been *reported* as successful.

The Manhattan Court Employment Project, mentioned previously in this chapter, omitted alcoholics and identifiable drug addicts from the program. While the overall statistics for the first three years of the Project's operation show that slightly less than half of the participants were successfully terminated from the Project (their charges were dropped), the figures for the third year show that rate to be over 60 percent. Recidivism rates show that those favorably terminated from the Project have a recidivism rate of one-half of those unsuccessfully terminated and also a recidivism rate of one-half of the control group's rate.[38]

The Dallas Police Department has developed a police diversion program aimed at juvenile offenders to help reduce the case load of juvenile court and to reduce juvenile recidivism. Briefly, their program consists of a unit of 12 civilian counselors and five sworn officers under the command of the department's youth section who operate through sub-programs. The first offender program consists of a four-hour lecture/slide program on the law which is conducted by sworn officers. A counseling program consists of a 16-hour skills training and skills application session along with his/her parents over a four to six month period for the serious offender. For youths requiring additional authority figures, a fireman counselor program is available. In this program, youths are matched to an on-duty fireman so that a big brother type of relationship may develop.

In the Youth Service Program (YSP) of the Dallas Police Department, data was obtained through analysis of police and juvenile court records. The results showed that the YSP had a direct effect on participants' further criminal activity during the follow-up time period. Re-arrest recidivism was reduced for YSP participants.[39]

In addition, all ratings showed a statistically significant improvement from a pre-to-post to post-post follow-up period for the following areas:

1. Skills total
    Physical fitness
    Interpersonal skills
    Study learning skills
    Reading

2. Home (living application) total
    Following rules and limits
    Doing chores
    Communicating with parents

3. School (learning application) total
    School behavioral problems
    Attendance
    Grades

4. Free time application total
    Participation in activity
    Participation in hobbies
    Part-time job
    Career development
    Type of friends

In short, the YSP had an effect on actual police practice not only by altering referral practices and alternatives, but also by creating a new operational program. The total referrals to the juvenile court were significantly down 12.3 percent between 1973 and 1975 while the juvenile population increased 2.3 percent. Juvenile court hearings were significantly down during the same period by 8.2 percent.[40]

Thus, the Youth Service Program directly diverted many youths out of the court system and affected future referrals to the juvenile justice system. Contrary to the opinion that many diversion programs only divert youth who would not enter the system again anyway, the data from the YSP indicate that those youths successfully diverted eventually would become involved again if it were not for the YSP.

Up Close and Personal

Mr. Marty Miller is the Director of the Pre-Trial Diversion Program, which is operated by the Sedgwick County District Attorney's Office in Wichita, Kansas. From April 1, 1978, through March 31, 1979, 450 applications for diversion were received. Of this number, 228 were approved for diversion. Those persons accepted for participation had usually committed one or more of the following types of crime: theft, violation of check laws, unemployment fraud, burglary and theft, criminal damage to property, forgery and burglary.

Mr. Miller introduced the following actual cases as characteristic examples of those which were evaluated to be appropriately diverted by the program. The names of the participants have been changed to insure their anonymity.[41]

Case No. 1: Sergeant Jones

Sergeant Jones is in his early twenties and stationed in Wichita at a military installation. Originally from Arkansas, he is a married man with two children. His wife works. Some friends of his from Arkansas came to visit him in Wichita and brought with them another man, a stranger to Sergeant Jones. When his friends departed, the stranger stayed behind with Sergeant Jones' consent. The stranger was from his hometown in Arkansas, enabling the two men to share experiences and talk about old times. Unknown to Sergeant Jones, the stranger was a burglar. Sergeant Jones went out drinking with his houseguest, and before long the stranger began to burglarize homes. Out drinking and driving around with him, Sergeant Jones began to participate with his houseguest in these burglaries. Finally, they were caught.

By this time they had hit five or six houses. The last place they hit they had inflicted approximately $800 in property damage. Although the diversion committee initially was inclined to reject Sergeant Jones' application for diversion, they consented after discovering that Sergeant Jones was very cooperative in helping recover most of the merchandise they had taken in the burglaries, some of which had been fenced. Additionally, a background check revealed that he had absolutely no prior offense record, either juvenile or adult, and that he had an excellent military record.

At the diversion interview, Sergeant Jones accepted responsibility for his actions, stating that he knew what he did was wrong and that he was willing to make restitution to those whom he had burglarized. Sergeant Jones was placed in the program for a period of 18 months in which he was required to make restitution, to come in for a personal meeting with the director and to call in weekly. Sergeant Jones has proven to be one of the program's better participants. He has paid more than his share of the restitution and stayed out of additional trouble. He is still in the military, although the military has placed him under certain restrictive conditions. Sergeant Jones is very appreciative of this opportunity. He firmly believes that it has saved his career and family life. He realizes that with his full confession, he could easily have been given a ten-year prison sentence. Sergeant Jones' co-defendant was denied acceptance into the program because of his extensive criminal history. He was returned to Missouri for earlier charges, was convicted, and is presently serving time in the Missouri State Penitentiary in Jefferson City.

Case No. 2: Jack

Jack is a 26-year-old male who was arrested for attempted theft. He, along with another man, went into a local music store with the intent of stealing a guitar. Having taken the guitar, Jack and his friend were on their way out of the store when the owner said, "I wouldn't do that." The police arrived shortly after a call from the owner's wife, and arrested the two men. Jack had spent two to three weeks in the local jail before being interviewed. He had had his initial appearance and was awaiting his preliminary hearing. His attorney was court appointed insofar as Jack was indigent. A routine background check revealed that he had no previous offense record, either adult or juvenile.

The pre-trial diversion interview with him at the jail revealed that he only recently had arrived in Wichita. In the interim he had been "bumming around" the country, taking odd jobs along the way. He had just started work on a hog farm at the time of his arrest. It was discovered that both Jack and his friend had been drinking the morning before the incident and that Jack had a severe alcohol problem. A decision was made to place Jack in the diversion program. He was referred to a local alcohol abuse residential treatment center and was additionally required to report to the pre-trial diversion program monthly for a progress report. Jack's participation in the program was to last 12 months. At the present time Jack has been in the program for four months and he is now involved in the program and participates in Alcoholics Anonymous. Recently the alcohol and drug abuse residential treatment center received an emergency call. Someone had overdosed on drugs and emergency assistance was requested. Jack asked to go on the call with a staff person. Arriving on the scene, Jack gave the person mouth-to-mouth resuscitation and cardiopulmonary resuscitation. Because of Jack's efforts, the person survived.

Jack's co-defendant, whom Jack had met at a party, also applied for but was denied diversion. It was discovered that he had a past criminal record and an interview revealed that he blatantly lied about his participation in the incident and showed no remorse.

Case No. 3: Mr. And Mrs. Hoffman

Mr. and Mrs. Hoffman are an elderly couple, over 65, who recently moved to Wichita from a northern state to be near a special medical clinic for their health problems. They had no family or friends in the community and, insofar as they were retired had no job related acquaintances. During one of the winter months they went to a local department store, picked up a suitcase, and began to fill it up with a variety of different articles. They were caught in the act by a security guard. They had approximately $200 in merchandise in their possession at the time. Interestingly, none of the merchandise such as clothing, was in their size. The Hoffmans' attorney contacted the District Attorney's office regarding the application of his clients for the pre-trial diversion program. A background check was conducted which produced excellent references from former employers and friends, proving neither of them had participated in any criminal activities in the past.

An interview with the couple revealed that they had sufficient financial resources to support themselves and had no alcohol or drug related problems. It was very difficult to identify any motivating factors for their actions. When queried as to why they did it, they responded that they did not know and broke down and cried. It appeared that they were simply trying to attract attention to themselves—they were trying to get caught. They were new to the community but did not feel a part of it. The Hoffmans were accepted into the program and were given assistance in meeting people in the community, joining pertinent community associations and obtaining church membership. In the estimation of the diversion committee, this was a fine couple simply in need of community involvement. The Hoffmans have successfully completed their 12-month program of diversion.

Case No. 4: Sally

Sally is a 19-year-old girl from Wichita. Until recently, she resided with her family. Sally wanted to get out on her own and establish some personal independence. She acquired her own apartment and held a couple of different jobs, including pumping gas at a service station and working at a machine shop. After approximately three months away from home, she began to experience financial difficulties. She ran out of money, her rent came due and she had car troubles, causing her an inability to meet financial obligations. Although she came from an upper-middle class family which was supportive, she did not want to go home, concerned that her family would say, "We told you so." Her return home would be tantamount to admitting that she was incapable of being independent. Working at a machine shop on Sunday afternoon, she decided to go to the gas station where she was formerly employed. She gave the station attendant a note demanding the money from the cash register and the attendant consented. She then drove away. Approximately three blocks away she correctly identified an unmarked police car, stopped and walked back to the car and stated, "I did it. I robbed the gas station." Sally was alone in the incident and did not possess a weapon. A routine background check on Sally revealed that she had no prior offense record.

In the diversion interview, Sally stated that she robbed the station because she was in a financial bind and she did not want to go home because she didn't want to admit to her parents that she couldn't make it on her own. Sally was placed in the diversion program for a period of 12 months during which she was required to report on a weekly basis to the director. In need of additional parental supervision, Sally is now living, for the time being, with her parents. She also is going to vocational training school and has acquired a part-time modeling job. Although Sally probably would have been placed on probation if she had been prosecuted and convicted because she has no previous record and no weapon was involved, diversion is desirable for Sally.

Persons arrested but not convicted do not need to report that arrest when applying for most jobs under Kansas law. Previously, persons convicted of some crimes could have their records expunged. This law extends that privilege.

The cases cited by Mr. Miller are success stories. However, occasionally persons accepted for diversion do not complete the program satisfactorily. In fact, of the 228 approved for diversion, 173 have completed their diversion program successfully and only six persons have committed additional crimes while enrolled in the program. The remainder are still enrolled in the program without incident.

Summary

Diversion programs flourished during the 1970's in both the juvenile and criminal justice systems.

The purpose of diversion programs is to provide a formally acknowledged and organized program to remove an offender from the traditional processing through the criminal or juvenile justice system. Based upon explicit criteria of eligibility, diversion programs generally seek to provide clients with counseling and other services in areas such as education, employment, finances, health, substance abuse and the like. Eligibility usually means that everyone concerned agrees that the offender does not present a clear and present danger to society and that no constructive purpose would be served by conviction and sentence. The suspension of the criminal prosecution for a specific period of time is to permit the offender either to successfully complete his/her program and/or to demonstrate a lawful lifestyle. Most diversion programs are conditional. If the offender fails to live up to the agreements or gets arrested for other acts, the offender is removed from the program and criminal prosecution is not only resumed for the first offense but also the second offense.

Informal diversion is the result of officials in the criminal justice system, i.e., police, prosecutors, etc., exercising their authority through their discretion to release offenders. Thus, in any given year, a community usually has more individuals coming into the justice system than actually reach the last stage of sentencing.

Under the topic of juvenile diversion programs, forestry camps and psychiatric training centers are illustrated. The Massachusetts experiment shows how a state could develop community-based programs by closing all the state training schools.

Adult diversion was developed as formalized programs to decrease the power of discretion and make the decisionmaker more accountable for the result. The President's Commission on Law Enforcement and Administration of Justice was one of the first authoritative expressions of the desirability of diversions during the 1960's. They argued that many offenders were in need of treatment or supervision rather than criminal sanctions. At that point, the American Bar Association developed standards and policy guidelines for pre-trial diversion. They also established a National Pre-Trial Intervention Service Center with the expressed purpose of stimulating pre-trial diversion programs and acting as a clearinghouse for gathering data on the progress, problems and measure of success.

Pre-trial diversion, which reflects diversion before the trial stage, shows the criteria used, the process and how termination occurs. Since pre-trial diversion is generally viewed so favorably, other diversion programs have been developed to affect offenders at the pre-arrest stage and the post-trial stage.

As admirable as diversion programs may seem on the surface, these programs are not without critics who identify many problems. Some of the problems center around the fact that the programs increase the numbers of persons needing to be formally handled by the justice system. Since some programs are only concerned with the unlawful behavior, the primary cause for the behavior gets lost in the paperwork. Even more unsettling has been the arguments that the programs lack constitutional procedural safeguards. The presumption of guilt, for example, causes alleged offenders to be placed in a probation type status under a contract which limits rights and individual freedoms.

On the other hand, the proponents of diversion maintain that the merits of diversion more than offset the perceived problem areas. They justify diversion on the following grounds: (1) diversion represents a more economical manner of dealing with the problem of crime in society; (2) diversion reduces the prospects of stigmatization of offenders by enabling them to avoid a criminal record; (3) diversion, by reducing the total case load, relieves an already overtaxed and overburdened criminal justice system which, in turn, permits the system to devote its efforts and energies on more serious criminals; (4) diversion, since it often seeks to provide clients with needed services and resources, is a more humane way of dealing with offenders; and (5) diversion serves as a means of segregating less serious offenders, such as misdemeanants and minor offenders, from more serious offenders, such as habitual felony offenders, who are processed through the criminal justice system.

Certain factors make it extremely difficult to assess the overall effectiveness of diversion programs. Some critics also suggest that successful diversion programs are much more likely to be evaluated and their results reported. These serious limitations need to be recognized. They suggest the difficulty of attempting to draw even general conclusions regarding the efficacy of diversion programs.

Notes

1. For additional information, see *Instead of Jail: Pre- and Post-Trial Alternatives to Jail Incarceration*, Volumes 1-5 (Washington, D.C.: Law Enforcement Assistance Admin., Oct. 1977)

2. United Nations, "The Origin of Probation in the United States," *Probation, Parole and Community Corrections* (2d ed.; New York: John Wiley & Sons, 1976), pp. 89-90.

3. Robert M. Mennel, *Thorns and Thistles* (Hanover, New Hampshire: The University of New Hampshire, 1973), pp. 14-29.

4. Ibid.

5. Nicholas N. Kittrie, *The Right To Be Different* (Baltimore, Maryland: Penguin Books, 1973), p. 109.

6. Mark M. Levin and Rosemary C. Sarri, *Juvenile Delinquency: A Comparative Analysis of Legal Codes in the United States* (Ann Arbor, Michigan; The University of Michigan, 1974), pp. 16-17.

7. 383 U.S. 541, 16 L.Ed.2d 84, 86 S.Ct. 1045, 1966.

8. President's Commission of Law Enforcement and Administration of Justice, *Task Force Report: Juvenile Delinquency and Youth Crime* (Washington: Government Printing Office, 1967); Edwin E. Schur, *Radical Non-Intervention* (Englewood Cliffs, N.J.: Prentice-Hall, 1973).

9. Steve Gettinger, "New York City's Juvenile Justice System," *Corrections Magazine*, 2 (June 1976), pp. 51-57.

10. Roger Hood and Richard Sparks, *Key Issues in Criminology* (New York: McGraw-Hill Book Company, 1979), p. 70.

11. Ibid., p. 74.

12. Ibid., p. 78.

13. Ruth Shonle Cavan and Theodore N. Ferdinand, *Juvenile Delinquency* (3rd ed. New York: J.B. Lippincott, 1975), pp. 428-29.

14. Fritz Redl and David Wineman, *The Aggressive Child* (New York: The Free Press, 1960).

15. Cavan and Ferdinand, op. cit., pp. 435-37.

16. Michael S. Serrill, "Juvenile Corrections in Massachusetts, *Corrections Magazine*, 2 (November/December 1975), pp. 3-12.

17. Robert M. Carter, "The Diversion of Offenders," *Federal Probation*, 36 (December 1972), pp. 31-36.

18. President's Commission on Law Enforcement and Administration of Justice, *Task Force Report: The Courts* (Washington: Government Printing Office, 1967), p. 6.

19. *General Report: The Challenge of Crime in a Free Society* (Washington: Government Printing Office, 1967), pp. 133-39.

20. For the beginnings of this project see *Informational Bulletin No. 13*, July 1972 (rev. January 1973) of the Commission on Correctional Facilities and Services of the American Bar Association.

21. National Pretrial Intervention Center, *Source Book in Pretrial Criminal Justice Intervention Techniques and Action Programs* (Washington: American Bar Association Commission on Correctional Facilities and Services, May 1974).

22. M.T. Nietzel and J.T. Dade, "Bail Reform as an Example of a Community Psychology Intervention in a Criminal Justice System," *American Journal of Community Psychology*, 1, 1973, pp. 238-47. See also C. Ares, A. Rankin, and H. Struz, "The Manahattan Bail Project: An Interim Report on the Use of Pretrial Parole," *New York University Law Review*, 38, 1973, pp. 67-95.

23. Joan Mullen, *Pre-Trial Services: An Evaluation of Policy-Related Research* (Cambridge, Mass.: Abt Associates, December 1974), pp. 22-28.

24. *Directions of Criminal Justice Diversion Programs, 1976*. Pretrial Intervention Service Center, Washington, D.C.

25. For more information, see *Instead of Jail: Pre- and Post-Trial Alternatives to Jail Incarceration*, Volumes 1-5 (Washington, D.C.: Law Enforcement Assistance Admin., Oct. 1977).

26. East Baton Rouge Parish, Louisiana, District Attorney, *Pre-Trial Intervention Program*, 1978.

27. John W. Palmer, "Pre-arrest Diversion: Victim Confrontation," *Federal Probation* 38 (September 1974), pp. 12-18.

28. *Instead of Jail: Pre- and Post-Trial Alternatives to Jail Incarceration*, Volume 1 (Washington: National Institute of Law Enforcement and Criminal Justice, 1977), p. 17.

29. Lucy Berlinger, "Child Sexual Abuse: What Happens Next?", *Victimology* 2 (2) 1977, pp. 327-331.

30. Richard J. Lundman, "Will Diversion Reduce Recidivism?" *Crime and Delinquency*, October 1976.

31. Ibid.

32. Robert W. Balch, "Referred Prosecution: The Juvenilization of the Criminal Justice System," *Federal Probation*, 2 (June 1974), pp. 46-50.

33. Joan Mullen, *The Dilemma of Diversion* (Washington: Government Printing Office, 1974), p. 17.

34. R. Baron, F. Funey, and W. Thornton, "Preventing Delinquency Through Diversions, The Sacramento County Diversion Project," *Federal Probation*, 37 (March 1973), pp. 13-19.

35. R. Gemignani, "Diversion of Juvenile Offenders from the Juvenile Justice System," in *Criminal Justice Monograph: New Approaches to Diversion and Treatment of Juvenile Offenders*, ed. P. Lejins (Washington: Government Printing Office, 1973), p. 10.

36. Statement by Marty Miller, director of the Pre-Trial Diversion Program, Sedgwick County District Attorney's Office, Wichita, Kansas, August 17, 1979.

37. John W. Palmer, *Pre-Arrest Diversion*, op. cit., p. 17.

38. Vera Institute of Justice. *Pretrial intervention: The Manhattan Court Employment Project*. Final report, New York, 1972.

39. Thomas R. Collingwood, "Defining Critical Factors in Police Diversion Programs," (paper presented to the Academy of Criminal Justice Sciences, Cincinnati, Ohio, March, 1979).

40. Ibid.

41. Statement by Miller, August 17, 1979.

Resources

Annual Journal 1978 (Washington, D.C.: Pretrial Service Resource Center, 1978).

Instead of Jail: Pre- and Post-Trial Alternatives to Jail Incarceration, Volumes 1-5 (Washington, D.C.: Law Enforcement Assistance Administration, October 1977).

Chapter 3
Probation

The literature in the field of criminal justice is inundated with definitions of probation. However, those definitions of probation developed by the Task Force on Corrections appointed by the President's Commission on Law Enforcement and Administration of Justice (1967), the American Bar Association Project on Standards for Criminal Justice (1970) and the National Advisory Commission on Criminal Justice Standards and Goals (1973) appear to be the definitions which are most commonly subscribed to and cited. Consequently, a review of these particular definitions of probation is in order.

Definition

In 1967, the Task Force on Corrections appointed by the President's Commission on Law Enforcement and Administration of Justice defined probation as: "A legal status granted by the court whereby a convicted person is permitted to remain in the community subject to conditions specified by the court."[1]

In 1970, the American Bar Association Project on Standards for Criminal Justice introduced the following definition of probation:

> A sentence not involving confinement which imposes conditions and retains authority in the sentencing court to modify the conditions of sentence or to resentence the offender if he violates the conditions. Such a sentence should not involve or require suspension of the imposition or execution of any other sentence... A sentence to probation should be treated as a final judgment for the purposes of appeal and similar procedural purposes.[2]

In 1973, the National Advisory Commission on Criminal Justice Standards and Goals defined probation in the following manner:

> In corrections, the word 'probation' is used in four ways. It can refer to a disposition, a status, a system or subsystem, and a process.
>
> Probation as a court disposition was first used as a suspension of sentence. Under probation, a convicted offender's freedom in the community was continued, subject to supervision and certain conditions established by the court. A shift is now occurring, and

probation is being used increasingly as a sentence in itself...

Probation as a status reflects the position of an offender sentenced to probation. For the offender, probation status has implications different from the status of either free citizen or confined offender.

Probation is a subsystem of corrections, itself a subsystem of the criminal and juvenile justice system... When used in this context, probation refers to the agency or organization that administers the probation process for juveniles and adults.

The probation process refers to the set of functions, activities, and services that characterize the system's transactions with the courts, the offender, and the community. The process includes preparation of reports for the court, supervision of probationers, and obtaining or providing services for them.[3]

Despite slightly different variations in orientation and terminology, a perusal of these definitions captures the essential elements and features of probation. They are, as follows:

1. *Probation* is a community-based correctional alternative that is utilized prior to imprisonment which permits the offender to remain in the community. A judge can impose a sentence of probation in different ways. For example, the judge may actually impose a prison sentence as determined by the law which has been violated, and then suspend the execution of that sentence and place the offender on probation. Another method is for the judge to defer the sentencing process and place the offender directly on probation. Furthermore, in some states, there is statutory ability to sentence the offender directly to probation.

2. Central to probation is the element of *conditional release*, that is, the liberty or the right of the offender to remain in the community is contingent upon his compliance with court-imposed conditions. If the offender fails to abide by the conditions of his probation, the probationer risks the possibility of having his probation revoked. If revoked, the offender generally is imprisoned to serve the time he would have received had probation not been granted.

3. *Supervision* represents another essential item of probation, at least in its ideal-type. An offender granted probation is placed under the supervision of a probation agency. As such, a probation officer is responsible for monitoring the probationer's behavior in the community and bringing to the attention of the court the failures of the probationer to comply with the conditions of his probation. In addition to this surveillance function of probation, supervision also involves a treatment dimension. In this context, supervision refers to the efforts of the probation officer to assist the offender in successfully adjusting to life in the community. Probationers may receive guidance and counseling from the probation officer and

referral services to appropriate community social service agencies, including programs for substance abuse, mental health, vocational training, employment and academic training.

Utilizing the aforementioned essential elements of probation, the following composite definition of probation is presented. Probation is: (1) a community-based correctional alternative (2) that involves a sentence imposed by the court upon an offender after a finding, verdict or plea of guilty, (3) which does not require the incarceration of the offender (4) but which allows the offender to remain in the community (5) subject to conditions imposed by the court and (6) supervision by a probation agency.

History

Probation, the supervised release of an offender to the community in lieu of incarceration, is credited as being clearly an American development. According to Newman, "Probation, both in conception and development, is America's distinctive contribution to progressive penology."[4] However, the origins of probation are usually traced to the English common law and such legal devices as "benefit of clergy," judicial reprieve, release on one's own recognizance, bail and the "filing" of cases. The common denominator of these practices, usually viewed as the direct precursors of probation, is that they were all used to temporarily suspend sentences in order to mitigate unduly severe sentences.

"Benefit of clergy," which dates back to the thirteenth century, is usually identified as a historical forerunner of probation. Initially, it was a method which was utilized to have the cases of criminally accused clerics transferred from secular courts to church courts. The Church insisted that only it had jurisdiction over members of the clergy. It should be emphasized that during this period numerous crimes were punishable by death. Consequently, it was advantageous and desirable to be tried in an ecclesiastical court because more lenient treatment could be expected. Eventually, this privilege was extended to all people who could read. It is interesting to note that to test the offender's ability to read and thereby qualify for the benefit of clergy, the offender was given a psalm to read. To feign literacy, many offenders memorized the psalms which were most frequently utilized. The benefit of clergy was employed in the American colonies prior to the Revolutionary War. This practice was finally abolished in England in 1841.

Another procedure which is normally identified as a historical antecedent of probation is judicial reprieve. A judicial reprieve was a temporary suspension of the imposition or execution of a sentence by the judge for the purpose of allowing the offender to petition the crown for clemency in the way of applying for an absolute or conditional pardon. The judge utilized his discretion when employing judicial reprieves in those instances where he was dissatisfied with the verdict or the evidence.

Recognizance and bail, according to Dressler, represented the first rudimentary stage in the development of probation.[5] The practice of releasing an individual on his own recognizance developed in the fourteenth century as a crime prevention measure. Under this method, a defendant gave assurance to the public by entering a bond or promise with the state that he would not commit crimes for a stipulated period of time and he would appear in court on a given date for trial or final disposition of the case. Recognizance was utilized for people who were suspected of committing crimes and for individuals who were actually arraigned in court for criminal offenses. Bail developed in medieval England. At that time the pre-trial release of the defendant was considered necessary since it was commonplace for accused persons to spend extended periods of incarceration before trial. Due to this condition, sheriffs were permitted to allow defendants to be conditionally released upon their promise, or the promise of another person, that they would appear for trial and would conduct themselves in a law-abiding manner. This procedure usually required sureties or bail and the person who stood surety had both the authority and responsibility to enforce the conditions of the offender's release. Therefore, the bailor provided a certain degree of supervision over the released offender. Carney notes that "The elements of suspension and supervision are what give recognizance and bail their relationship to probation."[6]

Another precursor of probation is the practice of "filing" a case. Having originated in the nineteenth century in Massachusetts, this device involved the procedure of suspending the imposition of a sentence when, after a guilty verdict, the court recognized circumstances which justified the mitigation of the penalty. The utilization of this device required the consent of both the prosecuting attorney and the defendant. The suspension of the sentence was also subject to the imposition of any special conditions the court deemed necessary. In some cases, sentences were suspended indefinitely. However, the court retained the power to reopen a case for sentencing at any time on the request of the prosecutor or the defendant.

As previously noted, probation, as it is known today, is considered an American development. The credit for the first utilization of probation in America is normally accorded to a prosperous Boston shoemaker, named John Augustus. Many of the present-day features and characteristics of probation were established by Augustus. These practices included: the careful investigation and screening of potential cases, the supervision of offenders, helping offenders to obtain employment and/or acquire an education, the development of a system of making progress reports to the court regarding the status of those offenders released under his supervision, the maintenance of a register on all the cases he handled and the provision of various other kinds of aid and assistance, such as arranging for housing. In view of the significant contributions made by Augustus to the concept and practice of probation, he is deservingly called the "father of probation."

Several additional events and dates warrant recognition regarding the development of probation in America. Massachusetts enacted the first actual probation statute in 1878 authorizing the city of Boston to appoint a paid probation officer. In 1880, legislation was passed in Massachusetts which authorized appointment of probation officers to all cities and towns in the state. In 1891, additional legislation extended probation services to all lower or inferior courts and in 1898, all superior courts of the state were authorized to appoint probation officers.

By 1900, six states, Massachusetts, Vermont, Illinois, Minnesota, Rhode Island and New Jersey had probation statutes. By 1915, a total of 33 states had passed laws authorizing adult probation. By 1925, probation for juveniles was employed in every state and by 1956 every state had a statute providing for adult probation. It should also be noted that a statute authorizing probation by federal courts was passed in 1925.

Probation is undoubtedly the most widely utilized community-based corrections program. Carlson, for example, mentions that in the United States probation constitutes as high as 70 percent of the sentences in some states and 54 percent in the federal system.[7]

In late 1976, the Bureau of the Census conducted the Criminal Justice Directory Survey of Probation and Parole Agencies for the Law Enforcement Assistance Administration of the U.S. Department of Justice. The survey revealed that:

> On September 1, 1976, there were almost 1.5 million (1,461,459) men, women, and children under State and local probation and parole supervision in the United States. Close to one million (923,064) were adult probationers... Another 328,854 were juveniles on probation.[8]

Table 3.1 clearly indicates the importance placed upon probation as an alternative to confinement in the criminal and juvenile justice systems.

Among the other selected findings of this survey were: 3,868 State and local probation and parole agencies were in operation, with 55,807 persons employed. There were also 20,263 volunteer workers in probation and parole agencies in addition to regular employees.[9]

Purpose

The proponents of probation stress its desirability as an alternative to incarceration, in appropriate cases, for several reasons. For example, in

Table 3.1 Number Of Persons Under Probation Or Parole Supervision On September 1, 1976 Compared To The Number Of Persons In Confinement (State And Local Governments Only)

Type of Offender	Under probation or parole supervision			In Confinement
	Total	On Probation	On Parole	
Total	1,461,459	1,251,918	209,541	457,528
Adults	1,079,258	923,064	156,194	370,515
Juveniles	382,201	328,854	53,347	87,013

Source: U.S. Department of Justice, *State and Local Probation and Parole Systems* (Washington, D.C.: U.S. Government Printing Office, 1978), p. 1.

1970, the American Bar Association Project for Standards for Criminal Justice approved the following:

Probation is a desirable disposition in appropriate cases because:

i. it maximizes the liberty of the individual while at the same time vindicating the authority of the law and effectively protecting the public from further violations of law;

ii. it affirmatively promotes the rehabilitation of the offender by continuing normal community contacts;

iii. it voids the negative and frequently stultifying effects of confinement which often severely and unnecessarily complicate the reintegration of the offender into the community;

iv. it greatly reduces the financial costs to the public treasury of an effective correctional system;

v. it minimizes the impact of the conviction upon innocent dependents of the offender.[10]

Maximization of Liberty/Protection of the Public

These objectives of probation are best understood if it is remembered that probation implies both a legal status and a treatment method.[11] Probation as a legal status involves a form of conditional release in which the offender is permitted to remain in the community under the supervision of a probation officer and subjected to certain conditions established by the court. It is the responsibility of probation agencies to ensure that probationers comply with the conditions of their release and to bring to the attention of the court reports of excessive violations of these conditions or the occurrence of new offenses. The court retains the authority to incarcerate the offender if he violates the conditions of probation. In this manner probation serves to enhance the safety and protection of the public.

As a treatment method probation enables the offender to experience a much greater degree of liberty and freedom than would be afforded him if he were institutionalized. By permitting the offender to remain in the community it allows him to receive the benefits associated with living in the community, such as maintaining supportive community relationships, assuming a greater degree of personal responsibility and reinvolving himself in society. Probation, in this sense, provides the offender with greater latitude in enacting a successful readjustment to living in the community.

Promotion of Rehabilitation

Advocates of probation maintain that probation advances the objective of rehabilitation. Rehabilitation is promoted by probation by permitting the offender to remain in the community and continuing normal community contacts, such as family, work, school and other supportive relationships. Therefore, community severance, an obstacle to rehabilitation associated with incarceration, is eliminated as a potential barrier to the rehabilitation process. In addition, the supervision of the offender by a probation officer, which may involve guidance, counseling and referrals to appropriate social service agencies, contributes to the rehabilitation of the offender.

Avoidance of Effects of Imprisonment

By allowing the offender to remain in the community, probation prevents the offender from experiencing the potentially damaging effects of incarceration in a correctional institution. These effects include: the consequences of community severance, the acquisition of a "criminal" label, lack of individual decisionmaking, loss of self-esteem and respect, exposure to episodes of institutional violence and contact with hard-core offenders.

Reduction of Financial Costs

Economic pressures and considerations are assuming a pivotal role in the correctional decisionmaking process. In a well-known and often seen television commercial, the following question is asked: "How do you spell 'RELIEF'?" In a correctional context "RELIEF" would be spelled P-R-O-B-A-T-I-O-N. Probation is indisputably one of the least expensive alternatives to incarceration. It is significantly cheaper in terms of both direct and indirect costs to place an offender on probation than to incarcerate him. The exorbitant costs of incarceration are avoided when utilizing probation as an alternative. In addition, by permitting the offender to remain in the community and to be employed, the offender can contribute to personal and family support, and pay federal and state taxes. Consequently, probation is ideally suited to offset the greater cost of institutional care.

Minimization of Impact of Conviction on Dependents

The correctional literature abounds with studies and descriptions of the potential impact of conviction on the offender himself. Rarely, however, is much discussion and attention focused on the impact of conviction on the innocent dependents of the offender, i.e., his family. The emotional, psychological, social and economical impact of the removal of the offender from the family unit due to imprisonment can, in some instances, be devastating. For example, in the case of a male offender, it may mean the removal from the family of a principal income producer, a spouse and a father. This might require major modifications and accommodations in life-style on behalf of the remaining family members. Such an experience could certainly constitute a "crisis period" for the offender's dependents. By allowing the offender to remain in the community, probation does not require the offender to sever his familial and community relationships.

Administration/Process

There are several areas of concern involved in the administration and process of probation. They are: (1) the organization of probation services; (2) the decision to grant probation; (3) conditions of probation; (4) the role of the probation officer; and (5) revocation of probation.

The Organization of Probation Services

Diversity, rather than uniformity, characterizes the organization of probation services in the United States. The complexity of probation organization is underscored by the following organizational differences. Some probation agencies have a singular function, such as being responsible for juvenile probation only or being responsible for adult probation only. Other probation agencies may have dual responsibilities for both juvenile and adult probation. In instances where adult probation may be separated from juvenile probation, there still may be further division of labor with one agency handling only adult misdemeanants and another agency handling adult felons. Still other probation agencies may be responsible for handling all of these types of probationers—juveniles, adult felons and adult misdemeanants.

Probation agencies also differ according to the branch of government, i.e., executive, judicial or both, and the level of government, i.e., state or local, which is responsible for probation. Some probation agencies are administered by an agency of the executive branch of government, such as the Division of Probation and Parole in Louisiana, whereas others are administered primarily by an agency of the judicial branch of government, such as the Office of Probation Administration in Nebraska. In addition, some probation agencies may be located in both branches of government with each branch having responsibility for particular aspects of the probation system. Probation services in some states are organized as a unified state system whereas in other states it is primarily a local service.

Add to this list of variations the fact that in some agencies parole services are sometimes combined with probation services. Therefore, some agencies may have dual functions of adult probation and parole or juvenile probation and parole. Some agencies even have responsibilities for three or four different functions regarding the provision of probation and parole services. It should also be noted that the federal system is separate.

There were 3,868 State and local government agencies with responsibility for probation, parole or some combination of the two, on September 1, 1976. Approximately three-fifths (2,364 or 61 percent) were state-level agencies; slightly less than two-fifths (1,430 or 37 percent) were county-level agencies and the remainder (74 or 2 percent) were municipal-level agencies.[12] Table 3.2 shows the number of agencies according to function(s) and level of government. Table 3.3 distributes the number of agencies in a different manner than Table 3.2 by showing the total number of agencies performing a particular function by level of government.

The data clearly indicate that the parole function is mainly a State responsibility. In fact, 85 percent of adult parole agencies and 81 percent of juvenile parole agencies were at the State level of government.[13] However, responsibility for probation services seems to be almost equally distributed between State and local governments. State governments have slightly more agencies for adult probation whereas local governments have slightly more agencies for juvenile probation. Of the 1,929 agencies having adult probation as a function, slightly less than three-fifths (1,087 or 56 percent) were State-level agencies and more than two-fifths (842 or 44 percent) were located at the county or municipal level. Of the 2,126 juvenile probation agencies, approximately three-fifths (1,210 or 57 percent) were local agencies and about two-fifths (916 or 43 percent) were State agencies.[14]

The Decision to Grant Probation

Two factors need to be emphasized regarding the probation decisionmaking process. First, it is the responsibility of the sentencing court to make a decision to grant probation. Secondly, although the decision to grant probation resides with the court, this decision must be made within the limits and restrictions of statutes regulating eligibility for

Table 3.2 Number of State And Local Probation and Parole Agencies by Function(s) and Level of Government, September 1, 1976

Function(s) of Agencies	State-Local Total	Level of Government		
		State	County	Municipal
Total Agencies	3,868	2,364	1,430	74
Agencies with a single function	1,628	827	758	43
Adult probation only	340	103	212	25
Juvenile probation only	808	249	543	16
Adult parole only	121	118	2	1
Juvenile parole only	359	357	1	1
Agencies with dual functions	1,832	1,270	532	30
Adult and juvenile probation	546	121	400	25
Adult and juvenile parole	20	20	—	—
Adult probation and parole	702	657	41	4
Juvenile probation and parole	564	472	91	1
Agencies with three or four functions	342	203	140	—
Parole authorities	65	64	—	1

—Represents zero.
Source: U.S.Department of Justice, *State and Local Probation and Parole Systems* (Washington, D.C.: U.S. Government Printing Office, 1978), p.2.

Table 3.3 Number of State and Local Agencies Performing Probation or Parole Functions, by Level of Government, September 1, 1976

Level of Government	Agency Function[a]									
	Probation				Parole					
	Adult Probation		Juvenile Probation		Adult Parole		Juvenile Parole		Parole Authorities	
	Number	%	Number	%	Number	%	Number	%	Number	%
State-local total	1,929	100	2,126	100	1,154	100	1,221	100	65	100
State	1,087	56	916	43	984	85	992	81	64	98
County	788	41	1,167	55	165	15	227	19	—	—
Municipal	54	3	43	2	5	(Z)	2	(Z)	1	2

—Represents zero.
Z Percent rounds to zero.
[a]Agencies having multiple functions are counted in more than one column. The figures therefore do not agree with Table 3.2, which counts agencies only once in single or multifunctional categories.

Source: U.S. Department of Justice, *State and Local Probation and Parole Systems* (Washington, D.C.: U.S. Government Printing Office, 1978), p. 2.

probation. Several states have enacted statutory restrictions on the utilization of probation. For example, statutes may prohibit the utilization of probation for offenders who have committed certain types of offenses, such as murder, rape or capital offenses, or offenders who have demonstrated a habitual pattern of similar serious offenses, or if the offender was armed at the time he committed the crime. Therefore, the decision to grant probation is characterized by the broad discretionary authority of the court operating within an umbrella of statutory limitations.

One of the primary devices utilized by the court to decide whether to grant probation is the pre-sentence investigation which is usually prepared for the court by a probation officer. The main purpose of the pre-sentence investigation is to provide the sentencing court with pertinent information concerning the offender so that it may have a sound basis on which to select the most appropriate sentencing alternative.

The American Bar Association Project on Standards for Criminal Justice recommends that a full pre-sentence report should contain the following items:

a. a complete description of the offense and the circumstances surrounding it, not limited to aspects developed for the record as part of the determination of guilt;

b. a full description of any prior criminal record of the offender;

c. a description of the educational background of the offender.

d. a description of the employment background of the offender, including any military record and including his present employment status and capabilities;

e. the social history of the offender, including family relationships, marital status, interests and activities, residence history, and religious affiliations;

f. the offender's medical history and, if desirable, a psychological or psychiatric report;

g. information about environments to which the offender might return or to which he could be sent should probation be granted;

h. supplementary reports from clinics, institutions and other social agencies with which the offender has been involved;

i. information about special resources which might be available to assist the offender, such as treatment centers, residential facilities, vocational training services, special educational facilities, rehabilitative programs of various institutions to which the offender might be committed, special programs in the probation department and other similar programs which are particularly relevant to the offender's situation;

j. a summary of the most significant aspects of the report, including specific recommendations as to the sentence if the sentencing court has so requested.[15]

The pre-sentence report concludes with a recommendation section if it is requested by the judge. This constitutes a crucial element of the report because it is in this section that the probation officer presents his recommendations to the court regarding what he believes to be the appropriate sentence for the defendant. In some cases the probation officer may conclude that the interests of the offender and society are best served by incarceration whereas in other cases he may conclude that probation is the most appropriate disposition. It should be noted that in a very high percentage of cases, estimated in some instances as high as 95 percent, the probation officer's recommendations are followed by the court. Several explanations have been suggested for this situation, including: (1) probation officers are in a strategic position to suggest the most appropriate sentencing alternative because of the thorough knowledge they have acquired through conducting the pre-sentence investigation and because judges are influenced by what they read in the report; (2) probation officers may deliberately suggest sentencing recommendations that will "mesh" with the beliefs, biases and prejudices of particular judges; (3) probation officers and judges may rely on similar factors in reaching sentencing decisions; and (4) some cases, to both judges and probation officers, may be interpreted as "clear-cut" cases warranting obvious dispositions of either incarceration or probation.

Normally, the recommendation of the probation officer also includes a treatment plan, given the recommended disposition. If the defendant is recommended for probation, the probation officer may propose suggestions for his probation, including plans for residence, education, employment, medical/psychiatric treatment and utilization of community resources.

Figure 3.1 is a copy of the Pre-Sentence Investigation Form which is utilized by the Eighteenth Judicial District Court, State of Kansas. The probation officer uses the information supplied on this form by the offender along with corroborating evidence he obtains from pertinent persons, agencies and resources to develop, in narrative form, the pre-sentence investigation report he presents to the sentencing court.

In addition to the Long Form Pre-sentence Report previously described, an abbreviated variant of this report, frequently called the Short Form Pre-sentence Report, is often utilized. A short form report normally consists of a cover sheet and the following data: official version of the offense, defendant's version of the offense, prior record, abbreviated version of the defendant's personal history and evaluative summary and recommendation. The impetus for the short form developed out of a recognition of enormous case loads and the inability of probation officers to always prepare full-length reports given the time-consuming nature of this task and the manpower available. Furthermore, a well prepared short

Figure 3.1 Pre-Sentence Investigation Form

```
                        PRE-SENTENCE INVESTIGATION FORM


   Name:_____Judge:_____

   Case No._____Attorney:_____

   K.S.A._____Class:_____Appointed:_____Retained:_____

   K.S.A._____Class:_____D.A._____

   K.S.A._____Class:_____Bond:_____Jail:_____

   Reduced To:_____No. of Counts:_____

   Today's Date:_____Sentencing Date:_____

   Assigned to C.S.O._____Interview Date:_____



                             DEFENDANT

   The Judge has ordered a Pre-Sentence Report made on you which begins with this
   questionnaire.  Fill in all blanks and dates.  Write legibly or print.  Use the
   back of a page if more space is needed.

   Full Name:_____Marital Status:_____
                 First    Middle     Last
   Aliases:_____

   Address:_____Phone:_____
               Street         City & State        Zip
   Alternate Phone No._____Name:_____
                                                        Relationship
   Date of Birth:_____Age:_____Height:_____Weight:_____

   Place of Birth:_____Race:_____
                        City & State
   Color of Hair:_____Color of Eyes:_____Scars:_____

   Complexion: Fair:_____Ruddy:_____Light Brown:_____Dark Brown:_____

   Social Security No._____D.L.No._____

   Employment:_____
                     Name                  Address
   Supervisor or Boss:_____Mo./Yrs.Employed:_____

   Year and Make of Car:_____Tag No._____

   Present Offense: Your version and physical condition at the time (drugs/alcohol).

   _____

   _____

   _____

   _____

   _____

   _____

   _____

   _____

   _____

   _____

   _____

   _____
```

Prior Record: Juvenile, Adult, Traffic and DWI

Type	City & State	Date	Disposition

Ever been on Probation? Explain for what and reaction to probation.

_____

_____

_____

_____

Personal and Family Data:

Your Childhood: Good, Bad? Explain._____

_____

Dicipline: Type._____

Activities: (Scouts, Youth Organizations?)_____

Your relationship with parents:_____

Your relationship with siblings:_____

Parents divorced during childhood?_____

If so, how did this affect you?_____

Responsibilities at home?_____

Age left home and circumstances:_____

_____

Family's attitude towards you for this offense:_____

EDUCATION

Name of School - Grades	Address	Date- Graduate
College:		
Trade School:		
High School:		
Intermediate:		
Grade:		

Did you like school?_____Average grades:_____Attendance:_____

Sport activities:_____ Clubs:_____

EMPLOYMENT

List your employment for the past five years starting with present or last job.

Employer	Address	Dates	Type of Work	Terminated? Why?

Job Skills:_____

MILITARY

Have you been in the Military Service?_____If so, what Branch?_____

Dates: Entered:_____Discharged:_____Type of Discharge:_____

Describe what you did:_____

Rank at time of discharge:_____Eligible for VA Benefits?_____

If so, explain:_____

Military Serial No._____

ECONOMIC STATUS

Monthly income:_____Is your spouse employed?_____If so, where:_____

What is his/her income?_____Do you have a checking account?_____

Do you have a savings account?_____Do you have a budget?_____

Do you owe attorney fees?_____If so, how much?_____Payments?_____

Other outstanding debts:

Owed To	For	Total Amount	Amount of Payments

HOUSING

Do you live in a room_____Apartment_____House_____Mobile Home_____Other_____

Do you own_____Rent_____Monthly rent or payment_____

Who do you live with?_____Relationship:_____

List the last three previous addresses where you lived. Why you moved.

Address, City & State	Dates	Reason for Moving

HEALTH

Childhood Diseases:_____

Any severe illness or injury?____Explain:_____

Hospital:_____Dates:_____

Under current medical treatment?_____Type:_____Dr._____

Any emotional problems?_____Explain:_____

Psychiatric Evaluation or Treatment?_____Explain and give dates:_____

_____

Where?_____

Name of Psychiatrist or Psychologist:_____

Address:_____

Ever use any drugs not prescribed?_____Use of alcohol?_____

Ever had treatment for drug usage?____Explain:_____

_____

SUBSTANCE USE

TYPE	Age You Began	Age(s)Used Regularly	Age Quit	How Often Used	Ever O.D.	Method:Drank, Ate Smoke,Inject,Snort
Alcohol						
Marijuana						
Tolec/Solvent						
Hallucinogens: LSD,PCP,THC, Acid, Mescaline, Psilocybin						
Amphetamines: White Crosses, Blacks, Xmas, Trees, Crystal, Methedrine, Desoxyn, Dexedrine						
Barbiturates: Reds, Downers, Amytal, Nembutal, Phenobarbital, Seconal, Tuinal						
Tranquilizers: Librum, Equinil, Qaaludes, Miltown, Valium, Placidyl, Methaqualone, Stellazine						
Cocaine						
Merhadone (Legal or Illegal)						
Heroin						
Other Narcotics: Morphine, Opium, Codeine, Demarol, Dilaudid, Percodan						

MARITAL STATUS

Have you ever been married?_____ How many times?_____ Chidren?_____
                                                                    (No.)

List your marriages, reason for divorce or termination and children's names:

First name & prior last name of Spouse	Reason of Divorce	Children

Are you living with someone?(opposite sex)_____ Who?_____

Are you paying Child Support?_____ How Much?_____ To?_____

Do you have custody of any children from a divorce?_____

RELIGIOUS PREFERENCE

Do you attend church?_____ Do you belong to a church?_____ Name:_____

Do you believe in: Witchcraft?_____ ESP?____ Astrology?_____ Some type of God?_____

Did you attend church as a child?_____ Protestant?_____ Catholic?_____

Other religion?_____

SIBLINGS (Brothers & Sisters)

Name	Relation	Age	Address & Phone	Occupation

Have any been arrested?_____ If so, for what?_____

Any been on drugs or alcohol?_____ Explain:_____

Relationship with brothers & sisters:_____

Do you have a continuing relationship with them?_____

Did they ever involve you in crime?_____ Explain:_____

Did they ever serve time in prison?_____

LEISURE - TIME ACTIVITIES

What do you do for recreation?_____

Do you have any hobbies?_____

Do like to read?_____ Watch TV?_____ Go to movies?_____

PARENTS

Natural Father:_____Address:_____

Phone:_____Employment:_____

Place of Birth:_____Age:_____Education:_____

Health:_____Alcoholic?_____Drug Abuse?_____

Psychiatric problems?_____Explain:_____

Marriages : To:_____Dates:_____

        To:_____Dates:_____

Natural Mother:_____Address:_____

Phone:_____Employment:_____

Place of Birth:_____Age:_____Education:_____

Health:_____Alcoholic?_____Drug Abuse?_____

Psychiatric Problems?_____Explain:_____

Marriages: To:_____Dates:_____

       To:_____Dates:_____

Who raised you?_____Any incest?_____

Stepparents: Father?_____

Address:_____Phone:_____

Occupation:_____Alcoholic?_____

Stepparents: Mother?_____

Address:_____Phone:_____

Occupation:_____Alcoholic?_____

How did your stepparent(s) treat you? _____

_____ _____

Did you feel your stepsister(s) or stepbrother(s) were favored over you? _____

Explain:_____

OTHER INFORMATION

Do you feel you should have probation?____Why?_____

_____

_____

Is there anything else you want the court to know about your circumstances?

_____

_____

_____

_____

_____

_____Information Given By

```
                    AUTHORIZATION FOR RELEASE OF INFORMATION

I,_____,  _____, hereby authorize
                                              (D.O.B)
_____
(name of agency, program or individual and title)
to disclose the following information from my records.(Specify extent or nature of
information to be disclosed.)  _____
_____

The purpose or need for such disclosure is _____
_____

Medical records are protected by Federal Regulations, Kansas Statutes and/or
Administrative Regulations and any further disclosure is prohibited without
the undersigned's consent.

This authorization is subject to revocation at any time except to the extent that
action has been taken in reliance thereon.

Specify the date, event or condition upon which this consent expires_____
_____
(If left blank, expiration date is sixty (60) days after the date entered below.)

If applicable, disclosure made pursuant to this authorization shall be accompanied
by a written statement regarding re-disclosure as provided for by Federal Regula-
tion 42C.F.R.  Part 2.


_____          _____
       Date                        Signed


_____          _____
      Witness                  Parent or Legal Guardian Signature


    (2-15-81)                                        5-11a
```

form would still contribute in a meaningful fashion to the sentencing decision of the judge.

Conditions of Probation

Probation is a form of conditional release, that is, the liberty of the offender to remain in the community is contingent upon his compliance with court-imposed conditions. Conditions of probation are usually identified as either "general" or "special" conditions. General conditions refer to conditions that are applicable to all probationers. Typical examples of general conditions that may be imposed are: the requirement that probationers should not violate any criminal laws of the United States and/or state in which probationer resides, or the requirement that probationers should not associate with persons who have criminal records. Special conditions relate to conditions that are imposed by the court in individual-specific cases. Their intent is to individualize the conditions of release in recognition that offenders have different needs and problems that may need to be addressed to maximize their chances for a successful probation outcome. The requirement that a particular probationer who is diagnosed as an alcoholic submit to treatment for his alcoholism or that a particular probationer who committed a crime that resulted in a financial loss to the victim due to property damage or loss or personal injury be required to pay restitution are common examples of special conditions that may be imposed.

The American Bar Association Project on Standards for Criminal Justice developed the following guidelines pertaining to the nature and determination of conditions of probation:

a. It should be a condition of every sentence to probation that the probationer lead a law-abiding life during the period of this probation. No other conditions should be required by statute; but the sentencing court should be authorized to prescribe additional conditions to fit the circumstances of each case. Development of standard conditions as a guide to sentencing courts is appropriate so long as such conditions are not routinely imposed.

b. Conditions imposed by the court should be designed to assist the probationer in leading a law-abiding life. They should be reasonably related to his rehabilitation and not unduly restrictive of his liberty or imcompatible with his freedom of religion. They should not be so vague or ambiguous as to give no real guidance.

c. Conditions may appropriately deal with matters such as the following:

   i. cooperating with a program of supervision;
   ii. meeting family responsibilities;
   iii. maintaining steady employment or refraining from engaging in a specific employment or occupation;
   iv. pursuing prescribed educational or vocational training;
   v. undergoing available medical or psychiatric treatment;
   vi. maintaining residence in a prescribed area or in a special facility established for or available to persons on probation;

 vii. refraining from consorting with certain types of people or frequenting certain types of places;

 viii. making restitution of the fruits of the crime or reparation for loss or damage caused thereby.[16]

The Role of the Probation Officer

The role of the probation officer revolves around two basic functions: (1) supervision and (2) investigation.

Supervision

One of the primary responsibilities of the probation officer is to provide supervision of probationers. This responsibility involves two distinct and conflicting components: surveillance and treatment.

In the context of supervision, surveillance refers to the probation officer's duty to realize one of the goals of probation—the protection of the public. In this capacity the probation officer is expected to monitor the probationer's behavior to make certain that the probationer obeys the law and abides by the conditions of his probation, and to recommend revocation of probation when warranted. Therefore, probation supervision involves a law enforcement dimension.

In addition to the component of surveillance, supervision also involves a treatment component in which the probation officer has an obligation to help the probationer in his reintegration into society through the provision of support, guidance and counseling services. The probation officer is expected to utilize his skills and resources to help the probationer resolve any difficulties that he may experience during the period of his probation, such as family, financial and/or employment problems, as well as any other social adjustment problems that the probationer may encounter. Consequently, probation supervision also encompasses a social work dimension.

In recent years, the treatment component of supervision has experienced somewhat of a redefinition. Due to a growing recognition and realization that probation officers are not able to satisfactorily serve as the sole treatment agent for probationers, as a result of time constraints (a significant amount of a probation officer's time is required to complete pre-sentence investigations and satisfy administrative responsibilities), the complexities of offender problems and lack of appropriate training and treatment skills, probation officers frequently prefer to envision one of their basic functions as serving as brokers or community resource managers. According to the National Advisory Commission on Criminal Justice Standards and Goals:

 ... This means that the probation officer will have responsibility for meshing a probationer's identified needs with a range of available services and for supervising the delivery of those services.

To carry out his responsibilities as a community resource manager, the probation officer must perform several functions. In helping a probationer obtain needed services, the probation officer will have to assess the situation, know the available (community) resources, contact the appropriate resources, assist the probationer to obtain the services and follow up on the case.[17]

Examples of appropriate community resources might be programs for substance abuse, employment, financial management, mental health services, education and vocational training. Figure 3.2 depicts the concept of resource brokerage.

One program that incorporates the broker or community resource manager approach to probation services is Community Resources Management Team, or CRMT. Heralded by its advocates as a coming method of operation for probation and parole in the United States, Community Resources Management Team represents a significant departure from traditional probation practices through its greater emphasis on the utilization of community resources, the pooling of case

Figure 3.2 Resource Brokerage

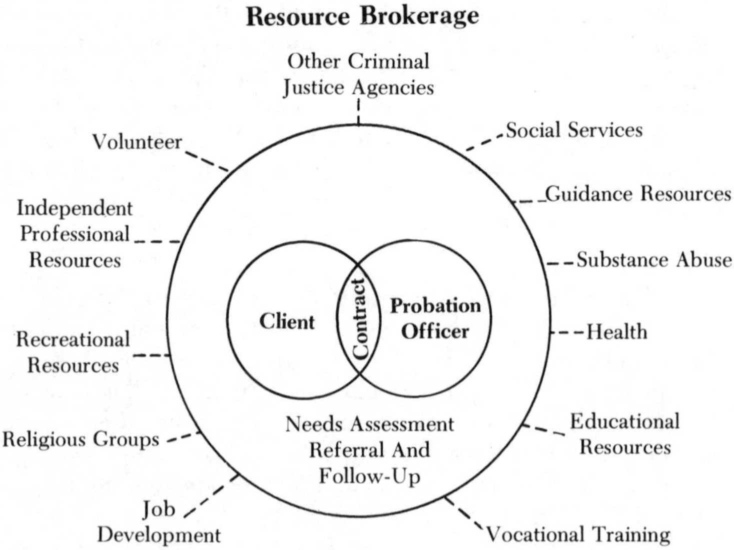

Resource Brokerage

Source: U.S. Department of Justice—National Institute of Justice, *Improved Probation Strategies: Trainer's Handbook* (Washington, D.C.: U.S. Government Printing Office, 1979), p. 176.

loads and team management instead of one-on-one counseling. Instead of operating on a traditional case load basis in which individual probation officers attempt to address all the problems of the clients on their case load personally, probation officers are organized into a team in which the group shares a case load of clients. Designed to improve the delivery of services to clients, the Community Resources Management Team assesses the needs of their clients, such as assistance in employment, education and vocational training, substance abuse, legal assistance and mental health. Oftentimes, certain team members specialize in certain client problem areas, such as education, employment and vocational services; other members may specialize in substance abuse services or mental health services. It is the role of the various Community Resources Management Team members to serve as resource brokers who link the probationers with the appropriate services in the community. Team members serve as advocates to ensure cooperation and the delivery of needed services for their clients from community service agencies. Team members are also responsible for monitoring the client's activities.

Investigation

In addition to the function of supervising probationers, probation officers also have the function of preparing investigative reports for the court. The principal investigation responsibility of the probation officer is the preparation of the pre-sentence investigation report for the court to help the court make appropriate dispositions of cases. Pre-sentence investigations are utilized extensively in felony cases. In misdemeanant cases they are seldom used; they are employed in selected cases. When employed in misdemeanant cases, an abbreviated format is normally used.

Revocation of Probation

The sentencing court has the authority to revoke the offender's probation at any time during the period of probation. Generally, there are two bases for the revocation of probation. In the first instance, the probationer may commit a "technical" violation, that is, he may violate the conditions of his probation. For example, a particular probationer may fail to comply with various conditions of his probation on a regular basis, such as failing to participate in an alcohol treatment program, to pay restitution or to report to his probationer officer as directed. This constitutes a grounds for revocation. In the second instance, the probationer may commit a new criminal offense. Therefore, if the probationer is in violation of the conditions of his probation or commits a new criminal offense, there is a possibility of revocation, that is, the removal of the offender from probation, which often results in the incarceration of the offender. However, not all violations necessarily lead the probation officer to recommend revocation or lead to a revocation hearing. Probation officers exercise broad discretion in this matter.

There is a noticeable lack of consensus concerning what constitutes an appropriate justification for the revocation of probation. It is maintained by some judges and probation officers that the only justifiable basis for revocation of probation is conviction for new offenses. Others contend that violations of conditions of probation other than the commitment of a new criminal offense also is a sufficient basis for revocation, especially when such violations are committed by a probationer who appears to be unconcerned and apathetic and who demonstrates a lack of willingness to cooperate with the probation agency and court. Still, another group believes that before recommending revocation of probation, the probation officer should carefully weigh and consider the circumstances of the violations, the general attitude and outlook of the probationer, his social adjustment during the period of his probation with his family, his job, overall probation plan and his community, along with his efforts to abide with the conditions of his probation.[18]

Too often in the past probation could be simply and speedily revoked without due process rights for the probationer. However, in recent years the United States Supreme Court has handed down decisions which have provided prodecural safeguards to apply at revocation of probation (and parole) proceedings. Three cases are of primary significance in this regard: *Mempa* v. *Rhay*, *Morrissey* v. *Brewer* and *Gagnon** v. *Scarpelli*.

In *Mempa* v. *Rhay*, 1967, the United States Supreme Court held that due process requires a hearing before probation can be revoked, that the probationer is entitled to adequate notice and that the probationer has a right to counsel at time of a revocation hearing where the imposition of the sentence has been suspended.[19] In 1972, the United States Supreme Court handed down the landmark decision on parole, in *Morrisey* v. *Brewer*.[20] The Supreme Court established specific guidelines for a two-step revocation hearing process according to the constitutional requirement of due process. One year later, in 1973, the United States Supreme Court handed down another significant decision. In *Gagnon* v. *Scarpelli* the United States Supreme Court ruled that all of the rights they had awarded to parolees in revocation proceedings also applied to probationers. Moreover, the court held that probationers and parolees had a qualified right to appointed counsel in revocation hearings.[21]

Problems

Despite its inherent advantages and widespread utilization as a community-based correctional program, probation has been subjected to

---

*At this time refer to the Section on "Revocation of Parole" in Chapter Four: Parole for a more detailed discussion of the *Morrissey* v. *Brewer* decision.

various criticisms by the public, criminal justice practitioners, scholars and probationers themselves. The principal criticisms include: (1) probation constitutes a form of leniency; (2) unmanageably large case loads contribute to the nominal supervision of probationers; (3) there is an inadequate allocation of financial resources and manpower to probation services; (4) the conditions of probation are oftentimes overly severe, punitive, arbitrary and ambiguous; and (5) the probation decisionmaking process is too discretionary.

A Form of Leniency

The public oftentimes perceives probation as a form of leniency which unjustly depreciates the seriousness of the behavior which has been committed by the offender. The argument is introduced that disrespect for law and order in society may be fostered because criminals are not appropriately punished. After all, imprisonment is appropriate punishment; releasing the offender back into the community is not—"it's nothing more than slapping the offender on the wrist and telling him he had better not do it again." Additionally, these critics maintain that, given the realities of the practice of probation today, the release of the offender back into the community (even if conditional and technically under supervision), does not satisfactorily insure the protection of the public.

In reaction to this line of criticism, the American Bar Association Project on Standards for Criminal Justice has recommended that probation should be the preferred sentence, rather than imprisonment, *unless*:

1. confinement is necessary to protect the public from further criminal activity; or
2. the offender is in need of correctional treatment which can most effectively be provided if he is confined; or
3. it would unduly depreciate the seriousness of the offense if a sentence of probation were imposed.[22]

Large Case Loads: Nominal Supervision

Another frequent criticism of probation is centered upon the unmanageably large case loads assigned to probation officers. Case loads between 50 and 100 are commonplace and even larger case loads are not uncommon. Case loads of this size preclude the attainment of the supervision dimension of probation. Due to the large percentage of time devoted by the probation officer to investigative functions, administrative tasks, general preparation and completion of pre-sentence investigations and other reports, the actual supervision of probationers is frequently relegated to a position of secondary importance. The result has been that supervision of the probationer in the community is often only nominal. Critics suggest that it would indeed be appropriate to describe the supervision component of probation as "supervision in name only" or as primarily a pretense or as "token supervision." Other critics maintain that many periods of probation are actually nothing more than unsupervised suspended sentences. The bottom line is: although supervision constitutes an essential element of probation in theory, in practice it does not appear to be an indispensable ingredient.

Various strategies have been suggested to address this problem, including the classification of probationers into different risk categories and the employment of programs requiring varying kinds and amounts of supervision, utilizing supervision as a variable condition of probation which may or may not be imposed in a particular case, discharging offenders from probation by court order when they have received the maximum benefit from supervision and utilizing volunteers in probation service.

Inadequate Allocation of Financial Resources and Manpower

Another common criticism of probation services is that they are inadequately funded and staffed, given the number of offenders under supervision. Critics maintain that probation services must be better organized, staffed and funded if the desired objectives of probation are to be achieved. According to the Chamber of Commerce of the United States:

> A major weakness in probation and parole services is that they have never received adequate funds for the number of offenders under supervision. Two-thirds of all offenders are under probation or parole supervision, but these services receive less than one-third of the moneys allocated for correctional efforts.[23]

Similarly, Morris and Hawkins note:

> Although...four-fifths of the correctional budget is spent and nine-tenths of correctional employees work in penal institutions, only one-third of all offenders are confined in them; two-thirds are under supervision in the community.[24]

These passages point to a glaring disparity between situation and resources.

Undesirable Conditions of Probation

An additional criticism relates to the conditions of probation. In some instances, they are berated as being overly severe, rigid, demanding, punitive, arbitrary and ambiguous. They are also frequently criticized as being concerned primarily with specifying behaviors in which probationers should not engage. It is often argued that probationers are expected to maintain elevated standards of behavior that even the average citizen would experience difficulty meeting. As a result of such criticisms, there has been a trend in recent years to reduce the number of conditions imposed on probationers and to make them more realistic, practical, enforceable and individualized according to the specific needs of the offender.

Discretionary Nature of the Selection Process

Although sentencing guidelines may assist the court in the probation decisionmaking process in some instances, considerable discretion is exercised in most probation decisions. The pre-sentence investigation report prepared by the probation officer remains the principal device utilized by the court in deciding for or against a sentence of probation. Although it provides the court with information about the offender, the ultimate decision may be based upon the personal beliefs and attitudes of the judge and probation staff regarding the particular offender and offense. To counter criticisms of discretion and sentencing disparity directed against the probation decisionmaking process, various decision guidelines for probation decisions have been developed in an attempt to predict the likelihood of successful probation, to minimize sentencing disparities and to promote consistency in decisionmaking. For example, the Vera Institute of Justice in New York developed a scoring system, based upon the factors of a defendant's prior criminal record, employment record and family relationships, to assist workers in making sentence recommendations.

Cost

According to Clear and Clear, "Economic considerations are going to play a key role in the development of the correctional system within the next decade.... The bottom line of the future is going to be economic accountability."[25]

Therefore, the future of probation should be bright. One very important aspect of probation in its favor is its cost. As the following examples will clearly demonstrate, probation constitutes, perhaps, the least expensive alternative to incarceration.

In 1967, the President's Commission on Law Enforcement and Administration of Justice reported that:

> The overall daily cost for a juvenile in an institution is 10 times more than the cost of juvenile probation or aftercare. For adults, State institutional cost is about 6 times that of parole and about 14 times that of probation.[26]

Cocoros and Fraizer et al. conducted a detailed cost investigation which compared incarceration and adult felon probation in Texas. They concluded, in 1973, that incarceration costs ten times more than probation per client.[27] In 1975, the Tennessee Law Enforcement Planning Commission reported quite similar findings on the basis of their study which compared probation and incarceration as correctional programs.[28] According to a report published by the Virginia Department of Corrections in 1976, the cost of imprisoning an offender in that state was $6,862, whereas the cost of placing an offender on probation was only $472. Thus, incarceration was discovered to cost 14 times more than probation.[29]

The fact is indisputable—it is substantially cheaper in direct costs to place an offender on probation rather than to imprison him. Furthermore, the utilization of probation will also yield great savings in terms of indirect costs. Since probation allows the offender to maintain employment in the community, the offender is in the position to contribute to personal and family support, as well as to pay federal and state taxes. In effect, potential losses brought on by incarceration in such areas as public assistance payments and tax revenue, would be reduced.

Effectiveness

Accountability is a key concern in today's world. Therefore, the question of probation effectiveness is of primary significance. However, this is not an issue that can be easily addressed. Keve, for example, states: "...research on the effectiveness of probation continues to be spotty and uncertain, and it probably is possible to find various study results to support any viewpoint.[30] Smykla mentions that: "A volume of research can be found to support just about any contention—pro and con—concerning probation...."[31] He characterizes the research on probation as garbled, contradictory and of poor quality.[32] Regarding the results of probation related research, Carlson reports that: "Unfortunately, the picture isn't all that clear...."[33] Therefore, rather than present a lengthy literature review of probation studies which might result in confusion instead of comprehension, discussion will be confined to the presentation of conclusions on probation effectiveness reached by Lipton, Martinson and Wilks and the Georgia Institute of Technology after reviewing probation effectiveness studies. However, before proceeding to an identification of these findings, it is important to cite the main factors which make it extremely difficult to evaluate probation effectiveness.

First, there is no general consensus regarding what measures should be utilized to determine probation outcome, that is, success or failure. Is it recidivism? If so, how is recidivism to be measured? There are numerous variations of what constitutes recidivism, including unsuccessful probation termination due to absconding, revocation or conviction, rearrest for a similar offense rearrest, for a similar or lesser offense and reconviction for an additional crime.[34] If traditional measures of recidivism are to be utilized as outcome measures, what follow-up period of time should be utilized? What about technical violations of conditions of probation? How should they be treated in assessing probation effectiveness? Definitional problems abound.

Another problem is the variations which exist in probation agencies and programs. Probation agencies and programs are different in terms of policies, practices and philosophies. Therefore, it is difficult to generalize findings from one agency or program to another.

An additional problem with probation evaluation studies is that they frequently do not utilize control groups for comparison purposes or for pertinent variables, such as type of offense and type and quality of probation service. When studies have utilized control groups they have experienced problems with the control groups not achieving the randomness desired. Consequently, some group differences may account for differences in outcome.[35]

The aforementioned factors should serve as a basis for exercising extreme caution in the review, analysis and interpretation of the results of probation effectiveness studies.

Lipton, Martinson and Wilks developed the following conclusions after reviewing analyses on juvenile and adult probation:

1. Intensive probation supervision (15-ward case load) is associated with lower recidivism rates for males and females under 18.
2. There were no statistically significant differences in the rates of new crimes committed by adult federal probationers under intensive supervision (15-man case load), ideal supervision (50-man case load), or minimal supervision (client-initiated contact), but intensive probation had a substantially higher rate on technical violations than the other two levels of supervision.
3. Probationers had a significantly lower violation rate than parolees. Among first offenders, probationers had a significantly lower violation rate than parolees. However, for offenders with one prior felony, and offenders with two or more prior felonies, there was no significant difference between the violation rates of probationers and parolees.
4. There is evidence that a larger proportion of offenders now imprisoned could be placed on probation instead, without any change in the reconviction rate of a jurisdiction, although with the selection of worse risks for probation, the gross success rate for probation might drop.
5. There is some evidence that a professionalized probation service with smaller case loads is capable of detecting more violations and of tolerating and managing more offenders who commit violations, than is a standard probation service.[36]

The Georgia Institute of Technology, as part of the National Evaluation Program on "Evaluation of Intensive Special Probation Projects," sponsored by the National Institute of Law Enforcement and Criminal Justice, arrived at the following conclusions on probation:

1. The literature is inconclusive that case load reduction results in a decrease in recidivism. In fact, many studies have shown increased

recidivisim which has been attributed to higher levels of surveillance.

2. Several recent case load reduction projects claim decreases in the recidivism rate, but the associated evaluation designs may not be strong enough to warrant such claims.

3. There is only weak evidence for success of volunteer probation projects.

4. Projects specializing in serving particular client groups offer evidence of successful outcomes.[37]

Juvenile Program Application

Adult probation has its counterpart in the juvenile justice system—juvenile probation. Juvenile probation constitutes one of the principal dispositional alternatives that may be imposed by a juvenile court judge who generally can exercise broad discretion in selecting an appropriate disposition from a range of possible alternatives, including dismissal of the case, suspended sentence, placement in a community treatment program and commitment to a juvenile institution.[39]

Juvenile probation, which is a legal status created by a court of juvenile jurisdiction, is "...the conditional release of a juvenile under formal supervision of the juvenile courts' probation service or other court related agency."[39] The juvenile is allowed to remain in the community, subject to conditions imposed by the court. These conditions may include general conditions, such as avoiding association with other delinquents or obeying the law, and specific conditions, such as attending school, participating in a vocational training program, obtaining employment, obeying parents and undergoing special treatment for such problems as substance abuse or psychological or emotional problems.

Juvenile probation has three interrelated objectives. They are: (a) preventing a repetition of the child's delinquent behavior; (b) preventing longtime deviate or criminal careers; and (c) assisting the child, through measures feasible to the probation service, to achieve his/her potential as a productive citizen.[40]

Although the history and development of probation has been described earlier in this chapter, it is important to introduce some additional information regarding juvenile probation and its history and utilization. First, it should be noted that the major development of juvenile probation in this country occurred in the twentieth century. Two factors of major significance in the development of juvenile probation were the wave of social reform which characterized the later half of the 19th century and the development of the juvenile court movement during the first few decades of the twentieth century.[41] The social reform movement was based upon the philosophy of a new and expanded public responsibility for the protection of the child. This movement was characterized by the passage of laws directed against cruelty to children, the development of philanthropic associations for the protection and aid of the dependent and neglected child and the establishment of specialized institutions for segregating the child offender from adult criminals.[42] In 1899, the first juvenile court in the United States was established in Cook County (Chicago), Illinois through the Juvenile Court Act of Illinois. The statute which established the juvenile court gave the court jurisdiction over all offenders up to the age of sixteen and authorized the court to appoint a probation officer in certain circumstances.[43] It was the perspective of the juvenile court that "the delinquent child had ceased to be a criminal and had the status of a child in need of care, protection, and discipline directed toward rehabilitation. As with the other two categories of children (dependent and neglected children), he became a ward of the state."[44] The first decades of the twentieth century witnessed the rapid development of the juvenile court. These two movements, that is, the wave of social reform which characterized the later half of the 19th century and the juvenile court movement which occurred during the first few decades of the 20th century, are generally credited with bringing about the development and enrichment of juvenile probation. By 1925, probation for juveniles was employed in every state.

The importance of juvenile probation today is underscored by the following figures. There were 328,854 juveniles under probation supervision on September 1, 1976. Slightly more than three-fourths of the juvenile probationers, 77 percent (251,781), were males and slightly less than one-fourth of the juvenile probationers, 23 percent (77,073), were females. Overall, almost three-fourths of the juvenile probationers, 72 percent (237,368), were delinquent offenders, that is, they had been adjudicated for an offense which would have been a crime if it had been committed by an adult. Seventy-six percent (191,427) of the male juvenile probationers and 60 percent (45,941) of the female juvenile probationers were delinquents. The remaining 24 percent (60,354) of the male juvenile probationers and 40 percent (31,132) of the female juvenile probationers were status offenders, that is, they had been adjudicated for an offense that would not have been a crime if it had been committed by an adult, such as running away from home or truancy.[45]

Up Close and Personal

Approximately three years ago, Roger Goodwin, a 54-year-old male, was charged with the second degree murder of a 50-year-old woman in a large city of a midwestern state. Through the plea bargaining process his charge was reduced to involuntary manslaughter to which he pleaded nolo contendere. He was given a one to five year sentence and placed on a four year probation. At the time of this interview, he had been on probation for two years, ten months.

QUESTION: Other than the crime you committed for which you were placed on probation, did you have any prior adult or juvenile record?

ANSWER: No, I did not have any prior adult or juvenile record. I had never been in any kind of trouble before.

QUESTION: Could you please recount the details of the crime for which you were placed on probation?

ANSWER: At the time of the crime I was working for a local trash service. I had been laid off from my regular construction job. One evening after work I returned to my apartment which I shared with George, a retired man who was approximately 71 years old. My roommate, George, and some other people were in the apartment playing dominoes. I had bought some bourbon at a liquor joint and I was drinking it with two friends of mine, Raymond and Tom, who had come over to the apartment. One of the people in the apartment was Raymond's sister, Gladys, who used to be a girl friend of mine although we hadn't lived together for quite some time. Gladys came over to me and asked me for some money. Like I said, I had been laid off from my construction job and I was working for a trash service. I was in debt. As a matter of fact, I had just paid my bills earlier that day. With what little money I had left, I bought some food. I told her that I didn't have any money to give her. Gladys got really upset—she was cussing and really raising some hell. I told her to go home and suggested to Raymond and Tom that we go somewhere else. So we went in my car to a liquor joint. A few hours later I went back home. My roommate told me that Gladys had returned to the apartment on two occasions while I was gone. Shortly after I returned to the apartment, Gladys came back to the apartment for what amounted to the fourth time. She came in the apartment. She was cussing and disturbing the peace. I told her to leave and I called the police. Gladys was a little crazy anyway. I knew that from before, and I didn't want any trouble. By the time the police arrived Gladys was on the sidewalk across from my apartment. I told the police that she was over there. I said: 'There she goes now.' The police talked to her briefly but they decided not to do anything. After the police left Gladys came back again. I went to call the police on the telephone for a second time. Gladys came into the apartment and I looked around just in time to see her coming at me with a butcher knife. She cut me. I could tell she wanted to kill me. I didn't want to hurt her but I had to protect myself. I struggled with her. She fell on a coffee table. I thought she had been knocked out. I called the police. The police felt her pulse. She was dead. When she fell the knife had apparently pierced her heart. I was arrested.

QUESTION: What crime were you charged with?

ANSWER: I was charged with second-degree murder. However, I plea bargained and the charge was reduced to involuntary manslaughter to which I pleaded nolo contendere.

QUESTION: What sentence did you receive?

ANSWER: I was given a one to five year sentence and placed on probation for a period of four years. (Probation was recommended by the probation officer who conducted the pre-sentence investigation and this recommendation was followed by the judge because the offender had no prior criminal record, the victim actually initiated the fight, the defendant had called the police twice regarding potential trouble at his apartment, the stabbing of the victim did not appear to be intentional and the defendant could possibly have been cut again by the victim or even killed if he had not tried to protect himself.)

QUESTION: What are the conditions of your probation?

ANSWER: Most importantly, that I stay out of trouble. I'm not supposed to break the law or associate with persons who have criminal records, and I'm to conduct myself as a good citizen. In addition, I'm not supposed to leave the state without the permission of my probation officer, I have to pay court costs and I must meet with my probation officer once a month. Another special condition was that I participate in an alcohol treatment program. (This last condition was imposed because an evaluation ordered by the court revealed that Mr. Goodwin was an alcoholic. He had been drinking for 18 years and had received no prior alcoholic treatment. His alcoholism had developed to the point that he was physically addicted to alcohol.)

QUESTION: You stated that one of the conditions of your probation is that you are required to meet with your probation officer once per month. What are your meetings with your probation officer like?

ANSWER: The first thing I usually do upon arriving at his office is to fill out a monthly probation report. I have to respond to questions concerning where I am living, where I'm working and what my salary is, if I'm unemployed and why, whether I have any problems that I need to discuss with my probation officer and whether I've been in any kind of trouble since the last probation monthly report. After I complete the report and my probation officer has an opportunity to look it over, we have a meeting which lasts about 20 minutes. He asks me how I'm doing and if everything is going alright. If I have any problems we talk about them.

QUESTION: During the period of your probation, have you experienced any problems? If so, did your probation officer discuss them with you and try to assist you in resolving them?

ANSWER: At the beginning of my probation I got into an awful lot of trouble. As part of my probation I was required to participate in an alcoholic treatment program. I received this treatment at the Veteran's Administration Hospital. Well, there at the start I wasn't adapting to the alcohol program very well. The head of the alcohol treatment program, Mr. Jones, and I were always getting into it about my drinking—I had started drinking again. On a few occasions the police were receiving telephone calls from my neighbors about my drinking and arguments I was having with my girl friend.

QUESTION: Did your probation officer try to help you with this problem?

ANSWER: Yes, he did. He helped me a lot. He talked with me about this problem. He tried to reason with me about the necessity to stop drinking. He emphasized the importance of my receiving alcoholic treatment at the Veteran's Administration Hospital. He talked with Mr. Jones and together they convinced me that I had to buckle down. If I didn't make a serious attempt at the program, they told me that they simply wouldn't go any further with me. My probation officer also reminded me that if I continued to drink and did not attend alcohol treatment as required as a condition of my probation, my probation could be revoked. He didn't say this to scare me but only to make me aware of the consequences of my irresponsible behavior. He helped me get through this difficult time. I haven't been in trouble since.

QUESTION: Do you think Alan is a good probation officer?

ANSWER: Yes, he sure is.

QUESTION: What qualities make him a good probation officer?

ANSWER: He's a very kind and concerned person. If you need help, he sincerely wants to help you. He will take as much time as is necessary to help you resolve your problems. He's fairly quiet but he is very easy to talk to. During the two years and ten months I have been on probation, I have learned a lot from him. What I have learned most of all is how to behave responsibly and how to avoid trouble.

QUESTION: Looking back at the crime you committed, do you think you should have been placed on probation or sent to prison?

ANSWER: I should have been placed on probation.

QUESTION: Why should you have been placed on probation?

ANSWER: I was at my own home when the trouble occurred. I called the police on two occasions in order to prevent this trouble from getting out of hand. The woman attacked me with a knife and cut me; she aimed to kill me. The situation just happened. I tried to get out of it but I couldn't. All I did was protect myself. Her death was an accident.

QUESTION: What would have happened if they would have sent you to prison instead of placing you on probation? What type of impact do you think that might have had on you?

ANSWER: If they had decided to send me to prison, I probably would have died. I wouldn't have been able to stand prison. I couldn't have made it. I just couldn't stand to be confined. I've heard so much about what happens in prison.

QUESTION: What have you heard about prison?

ANSWER: I've heard about the violence. How if you see someone get killed you are supposed to 'see nothing, hear nothing, do nothing.' I've also heard about how they offer you cigarettes and expect you to have sex with them. I wouldn't have gone for it.

QUESTION: What is the advantage of having been placed on probation?

ANSWER: It gives me my freedom! That means more to me than anything else on earth!

QUESTION: Do you think you will complete your probation satisfactorily?

ANSWER: Yes, I try to live right. I try to avoid trouble and I've received the help I needed to control my drinking. Before, I used to drink like a fish. That got me in trouble and occasionally cost me my job. This one criminal incident is the only serious trouble I have ever gotten into. I'm sorry it happened, truly sorry. I never intend to ever let something like that happen again.

Summary

Probation is (1) a community-based correctional alternative (2) that involves a sentence imposed by the court upon an offender after a finding, verdict or plea of guilty (3) which does not require the incarceration of the offender (4) but which allows the offender to remain in the community (5) subject to conditions imposed by the court and (6) supervision by a probation agency.

Probation, the supervised release of an offender to the community in lieu of incarceration, is credited as being a clearly American development. However, the origins of probation are usually traced to the English common law and such legal devices as "benefit of clergy," judicial reprieve, release on one's own recognizance, bail and the "filing" of cases. The common denominator of these practices is that they were all used to temporarily suspend sentences in order to mitigate unduly severe sentences. The credit for the first utilization of probation in America is normally accorded to John Augustus. From 1841-1859 Augustus is credited with having supervised or "bailed on probation" almost 2,000 persons. Many of the present-day features and characteristics of probation were established by Augustus. In view of the significant contributions made by Augustus to the concept and practice of probation, he is deservingly called the "father of probation." By 1925 probation for juveniles was employed in every state and by 1956 every state had a statute providing for adult probation. A statute authorizing probation by federal courts was passed in 1925.

The proponents of probation stress its desirability as an alternative to incarceration, in appropriate cases, for several reasons. The American Bar Association Project on Standards for Criminal Justice summarized the possible benefits of probation as follows:

 i. it maximizes the liberty of the individual while at the same time vindicating the authority of the law and effectively protecting the public from further violations of law;
 ii. it affirmatively promotes the rehabilitation of the offender by continuing normal community contacts;
iii. it voids the negative and frequently stultifying effects of confinement which often severely and unnecessarily complicate the reintegration of the offender into the community;
iv. it greatly reduces the financial costs to the public treasury of an effective correctional system;
 v. it minimizes the impact of the conviction upon innocent dependents of the offender.[46]

There are several areas of concern involved in the administration and process of probation. They are: (1) the organization of probation services; (2) the decision to grant probation; (3) conditions of probation; (4) the role of the probation officer; and (5) revocation of probation.

Diversity, rather than uniformity, characterizes the organization of probation services in the United States. The complexity of probation organization is underscored by the following organizational differences. Some probation agencies have a singular function, such as being responsible for juvenile probation only or being responsible for adult probation only. Other probation agencies may have dual responsibilities for both juvenile and adult probation. In instances where adult probation may be separated from juvenile probation, there still may be a further division of labor with one agency handling only adult misdemeanants and another agency handling adult felons. Still other agencies may be responsible for handling all of these types of probationers—juveniles, adult felons and adult misdemeanants. Probation agencies also differ according to the branch of government, i.e., executive, judicial or both, and the level of government, i.e., state or local, which is responsible for probation. Add to this list of variations the fact that parole services are sometimes combined with probation services in some agencies. It should also be noted that the federal system is separate.

Two factors need to be emphasized regarding the probation decisionmaking process. First, it is the responsibility of the sentencing court to make a decision to grant probation. Secondly, although the decision to grant probation resides with the court, this decision must be made within the limits of statutes regulating eligibility for probation.

Therefore, the decision to grant probation is characterized by the broad discretionary authority of the court operating within an umbrella of statutory limitations. One of the primary devices utilized by the court to decide whether to grant probation is the pre-sentence investigation report which is usually prepared for the court by a probation officer. The main purpose of the pre-sentence investigation report is to provide the sentencing court with pertinent information concerning the offender so that it may have a sound basis on which to select the most appropriate sentencing alternative.

Probation is a form of conditional release, that is, the liberty of the individual to remain in the community is contingent upon the probationer's compliance with court-imposed conditions. Conditions of probation are usually indentified as either "general" or "special" conditions. General conditions refer to conditions that are applicable to all probationers. Special conditions relate to conditions that are imposed by the court in individual-specific cases.

The role of the probation officer revolves around two basic functions: (1) supervision and (2) investigation. The function of supervision involves two distinct and conflicting components: surveillance and treatment. Surveillance refers to the probation officer's duty to realize one of the goals of probation—the protection of the public. In this capacity the probation officer is expected to monitor the probationer's behavior, making certain the probationer obeys the law and abides by the conditions of his probation and recommending revocation of probation, when warranted. Supervision also involves a treatment component in which the probation officer has an obligation to help the probationer in his reintegration into society through the provision of support, guidance and counseling services. In recent years, the treatment component has experienced somewhat of a redefinition. Therefore, probation officers frequently prefer to envision one of their basic functions as serving as brokers or community resource managers. Probation officers also fulfill an investigation function. The principal investigation responsibility of the probation officer is the preparation of the pre-sentence investigation report for the court to help the court make appropriate dispositions of cases.

The sentencing court has the authority to revoke the offender's probation at any time during the period of probation. Generally, there are two bases for the revocation of probation. In the first instance, the probationer may commit a "technical" violation, that is, he may violate the conditions of his probation. In the second instance, the probationer may commit a new offense. Therefore, if the probationer is in violation of the conditions of his probation or commits a new criminal offense there is a possibility of the removal of the offender from probation, which often results in the incarceration of the offender. However, not all violations necessarily lead the probation officer to recommend revocation or lead to a revocation hearing. Probation officers exercise broad discretion in this matter. In recent years, the United States Supreme Court has handed down cases which have provided procedural safeguards to apply at revocation of probation (and parole) proceedings. Three cases are of primary significance in this regard: *Mempa* v. *Rhay*, in 1967, *Morrisey* v. *Brewer*, in 1972 and *Gagnon* v. *Scarpelli*, in 1973.

Despite its inherent advantages and widespread utilization as a community-based correctional program, probation has been subjected to various criticisms by the public, criminal justice practitioners, scholars and probationers themselves. The principal criticisms include: (1) probation constitutes a form of leniency; (2) unmanageably large case loads contribute to the nominal supervision of probationers; (3) there is an inadequte allocation of financial resources and manpower to probation services; (4) the conditions of probation are oftentimes overly severe, punitive, arbitrary and ambiguous; and (5) the probation decisionmaking process is too discretionary.

One very important aspect of probation in its favor is its cost. The fact is indisputable—it is substantially cheaper in direct costs to place an offender on probation rather than to imprison him. Furthermore, the utilization of probation will also yield great savings in terms of indirect costs. Since probation allows the offender to maintain employment in the community, the offender is in the position to contribute to personal and family support, as well as to pay federal and state taxes. In effect, potential losses in such areas as public assistance payments and tax revenue brought on by incarceration, would be reduced. It is probable that probation constitutes the least expensive alternative to incarceration.

Accountability is a key concern in today's world. Therefore, the question of probation effectiveness is of primary significance. However, this is not an issue that can be easily addressed because there are several factors which make it extremely difficult to evaluate probation effectiveness. First, there is no general consensus regarding what measures should be utilized to determine probation success or failure. Second, probation agencies and programs are characterized by variations in policies, practices and philosophies. Therefore, it is difficult to generalize findings from one agency or program to another. Third, probation evaluation studies frequently do not utilize control groups for comparison purposes.

Adult probation has its counterpart in the juvenile justice system— juvenile probation. Juvenile probation is "...the conditional release of a juvenile under formal supervision of the juvenile courts' probation service or other court related agency."[47] The juvenile is allowed to remain in the community, subject to conditions imposed by the court. These conditions may include general conditions, such as obeying the law, and specific conditions, such as attending school, participating in a vocational training program, obtaining employment, obeying parents and undergoing special treatment for such problems as substance abuse or psychological or emotional problems. Two factors were of major significance in the development of juvenile probation: (1) the wave of social reform which characterized the latter half of the 19th century and (2) the juvenile court movement which occurred during the first few decades of the 20th century. By 1925, probation for juveniles was employed in every state.

Notes

1. President's Commission on Law Enforcement and Administration of Justice, *Task Force Report: Corrections* (Washington, D.C.: U.S. Government Printing Office, 1967), p. 206.

2. American Bar Association Project on Standards for Criminal Justice, *Standards Relating to Probation* (New York: American Bar Association, 1970), p. 9.

3. National Advisory Commission on Criminal Justice Standards and Goals, "Probation: National Standards and Goals," *Corrections* (Washington, D.C.: U.S. Government Printing Office, 1973), p. 312.

4. Charles L. Newman, *Sourcebook on Probation, Parole and Pardons*, 3d ed. (Springfield, Illinois: Charles C. Thomas, 1968), p. 12.

5. David Dressler, *Practice and Theory of Probation and Parole*, 2nd ed. (New York: Columbia University Press, 1969), p. 20.

6. Louis P. Carney, *Probation and Parole: Legal and Social Dimensions* (New York: McGraw-Hill Book Company, 1977), p. 77.

7. Norman A. Carlson, "The Future of Prisons," *Trial* 12 (March, 1976), p. 32.

8. U.S. Department of Justice, *State and Local Probation and Parole Systems* (Washington, D.C.: U.S. Government Printing Office, 1978), p. 1.

9. Ibid., p. vii.

10. American Bar Association Project on Standards for Criminal Justice, *Standards Relating to Probation*, p. 27.

11. Douglas Lipton, Robert Martinson and Judith Wilks, *The Effectiveness of Correctional Treatment: A Survey of Evaluation Studies* (New York: Praeger Publishers, 1975), pp. 9-10.

12. U.S. Department of Justice, *State and Local Probation and Parole Systems*, p. 2.

13. Ibid.

14. Ibid.

15. American Bar Association Project on Standards for Criminal Justice, *Standards Relating to Probation*, pp. 34-35.

16. Ibid., pp. 44-45.

17. National Advisory Commission on Criminal Justice Standards and Goals, *Corrections*, pp. 322-323.

18. Eugene C. Dicerbo, "When Should Probation be Revoked?," in *Probation, Parole and Community Corrections*, edited by Robert M. Carter and Leslie T. Wilkins (New York: John Wiley & Sons. Inc., 1976), p. 448.

19. Mempa v. Rhay, 389 U.S. 128, 88 S. Ct. 254, 19 L. Ed. 2d 336 (1967).

20. Morrissey v. Brewer, 408 U.S. 471, 92 S. Ct. 2593, 33 L. Ed. 2d 484 (1972).

21. Gagnon v. Scarpelli, 411 U.S. 778, 93 S. Ct. 1756, 36 L. Ed. 2d 656 (1973).

22. American Bar Association Project on Standards for Criminal Justice, *Standards Relating to Probation*, p. 10.

23. Chamber of Commerce of the United States, *Marshalling Citizen Power to Modernize Corrections* (1972), p. 3.

24. Norval Morris and Gordon Hawkins, *The Honest Politician's Guide to Crime Control* (Chicago: University of Chicago Press, 1970), p. 134.

25. Val Clear and Scott Clear, "Some Other Issues," in *Corrections: An Issues Approach*, edited by Martin D. Schwartz, Todd R. Clear, and Lawrence F. Travis III (Cincinnati: Anderson Publishing Company, 1980), p. 88, 90.

26. President's Commission on Law Enforcement and Administration of Justice, *Task Force Report: Corrections*, p. 194.

27. John A. Cocoros, Robert Lee Fraizer, Charles M. Friel and Donald J. Weisenhorn, *Incarceration and Adult Felon Probation in Texas: A Cost Comparison*, Criminal Justice Monograph, Vol. 4, No. 3 (Huntsville, Texas: Institute of Contemporary Corrections and the Behavioral Sciences, Sam Houston State University, 1973).

28. Tennessee Law Enforcement Planning Commission, *Probation and Parole*, by Pamela Collins, Ron Fryar, Linda Myers, Romon Sanchez-Villas. Joint Report of the Tennessee Department of Corrections and the Tennessee Law Enforcement Planning Commission (Nashville, Tennessee: Tennessee Law Enforcement Planning Commission, 1975).

29. Virginia Department of Corrections, "Corrections Options for the Eighties," 1978, p. 80.

30. Paul W. Keve, *Corrections* (New York: John Wiley and Sons, Inc., 1981), p. 260.

31. John Ortiz Smykla, *Community-Based Corrections* (New York: Macmillan Publishing Co., Inc., 1981), p. 148.

32. Ibid.

33. Rick J. Carlson, *The Dilemmas of Corrections* (Lexington, Massachusetts: D.C. Heath and Company, 1976), p. 94.

34. U.S. Department of Justice, *National Evaluation Program: Evaluation of Intensive Special Probation Projects* (Washington, D.C.: U.S. Government Printing Office, September, 1977), p. 5.

35. Ibid.

36. Douglas Lipton, Robert Martinson, and Judith Wilks, *The Effectiveness of Correctional Treatment: A Survey of Treatment Evaluation Studies* (New York: Praeger, 1975), pp. 59-61.

37. U.S. Department of Justice, *National Evaluation Program: Evaluation of Intensive Special Probation Projects*, p. iii.

38. Joseph J. Senna and Larry J. Siegel, *Introduction to Criminal Justice* (St. Paul, Minnesota: West Publishing Company, 1981), p. 613.

39. Douglas R. Besharov, *Juvenile Justice Advocacy* (New York: Practising Law Institute, 1975), p. 379.

40. President's Commission on Law Enforcement and Administration of Justice, *Task Force Report: Corrections*, p. 131.

41. Ibid.

42. Ibid.

43. Rodney J. Henningsen, *Probation and Parole* (New York: Harcourt Brace Jovanovich, Inc., 1981), p. 16.
44. Ruth S. Cavan, *Juvenile Delinquency* (Philadelphia: J.B. Lippincott Co., 1962), p. 362.
45. U.S. Department of Justice, *State and Local Probation and Parole Systems*, p. 3.
46. American Bar Association Project on Standards for Criminal Justice, *Standards Relating to Probation*, p. 27.
47. Douglas R. Besharov, *Juvenile Justice Advocacy*, p. 379.

Chapter 4
Parole

Between 96 and 99 percent of the offenders who have been imprisoned will eventually return to society.[1] Therefore, a principal preoccupation of most prisoners is getting out of prison. They look forward with great anticipation to the day when they will be released. Among the ways in which a prisoner may be released are discharge at expiration of full sentence, release at the expiration of the maximum term of imprisonment minus good time or mandatory release, pardon and commutation of sentence. However, parole is the primary concern of most prisoners as it constitutes the dominant method of release from prison for offenders. According to the National Advisory Commission on Criminal Justice Standards and Goals, in 1966, 61 percent of prisoners were released from prison via parole, while this figure increased to 72 percent by 1970.[2] Cole and Talarico note that in 1976 approximately 60 percent of adult felons were released from prison on parole.[3] Stanley mentions that more than 60,000 felons are released on parole every year.[4]

Definition

Although there are several prevalent definitions of parole, many of them concentrate exclusively upon its legal aspects. However, to perceive of parole in its fullest sense as a community-based program, it is necessary to allude to its social objectives. Giardini, for example, asserts that a purely legalistic definition "does not convey the real meaning of parole as a service, the aim of which is to bring about a social readjustment in the life of an individual in conflict with society."[5] In a similar vein, Lipton, Martinson and Wilks suggest that parole should be viewed both as a legal status and a treatment method.[6] Therefore, parole may be defined, in an ideal-type sense, as a correctional method through which an offender, who has already served a portion of his sentence in prison, is conditionally released from a correctional facility to serve part of the unexpired sentence in the community under the continued custody of the state and under the supervision and treatment of a parole officer, with successful social reintegration as the objective.

This definition specifically refers to several underlying dimensions of the practice of parole. First, parole is granted after an offender has served a portion of his full sentence in prison. This alludes to the fact that the practice of parole is closely related to the concept and procedure of the indeterminate sentence. An indeterminate sentence, in its truest sense, has no minimum and maximum time specifications. Most indeterminate sentence laws, in actuality, specify that imprisonment shall be for a period of "not less than" a certain period of time "nor more than" a certain period of time. Therefore, the release of an offender is entirely dependent on an evaluation by the paroling authority of the offender's readiness for release from prison within the time limits fixed by the court. Second, society is protected by the legal status of parole which consists of placing the offender under restrictions and conditions of conduct which, if violated, can result in his reincarceration in a correctional facility. Third, the offender remains under the custody and control of the state while on parole. Fourth, as a treatment method parole is designed to assist the offender in becoming socially reintegrated into the community through the supervision and assistance of a parole officer.

History

An appreciation of present-day parole requires a review of its historical antecedents. This is necessary since not one but several independent penal practices contributed to its development. The following measures and practices were of special significance in the development of parole: (1) the conditional pardon; (2) the transportation of criminals to America and Australia; (3) apprenticeship by indenture; (4) the "ticket-of-leave" system; and (5) American prison reform in the 19th century.[7]

Conditional Pardon/Transportation/Indenture

Early in the seventeenth century England began to transport its criminals to the American colonies. This policy can be traced to the passage of a law in 1597 which provided for the banishment of dangerous criminals. The development and utilization of this practice by the English government can be attributed to two complementary factors. First, at that time England was plagued by severe economic pressures as evidenced by acute economic conditions, high taxes, an overcrowded labor market and rising rates of unemployment. Second, although there was an overabundance of labor in England, there were insistent demands for labor in the American colonies due to colonization. The criminals, in essence, constituted a captive "labor pool." As a result of these complementary conditions, the King of England approved a plan to grant reprieves and stays of execution to convicted felons who satisfied the requirement of being physically able to be employed. Originally, there were no specific conditions imposed on those criminals who received pardons. This practice was later amended in 1655 to include specific conditions and to provide for the revocation of the pardon if the offender failed to comply with the conditions and restrictions imposed on him. This amendment was necessitated because many of those criminals who were granted pardons avoided transportation or returned to England before their terms had officially expired.

During the early period of the transportation program, each contractor was paid a fee by the English government for each prisoner transported. This practice was terminated in 1717 after the enactment of a new law which stipulated that the contractor or shipmaster was to be given "property in service" of the prisoner until his full term had been completed. Upon delivery of the prisoner to the contractor or shipmaster, the government abandoned its interest in the well-being or behavior of the prisoner except if he violated the conditions of the pardon by returning to England before his term expired.

Upon their arrival in the Colonies, the services of the pardoned criminals were sold to the highest bidder. This resulted in the transfer of the "property in service" agreement from the shipmaster to the new master. Henceforth, the criminal was no longer called a convicted criminal; he was an indentured servant. Conditions imposed upon indentured servants were specified in an indenture agreement. This is similar to the procedure presently employed with parolees who agree in writing to abide by certain conditions for their release. A release form specifying such conditions is normally signed by the members of the parole board and the prisoner.

The termination of the Revolutionary War brought an end to the transportation of criminals to America. However, after the discovery of Australia in 1787, England sent her felons to Australia to exploit the land. This practice continued in Australia until 1867.

The Ticket-of-Leave: The Australian, English and Irish Experiences

Alexander Maconochie, considered to be one of the major pioneers in parole, served as superintendent of the Norfolk Island Prison Colony off the coast of Australia. Under his leadership several reforms in the Australian penal system were instituted, many of which represented a harsh attack on the basic structure and philosophy of the system itself. At the "heart" of the system which Maconochie introduced to the Australian prison at Norfolk Island was the "mark/ticket-of-leave system." The "mark system" represented a significant departure from the existing penal system wherein a prisoner was required to serve a definite sentence. However, the mark system instituted by Maconochie enabled a prisoner to earn early release through the accumulation of "marks" which were earned through hard work and behaviors compliant with prison regulations. Marks could be utilized to purchase rations or to reduce a prisoner's sentence. Consequently, the mark system provided inmates with a new feeling of optimism and hope for an earlier return to England and it encouraged hard work and good behavior on the behalf of inmates. Along with the "mark system" Maconochie incorporated into the penal system, a five-stage program of "graduated release" was designed to prepare inmates for release and return to life in the community. The five stages were as follows: (1) strict custody; (2) labor in government work gangs; (3) limited freedom within a prescribed area; (4) "tickets-of-leave"; and (5) total freedom.[8] When an inmate progressed to the fourth stage through the accumulation of a sufficient amount of marks he was entitled to a "ticket-of-leave" which, in essence, was the granting of freedom to the inmate, subject to restrictive conditions.

The English Penal Servitude Act of 1853, which governed prisoners in England and Ireland, substituted imprisonment for transportation. It also made it possible to grant a conditional release on "ticket-of-leave" to prisoners for good conduct, usually after they had served a specified part of their sentences. It was made clear to those offenders who were conditionally released on "ticket-of-leave" that it was not necessary for them to be convicted of a new crime to have their license revoked. If an offender associated with disreputable persons, led an idle or dissolute life or was unable to secure satisfactory employment to make an honest living, it would be interpreted that the offender was about to return to a criminal lifestyle. He would then be immediately apprehended and reimprisoned. A license specifying the conditions under which the offender was granted a "ticket-of-leave" was to be carried by the offender at all times and presented on demand.

During the early part of the "ticket-of-leave" program there was no provision for the supervision of released prisoners. However, this situation was eventually changed when public uproar attributed the blame for most of the serious crimes committed on prisoners released on "ticket-of-leave." The citizen demand that either the program be terminated or the prisoners be supervised resulted in the supervision of the prisoners first by police and later by agents employed by Prisoner's Aid Societies. These agents provided various services to the prisoners, such as helping them to secure employment, locate a place to live and resolve personal problems. Additionally, they explained the program to employers, attempted to enlist the cooperation of employers and provided a surveillance function by enforcing the conditions of leave imposed upon the released prisoners.

One year after the enactment of the English Penal Servitude Act in 1853, Sir William Croften became the head of the Irish prison system. The Irish prison system, under Crofton's administration and leadership, became well-known for its three-stage model of penal servitude, with each stage designed to bring the offender closer to the free community. Of course, Crofton is indebted to Maconochie for the concept of supervised stages of imprisonment. The first stage, or strict imprisonment stage, was characterized by strict custody, solitary confinement and monotonous work. The second stage, or intermediate stage, involved the placement of prisoners on public work projects and the opportunity for prisoners to earn "marks" toward release. The third stage was essentially supervised parole. During this last stage, prisoners were assigned to an intermediate prison where they worked unsupervised and were permitted to move in and out of the free community. If prisoners continued to exhibit appropriate behavior and were able to secure employment, they were granted a conditional pardon on a "ticket-of-leave" and returned to the community.[9] Crofton instituted a system of supervision of prisoners on "ticket-of-leave" whereby they were supervised in rural areas by the police, and in the City of Dublin by civilian employees who possessed the title of Inspector of Released Prisoners. Inspectors of Released Prisoners performed a number of services, including assisting "ticket-of-leave" prisoners obtain employment, visiting their homes bi-weekly, requiring them to report at periodic intervals, verifying their employment and working cooperatively with the police.[10] Consequently, at this point in the evolution of parole, all of the necessary elements of contemporary parole existed: supervision, treatment and a paid parole worker.

Parole in the United States

Three preconditions were necessary for the development of parole in the United States. These were: the reduction of the term of imprisonment for good conduct, the indeterminate sentence and supervision.[11]

The principle of reducing the term of imprisonment for good conduct was initially recognized by the passage of the commutation or "good time" law in New York in 1817. It permitted prison inspectors to allow time off the definite sentence of an offender for good behavior and work willingly performed. However, commutation was not tantamount to parole. Those prisoners who were able to take advantage of "good time" laws enacted in New York and other states were released earlier, but unconditionally and usually without supervision.

Parole was also dependent on the emergence of the indeterminate sentence. Although an indeterminate sentence, in its truest form, has no minimum and maximum period of time specifications, most indeterminate sentence laws, in actuality, specify that the penalty for any given offense will be stated in terms of a minimum and maximum period of time. Consequently, the length of time served is an indeterminate period of time within the statutory minimum and statutory maximum limitations which is determined on the basis of an evaluation by the paroling authority of the offender's readiness for release. Zebulon Brockway, the noted penal reformer, became the Superintendent of the New York State Reformatory at Elmira, usually called the Elmira Reformatory, when it opened in 1876. He campaigned for the utilization of the indeterminate sentence and in 1876 the state of New York passed the necessary authorization. However, prisoners under definite sentence were committed to the Elmira Reformatory by the state courts until the Indeterminate Sentence Act became law in 1877. Therefore, it was in New York that the first indeterminate sentence, with minimum and maximum limits, was made law.

The third necessary precondition of parole in the United States was supervision. The supervision of persons released from prison was initially satisfied by the use of volunteers. Oftentimes, members of prison societies served in the capacity of volunteer supervisors of released offenders. In fact, the value of assisting released prisoners was recognized by the Philadelphia Society for Alleviating the Miseries of Public Prisons in 1822.[12] About three decades later, in 1851, this organization appointed two agents to assist prisoners who were released from the Philadelphia County Prison and the penitentiary.[13] It is generally believed that the State of Massachusetts appointed the first paid public employees to assist released prisoners in 1845.[14]

Elmira Reformatory was the site of the inception of parole in the United States in 1876 with Zebulon Brockway as superintendent. Several important penal practices were employed at that institution, including the use of the indeterminate sentence, the prisoner's release date determined by the number of "good marks" earned, and the continued jurisdiction of the prison over the released offender for a period of six months. During that six-month period the released prisoner was required to report on a regular basis to a volunteer guardian or sponsor. Therefore, the essential elements of parole, the indeterminate sentence, reducing the term of imprisonment for good conduct and supervision, were all present.

By 1880, only three states had passed parole laws. However, parole spread gradually throughout the country and by 1945 some form of parole legislation was passed in every state. Parole existed in every state, the District of Columbia and at the federal level until the mid-1970's. Since that time a few states have passed determinate sentencing laws. Consequently, some states no longer parole offenders.

Purpose

The proponents of parole maintain that there are, in principle, several advantages which accrue to both the offender and the community through its utilization. In general, these advantages relate to: the release of the offender when he is ready, the provision of a feeling of hope for the offender, the opportunity for the offender to reassume family and community responsibilities, financial savings for the taxpayer, the protection of society and the provision of supervision and assistance to the offender through the use of a parole agent.

Readiness for Release

In principle, the practice of parole rests firmly upon several underlying assumptions. First, it is assumed that offenders can be classified into certain diagnostic categories. Second, it is assumed that appropriate institutional treatment programs can be designed and employed which will result in the necessary attitudinal and behavioral changes in offenders for them to successfully adjust to community living upon release from prison. Third, it is assumed that there is a need to evaluate an offender on a continuing basis to determine if he is ready to be released or if he is still unsafe to be released. Fourth, it is assumed that the paroling authority is capable of making an objective release decision. In other words, it is assumed that the paroling authority can determine an offender's optimal time for release within the original sentence imposed by the court. Consequently, one of the supposed merits of parole is that it enables the offender to be released from prison when he is psychologically and socially best suited for release. If this time can be correctly determined, it is reasoned that this will increase the offender's prospects for a successful readjustment to living in the community.

Feeling of Hope

Most inmates desire to get out of prison by serving as little time as possible. Inmates recognize that positive changes in behavior can result in early release from prison via parole, prior to the completion of their maximum sentence. Parole advocates argue that the prospect of being paroled provides inmates with a feeling of hope and encourages them to abide by institutional rules and regulations and to participate in activities directed at self-improvement and self-betterment in attitudes and patterns of behavior.

Reduction in Period of Community Severance

Since parole permits the offender to be at liberty in the community, it reduces the period of time in which he is separated from participation in the normal social life in the free community. Institutionalization interrupts participation in critical familial, occupational and communal roles, often for lengthy periods of time. Usually, the longer the period of community severance, the more difficult it is for the offender to reassume successfully such roles as father, spouse, employee and citizen. Imagine, for example, the offender who as a father and spouse is separated from his wife and young children. He may have only been able to occasionally visit with them during his period of incarceration. When he is released, he must try to pick up where he left off, knowing all too well that he has missed out on many important family life events. Not only must he successfully reenter society, he must successfully reenter a family which has adjusted to life without him.

Furthermore, since the offender is released into the community earlier on parole, it is possible for the offender to avoid the additional damaging effects of continued institutionalization.

Financial Savings

Cost considerations make parole a desirable alternative to further institutionalization. A comparison of the differences between prison and parole costs are sizeable and it is readily apparent that it is cheaper to parole an offender than to imprison him. Staunch supporters of parole who are unable to convince skeptics of the philosophical and humanitarian merits of this practice are accustomed to pointing out the monetary savings of parole in order to attract, at least, their partial support.

Protection of Society

Another basic purpose of parole is the protection of society. Ideally, it satisfies this function through releasing the offender at the optimal time of release for maximizing his chances of achieving a noncriminal lifestyle, by reserving the right to return him to prison for all or part of the balance of his sentence if he fails to comply with the conditions imposed upon him by the paroling authority and through the provision for supervision of the offender which entails a surveillance and law enforcement function for the parole officer in making sure that the parolee conforms to the conditions governing his release. Some parole officers, in fact, are authorized to carry firearms and make arrests.

Supervision and Assistance

Parole, in principle, is a method of supervised release of the offender from prison. Rather than leaving the offender on his own to adjust to the complexities of life in the community after a period of imprisonment, the offender is assigned a parole agent who should, if necessary, provide assistance to the released offender in such areas as counseling, obtaining employment, securing housing and referral to appropriate community agencies which can provide needed services for the parolee. Hopefully, the assistance provided by the parole agent will increase the probability of the offender's successful adjustment in the community.

Administration/Process

There are five major areas of concern involved in the administration and process of parole. They are: (1) the administrative structure of the parole board; (2) the selection of prisoners to be placed on parole; (3) the establishment of conditions imposed upon the parolee; (4) the provision for supervision of the parolee; and (5) the determination of the basis for revocation.

The Administrative Structure of the Parole Board

The parole board is invested with the authority to grant parole. Generally, there are two basic organizational parole board models utilized today: (1) the independent board and (2) the consolidated board.

Under the independent parole board model the parole decisionmaking powers rest with an independent authority or agency. Much of the impetus for the independent parole board model was generated by growing dissatisfaction with an earlier model referred to as the institutional model, or prison parole board model, in which parole decisionmaking was administered by prison authorities under the assumption that the correctional institution's staff was in the best position to make decisions affecting the offender because of its close contact with the offender. The institutional model was bombarded with criticisms, including: (1) the basis for parole decisions made by institutional parole authorities too frequently reflected institutional concerns, such as an insistence or desire to completely enforce all institutional rules and regulations, to reduce overcrowding and/or to eliminate "troublemakers" from the institutional population; (2) prison parole boards were too easily influenced by the subjective, unsubstantiated input of correctional staff persons; and (3) the institutional parole decisionmaking process, relatively removed from public visibility and control, was conducive to the employment of informal procedures which might jeopardize its ability to reach fair decisions or turn such proceedings into routine actions that treated prisoners, for whom the impending decision was of paramount significance, as only secondary in importance to the outcome itself. Such criticisms contributed to the decline of the institutional model and the development and adoption of the independent parole board model. Its advocates have stressed its ability to reach more objective parole recommendations than were possible by prison paroling authorities which were too closely aligned with the correctional system to render truly objective decisions. Despite its purported and objective decisionmaking benefits, the independent parole board model has also been subjected to harsh criticism. The opponents of the independent parole board have charged that its value in parole decisionmaking is severely hampered by its lack of knowledge, especially that acquired by firsthand experience, regarding correctional institutions, programs, policies and conditions. The National Advisory Commission on Criminal Justice Standards and Goals has summarized more specifically those criticisms leveled against this model. It states:

> In the adult field, a good deal of reform was associated with the removing of parole decision making from institutional control to an

independent authority... Whatever its merits in fostering objectivity the independent parole board has been criticized on several counts. First, the claim is made that such boards tend to be insensitive to institutional programs and fail to give them the support they require. Second, independent boards are accused of basing their decisions on inappropriate considerations, such as the feelings of a local police chief. Third, their remoteness from the institutional program gives independent boards little appreciation of the dynamics in a given case; their work tends to be cursory, with the result that too often persons who should be paroled are not, and those who should not be paroled are released. Fourth, the argument is made that independent systems tend to place on parole boards persons who have little training or experience.[15]

As a result of the harsh criticisms directed against the institutional and independent models, another model, known as the consolidation model, emerged and gained considerable support and popularity. Under this model, the authority for parole decisionmaking usually resides in a central decisionmaking authority which is organizationally situated within an overall department of corrections. This model is related to the general move toward the consolidation of all types of correctional services and programs, such as institution-based programs, community-based programs and after-care programs, under an overall department of corrections. Proponents of this model claim that several clear advantages adhere to the consolidation model that make it preferable to other parole board models. First, it promotes objectivity (a purported shortcoming of the institutional model) and sensitivity toward correctional programs, policies and conditions (a purported shortcoming of the independent model) since it removes the decisionmaking authority from the correctional institution itself but still keeps it within the correctional system. Second, since decisionmaking is removed from the control of correctional institutions, other pertinent considerations, aside from just institutional concerns, will be considered in rendering parole decisions. Third, the consolidation model is conducive to the selection of career correctional personnel as parole board members. Such members are more capable of providing insight into parole decisionmaking matters than members who are politically appointed. Fourth, the consolidation model views the treatment of the offender as a continuum, rather than as just a series of experiences which are totally separate and unrelated, that should fall within a single administration. Despite these perceived advantages, considerable concern exists that the consolidated board may have difficulty in maintaining its autonomy.

Today, the consolidation model operates in thirty states, while the independent model is employed in twenty states.

The American Correctional Association has identified four main functions for state parole boards. These functions are: (1) the selection of inmates for parole; (2) the provision of assistance, supervision and continuing control of parolees in the community; (3) a determination of when the parole objective is completed, leading to discharge from parole; and (4) a determination as to whether parole should be revoked in the event that a parolee should violate the conditions of his parole.[16]

Parole boards vary from jurisdiction to jurisdiction in terms of their size, methods of appointment of members, the ways in which parole decisions are made and in the determination of parole eligibility dates. Controversy and criticism have often resulted from the differential resolution of these issues by the various jurisdictions.

Parole boards vary in size from three to twelve members. However, in a large majority of jurisdictions they are comprised of either three or five members. Methods of selection of parole board members include: appointment by the governor, appointment by the governor and other state officials, appointment from a civil service list and appointment by another state department head or civic official from a prepared list. However, in most jurisdictions, the prevalent mode of selection is by gubernatorial appointment.

The way in which actual parole decisions are made also varies from jurisdiction to jurisdiction. This decision is usually made at what is called a parole grant hearing at which time the parole board has the opportunity to meet with the offender, interview him and make a decision regarding his "readiness" for release from prison into the community. Some jurisdictions require the full board membership be present at the hearing, while other jurisdictions require only part of the board be present. In a few instances, hearing examiners interview parole candidates. Some jurisdictions rely strictly upon written reports and do not require interviews with parole candidates.[17]

Variance also exists from jurisdiction to jurisdiction regarding eligibility dates for parole. Some jurisdictions make an inmate eligible for parole only after he has completed his minimum period of imprisonment, while others permit the good time that an inmate has accumulated to be deducted from the minimum sentence in computing a parole eligibility date. In still others, inmates become eligible for parole consideration after they serve one-third of their maximum sentence. Finally, in some jurisdictions eligibility is set by the length of the sentence or by the number of previous felony convictions an inmate possesses.

The Selection of Parolees

Oftentimes, there are no codified rules, standards or guidelines that a parole board must follow in reaching a parole decision. Consequently, this has resulted in criticisms of parole board decisions as being subjective, inconsistent, discretionary and unfair. Despite the lack of a "magical" formula, there are a number of factors that are routinely taken into consideration by the parole board in making a decision to grant parole. Most of this information is contained in a case file which parole board members have the opportunity to review prior to the parole grant hearing. Among the principal factors considered in the parole decision are: criminal record—past and present, parole plan—employment/residence/special programs, prior community supervision experiences, participation in institutional programs, institutional adjustment, psychological change, circumstances of the offense and appropriate period of imprisonment. Oftentimes, these factors are subjectively weighed in a differential manner by parole board members in making a decision to grant parole.

Before discussing these factors, however, it should be noted that the U.S. Parole Commission has developed and implemented a procedure to structure and formalize parole release decisionmaking guidelines as they relate to the federal parole process.[18] Simply stated, this procedure involves the development of decision guidelines through the identification of salient factors, such as the number of prior convictions, number of prior incarcerations, age at first commitment, type of offense for which committed, employment record, history of drug dependency and prior experiences on parole and/or probation and the assignment of a weight to each factor. Through this process an individual offender is evaluated according to the aforementioned offender characteristics and assigned a salient factor score which indicates a "parole prognosis" such as very good, good, fair or poor. The salient factor score is considered along with an inmate's offense characteristics (that is, the severity of crime he committed which is categorized as either low, low moderate, moderate, high, very high, greatest I or greatest II) and prior jail and prison duration he has served in determining a recommended time that an offender should serve before parole is granted. Naturally, these guidelines are predicated upon appropriate institutional conduct and performance. The predictive validity of the salient factor formula is continuously monitored so that necessary refinements and changes can be made.

In the past, state parole authorities usually did not rely on prediction methods and many still don't. However, the merits of utilizing explicit decisionmaking guidelines are being increasingly recognized by state parole authorities, such as those in Oregon, Louisiana, Minnesota, New Jersey, North Carolina, Virginia and Washington.[19]

Criminal Record—Past and Present

For many parole board members "actions speak louder than words." Therefore, a primary consideration in assessing a candidate's likelihood of committing another crime is based upon a perusal of the inmate's past criminal record and the offense(s) for which he is currently imprisoned. The seriousness of the offense(s) are, oftentimes, especially significant in decisionmaking. Many questions are entertained by the parole board in weighing the importance of this factor in the overall decisionmaking process. Is the inmate a "first-time" offender who is unlikely to commit a new criminal offense if released? Is the inmate a habitual offender who is likely to commit a new crime if released? In the event an inmate should be released on parole and our evaluation has been incorrect, is the parolee more likely to commit a serious or a minor offense? Does the candidate have a history of alcoholism or drug addiction which has contributed to his past criminal lifestyle? These are just a few examples of the kinds of questions that flash before a parole board member's mind. Despite the existence of other indicators of "readiness" for parole, it is often the case that the parole board member simply can't bring himself to believe that a prisoner with a lengthy or serious criminal record has reformed sufficiently to be ready for release. A common complaint among parole candidates is that parole board members "won't look past the inmate's record" in reaching a decision. Furthermore, the complaint often arises that offenders who are actually the best parole risks, that is, offenders who have committed such crimes as homicide, manslaughter, or certain types of sex crimes, are routinely given unfavorable decisions solely because of the type(s) of crime(s) they have committed. Parole board members are often placed in a difficult position. They may strongly suspect that a parole candidate is, in fact, "ready" for parole based upon an examination of available indicators, but they realize they may be publicly criticized for paroling an inmate with a bad criminal record. It is difficult for board members not to react to such pressures. Often in the back of their minds is the question: How will the public react if we release an offender with a known past record of serious criminal behavior and he should commit a serious crime while on parole?

Circumstances of the Offense

In addition to the candidate's criminal record itself, the parole board may be influenced in its decision if there is evidence that the offense which was committed by the inmate was situational in nature or his participation was due to extenuating circumstances. A favorable parole decision may be rendered if, in the board's opinion, the pertinent situational factors have changed or been eliminated.

Parole Plan—Employment/Residence/Special Programs

As part of the parole process, prisoners are often required to make a parole plan. This consists of the offender arranging for suitable employment, residence and possibly participation in special programs, such as an educational or vocational training program, Alcoholics Anonymous or a drug program, upon his release. An acceptable parole plan may be interpreted as a good indication that the inmate is seriously pondering his future, whereas an unacceptable plan may be considered as a basis for denying parole or deferring it until an acceptable parole plan is developed. Parole board members want to know the answers to the questions: Where do you intend to live? How do you intend to support yourself and your family? Do you intend to enroll in community programs that may provide assistance to you in personal problem areas, such as education, vocational training or substance abuse? Parole boards are well aware that parolees must face several reentry problems immediately upon release and they believe it is necessary to know something about how candidates intend to realistically and specifically deal with these problems. In some cases, the paroling authority may require that a candidate's parole plan include a stay at a halfway house. If openings are unavailable in such programs, parole may be deferred until such openings occur. It is important to note, however, that parole plans submitted by parole candidates are not always what they appear to be. For example, Erickson et al. report that "... many ex-cons and professionals believe that 90% of the jobs in release are 'fictitious,' i.e., promised by friends and relatives where in fact no 'real' job exists."[20]

Prior Community Supervision Experiences

Many inmates who are parole candidates have had prior community supervision experiences either while on probation or during an earlier parole. In fact, some inmates may be serving their present sentence due to the revocation of their prior supervision. The parole board recognizes the difficulty in predicting successful community adjustment on the basis of institutional adjustment factors. Therefore, information related to the outcome of a candidate's prior community supervision experiences may provide some important insight into how the candidate may adjust to being released into the community on parole. If the candidate had a prior successful parole or probation the board may be favorably impressed, whereas a prior revocation of parole or probation may create considerable doubt among board members as to the desirability of placing a former "failure" in a similar program again.

Participation in Institutional Programs

An inmate's attempt at self-improvement at the institution is carefully scrutinized by parole board members. Participation in "rehabilitative" programs, such as education, vocational training, individual or group methods of therapy, substance abuse programs or religious programs, is usually perceived positively. Inmates who have participated in these programs are often viewed as being interested in improving themselves and as constituting better risks for parole than inmates who have not participated in such programs. Nonparticipants may be perceived as inmates who are just interested in "doing their time" rather than as individuals interested in preparing themselves in a conscientious fashion to successfully reenter society. Reports from work supervisors, counselors and academic and vocational training instructors may be of assistance to parole board members in assessing the benefits derived from institutional programs by the parole candidates. It may help them determine answers to such questions as: How much progress has the inmate made while at the institution? Is he seriously concerned with improving himself? What skills and abilities has he acquired while at the institution which may increase his chances of successfully adjusting to life in the free community? Did he participate in these programs just as a matter of "going through the motions" or with a positive attitude towards improving himself?

Institutional Adjustment

Another factor normally considered by the parole board is the inmate's record of behavior while at the institution. Did the inmate comply with institutional rules and regulations or did he violate such rules and regulations? How many disciplinary write-ups does an inmate have? What are the nature of these write-ups? Were they minor or major disciplinary infractions? Were there any extenuating circumstances involved in these rules violations? A good institutional behavioral record might be perceived as an indication of the inmate's ability and willingness to comply with behavioral expectations of the society when released. A poor institutional record, on the other hand, may cast grave doubts about his ability to comply with societal behavioral expectations. Inmates often complain that parole boards are just looking for something negative by counting the number of "pink slips" contained in an inmate's file. Furthermore, they argue that, oftentimes, disciplinary write-ups appear in their files because they were "framed," or a correctional officer who "had it in for them" was trying to get back at them by writing them up, or that they had to violate a rule in order to protect themselves from other inmates. However, they maintain that the board doesn't take these factors into consideration when evaluating their institutional adjustment. Consequently, an inmate's record may be interpreted as being worse than it actually is, according to the inmate's perspective. Reports submitted by correctional personnel, such as unit team members, work supervisors and treatment staff, may also provide additional input into this area for members of the parole board.

Psychological Change

Another significant factor in the parole decisionmaking process is the psychological change experienced by the inmate. The board is favorably impressed with signs that an inmate has developed insight into those problems that contributed to his offense, that he has attempted to overcome these problems while at the institution and that he is now willing to accept responsibility for his behavior. Failure to admit guilt for his crime(s), to continue to insist that he was "framed" or that he was a "political prisoner" or to fail to show remorse for one's past criminal actions may be interpreted to mean that an inmate is not psychologically "ready" to be released into the community on parole. The parole board is interested in whether or not the inmate has taken advantage of the opportunity to participate in individual or group therapy and counseling programs at the institution. The board also carefully reviews psychological reports submitted by psychologists, psychiatrists or leaders of therapy groups regarding the psychological progress experienced by inmates.

The "Appropriate" Period of Imprisonment

Parole board members often have strong feelings regarding how much time an inmate should serve in prison for certain types of crimes. This may exert an influence upon the parole board in making its parole decision. Sometimes parole board members may feel that the seriousness of the offense would be minimized by paroling an inmate too soon. Therefore, an inmate could conceivably be "ready" for release via parole, according to available indicators, but still be denied parole because it would constitute an "injustice" from the subjective standpoint of the parole board members. Generally, the rule of thumb is that the more serious the offense, the longer an inmate should be imprisoned before being paroled.

There is considerable concern regarding which factors, in actuality, carry the most weight among parole board members in making a decision to grant parole. The above-mentioned factors are commonly considered. However, this is certainly not an exhaustive list. A parole decisionmaking study conducted by Talarico offers some insight into this matter. According to this study, approximately three-fifths of the decisions made by the parole board in Connecticut could be attributed to 21 variables. Eleven of these 21 variables were discovered to carry the most weight. They were, in order: "(1) parole plans—job; (2) job training or work; (3) work or educational release; (4) parole plans—residence; (5) family stability; (6) parole revocations; (7) drug treatment; (8) alcohol treatment; (9) family criminal record; (10) violence in offense; and (11) history of violence."[21] It is interesting to note that the criteria employed were primarily related to "...external conditions over which the offender had little control...or to conditions in the offender's past..."[22]

Another study of parole decisionmaking was conducted by the National Parole Institutes. Based on the responses to a questionnaire completed by almost one-half of the parole board members in the United States, this study identified those items selected by at least one-fifth of the responding parole board members as being among the five most important factors in parole decisions. Table 4.1 presents these items in order of the percentage of the respondents who included them as one of the five most important considerations. The first three items identified pertained to the

Table 4.1 Items Considered by Parole Board Members to be Most Important in Parole Decisions

Item	Percent Including Item as One of Five Most Important
1. My estimate of the chances that the prisoner would or would not commit a serious crime if paroled.	92.8
2. My judgment that the prisoner would benefit from further experience in the institution program, or, at any rate, would become a better risk if confined longer.	87.1
3. My judgment that the prisoner would become a worse risk if confined longer.	71.9
4. My judgment that the prisoner had already been punished enough to "pay" for his crime.	43.2
5. The probability that the prisoner would be a misdemeanant and a burden to his parole supervisors, even if he did not commit any serious offenses on parole.	34.3
6. My feelings about how my decision in this case would affect the feelings or welfare of the prisoner's relatives or dependents.	33.8
7. What I thought the reaction of the judge might be if the prisoner were granted parole.	20.9

Source: The National Advisory Commission on Criminal Justice Standards and Goals, *Corrections* (Washington, D.C.: U.S. Department of Justice, 1973), p. 394, from National Parole Institutes, *Selection for Parole* (New York: National Council on Crime and Delinquency, 1966).

protection of the public or the risk of committing new criminal acts, whereas the last four items were related to the "appropriate" period of imprisonment, the probability of the prisoner being a misdemeanant or burden to the parole agent, the impact of the decision on the prisoner's family and the reaction of the judge.[23]

Parole decisions usually take one of the following forms: (1) the prisoner is granted parole effective in six months and a work release assignment is recommended as soon as possible to prepare him for his upcoming release on parole; (2) the prisoner is denied parole at the present time with the offender remaining in prison and his parole to be reconsidered at a later date; or (3) the prisoner is denied parole with the offender remaining in prison until expiration of the prisoner's maximum sentence.

Conditions of Parole

As specified in the definition of parole introduced earlier, parole is a form of conditional release. That is, an offender's release into the community on parole is contingent upon his compliance with a set of rules and regulations. Although conditions vary from state to state and jurisdiction to jurisdiction, conditions of parole are somewhat standardized. Arluke's study of parole conditions in the various states revealed that parole conditions generally can be classified into 29 basic categories. The nine most prevalent conditions were: (1) prohibiting association with undesirable persons, persons having a criminal record or persons engaged in illegal activity; (2) prohibiting the use of controlled substances, narcotics, drugs and alcoholic beverages; (3) approval of changes in marital status, such as marriage or divorce, require prior notification and approval; (4) compliance with the law is compulsory; (5) parolees are prohibited from owning, possessing, purchasing, receiving, selling or transporting any deadly weapons or firearms; (6) parolees may not own, buy or provide money for the purchase of any motor vehicle or drive a vehicle without permission; (7) prior permission must be obtained to travel outside the state; (8) place of residence or employment status and changes related thereto, must be reported; and (9) written reports must be submitted regularly on the specified date to the parole officer.[24] As a result of court decisions which have held that certain conditions which have been imposed on parolees in the past were often impossible and/or unreasonable and/or unfair, there has been a strong trend in recent years toward reducing the number of parole conditions.

Supervision of Parolees

Parole, in concept, provides for supervision of the offender, once he has been released from prison. The provision of community supervision is based upon two underlying principles: (1) the need to protect the public and (2) the need to provide assistance to the parolee in becoming "reintegrated" into the community. Consequently, the parole officer or agent, who is the cornerstone of parole supervision, is often perceived as having to occupy and perform in two potentially conflictual roles: that of a policeman and social worker.

Parole supervision entails a law enforcement function. In order to achieve the goal of the protection of the public, parole agents often perform a number of "policing" or "surveillance" duties. These include making sure the parolee adheres strictly to the conditions of his parole and initiating revocation procedures if a violation of the rules occurs. In some jurisdictions, parole officers are even required to carry firearms and to arrest parole violators.

It is well-known and documented that the offender must face several problems upon his "reentry" into society. That he is not always successful in addressing and resolving these important problems is evidenced by the fact that a high percentage of post-prison failures occur within the first six months after release. A study conducted by Erickson et al. provides important insight into the potential "reentry" problems for parolees. When queried as to their needs upon release, the needs identified by parolees were "predominantely physical/material" in nature, such as the need for a job, money, general assistance, transportation, clothes, housing and medical/ dental treatment. In addition, "predominantely social needs," such as the need for general acceptance (expressed as needs for understanding, love and respect), and the need for social anchoring and primary group support from friends, wife, mate and family, and "predominantely psychological needs," such as self-attribute needs, harm-avoidance needs and altruistic needs were also strongly expressed.[25] Parolees were also asked to rank order a list of needs and to rate each of the same needs regarding how adequately they were being fulfilled. Ranked first in order of priority were education, money and job.[26]

Recognizing the existence of such problems, the parole agent in his role as a social worker may provide much needed assistance in several ways to the parolee. The parole agent may provide assistance to a parolee in securing employment, finding a place to live or obtaining benefits, such as social security. He may also refer the parolee to community social service agencies which may, in turn, be of direct assistance to the parolee in providing him with health, welfare, employment placement and educational or legal services. If the parolee and his family are encountering special problems which they are having difficulty resolving, the parole agent may provide supportive counseling and/or advising.[27]

Revocation of Parole

The parolee faces the prospect of having his parole revoked if he violates one or more conditions of his parole or if there is evidence that he has participated in new criminal conduct. The parole agent occupies a strategic position in this process insofar as he has the power to recommend revocation of parole.

The decision to recommend revocation of parole can be a complicated one. Although some situations dictate a recommendation for revocation, such as the parolee being convicted of a new felony or the possession of evidence by the parole agent that the parolee has engaged in serious criminal conduct, not all cases are clear-cut. In these later instances the parole officer must exercise discretion in making a decision to initiate the revocation process. Together with the marginal nature of the case, the parole agent must often balance his potentially conflicting roles of "policeman" and "social worker." Even though a parolee may have committed one or more technical violations, a parole agent may decide not to recommend revocation of parole due to various mitigating factors. Such factors might include: the parole agent's belief that the consequences of revocation to a parolee may be too severe; the parole agent's belief that the parolee has made a basically sound adjustment to life in the community despite the existence of one or more violations; the parole agent's belief that further imprisonment will not be of any value to the parolee; or the parole agent's knowledge that the time remaining on parole is of short duration.[28] In making these difficult decisions the parole agent must resolve, on the basis of personal beliefs, values, personality, experience, agency policy or circumstances of the case, the conflicting objectives of community supervision: protection of the public and rehabilitation of the offender.

The essential elements of due process have been noticeably absent from parole revocation proceedings in the past. However, in 1972, the U.S. Supreme Court handed down the landmark decision on parole, *Morrissey* v. *Brewer*.[29] The Supreme Court established specific guidelines for a two-step revocation hearing process according to the constitutional requirement of due process. The first step of the two-step revocation hearing process is a preliminary hearing which is supposed to be held shortly after the arrest of the parole violator and close to the location of the alleged violation or arrest. The primary purpose of the preliminary hearing is to determine if there is probable cause or reasonable grounds to believe that the parolee committed acts which violated his parole. The hearing officer at the preliminary hearing is supposed to be an independent decisionmaker, other than the parole officer who made the report of parole violations or recommended revocation of parole. The hearing officer does not have to be a judicial officer. The parolee is required to be notified of the preliminary hearing and its purpose, and to be apprised of the alleged violation(s). The parolee is permitted to appear at the preliminary hearing and speak on his own behalf and to present pertinent materials and/or witnesses. The parolee is also entitled to query those persons who have introduced information on which the allegations of parole violations are based. It is the responsibility of the preliminary hearing officer to summarize the proceedings, make a determination as to whether there is probable cause or reasonable grounds to hold a parolee for a full revocation hearing and to identify the reasons for his decision and specify the evidence which led to his decision. The second step of the revocation hearing process—a full revocation hearing—is required if it is determined that probable cause or reasonable grounds exist that the parolee participated in acts which violated his parole. Its purpose is to make a final evaluation of any disputed or contested facts and to determine if revocation is warranted on the basis of the evidence presented. A decision is made as to whether the parole violator should remain in the community or be returned to prison and, if so, for how long. The parolee is entitled to the following minimum requirements of due process at the revocation hearing:

> ... (a) written notice of the claimed violations of parole; (b) disclosure to the parolee of evidence against him; (c) opportunity to be heard in person and to present witnesses and documentary evidence; (d) the right to confront and cross-examine adverse

witnesses (unless the hearing officer specifically finds good cause for not allowing confrontation); (e) a 'neutral and detached' hearing body such as a traditional parole board, members of which need not be judicial officers or lawyers; and (f) a written statement by the fact finders as to the evidence relied on and reasons for revoking parole.[30]

In 1973, less than a year after the U.S. Supreme Court handed down the landmark decision on parole, *Morrissey* v. *Brewer*, the U.S. Supreme Court handed down another significant decision. In *Gagnon* v. *Scarpelli*, the U.S. Supreme Court held that parolees and probationers had a qualified right to counsel in revocation hearings.[31]

Problems

There are a variety of problems plaguing the system of parole. Much of the dissatisfaction with parole relates to the difference between how parole is ideally designed to work and how it actually works in practice. Much of the criticism has been centered upon parole board performance, decision-making and selection, the conditions of release, the merits of supervision and legal issues surrounding the process and administration of parole.

Parole boards have been the target of much of the criticism directed against the parole system. The criticisms against parole boards take many forms. First, parole boards are often criticized for the arbitrary character of their decisionmaking. Critics maintain that, in making decisions to release a prisoner on parole or to continue his imprisonment, parole boards frequently rely on highly subjective criteria, such as personal theories of criminality, moralistic judgments, personal prejudice against certain types of offenders or even pure guesswork or hunches, rather than on more objective criteria or a set of guidelines designed to guide parole board members in making predictive decisions. Second, the complaint is often registered that parole board members are oftentimes political appointees who are nonprofessionals lacking sufficient expertise and training in the correctional field which would enable them to properly evaluate and assess relevant parole decisionmaking materials. Third, given the crucial nature of parole decisionmaking in determining human destinies, parole boards do not give sufficient attention to the analysis and dynamics of individual cases. Critics of the parole process point out that parole board hearings are too brief, superficial and cursory. In fact, on a national average, parole boards devote only about ten minutes to each case.[32] A heavy work load contributes substantially to this lack of attention. A study of the average number of cases heard per day during parole consideration hearings in 51 jurisdictions revealed that an average number of 1-19 cases were heard per day by 11 parole boards, 20-29 cases were heard per day by 15 boards, 30-39 cases were heard per day by 14 boards and 40 or more cases were heard per day by 11 parole boards.[33]

The conditions imposed upon parolees have also drawn strong criticism. They have been characterized as being too numerous, too vague, too coercive, too intrusive and subject to the discretionary enforcement of parole agents. Consequently, such conditions are perceived as hindering rather than facilitating the parolee's reintegration into society after release from prison. A comprehensive review of parole conditions by Arluke led him to conclude that:

> Some parole conditions are moralistic, most are impractical, others impinge on human rights, and all reflect obsolete criminological conceptions. On the whole, they project a percept of a man, who does not exist.[34]

The supposed merits of parole supervision have also come under heavy attack. Although community supervision of the parolee is theoretically designed to protect the public and increase the probability of the prisoner successfully reentering society, critics cast grave doubts about the realistic prospects of attaining such goals for several reasons. Large case loads, the lack of providing different kinds of supervision required by different types of cases, the conflicting roles of law enforcement officer and social worker performed by parole agents, an over reliance on the law enforcement function of supervision, the psychological stress placed on parolees in the community by expecting compliance with such an umbrella of rules and the reluctance of parolees to seek help and assistance from parole agents, due to their conflicting roles of law enforcement officer and social worker, are all factors which make the attainment of the two principal goals of community supervision, protection and treatment, unlikely.

Although court decisions have focused increasing attention on the due process safeguards for a parole candidate or a parolee facing a parole-related hearing, there are still many pertinent legal issues and problems that remain unsettled and unresolved. Illustrative of such legal issues are: the right of the parolee to legal representation, whether or not testimony given upon the promise of immunity from a criminal prosecution can be used at a parole revocation hearing, the right to utilize evidence seized in violation of the Fourth Amendment at a revocation hearing, the effect upon a revocation hearing of a prior acquittal from criminal proceedings and the problem of determining what kind of due process one is entitled to at the parole grant hearing.[35] Until these and other essential legal issues are resolved, criticisms will continue to be made that parole-related hearings and proceedings are inadequate and unfair by traditional criminal justice standards.

The aforementioned shortcomings of parole have not led critics from traditionalist and moderate camps to abandon parole but instead to suggest various types of needed reforms which generally accept the principal premises of parole. Among the suggested changes which are geared to changes in parole practices, are: formalizing the release decisionmaking guidelines in order to limit the discretion of the parole board, imposing more demanding and pertinent qualifications for parole board membership, increasing the number of parole officers, reducing the case load size of parole officers, redefining and reprioritizing the roles of the parole officer such that there will be a de-emphasis of their law enforcement role and an attendant increase in their social service role and increasing the protection of inmates against the potential arbitrary and abusive actions by parole board members through the enactment of more rigorous and comprehensive due process and review procedures.[36]

However, there are also critics of parole who advocate its total elimination or abolition on the grounds that it is ineffective, an outdated practice, based upon erroneous assumptions and simply inoperable in practice according to its intended objectives. This group of critics, collectively known as the "abolitionists," question the potential impact of many of the more common reforms in parole procedures and practices.

The Citizens' Inquiry on Parole and Criminal Justice, Inc., a private, nonprofit research corporation, conducted a comprehensive study of the New York parole system. The following statement opened the section of the report entitled "Long-term Recommendations":

> The Citizens' Inquiry Report concludes that parole in New York is oppressive and arbitrary, cannot fulfill its stated goals, and is a corrupting influence within the penal system. It should therefore be abolished.[37]

Concerning the potential impact of the more common reforms in parole practices and procedures, the Citizens' Inquiry Report states:

> Whether these reforms would improve parole depends on the validity of the basic premises of the system and the quality of its goals. Parole rests on invalid premises. Thus, if the above or other reforms were implemented, the effectiveness of the system would not be significantly improved. Admittedly, it would be less oppressive and possibly more fair to the people under its control, but it would not be any more effective in doing what it intends to do.[38]

Another harsh critic, David Fogel, in elaborating a "middle range strategy" for the transformation and termination of what he calls the "fortress prison," recommended a return to flat time sentences with "...the elimination of both the parole boards and parole agencies as we have known them."[39]

David Stanley's inquiry into the purposes and performance of parole systems in the United States led him to suggest the necessity for an alternative system that would include, among other things, the termination of indeterminate sentencing, the elimination of parole release and supervision and improvements in community assistance to ex-offenders.[40]

The call for abolition of parole has also been strongly chanted by staunch supporters of a return to "flat" or determinate sentencing. For example, the state of Maine has instituted determinate sentencing and abolished parole. Several other states are considering sentencing structure reforms and the abolition of parole. The future of parole, at least as we have known it in the past, is seriously threatened by such developments.

Cost

A comparison between prison and parole costs reveals significant monetary differences. An examination of representative figures shows that it is clearly cheaper to parole an offender rather than to imprison him.

In 1972 the Vera Institute's Manhattan Court Project reported that there was a $3,200 differential between maintaining an offender in prison as contrasted to maintaining an offender on parole in the Manhattan, New York area. At that time, prison costs averaged $5,000 per year per inmate versus parole costs of $1,800 per year per offender.[41]

A startling institutional-parole cost comparison was also reported for Pennsylvania in 1972. In Pennsylvania the respective costs per year per offender for imprisonment and parole were $7,000 versus $700.[42]

Stanley reported prison-parole cost comparisons for various states, including Maine, Georgia and Wisconsin. In 1972, in Maine, it cost $12.80 per person per day to maintain an offender in prison versus $.81 per person per day to maintain an offender on parole. This represented a cost differential ratio of approximately 16:1 in favor of parole. In 1973, in Georgia, it cost $8.45 per person per day to maintain an offender in prison versus only $.95 per person per day on parole. This constituted a cost differential ratio of approximately 9:1 in favor of parole. In 1973, in Wisconsin, it cost $18.60 per person per day to maintain an offender in prison versus only $1.48 per person per day to maintain an offender on parole. In this instance, there was a cost differential ratio of approximately 13:1 in favor of parole.[43]

In 1976, in California, the respective prison and parole costs were $7,800 versus $550 per offender per year. This resulted in an annual savings of $7,250 per parolee.[44]

Finally, Waller reported that in Canada the Canadian Federal Penitentiary Service spent an average of more than $5,000 per year per inmate in prison, whereas the Canadian National Parole Service spent an average of only $500 per year per person to maintain an offender on parole.[45]

Although the costs of imprisonment and parole both continue to increase due to changes in the economy, the differential between prison and parole costs remains. The conclusion is clear: there is a substantial savings to be realized when utilizing a parole strategy over imprisonment.

Furthermore, it must be recognized that there are additional cost factors to be considered besides operational costs in estimating the overall economic benefits of parole. When released into the community, parolees have the opportunity to be gainfully employed. Wages earned on such jobs can be utilized by parolees to pay for personal and family support, legitimate debts, restitution and state and federal taxes. Their counterparts in prison, however, are not likely to be in the position to make such personal and societal contributions. Instead, they must often depend upon the state for the support of both themselves and their families.

Effectiveness

A significant proportion of the prior research in parole has been restricted to the presentation of "...simple summary data on the number of cases considered, the type of decisions made and the outcome in terms of revocation."[46] It would seem, on the surface, that the assessment of the effectiveness of parole as a correctional strategy in reducing recidivism would be a relatively easy task. However, the existence of several factors so complicates this process that it is problematic to estimate, on a nationwide basis, the overall merit of parole in reducing recidivism.

Before reviewing the results of some of the parole effectiveness studies which have been conducted, it is necessary to identify some of the principal factors which make it difficult to evaluate parole effectiveness. First, parole effectiveness studies frequently compare the recidivism rates of paroled prisoners with prisoners who have been discharged from prison on mandatory release or at the expiration of their sentences. However, oftentimes, there has been no attempt undertaken to control for the potential differences in the selection of these different groups. In other words, aside from the differences among prisoners according to their mode of release from prison, parole or non-parole, other significant differences may exist among prisoners. For example, offenders may differ with respect to their potential for committing new offenses. In fact, some researchers maintain that better risks may be selected for release from prison on parole. Therefore, the differential recidivism rates experienced by paroled and non-paroled groups may not be so much a function of the mode of release per se but of the selection process. Consequently, there may be noteworthy bias in making such comparisons. Second, there are a multitude of post-release factors which might exert an influential effect on the prisoner's conduct in the community after he is released from prison. These factors may contribute in a significant manner to a "successful" or "unsuccessful" parole outcome. It may not be the mode of release itself but post-release factors surrounding the prisoner's release experience, such as family environment, marital situation, employment or mental or physical health, which might make the difference between a "successful" or "unsuccessful" post-release experience. Third, there is no general consensus on what constitutes a "successful" parole outcome. Is it recidivism? If so, how is recidivism to be defined? What period of follow-up time should expire after the prisoner's release from prison before determining that a parolee has a successful outcome? Should it be calculated from the time of release until discharge from parole or should it be after a specified number of years have expired following release from prison? What constitutes an "unsuccessful" parole outcome? The commission of a new offense? A technical violation? Both? Obviously, definitions of recidivism may vary as can the ways in which recidivism rates in the parole field can be computed. Fourth, insofar as paroling policies, including philosophy, selection, supervision, staffing and revocation, practices may differ from jurisdiction to jurisdiction, it is difficult, if not impossible, to generalize about parole effectiveness from one jurisdiction to another or to the nation as a whole. The aforementioned factors should serve as a basis for exercising caution in the review, analysis and interpretation of the results of parole effectiveness studies.

A study completed in collaboration with the U.S. Board of Parole compared the success rates of prisoners released according to three different modes of release: parole, mandatory release and discharge at expiration of sentence. For purposes of this particular study, a successful release outcome was defined as the lack of any criminal conviction during a two-year follow-up period. The study revealed that prisoners who were released from prison on parole succeeded 89 percent of the time, while inmates released on mandatory release succeeded 74 percent of the time and prisoners discharged at the expiration of their sentences succeeded 68 percent of the time. Stated somewhat differently, 11 percent of the parolees had new convictions before two years had expired after release while the figures for mandatory releasees and prisoners released at the expiration of their sentences were 26 percent and 32 percent, respectively. After attempting to control for potential differences in "risk of new convictions" among type of release groups, the study indicated that the "corrected" success rates were 83 percent for the parolees, 77 percent for mandatory releasees and 71 percent for prisoners discharged from prison at the expiration of their sentences.[47] Despite the attempt to control for the risk factor, it is still difficult to account for the differences between the various release groups. The differences might be attributable to the way in which a "successful outcome" was defined, other unknown release selection factors or uncontrollable post-release factors, or a combination of all or some of these factors.

A five-year-out report released by the board of parole in New York examined the results of prisoners released to original parole either from the time of release until discharge from parole or until the expiration of five years following release from prison, whichever was earlier. The report indicated that during the five years following release, about one-half (approximately 50 percent) of all prisoners released on original parole were delinquents and of the delinquents, about four-fifths (approximately 80 percent) were returned to prison. Approximately 60 percent of those parolees who were returned to prison were returned because they were arrested for a further crime, while about 40 percent were returned for the commission of technical violations or for absconding.[48] The Citizens' Inquiry on Parole and Criminal Justice, Inc. maintains that "...New York has no statistical evidence demonstrating the social service it provides to parolees reduces recidivism."[49]

The *Uniform Parole Reports* of 1972 and 1973 reported that slightly under one-fifth (18.9 percent) of the prisoners paroled in 1970 were returned to prison at the end of one year[50] while over one-fourth (27 percent) of the prisoners paroled in 1969 were returned to prison within two years after release.[51] It is interesting to note that the vast majority of the 18.9 percent of the inmates who were paroled in 1970 and returned to prison within one year after release were returned for the commission of technical violations as contrasted to the conviction of a new major criminal offense(s). In fact, only about 25 percent of those returned to prison were returned with a new major criminal conviction.[52] The percentage of parolees who recidivated within the first year after release was reduced to only 5-8 percent if recidivism was defined not as simply return to prison for any reason but instead was defined as return to prison for a new major conviction. The overwhelming majority of those 5-8 percent returned to prison for a new major conviction were returned for nonviolent property crimes or drug violations. Less than one percent were returned for conviction or suspicion of a violent offense, such as homicide, manslaughter, forcible rape and/or aggravated assault, and just slightly over one percent were returned for potentially violent offenses such as armed robbery and unarmed or "strong-armed" robbery.[53] It should be reiterated that such results are difficult to interpret due to the aforementioned evaluative factors and, therefore, the low recidivism rates are not necessarily indicative of an extremely effective parole release system.

An analysis of parole outcome conducted by Gottfredson, Neithercutt, Nuffield and O'Leary examined 104,182 first time parolees who were released from every state in the United States and the District of Columbia between 1965 and 1970. Among their principal findings were: (1) in every criminal offense category offenders who did not possess a prior criminal record had higher parole outcome success rates than offenders with prior criminal records; (2) the highest parole outcome success rates, according to offense type, were for crimes against persons, such as homicide, manslaughter and sex crimes (felony sex offenses other than forcible rape); (3) the highest parole violation rates were generally for those offenses associated with younger offenders, such as vehicle theft, burglary and theft or larceny; (4) according to age, younger offenders possessed the worst parole outcome records while middle-aged offenders possessed the best parole outcome records; (5) there is a non-statistically significant correlation between time served in prison by inmates and parole outcome; and (6) there does not appear to be a strong relationship between the serving of time and parole outcome after the variables of age, offense and prior criminal record are taken into account.[54]

An examination of adult and juvenile parole studies by Lipton, Martinson and Wilks led to several conclusions regarding the effectiveness of parole as it related to mode of release, employment status, case load size and adequacy of supervision. Concerning mode of release, it was concluded that during an identical follow-up period parolees are less likely to be returned to prison than inmates who are discharged from prison without parole. However, following their release from parole, adult parolees experienced a comparable rate of return to prison as that experienced by prisoners who were discharged from prison on non-parole modes of release. Regarding employment status, it was discovered that adult prisoners may be released on parole without the certainty of employment without increasing the potential harm to the community. Evidence was discovered that offenders released to parole-developed jobs are considerably more likely to be related to parole failure than releasing offenders to jobs arranged by family and friends. With respect to case load size, the researchers revealed that there was no substantive evidence with either juvenile or adult parolees that small case loads are significantly different from large case loads in the percentage of offenders returned to prison or experiencing a major criminal arrest. On the topic of adequacy of supervision, it was determined that adequate supervision is related to success on parole for juveniles and that adequate supervision is more usually provided in smaller case loads. It was also discovered that some evidence exists to suggest that for adults adequate supervision was an instrumental variable when it was combined with a policy of high return to prison since it deterred offenders in all risk categories from committing new criminal offenses.[55]

Juvenile Program Application

Juvenile parole or aftercare constitutes a significant component of juvenile corrections. Its significance is better understood and appreciated through a perusal of the following six sequential steps related to juvenile case severity.

1. The family, school and church can 'fail,' but the new police role in prevention and diversion is possible.
2. Police prevention and diversion can 'fail,' but informal probation alternatives are possible.
3. Informal probation alternatives can 'fail,' but juvenile court-ordered probation is possible.

4. Probation can 'fail,' but correctional institutions are possible.

5. Correctional institutions can 'fail,' but parole is possible.

6. If parole 'fails,' society is then coping with an adult criminal.[56]

In this perspective, juvenile parole is viewed as "...society's last ditch defense against juvenile delinquents becoming adult criminals."[57]

In general, parole, both in the adult and juvenile areas, is similar in terms of definition, purposes, concept, essential ingredients and orientation. However, whereas the paroling authority for adults is the central parole board, for juveniles the paroling authority is oftentimes vested in the training school staffs or in boards, agencies or departments which are independent, in varying degrees, of the training school itself.[58] Although releasing adults and juveniles from correctional institutions involves similar concerns, such as where the parolee will live, work and what type of supportive services in the community can be used to assist the offender's readjustment and reintegration into the community, there is a somewhat differential emphasis in these areas due to age-related factors. Whereas there is a strong emphasis upon job placement among adults, the emphasis for juveniles is usually upon appropriate and suitable placement in educational and vocational training programs, or both. Additionally, whereas the adult parolee may establish an independent residence arrangement, the juvenile released from the institution may be placed back in his home but oftentimes the family home may not be a desirable living arrangement because family instability and problems may preclude the possibility of an adequate adjustment. Consequently, alternative settings, such as foster homes or group homes, may be utilized.

Up Close And Personal

Charles Goodman is a 32-year-old male who is presently serving a sentence of 4 to 20 years for rape. In the past he has been convicted of and served time for forcible rape, statutory rape and theft. He has been paroled a total of three times. In each instance, his parole was revoked because he committed a new offense. He is presently imprisoned in a maximum security correctional facility in the midwest. The following interview was conducted on July 28, 1980, at the prison. Mr. Goodman's parole eligibility date is this coming October. However, he is very pessimistic about his chances for parole this time.

QUESTION: The first time you were imprisoned what crime did you commit?

ANSWER: Rape.

QUESTION: How much time did you serve before you were paroled?

ANSWER: About 29 months.

QUESTION: Prior to actually going before the parole board what did you think your chances of being granted parole were?

ANSWER: I thought I would get out. I had a good institutional record. I did have one court line and I was put in the hole. But they let me out. I thought I would get out primarily because this was the first time I had committed a crime.

QUESTION: What do you remember about your first parole board hearing?

ANSWER: I was scared. I wondered whether they would let me get out. The hearing lasted about 15 minutes. They asked me all kinds of questions.

QUESTION: When you were released from prison on parole what was it like?

ANSWER: It seemed like I was lost. I was locked up about 29 months. Life on the outside was tough to get used to. Things had changed.

QUESTION: What was your parole experience like?

ANSWER: I was paroled to my hometown. I had a good job as a laborer with one of the railroads. I lived with my dad and stepmother. I paid them money for rent.

QUESTION: Did you meet regularly with a parole officer?

ANSWER: Yes. I had contact with a woman parole officer about once a month. We would talk about things—how things were going, if the job was working out. She was real helpful.

QUESTION: Did you successfully complete your parole?

ANSWER: No.

QUESTION: Why not?

ANSWER: After I got out I met a girl. I broke up with her about three months later. After I broke up with her, her cousin was sent over to my house. She told me my ex-girl friend was pregnant. They wanted money for an abortion and they didn't want her family to find out. I wouldn't pay. I had intercourse with her but I didn't get her pregnant. As a matter of fact, the reason I broke up with her was because she was messing around with some other guys, including my brother. When I wouldn't pay they had statutory rape charges filed against me. There was a law stating that you couldn't have intercourse with a girl under age 16. She was 15 and I was about 21.

QUESTION: What happened to you next?

ANSWER: First, I was sent to one of the state mental hospitals. I stayed there about eight months. It was like a maximum security prison. People were always under medication. They wanted to see how you clicked.

QUESTION: Why were you sent to a mental hospital?

ANSWER: I tried to play crazy. I didn't think the statutory rape charge was right. So, I thought I could go to the hospital and then get out.

QUESTION: Did you go to trial?

ANSWER: Yes, I eventually went to trial. I was found guilty. I admit I had intercourse with her—but I know that the baby was not mine. I had been out on parole for almost 22 months at the time of the supposed incident. I only had two more months left on parole. Instead, I was sent to one of the state's other maximum security prisons on a statutory rape conviction for a sentence of from one to 21 years.

QUESTION: What was the prison like?

ANSWER: It was a madhouse. Every time you turned around you would see blood, a stabbing, a shank or a killing.

QUESTION: Did you participate in any programs while you were there?

ANSWER: Yes. I was in Alcoholics Anonymous, got my G.E.D. and even took some college courses.

QUESTION: How much time did you spend in prison the second time?

ANSWER: I was there for just under three years. Then I was paroled to a halfway house in my hometown.

QUESTION: What were your thoughts when you were about to go before the parole board that time?

ANSWER: I didn't think they would let me out. In fact, I was passed over two or three times before I was granted parole. One time they told me I should take more education courses. I didn't have any disciplinary write-ups. I had a court line but it was dropped. I really didn't know if I would get paroled. I had a good institutional record but what they really look at is your past record.

QUESTION: How long did you stay at the halfway house? Did you think it was necessary to parole you to a halfway house?

ANSWER: It wasn't necessary. They probably did that because I violated my parole the first time I was out. I was at the halfway house for about three months. I lived there and worked at a job as a janitor at a local hospital.

QUESTION: Did you successfully complete your parole that time?

ANSWER: No. About one year after leaving the halfway house I was charged with burglary. I didn't do it. My brother was also charged with burglary. We were driving in a car and we were stopped on the highway by the police. My brother had some merchandise on the front seat which he said he had bought from some guy on the street. I was going to have to go to trial but my lawyer advised me to plead guilty to theft rather than to stand trial on burglary so that whatever time I got would run concurrently with my other time. I also pleaded guilty so that they didn't get me for being a habitual criminal.

QUESTION: Where were you sent then?

ANSWER: I was sent back to the prison where I first spent time. But I was paroled for a third time about two years later. However, the parole board wouldn't let me parole back to my hometown because the sheriff didn't want me there or something like that. They didn't want me there. But I got a lawyer and I was able to parole back to my hometown again.

QUESTION: What was your parole experience like this third time?

ANSWER: I had my own place to live. I also had a job lined up as a custodian at a local shopping mall and as a dishwasher at a truck stop. Boy, I've had to do a little bit of everything.

QUESTION: How often did you have to see your parole officer? Was he helpful?

ANSWER: For a while I had to see him every two weeks. Then it was about once a month. He talked to me, told me what would be best for me and how to avoid trouble. He was helpful.

QUESTION: Were you successful on parole this third time?

ANSWER: No. I got pinned with another rape case. I think my past record had a lot to do with it. I met this girl at a tavern

with some other girls and a guy. When the tavern was about
to close we asked the girls if they wanted to have an orgy.
They said it was alright. Later this one girl said I threatened
to kill her if she didn't take her clothes off. I didn't do that.
They all wanted to have an orgy. I had a fall partner. But
they dropped the charges on him but convicted him on
another charge. My fall partner supposedly took this one
girl to his apartment and beat her up—broke her nose,
blackened her eyes. Sure I had intercourse but they all
wanted to have an orgy. I didn't threaten anybody.

QUESTION: Did you go to trial?

ANSWER: Yes, I was convicted and got 4 to 20 years. I've
served about 32-33 months of that now.

QUESTION: It seems that girls appear to be one of the big
problem areas for you on parole?

ANSWER: Yeah. I've messed with quite a few. I like to party.
When I got out I just ran out with my brother, drank and
smoked weed. But I really didn't rape anybody. When
you've got a conviction for rape and you get out and a rape
occurs the police start looking for you. They pull you over a
lot and ask you about this robbery or that rape. They don't
want you there.

QUESTION: When are you eligible for parole? Do you think you
will get parole this time?

ANSWER: In about three months. (Chuckle). I won't get it! So,
I'm trying to get a new trial because I didn't have proper
legal representation.

QUESTION: What do inmates honestly think about parole?

ANSWER: They think it is too strict. You can't go to the bars, you
can't associate with this guy or that guy, you can't do this,
you can't do that. But it does make a lot of sense. When you
are locked up you are taken away from a lot of things. You
can't handle a lot of situations when you get out. You can't
just do what you want to do.

QUESTION: How would you change the parole system?

ANSWER: The parole board pulls out your past record. That's
what they decide on. They look at records—they don't
actually look at your case. If it's your second time around
they don't look at what you're here for now but they look at
your record from before. Sure, they have to look at
something but they use your past to deny you parole.

QUESTION: Final question. If, for some reason, you are granted

parole one more time, what must you do to be successful?
What will prevent you from returning to prison?

ANSWER: First, what I must do is to get out of this state.
If I don't I know I will have trouble. They will get me for the
habitual criminal act if I should do something wrong. I have
acquired some better job skills now. If I can just get out of
this state, I shouldn't have any problems. If I mess up one
more time, they will lock me up and throw away the keys.

Summary

Parole may be defined, in an ideal-type sense, as a correctional method
through which an offender who has already served a portion of his sentence
in prison is conditionally released from a correctional facility to serve part
of the unexpired sentence in the community under the continued custody
of the state and under the supervision and treatment of a parole officer,
with successful social reintegration as the objective.

An appreciation of present-day parole requires a review of its
historical antecedents. The following measures and practices were of
special significance in the development of parole: (1) the conditional
pardon; (2) the transportation of criminals to America and Australia; (3)
apprenticeship by indenture; (4) the "ticket-of-leave" system; and (5)
American prison reform in the 19th century.

The proponents of parole maintain that there are, in principle, several
advantages which accrue to both the offender and the community through
its utilization. In general, these advantages relate to: the release of the
offender when he is ready, the provision of a feeling of hope for the
offender, the opportunity for the offender to reassume family and
community responsibilities, financial savings to the taxpayer, the
protection of society and the provision of supervision and assistance to the
offender through the use of a parole agent.

There are two basic organizational parole board models: (1) the
independent board and (2) the consolidated board. The four principal
functions for state parole boards are: (1) the selection of inmates for parole;
(2) the provision of assistance, supervision and continuing control of
parolees in the community; (3) a determination of when the parole
objective is completed and discharge from parole; and (4) a determination
as to whether parole should be revoked in the event that a parolee should
violate the conditions of his parole. Parole boards vary in size from three to
12 members. However, in a large majority of jurisdictions they are

comprised of either three or five members. There are various methods of selection of parole board members. The prevalent mode of selection is by gubernatorial appointment.

Among the principal factors considered in the parole decision are: criminal record—past and present, parole plan—employment/residence/ special programs, prior community supervision experiences, participation in institutional programs, institutional adjustment, psychological change, circumstances of the offense and "appropriate" period of imprisonment.

An offender's release into the community on parole is contingent upon his compliance with a set of rules and regulations. Among the most prevalent conditions are: (1) prohibiting association with undesirable persons, persons having a criminal record or persons engaged in illegal activity; (2) prohibiting the use of controlled substances, narcotics, drugs and alcoholic beverages; (3) approval of changes in marital status, such as marriage or divorce, require prior notification and approval; (4) compliance with the law is compulsory; (5) parolees are prohibited from owning, possessing, purchasing, receiving, selling or transporting any deadly weapons or firearms; (6) parolees may not own, buy or provide money for the purchase of any motor vehicle or drive a vehicle without permission; (7) prior permission must be obtained to travel outside the state; (8) place of residence or employment status, and changes related thereto, must be reported; and (9) written reports must be submitted regularly on the specified date to the parole officer. There has been a strong trend in recent years toward reducing the number of parole conditions.

Parole provides for the supervision of the offender once he has been released from prison. The provision of community supervision is based upon two underlying principles: (1) the need to protect the public and (2) the need to provide assistance to the parolee in becoming "reintegrated" into the community. Consequently, the parole officer or agent, who is the cornerstone of parole supervision, is often perceived as having to occupy and perform in tow, potentially conflictual, roles: that of policeman and social worker. In order to achieve the goal of the protection of the public, parole agents often perform a number of "policing" or "surveillance" duties. These include making sure that the parolee adheres strictly to the conditions of his parole and initiating revocation procedures if a violation of the rules occur. In some jurisdictions, parole officers are even required to carry firearms and to arrest parole violators. The parole agent in his role as social worker may provide assistance to a parolee in securing employment, finding a place to live or obtaining benefits, such as social security. He may also refer the parolee to the appropriate community social service agencies for the provision of specific services.

The parolee faces the prospect of having his parole revoked if he commits a technical violation, that is, he violates one or more conditions of his parole, or if there is evidence that he has participated in new criminal conduct.

The essential elements of due process have been noticeably absent from parole revocation proceedings in the past. However, in 1972, the U.S. Supreme Court handed down the landmark decision on parole, *Morrissey* v. *Brewer*. The Supreme Court established specific guidelines for a two-step revocation hearing process according to the constitutional requirement of due process. In 1973, the U.S. Supreme Court handed down another significant decision. In *Gagnon* v. *Scarpelli* the U.S. Supreme Court held that parolees and probationers had a qualified right to counsel in revocation hearings.

There are a variety of problems plaguing the system of parole. Parole boards have been the target of much of the criticism directed against the parole system. Parole boards are criticized for the arbitrary character of their decisionmaking, for the lack of attention they give to the analysis and dynamics of individual cases and for the selection process of members which often results in the political appointment of nonprofessional members who lack sufficient expertise and training in the correctional field which would enable them to properly evaluate and assess relevant parole decisionmaking materials. The conditions imposed upon parolees have also drawn strong criticism. They have been characterized as being too numerous, too vague, too coercive, too intrusive and subject to the discretionary enforcement of parole agents. The supposed merits of parole supervision have also come under heavy attack. Large case loads, the lack of providing various kinds of supervision required of different types of cases, the conflicting roles of law enforcement officer and social worker performed by parole agents, an over reliance on the law enforcement function of supervision, the psychological stress placed on parolees in the community by expecting compliance with such an umbrella of rules, and the reluctance of parolees to seek help and assistance from parole agents due to their conflicting roles of law enforcement officer and social worker are all factors which make the attainment of the two principal goals of community supervision, protection and treatment, unlikely. Although court decisions have focused increasing attention on the due process safeguards, such as a parole grant hearing or revocation proceedings, there are still many pertinent legal issues and problems that remain unsettled and unresolved. Until they are resolved in a satisfactory manner parole related hearings will continue to be described by the critics as being "unfair" and inadequate according to traditional criminal justice standards. The aforementioned shortcomings of parole have not led critics to abandon parole but instead to suggest various types of needed reforms which generally accept the principal premises of parole. However, there are also critics, collectively known as the "abolishionists," who advocate its total elimination or abolition on the grounds that it is ineffective, an outdated practice, based on erroneous assumptions and simply inoperable in practice according to intended objectives.

A comparison between prison and parole costs reveals significant monetary differences. An examination of representative figures shows that it is clearly cheaper to parole an offender rather than to imprison him.

It would seem, on the surface, that the assessment of the effectiveness of parole as a correctional strategy in reducing recidivism would be a relatively easy task. However, the existence of several factors so complicates the process that it is problematic to estimate, on a nationwide basis, the overall merit of parole in reducing recidivism.

Notes

1. Dwight C. Jarvis, *Institutional Treatment of the Offender* (New York: McGraw-Hill Book Company, 1978), p. 121.
2. National Advisory Commission on Criminal Justice Standards and Goals, *Corrections* (Washington, D.C.: U.S. Department of Justice, 1973), p. 389.
3. George F. Cole and Susette M. Talarico, "Second Thoughts on Parole," *American Bar Association Journal*, Volume 63 (July, 1977), pp. 973-976.
4. David T. Stanley, *Prisoners Among Us: The Problem of Parole* (Washington, D.C.: The Brookings Institution, 1976), p. 1.
5. G.I. Giardini, *The Parole Process* (Springfield, Illinois: Charles C. Thomas, 1959), p. 263.
6. Douglas Lipton, Robert Martinson, and Judith Wilks, *The Effectiveness of Correctional Treatment* (New York: Praeger Publishers, 1975), pp. 9-10.
7. New York State Division of Parole, *Manual for Parole Officers*, 1953, as reprinted in George G. Killinger and Paul F. Cromwell, Jr., *Corrections in the Community: Alternatives to Imprisonment* (St. Paul, Minnesota: West Publishing, 1974), p. 400.
8. Rodney J. Henningsen, *Probation and Parole* (New York: Harcourt Brace Jovanovich, 1981), pp. 55-56.
9. Harry E. Allen and Clifford E. Simonsen, *Corrections in America: An Introduction* (Beverly Hills, California: Glencoe Press, 1975), p. 51.
10. Killinger and Cromwell, *Corrections in the Community*, 1st edition, p. 414.
11. Paul Cromwell, George Killinger and Hazel Kerper, *Probation and Parole in the Criminal Justice System*, 1976, as reprinted in George G. Killinger and Paul F. Cromwell, Jr., *Corrections in the Community*, 2nd edition (St. Paul, Minnesota: West Publishing, 1978), p. 240.
12. Ibid.
13. Ibid.
14. Ibid.
15. National Advisory Commission on Criminal Justice Standards and Goals, *Corrections*, p. 396.
16. William Parker, *Parole: Origins, Development, Current Practices and Statutes* (College Park, Maryland: American Correctional Association, 1972), p. 23.

17. Frank P. Prassel, *Introduction to American Criminal Justice* (New York: Harper and Row, 1975), p. 208.
18. 28C.F.R.§2.52, 38 Federal Register 222 (November 19, 1973) as amended.
19. Henningsen, *Probation and Parole*, p. 78.
20. Rosemary J. Erickson, Wayman J. Crow, Louis A. Zurcher, Jr. and Archie V. Connett, *Paroled But Not Free* (New York: Behavioral Publications, 1973), p. 65.
21. Reported in Cole and Talarico, "Second Thoughts on Parole," p. 974.
22. Ibid.
23. National Parole Institutes, *Selection for Parole* (New York: National Council on Crime and Delinquency, 1966).
24. Nat R. Arluke, "A Summary of Parole Rules—Thirteen Years Later," *Crime and Delinquency*, Volume 15 (April, 1969), p. 267 and pp. 272-273.
25. Erickson et al., *Paroled But Not Free*, pp. 66-73.
26. Ibid., p. 68.
27. Citizens' Inquiry on Parole and Criminal Justice, Inc., *Prison Without Walls* (New York: Praeger Publishers, 1975), pp. 74-78.
28. Ibid., pp. 134-136.
29. 408 U.S. 471, 92 S. Ct. 2593, 33 L. Ed. 2d 484 (1972).
30. Ibid.
31. Gagnon v. Scarpelli, 411 U.S. 778, 93 S. Ct. 1756, 36 L. Ed. 2d 656 (1973).
32. Board of Directors, National Council on Crime and Delinquency, "Parole Decisions: A Policy Statement," *Crime and Delinquency*, April, 1973, p. 137.
33. Vincent O'Leary and Joan Nuffield, *The Organization of Parole Systems in the United States*, 2nd edition (Hackensack, New Jersey: National Council on Crime and Delinquency, 1972), p. xxx.
34. Arluke, "A Summary of Parole Rules," p. 269.
35. Eugene N. Barkin, "Legal Issues Facing Parole," *Crime and Delinquency*, April, 1979, pp. 219-235.
36. Citizens' Inquiry on Parole and Criminal Justice, Inc., *Prison Without Walls*, pp. 166-167.
37. Ibid. p. 178.
38. Ibid., p. 167.
39. David Fogel, *"We Are The Living Proof": The Justice Model for Corrections* (Cincinnati: The W.H. Anderson, Co., 1975), p. 204.
40. Stanley, *Prisoners Among Us*, pp. 184-191.
41. Cited in National Advisory Committee on Criminal Justice Standards and Goals, *Task Force Report: Courts* (Washington, D.C.: U.S. Government Printing Office, 1973), p. 37.
42. Louis P. Carney, *Probation and Parole* (New York: McGraw-Hill Book Company, 1977), p. 156.
43. Stanley, *Prisoners Among Us*, p. 182.
44. Carney, *Probation and Parole*, p. 156.
45. Irvin Waller, *Men Released From Prison* (Toronto, Canada: University of Toronto Press, 1974), pp. xiv-xv.
46. Donald J. Newman, "Legal Model for Parole: Future Developments," in *Contemporary Corrections*, edited by Benjamin Frank (Reston, Virginia: Reston Publishing Company, 1973), pp. 251-252.

47. Don M. Gottfredson, "Some Positive Changes in the Parole Process," in *Offenders and Corrections*, edited by Denis Szabo and Susan Katzenelson (New York: Praeger Publishers, 1978), pp. 214-216.

48. Citizens' Inquiry, *Prison Without Walls*, p. 160.

49. Ibid., p. 166.

50. National Probation and Parole Institutes of the National Council on Crime and Delinquency, *Uniform Parole Reports* (November, 1972).

51. Ibid., February, 1973.

52. Ibid., November, 1972.

53. Ibid.

54. Don M. Gottfredson, M.G. Neithercutt, Joan Nuffield, and Vincent O'Leary, *Four Thousand Lifetimes: A Study of Time Served and Parole Outcomes* (Davis, California: National Council on Crime and Delinquency, Research Center, June, 1973).

55. Lipton, Martinson, and Wilks, *The Effectiveness of Correctional Treatment*, pp. 149-150.

56. Alan R. Coffey, *Juvenile Corrections: Treatment and Rehabilitation* (Englewood Cliffs, New Jersey: Prentice-Hall, Inc., 1975), p. 212.

57. Ibid., p. 213.

58. Hassim M. Solomon, *Community Corrections* (Boston, Massachusetts: Holbrook Press, 1976), pp. 205-206.

Chapter 5
Work Release

Work release is a correctional program under which certain selected inmates of a local county jail or a state or federal correctional institution are allowed to be gainfully employed on a full-time basis in the community. The selected inmates return to authorized custody during nonworking hours, whether it be the inmates' resident institution or contracted housing nearer the source of employment, such as halfway houses, work release centers or county jails.

History

A correctional milestone occurred in 1913 with the passage of the first work release law in Wisconsin. Known as the Huber Law, after its sponsor, Senator Henry A. Huber, this legislation allowed misdemeanants in county jails to be gainfully employed during the day in the community as farm laborers for a minimum of ten and a maximum of 12 hours per day and returned to custody at night. Historically work release was not born out of a lofty quest for rehabilitation but for retribution. It was meant to serve as a form of punishment. Its advocates considered it unjust for criminal offenders to waste their time in idleness and vice while respectable citizens labored. Despite the passage of the Huber Law, there was very little actual application until 1943. In 1943, to meet the rising labor needs brought on by World War II, Municipal Court Judge Oscar J. Schmiege of Outagamie County, Wisconsin, made more extensive use of the law by initiating a work release program under which non-dangerous offenders could be gainfully employed outside the jail and pay for their own room and board.[1]

After its early beginning in Wisconsin, work release went into an extended dormant period during which it failed to attract much support. By 1950, only four states, Wisconsin in 1913, Nebraska and West Virginia in 1917, and Hawaii (then the Territory of Hawaii) in 1935, had provisions for work release.

In 1957, state legislation in North Carolina authorized the establishment of the most extensive work release program up to that time. For state prisoners rather than jail inmates, the first work release statute in North Carolina restricted eligibility to misdemeanants. Later the statute was liberalized to extend the privilege to felons making North Carolina the first state to extend the privilege of work release to felons.[2]

Interest in work release appreciably increased following the successful experience of the North Carolina work release program and the provision for work release participation for inmates incarcerated in federal correctional institutions by the passing of the Prisoner Rehabilitation Act of 1965. This period of substantial growth and development for work release following these two significant events, is confirmed by the fact that by 1966, 29 jurisdictions comprised of 27 states, the federal government, and the District of Columbia had authorized work release and 40 jurusdictions provided for work release programs by 1968. Further growth and development occurred through 1973 when there were 36 states which authorized work release programs in state institutions and 26 states authorized work release programs in county or municipal institutions.[3] By 1975, only two states, Utah and Wyoming, lacked statutory authorization for work release, although both operated such programs.[4]

Despite the existence of laws permitting work release, usually no more than ten percent of a state's inmates participate in work release while on the average, only one or two percent usually participate.[5] There is great disparity among states in terms of their utilization of such programs. Those states with the largest work release programs are Florida, Michigan and North Carolina. Florida, with approximately 20,000 inmates, has 1,900 inmates on work release; Michigan places more than 1,000 inmates on work release; and North Carolina has 1,500 persons on work release out of an overall prison population of 13,500. By comparison, Illinois, which has a prison population comparable in size and character to Michigan, has only 160 persons on work release; Texas with an institutional population of 24,000 inmates has almost no inmates on work release; and Mississippi, with an institutional population of only 3,000, has approximately the same number of inmates on work release as the states of New York and California which have prison populations of more than 20,000 inmates.[6]

Purpose

The principal purposes or objectives of work release programs relate to economic, rehabilitative and humanitarian themes. They can be summarized as follows:

Graduated Release

Work release is a program of graduated release which is designed to help selected inmates prepare for release and to assist them in making a successful transition from the structured institutional environment back into the free community. As such it provides a structured pre-release experience for inmates which can eliminate or reduce the degree of psychological and cultural shock that can often occur for inmates who are directly and suddenly released from an institution back into the community. This situation, in part, may account for why the highest percentage of post-prison failures occur within the first six months after release. Inmates are frequently incapable of making a successful adjustment from a situation of total incarceration to complete freedom. Work release is intended to bridge the gap between imprisonment and freedom in the community for inmates and enable them to become gradually adjusted to life in the community and the responsibilities community living entails.

Indicator of Readiness for Parole

As a general rule, inmates placed in work release programs must be within a certain time period of their earliest possible release date. Oftentimes, this is a period of six months. Insofar as work release is a community-based oriented program, it gives the paroling authority an important additional means of testing and observing the inmate's suitability for release into the community via parole before a final decision is made. Although a careful perusal of an inmate's institutional adjustment record is one of several critical measures used in determining readiness for parole, it represents essentially an adjustment to a total institution, not the free community. Therefore, the additional information provided by the inmate's work release experience complements other available data in determining an inmate's readiness for parole. Successful institutional adjustment in and of itself is no guarantee of successful community adjustment.

Savings to Taxpayer

Money earned by work release participants is often used to pay: (1) federal and state taxes, (2) program maintenance (room and board) and transportation costs, (3) support to dependents who may be on welfare or public assistance rolls, and (4) legitimate debts, court costs and/or restitution. Money may also be deposited in an inmate savings account to be utilized upon release. These payments, made with money earned by inmates on work release, represent a substantial savings to the taxpayer and appreciably diminish the state's welfare burden.

Improvement in Self-Esteem

Among the core values found in American society is the value placed upon work.[7] Success in this area is often essential in maintaining one's self-esteem and self-respect. However, in prison inmates frequently are placed in menial jobs that are related to the maintenance of the prison. Additionally, there is little incentive to take pride in one's work insofar as prison pay is often ridiculously low by societal standards. These factors, together with the inability of the inmate to assist in the support of his family, contribute to a loss of self-esteem and self-respect. By allowing inmates to be constructively employed at standard wages and to utilize their earnings to contribute to the support of themselves and their dependents, rather than relying totally on the welfare system of the state, work release enables inmates to develop a feeling of self-worth and accomplishment.

Possible Job Retention

A bona fide job in the community is an absolute necessity for the ex-offender. Upon release from prison, ex-offenders are suddenly faced with numerous expenses. They must purchase clothing, food, find a place to live and possibly reassume family responsibilities. Funds provided by the institution to the inmate upon release are usually insufficient to adequately cover these immediate expenses. Furthermore, the ex-offender must confront several problems when seeking employment, such as unrealistic employment expectations, the burden of his criminal record and possible discrimination in both the public and private employment sectors. Consequently, not only is a job an economic necessity but it can also greatly influence his ability to successfully reenter the community. Ideally, the specific training or experience in actual work release situations is related to the inmate's prior educational or occupational training. Hopefully, work release will in some instances, place the offender on a job he can retain after release and, therefore, eliminate the eventual difficulty of having to find a job and its concomitant problems.

Preservation of Family and Community Ties

Many work release programs permit their participants to leave the facility of their confinement periodically on passes. Passes may be issued to work releasees to visit their families for the purpose of establishing ties, to participate in religious services or activities within the community, to participate in counseling or treatment services provided by agencies in the community or to participate in recreational activities. Work release, therefore, can serve as a vehicle through which inmates can preserve positive family and community ties.

Administration/Process

There are several important matters involved in the administration and process of work release programs. These include the establishment of eligibility requirements for selecting inmates for participation, the actual procedural steps in making an application for work release, identifying conditions for removal from work release status and the execution of work release plan agreements. In all of these areas, great concern should be exercised for the well-being and security of the community and for the safeguard of its property while at the same time attempting to make work release an optimally valuable experience for the inmate and preventing the possible exploitation of the inmate.

Eligibility Requirements

The selection of participants for work release includes numerous factors. Participation in work release is usually voluntary. Although eligibility requirements vary from program to program, a recent poll of 24 work release programs revealed that there are six common criteria for exclusion from participation in work release programs which relate to offense type or background: violence, sexual crimes, narcotics sale, narcotics use, notoriety and organized crime. Offenders convicted of assaultive or violent and/or aggressive crimes were excluded from participation in 20 of the 24 programs polled; offenders convicted of sexual offenses were excluded in 18 of the 24 programs polled; offenders convicted of selling narcotics were excluded in 16 of the 24 programs polled; offenders convicted of narcotics use were excluded in 12 of the 24 programs polled; offenders characterized by notoriety which was likely to evoke adverse public reactions were excluded in 12 of the 24 programs polled; and offenders with past involvement in organized crime were excluded in 10 of the 24 programs polled. In addition to these criteria, two other factors were also prominent: offenders who were considered escape risks and offenders with serious mental, emotional or personality problems.[8]

In addition to excludable offenses, participation in work release programs also hinges upon other factors. Usually inmates have to be within a certain number of months of their probable release date or earliest projected parole hearing. This may vary from three to 24 months, with six months being the most common. Stipulations also frequently exist requiring that a certain proportion of the offender's sentence must be served before he is eligible. Some states require the offender to serve half his sentence before he is eligible while others require a shorter period of time remaining to be served.[9] For example, in North Carolina offenders for whom work release is viewed as a transitional program between incarceration and release must have served a minimum of 10 percent of their maximum sentence to acquire eligible status. However, in North Carolina the court can recommend immediate work release for nonserious offenders who are serving sentences of five years or less.[10]

Oftentimes, other conditions must also be satisfied to be eligible for work release participation. Several programs require applicants to have satisfactorily completed a minimum number of days in minimum custody before being eligible. Applicants are also frequently required to have satisfactorily adjusted while incarcerated as evidenced by a good institutional record. Applicants must also be in good physical condition, sufficient to be able to acquire and maintain employment. Preference is frequently given to inmates who are residents of the state insofar as they may often be placed in programs near their families and their intended place of residence after release. Additionally, many states would prefer to extend such program participation to their own residents who are likely to remain in the state after release, versus nonresident inmates who may leave the state soon after release.

Processing of Work Release Applications

Although the administrative procedures for work release applications vary from program to program, there are a set of procedures common to those work release programs which are considered transitional programs between incarceration and release.

Inmates requesting work release privileges must usually submit applications within a fixed time period related to a specified number of months prior to the earliest parole date or the earliest discharge date. In order to initiate the request for application to work release the inmate must normally contact a classification officer or a member of their unit team or the work release coordinator of the institution in which he is incarcerated to secure an application. Figure 5.1 is a copy of the Inmate Work Release Application employed by the State of Kansas, Department of Corrections. The applicant is oftentimes also required to complete a Work Release Inmate Statement of Intent specifying why he is requesting work release. Figure 5.2 is a copy of the form utilized by the State of Kansas, Department of Corrections.

The application materials are normally completed with the assistance of the aforementioned institution contact person and is then forwarded for review to a committee at the respective institution. This committee will make a recommendation for or against approval of work release. If the inmate's request should be denied, the reason for that recommendation is noted. The application next is usually forwarded to the Work Release Division at Department Headquarters where it will be evaluated by members of the Division for their recommendation. They may recommend approval, denial or consideration at a later date. Reasons are specified for their decision. Often the application is then submitted to the Director,

Assistant Director or Secretary of the Department of Corrections for a final decision. Upon that determination, the inmate is notified of that decision.

Members of the work release unit normally assist approved applicants in finding suitable employment, arranging necessary job interviews and scheduling transportation to and from work.

Figure 5.1 Inmate Work Release Application

INMATE WORK RELEASE APPLICATION

TO: Secretary of Corrections

I, ..., NO. ...., INSTITUTION .... ,
respectfully submit application for participation in the Work Release Program.

1.   I am requesting Work Release privileges in .... County.
     I will/will NOT accept Work Release privileges in any County designated by the Secretary.

2.   List close relatives or other resources (friends, sponsors, etc.) currently residing in or near the county in which Work Release is requested.

NAME	AGE	ADDRESS	RELATIONSHIP
....	....	....	....
....	....	....	....
....	....	....	....

3.   Current martial status: Single ....   Married ....   Divorced ....

4.   Number of legal dependents .... Are these dependents now receiving public assistance through the Department of Social and Rehabilitation Services? ....

5.   I   (A) am NOT under court order to support my dependents at this time.
             (B) am under court order to support my dependents at this time. This court order was rendered in .... County.

6.   List individuals or business concerns to which you are obligated as a result of a loan, purchase, court ordered restitution or other legally incurred debt.

BUSINESS CONCERN	ADDRESS	AMOUNT OWED
....	....	....
....	....	....
....	....	....

7.   List your education background:

     1-6 7 8 9 10 11 12 GED   AA DEGREE BA/BS DEGREE   TOTAL COLLEGE HOURS ....
     If vocational school, list type of training received while in the institution: ....
     ....

8.   List work skills and occupations: ....
     ....

     Do you have your own tools?   Yes ....   No ....   List past employment:

FIRM NAME	ADDRESS	YOUR JOB	DATES
....	....	....	....
....	....	....	....
....	....	....	....

Figure 5.1—Concluded

9. Social Security Number: ................-..............-..................

10. Do you have any writs (habeau corpus, certiorari, etc.) pending in a court? ....

    If yes, in which court? ....

    Do you have any detainers lodged against you?   Yes ....   No ....

    If yes, from what jurisdiction and for what type of offense? ....

11. Are you eligible for a parole hearing?   Yes ....   No ....

    If yes, when are you due to see the Kansas Adult Authority? ....

    List any physical disabilities, if any: ....

    Are you taking medication?   Yes ....   No ....

    If yes, describe the type and purpose of the medication: ....

In applying for Work Release candidacy, I hereby authorize the Department of Corrections to reveal any portion of my offense record to prospective parties and/or agencies involved in considering my application. I further agree to exempt the Department of Corrections from all liabilities arising from the disclosures of said information. I agree to abide by all rules and regulations concerning my assignment to the Work Release Program.

....
(Date)   (Inmate's Signature)

....
(Witness)   (Witness)

(WITNESSES MUST BE EMPLOYEES OF THE DEPARTMENT OF CORRECTIONS)

DISTRIBUTION: Secretary of Corrections (2)
               Unit Team
               Institution File

Prior to the approval of a participant's Work Release Employment Plan, work release program personnel often conduct a pre-exit investigation. The purpose of this investigation is to verify the validity of the inmate's proposed work release plan, to determine that there will be no exploitation of the inmate, insure that the inmate will receive compensation

Figure 5.2 Work Release Inmate Statement of Intent

WORK RELEASE
INMATE STATEMENT OF INTENT

I, _____
                    (Name)   (Number)

request Work Release privileges in _____
                                        (County)   (State)

I plan to parole in _____ which would make
                    (County)   (State)

this a _____ request. The reason I
                (Temporary or Permanent)

request Work Release in _____ is because:
                            (County)   (State)

_____

_____

_____

_____

_____

_____

_____

_____

_____

_____

_____

_____

_____

_____

_____

P-203

equal to that of comparable workers and that they will not be employed under adverse or unacceptable working conditions.

Removal from Work Release Status

Once accepted as a work release participant, work releasees are often required to consent to a set of rules or conditions regarding their participation in the program. Figure 5.3 lists the conditions of work release required of participants in the work release program administered by the State of Kansas, Department of Corrections. They are representative of most work release programs.

Explicit reasons are also usually specified which will result in the termination or suspension of an offender's participation in work release.

Figure 5.3 Conditions of Work Release Agreement

STATE OF KANSAS

DEPARTMENT OF CORRECTIONS

CONDITIONS OF WORK RELEASE AGREEMENT

NAME_____ _____NUMBER_____

WORK RELEASE FACILITY_____

For the privilege of participating in the Work Release Program, I hereby agree to the following rules:

1. I will at all times conduct myself with propriety so as not to bring discredit upon myself, the Work Release Program, my employer, or the institution/facility of my confinement.

2. I will obey all Federal, State, and local laws and departmental regulations and instructions of the facility wherein I am housed.

3. I will not change nor deviate from my approved work plan without consultation with the counselor and an alternate plan has been approved.

4. I will directly and promptly proceed to and return from my designated location by the approved method of transportation, route and time.

5. I will remain within the designated area of my Work Release plan.

6. I will return to my Work Release Facility immediately and without delay if approved work, training, or service ceases prior to the end of the scheduled time for the termination thereof.

7. I will make no contact either personal, telephone, or otherwise, with any individual on behalf of another inmate confined within an institution.

8. I will refrain from consuming any alcoholic beverages and/or any narcotics, or other drugs not prescribed as medication.

9. In the event of a strike, I will express no sentiments either for or against labor or management.

10. In the event of difficulty, I will contact the Work Release Center at the earliest possible time.

11. I understand that if I should willfully fail to remain within the extended limits of confinement or to return within time prescribed to the place of confinement, such shall be deemed as an aggravated escape from custody and shall be punishable by law.

DC/wr 4 (Rev. 1-81)

Figure 5.3—Concluded

12. I understand that the Department of Corrections will credit my account with wages paid and furnish me a receipt together with a statement of deductions made by my employer. I further understand that while the Department of Corrections will account for the wages and deductions according to the agreement that it is my responsibility to see that wages and deductions have been properly computed by my employer.

13. I hereby waive my right to make any claim for property which is lost, stolen or damaged in the Work Release Center if such property was not on the work release center list of permitted property; or if such property, whether a single item or collection of items, exceeds a value of $200.00; or if I have escaped from custody; I further understand and agree that according to K.A.R. 44-16-105 I own property at my own risk and shall not recover on any claim for loss or damage unless I can prove that it directly resulted from the intentional or grossly negligent act or omission of a correctional employee and unless the loss or damage was promptly and properly reported. I agree to make no claim for property lost, damaged or stolen from my room or locker if I am absent and this room or locker is unlocked.

14. I understand that Work Release is a privileged program and if I do not abide by the rules, regulations and work release general orders, I can be administratively removed from the program.

I hereby certify that the above Work Release conditions have been read and explained to the inmate.

The above Work Release conditions have been read and explained to me, and I do hereby agree to abide by these conditions.

Date _____

Inmate Signature _____

Witness _____

Officer in Charge _____

Generally, most programs will remove an inmate from work release if he is granted parole, is unable to satisfactorily adjust to his job as indicated by poor job performance or the establishment of unsatisfactory relationships with the employer and/or employees, participates in criminal behavior, displays a lack of interest or motivation in securing employment or refuses to accept offers of gainful employment, violates program rules or leaves his place of employment or work release housing area without authorization. Participants are also normally permitted to request voluntary withdrawal from the program if they believe that continued participation is not in their best interests.

Work Release Plan Agreements

An important dimension of work release participation involves the execution of a written agreement between the administering agency of the work release program and the participant. Such agreements outline the agreed upon work release plan for the participant. It specifies such information as at what work release facility the participant will be housed, conditions of employment, including place of employment, job title, salary and work schedule, transportation arrangements to and from work and disbursement of the participant's earnings for room and board, clothing, transportation, incidental expenses, support of dependents, payment of legal debts and savings. Figure 5.4 is a copy of the Inmate Work Release Plan Agreement utilized by the State of Kansas, Department of Corrections.

Additionally, a work release agreement is usually executed between the administering agency of the work release program and the employer. It normally provides information to the employer regarding the work release program and its regulations and the employment offer made to the inmate including job title, wages, work schedule and intended period of employment. Figure 5.5 is a copy of the Employer's Work Release Agreement used by the State of Kansas, Department of Corrections.

Problems

The implementation, administration and continuation of work release programs involves several peculiar problems. These problems must be skillfully addressed and resolved if the program is to be successful.

Community Resistance

Community resistance and opposition to work release programs often constitutes a major concern to work release administrators. Public suspicion exists insofar as many people believe that work release programs take away jobs from law-abiding persons, that work release inmates may commit crimes while involved in such programs and that work release centers located in the community may bring down property values. In addition, some employers may be reluctant to hire inmates on work release programs because of doubts they have regarding the ability of inmates to do the job or to behave in a consistently responsible manner.

Attempts to alleviate or neutralize community opposition often include the utilization of community involved citizens' advisory boards, media coverage of work release related human interest stories, immediate

Figure 5.4 Inmate Work Release Plan Agreement

FORM WR-05
P-21 (12-10-79)

STATE OF KANSAS
DEPARTMENT OF CORRECTIONS

INMATE WORK RELEASE PLAN AGREEMENT

NAME _____ NUMBER _____

_____WORK RELEASE FACILITY:_____

In accordance with the provisions of K.S.A. 1973 Supp. 75-5267 and 75-5268 and Rules established by the Department of Corrections for the administration of a Work Release Program, the Department of Corrections does hereby extend the limits of confinement for the above named inmate to allow him to participate in the following (work) (study) Release Plan:

This inmate will be housed in a Work Release facility located in: _____

1. Designated Location: (Employer, School, Facility, or Other)

    Employer's Name _____

    Address _____ Telephone Number _____

    Job Title _____ Immediate Supervisor _____

    Wages _____ Working Days Per Week Are _____ Through _____

    Working Hours Will Begin At _____ And End At _____

2. Transportation: Times, Route, and Method are as follows:

    Leave Work Release facility at _____ a.m. / p.m., with method of transportation

    being _____ . Return to Work Release facility by _____ a.m. / p.m.

    Method of transportation _____

    Route to and from work _____

Figure 5.4—Concluded

---

3. Earnings shall be paid or payable directly to the participant by the employer. It shall be accounted for as described in paragraph # 12, Form WR-04 of the agreement. As provided by statute, earnings will be distributed by the Department of Corrections in the following manner:

(a) Board and room at the rate of _____ per _____ .

(b) Clothing and/or tools as necessary.

(c) Necessary travel expense to and from work at the rate of $ _____ per _____

(d) Incidental expenses at the rate of _____ per _____ .

(e) Support of Dependents, if any, at the rate of 75% of net pay following deductions of a, b, c, and d above to be paid to:

_____   _____
(NAME)   (ADDRESS)

(f) Payment of legal debts, either acknowledged in writing or reduced in judgment, at the rate of 25% of net pay if item "e" above is not applicable.

$ _____ per _____ to _____

$ _____ per _____ to _____

(g) The balance of participant's earnings, if any, shall go to the participant's Work Release Account.

I hereby certify the above Work Release Plan has been   The above Work Release Plan has been read and explained
explained to the inmate.   to me, and I do hereby agree to participate under said
                                                             conditions.

_____ _____   _____ _____
(Date)   (Title)   (Date)   (Inmate)

---

official attention to unfavorable publicity or incidents which may damage the image of the program among the public and the use of program personnel to explain the aims of the program to the public, including a strong emphasis of the advantages of the program to the community in general and employers in particular.[11] Several steps may be taken by work

Figure 5.5 Employer's Work Release Agreement

STATE OF KANSAS

DEPARTMENT OF CORRECTIONS

EMPLOYER'S WORK RELEASE AGREEMENT

EMPLOYMENT OFFER FOR INMATE: _____ INSTITUTIONAL NO. _____

JOB TITLE: _____

WAGES: RATE _____ PER _____ PAY PERIOD _____

(OVERTIME) _____ PER _____

(I will notify the Department of Corrections if there are any changes in rates or wages.)

WORK HOURS: BEGINNING AT _____ ENDING _____

WORK DAYS: _____ THROUGH _____

EMPLOYMENT TO BECOME EFFECTIVE _____

(1) No inmate in the Work Release Program is to be considered an agent of the State of Kansas.

(2) While employed he shall be covered by the employer's insurance, and/or workmen's compensation insurance as required by law.

(3) In the event of a strike, the inmate will be withdrawn from the employment for the duration of the strike.

(4) The consumption of alcoholic beverages by the inmate is prohibited.

(5) The consumption of narcotics, or other drugs not lawfully possessed by the inmate is prohibited.

(6) The inmate must return to the facility immediately upon the conclusion of each day's work.

(7) The wages of Work Release participants are to be made payable to the participant. This remittance may be on a standard payroll check. Accompanying the check should be a statement of deductions made, showing also the name of the employee, the pay period, the institutional NO., and the computation of the gross wages.

It is further understood that Work Release employees are subject to the same deductions for tax and social security as any other employee.

(8) This Work Release Plan neither constitutes nor implies a contractual agreement between the Department of Corrections and the employer.

NAME: _____

_____ TITLE _____

ORGANIZATION OR COMPANY: _____

ADDRESS: _____

DATE: _____ TELEPHONE NUMBER: _____

release program personnel to reduce employer reluctance to hire work release inmates. The major steps are as follows:

1. Prospective employers may be provided with testimonials from other employers who had satisfactory work experiences with work release participants.

2. Prospective employers may be provided with a thorough explanation of the careful screening procedures utilized in selecting work release participants.
3. Prospective employers may be given the opportunity to have face-to-face contact with prospective work release employees prior to actual employment.
4. Work release staff can stress to prospective employers just how much the work release inmate has at stake in successfully completing his work release program, including his job.
5. Prospective employers may be provided with information demonstrating a proven record of success for the work release program for the past few years.
6. Prospective employers may be assured that they do not have to "babysit" the work release participants.
7. Work release staff may suggest hiring work release participants on a trial basis to extremely reluctant prospective employers.
8. Prospective employers may be assured that program staff will be available 24 hours a day in case of an emergency.[12]

Labor Market Needs

The success of work release programs in participant placements is highly dependent upon the supply-demand relationships in the local labor market.[13] Institutional and work release staff must be keenly aware of the numbers and types of jobs that are likely to be available at present and in the future in the local labor market, as well as the job skills required of prospective job candidates. Problems can occur for a work release program if the skills acquired by prisoners through education and vocational training offered at the institution do not coincide with the kinds and quality of jobs available in the local job market. Therefore, it is essential if this potential problem is to be minimized, that institutional and work release program personnel keep closely abreast of present and future local labor market needs and have this information incorporated into planning vocational training and educational programs for the inmates at the institution.

Problems with Employers

Problems have periodically been encountered with employers who have hired work releasees. Occasionally, employers have failed to reimburse work release employees. Also, realizing that they have a captive labor pool at their disposal, some employers have exploited work releasees by paying them less than minimum wage, forcing them to work overtime and making prisoners work undesirable shifts. Employers have also hired work releasees for ulterior purposes in using them as strike breakers.

Additionally, employers have also failed to report the absences of work release employees and failed to fulfill their bookkeeping responsibilities.[14]

In order to prevent these difficulties, most work release programs determine, prior to approval of a work release employment plan, that there will be no exploitation of the inmate on the job, that the inmate will receive compensation equal to that of comparable workers and that the inmate will not be employed under adverse or unacceptable working conditions. Additionally, a written agreement between the administering agency of the work release program and the employer detailing the conditions of employment must be completed prior to the commencement of employment by a work releasee.

Housing/Contraband/Transportation

Employment opportunities for work releasees tend to be concentrated in urban areas. However, prisons are often located in remote areas isolated from population centers. Consequently, since it is not always feasible to return work releasees to their resident institution during their nonworking hours, separate housing facilities closer to the job site are often required for work release participants. Work releasees may, therefore, be housed at city jails, privately operated halfway houses or quarters leased by the work release program administering agency to be used as work release centers. Nevertheless, the housing of work releasees may pose problems when a principal purpose of work release is to minimize costs. Additional problems may also be realized. Insofar as work releasees have regular access to the community, other non-work release inmates may exert pressure upon them to smuggle contraband into the institution. The inclusion of a special category of work release inmates with other inmates may also present problems for the staff, such as the necessity of conducting special counts and providing different feeding schedules.

Transportation arrangements must also be made for work releasees to and from work. This is especially difficult if work releasees are housed at a correctional institution which is not located near an urban area where inmates are most likely to find jobs.

Marginal Status

One of the supposed strong points of work release is that it represents a form of graduated, rather than abrupt, release of offenders back into the community. However, this same program characteristic is perceived by some as holding the potential for constituting a serious problem for work release participants themselves. Insofar as a work releasee is both part of the world of work in the free community and, at the same time, part of the world of prison he is a marginal man. This "half-free" status may pose serious problems of identification for the work releasee. He may have difficulty in resolving the question as to whether he is an inmate or a free person.

Escapes/Violations

Great precaution is normally exercised in the selection of work release participants. However, there always exists the possibility that participants in programs like work release, which are less restrictive in terms of the amount of overt supervision exercised, may escape or commit crimes. Such eventualities can pose serious problems for the continuation of work release programs. A few violent incidents involving work releasees killed the California Department of Corrections work release program and lead to severely restrictive new legislation in New York and dramatic program cutbacks in New Jersey.[15] The old saying, "one bad apple can spoil the whole barrel," certainly rings true for work release programs.

Administration

The implementation and operation of a work release program also presents additional administrative problems. Prison or jail administrators must assume such added duties as locating employment for work release participants, screening work release applicants, maintaining records, supplying special housing for work releasees, furnishing transportation and providing field supervision of inmates.

Selection of Participants

The selection of work release participants also poses a problem which should not be underestimated. Many work release administrators feel strapped by heavy statutory restrictions placed on prisoner eligibility. A study of 46 work release administrators across the country revealed that practically every respondent identified various aspects of the law which affected their operating activities. In fact, most experienced administrators perceived existing legislation as inhibiting some of their efforts and only three administrators believed the law was flexible enough to permit them to function at maximum efficiency. A hindering aspect of work release legislation commonly noted by the administrators was the undue restrictions that prevent certain individuals from participation in work release despite the lack of scientific evidence for such exclusions. In several states, homosexuals, persons without a history of previous employment, people with physical, mental or emotional handicaps and persons who have committed violent crimes are excluded from work release program consideration.[16]

Cost

Although the rehabilitative value of work release is debatable, given the present lack of a sufficient number of well designed empirical investigations, there are definite demonstrable economic savings to the community offered by work release programs. Indeed, the principal justification for the implementation and continuation of many work release programs has been the economic benefits which accrue from the operation of such programs. The taxpayer's burden is certainly alleviated by the disbursement of monies earned by work release participants to pay (1) federal and state taxes; (2) program maintenance (room and board) and transportation costs; (3) support to dependents who may be on welfare or public assistance rolls; and (4) acknowledged legal debts, court costs and/or restitution. Additionally, work release participants may accumulate savings for much needed use upon their release.

Federal, state and county operated work release programs have prided themselves upon their economic success stories. Work releasees in Florida earned more than $43 million in wages during the past decade. These earnings were utilized to pay $13 million in room, board and transportation, $6 million in taxes and other payroll deductions and $3 million in support to dependents.[17]

The 100 inmates who participated in work release in Kansas in 1979 earned gross wages of $497,123.35. In turn, the work releasees paid $9,599.79 in state taxes, $61,167.90 in federal taxes, $86,863.30 in maintenance to the state, including room, board and transportation, $33,867.59 in support to dependents and $57,909.66 in legal debts.

More than 2,000 prisoners participated in the federal work release program during its initial 15 months of operation. During this period work releasees earned $2,147,000 out of which was paid $373,000 in support to dependents, $203,000 to the Federal government for room and board and $303,000 in federal, state and local security taxes. Additionally, $575,000 was spent by participants at local businesses near their institutions. The remainder was placed in the inmates' savings accounts for utilization upon their release.[18]

A total of 1,263 trainees participated in the work release program at the Rehabilitation Center in Buck County, Pennsylvania from October, 1963 to May, 1973. During this period $811,509 in wages were earned by work releasees. From this amount $158,811 was paid in board to the county, $96,304 was paid in court costs and fines, $57,866 was paid in support and on debts, $86,843 was paid in voluntary support to dependents, $14,162 was paid in restitution, $73,279 was paid on miscellaneous expenses, $131,470 was paid for transportation, $181,494 was paid in federal board to the county, $40,037 was utilized for personal expenses and $232,811 was spent at the canteen or placed in savings accounts.[19]

Taxpayers realized a net savings of $74,673.00 during the first two years of operation of the Orange County, California work release program. Program operating costs, including salaries, clerical support, maintenance and operation and capital outlay amounted to $32,500 whereas savings due to a work release strategy totaled $107,173. Prisoner earnings from work release participation resulted in reimbursements of $42,414, fines of $1,393 and support to dependents of $63,366.[20]

Cost analysis of a work release program operated by the District of Columbia Department of Corrections also revealed dramatic economic savings. The cost of maintaining an average of 54 felons and 44 misdemeanants during the initial phase of the program, when it was based in a countryside prison, was $104,209. This represented a savings to the Department of Corrections of $59,548 when compared with the maintenance of regular, non-work-release prisoners. During the initial phase, participants in the work release program earned $387,376. From their earnings, work releasees paid $94,006 to the government for room, board and taxes. In addition, they paid $74,104 to support their dependents and to pay on legitimate debts. They retained $219,265 for personal use in the program and for savings to be utilized after their release. From their earnings, the government received an average return of $769 per felon work-release-year and $580 per misdemeanant work-release-year. Felons returned an average of $1,363 and misdemeanants $1,071 to the government and community (dependents and creditors) per participant year. When additional departmental cost reductions were taken into consideration, the total benefits from work release came to $2,315 per felon work-release-year and $2,023 per misdemeanant work-release-year.[21]

During the second phase of the District of Columbia Department of Corrections work release program, when it was based in a jail in D.C., there was an estimated savings of $109,342. Work releasees earned a total of $370,524 in wages during this period. From this amount, $125,559 was paid to the government for room, board and taxes, $59,873 was paid to dependents and creditors and $185,091 was retained for personal use. The average return to the government alone was $789 per participant work-release-year while the average return to the government and the community (dependents and creditors) was $1,166 per man-year. When departmental maintenance cost reductions due to a work release strategy are also considered, the total benefits from work release to persons other than the participants came to $2,363 per program-man-year. Overall, the placing of inmates on work release, rather than in an institution, saved society about one-half the cost of maintaining an inmate in the Department of Corrections.[22]

Work release, therefore, appears to be on solid footing strictly from a fiscal standpoint. However, it has been suggested by some that its fiscal attractiveness has been exaggerated due to the failure of work release advocates to take into appropriate consideration the costs involved in administering such programs. These costs relate to the provision of counseling services, implementation of selection procedures, testing of potential participants, the necessity of keeping records, supplying special housing for work releasees, feeding at unusual hours and field supervision of inmates. Nevertheless, the verdict is clear: work release is less costly than institutionalization.

Effectiveness

Those studies addressing the general area of work release effectiveness have concentrated upon the following areas:

1. the effectiveness of work release in reducing recidivism;
2. the discharge of participants on work release without incident;
3. those variables which have the most power in predicting work release participant success;
4. attitude change attributed to participation in work release programs; and
5. escape rates of persons on work release.

Reducing Recidivism

There is no clear-cut evidence regarding whether work release is effective in reducing recidivism. Studies conducted of work release programs in California, Pennsylvania, the District of Columbia and North Carolina report conflicting findings.

Some studies have concluded that work release inmates have lower recidivism rates than inmates not involved in work release. Despite formidable methodological difficulties, a study conducted by the Parole and Community Services Division of the California Department of Corrections indicated that inmates who participated in work release had a prison return rate of 12.3 percent after one year while the statewide felon return rate was 21 percent after one year.[23]

A study of work release at the Bucks County Prison in Pennsylvania, also plagued by methodological problems, showed that 18 months after their release only eight percent of work release inmates had committed new offenses. This compared favorably with a rate of 15 percent experienced by a group of inmates who had not participated in the work release program.[24]

A quasi-experimental evaluation of the work release program operated by the District of Columbia Department of Corrections compared the post-release performance of 120 work release inmates who were "in-program" successes and 119 inmates who were directly released from prison via parole. The two groups were matched on various characteristics that were judged to be related to post-release performance. Each of the two groups were additionally subdivided into four groups according to offense type, felony or misdemeanor, and the presence or absence of problems, including drugs, alcohol abuse and/or emotional difficulties. The work release group and institutional release group, therefore, each consisted of four subgroups: non-problem felons, non-problem misdemeanants, problem felons and problem misdemeanants. Overall, the post-release failure rate for the work releasees was 18.4 percent compared to a post-release failure rate of 30.2 percent for the institutional releasees. Post-release failure rate was defined as the return to the system within eight months by parole revocation or by sentence of 30 days or more. A comparison of the four subgroups indicates that non-problem felon work releasees had a failure rate of 8.6 percent compared to a failure rate of 21.7 percent for non-problem felon institutional releasees; non-problem misdemeanant work releasees had a failure rate of 2.7 percent versus a failure rate of 14.3 percent for non-problem misdemeanant institutional releasees; and problem felon work releasees had a failure rate of 33.3 percent compared to a failure rate of 47.4 percent for problem felon institutional releasees. However, the failure rate for problem misdemeanant work releasees was 41.7 percent versus 39.1 percent for problem misdemeanant institutional releasees. Therefore, work release appeared to be the superior release modality overall and in three of the four subgroups.[25]

Studies conducted in North Carolina and Santa Clara County, California have been much less conclusive. A study of work release in North Carolina reported that overall work releasees and orthodox parolees did not differ significantly in parole outcome. An analysis by ethnic background indicated that 29 percent of the white work releasees compared to 31 percent of the white orthodox parolees were returned to prison. For blacks, 40 percent of the work releasees compared to 30 percent of the orthodox parolees were returned to prison.[26]

A study of work release in Santa Clara County, California indicated that there was a comparable number of arrests in the post-release period for both the work release and non-work release groups. However, during the same time period the work release group, on the average, went twice as long between arrests as the non-work release group.[27]

Another study of work release in the District of Columbia cast serious doubt upon the effectiveness of work release. A total of 281 participants in work release, 156 felony offenders and 125 misdemeanant offenders, who entered the program during the first 16 months after its inauguration were traced through the program and for one year after release. Approximately one-third of the 156 felons (32 percent) absconded or had their participation revoked. These inmates, in turn, became part of the general D.C. jail population and served an average of 4.9 additional months before their release. One year after the release of the 156 felons, about one-fourth (26 percent) returned to the District of Columbia jail while the remaining three-fourths (74 percent) were defined as successes. The 125 misdemeanants had an in-program failure rate of 29 percent. Their 12 month failure rate was 24 percent. A comparison of the work release felon group with a group of 432 non-work release felons discharged from the District of Columbia Reformatory after a period of one year on release revealed a success rate of 76 percent for the work release group compared to a success rate of 85 percent for the non-work release group.[28]

Discharge without Incident

The effectiveness or success of work release has been assessed in other ways than examining its impact on reducing recidivism. Its effectiveness or success is also frequently defined as the discharge without incident of work release participants after completion of sentence and the work release portion of it.

Reports from North Carolina, California and Rhode Island provide some insight regarding the effectiveness of work release utilizing this criterion. Defined as discharge without incident, work release is judged to be 71 to 73 percent successful in North Carolina. In California, work release is evaluated as 90 percent successful in 21 counties and 80 percent successful in Los Angeles County. In Rhode Island, the success of work release programs ranges from 60 to 72 percent.[29]

Variables Which Predict Success

Other studies have focused upon identifying those variables that can significantly distinguish successful participants from unsuccessful participants on work release. The identification of candidates who will prove successful on work release should contribute to the overall effectiveness of work release programs.

A study conducted by Elder and Cohen examined youthful, nonviolent male offenders incarcerated in a minimum security federal institution. Their findings indicated that the best predictors of success on work release were the level of institutional adjustment immediately before entering the program, whether the inmate had been convicted of auto theft, history of drug use and age at first arrest.[30] In other words, those offenders who were better behaved in the institution, who had not been convicted of auto theft, who did not have recurrences of drug related behaviors and those who were first arrested at a relatively older age, as contrasted to a relatively younger age, were more likely to have a successful work release experience.

Lebowitz also conducted a predictive study in a federal institution. He discovered that work release entry age, offense for which committed, commitment age and sentence category had the most power in predicting work release success.[31]

Fair, Issac & Company, Inc. also conducted a federal prediction study of work release success. They discovered the following factors to be the strongest predictors of success on work release: whether the inmate had been placed in the institution's segregation unit, custody status immediately prior to work release, time remaining from the beginning of participation in work release to the completion of the total sentence, length of time spent on the longest previous institutionalization, length of time left from beginning of participation in work release to the completion of incarceration, number of institutional disciplinary violations, age at first conviction, type of offense, number of prior convictions and longest period of time spent in the community during any two prior periods of incarceration.[32]

A study conducted by Brookhart, Ruark and Scoven examined 21 pre-program characteristics of 250 adult male felons who had participated in a work release program operated by the Virginia Department of Corrections. Of the 250 work release participants, 119 successfully completed the work release program while 131 were unsuccessful in completing the program. The researchers discovered that eight of the 21 pre-program characteristics evidenced significant value in discriminating successful work release program participants from unsuccessful work release program participants. The eight pertinent pre-program characteristics were: emotional maturity, relationship to parole eligibility, number of adjustment reports, time to discharge, number of total convictions, number of felonies, type of offense and occupation. Generally, those inmates who received higher ratings of emotional maturity, entered work release after their date of parole eligibility, had fewer adjustment committee reports, had a greater number of months to discharge, had a fewer number of total convictions, had a fewer number of previous felonies, were convicted of less serious offenses and possessed lower skill levels had a greater probability of success on work release.[33]

Attitude Change

Another approach to evaluating the effectiveness of work release has been to assess its value in changing the attitudes of work release participants. Illustrative of this approach is a study on attitude change among work release inmates conducted by Waldo, Chiricos and Dobrin.

They compared a group of non-work release inmates with a group of work release inmates who possessed similar backgrounds and demographic characteristics in a study of attitudes related to legitimate opportunity, achievement motivation, legal self-concept, self-esteem and focal concerns. Their analysis showed that there was no significant change in attitudes in these areas that could be attributed to participation in work release.[34]

Escape Rates

Escape rates constitute, for some, an important indicator of work release effectiveness. Ayer notes that slightly more than one-third of federal work release inmates (35 percent) fail to complete their work release program while at state and local levels, slightly less than one-third of work release inmates (about 30 percent, sometimes higher) fail to complete their programs. Removals for reasons of escape averages about 6.5 percent at the federal level and approximately 4 to 6 percent at state and local levels.[35]

Juvenile Program Application

Work release, in its strictest sense, is almost exclusively an adult correctional program. This is understandable insofar as in juvenile corrections a premium is placed upon the provision of academic instruction. This makes sense in that, on the outside, children between the ages of six and 16 spend a substantial proportion of their waking hours at school.[36] In fact, this concentration upon education, at least to the eighth grade or until age 16, is mandated by law, although this varies somewhat from state to state. Furthermore, work release programs for juveniles would be hampered by child labor law restrictions. Additionally, emphasis is placed on vocational training since this age group, comparatively speaking, possesses a low level of skill or no skill training. Individual and/or group methods of therapy also comprise an important aspect of the overall program for juveniles.

Up Close and Personal

Roger Turner is a 23-year-old male inmate at the Kansas State Industrial Reformatory in Hutchinson, Kansas. Admitted in July, 1979, for burglary, this is his second burglary conviction. Previously, he served two years for burglary at Algoa—the Missouri Intermediate Reformatory for Young Men. Raised in southwest Missouri, he recently was granted parole. His parole plan calls for him to go to Kansas City, Missouri. He participated in the work release program at the Kansas State Industrial Reformatory for about three months—up until he was granted parole. This interview occurred on June 30, 1980.

QUESTION: Why did you apply for work release?

ANSWER: Participation in work release is voluntary. I applied because I had set some personal goals to make parole. I had some educational and vocational goals which I met. I completed my G.E.D. and an electrical appliance repair manpower course which required 750 clock hours. I really wanted to get a certificate for the appliance repair course. In order to get one, you really have to know something; it's not just the hours. After achieving these goals I still had some time until parole. I would rather be on the outside and making money than to be behind walls. There's a pressure there. Behind the walls there are different rules—bullshit rules. You have to be uniformed and wear the same type of clothes as everyone else. You also have to put up with more people. On work release there is a more relaxed atmosphere, there are less people to put up with, there are less bullshit rules, and you can wear any type of clothes. Also, on work release here you can make more verbal contact with your family because you are allowed to use the phone much more. Also work release can help you to deal with people on the street.

QUESTION: Where are you employed on work release and what do you do there?

ANSWER: I work at a local mobile home construction firm as an electrician. I string wires to wire fixtures.

QUESTION: How much do you get paid per hour and how does this compare with the wages earned by your fellow workers?

ANSWER: I get paid the same wages as anyone else. I started out at $4.62 per hour and left at $4.72 per hour.

QUESTION: How would you respond to someone who felt that you, as an inmate on work release, were taking away a job from a normal law-abiding citizen?

ANSWER: I would tell them that I have to eat too.

QUESTION: But what if they countered by saying that the institution can feed you?

ANSWER: I would tell them that I want to be self-sufficient. I don't want to rely on the state.

QUESTION: How do you spend the money you earn on work release?

ANSWER: After taxes I take home about $115 per week. Just like anyone else, I have federal and state taxes deducted from my paycheck. I pay $5.00 per day, 7 days per week for room and board and 17 cents per mile for transportation to and from work. I draw about $20.00 per week for incidental personal expenses, like phone calls, cigarettes and other purchases from the canteen. I am able to put about $50.00 per week in my savings account.

QUESTION: How do you get to and from work?

ANSWER: Vans, driven by an officer or counselor, are used to take work releasees to and from work. The vans usually leave here between 6:30 a.m. and 6:45 a.m. I start work at 7:00 a.m. and get off at 3:30 p.m. I am picked up at that time by the van and taken back to the work release quarters at the institution.

QUESTION: At the time of your job interview, how did your employer treat you?

ANSWER: I imagine he treated me just like anyone else. He told me he wanted reliable employees because they had a high turnover rate. It didn't seem to make any difference to him that I was an inmate, only if I would do a responsible job.

QUESTION: Do your fellow workers know that you are an inmate?

ANSWER: Yes. They see me getting dropped off and picked up by the Department of Corrections van every day.

QUESTION: How do your fellow workers treat you?

ANSWER: Just like anyone else—normal. People treat me just like I treat them—with respect.

QUESTION: Did your training at the institution relate to the job you have on work release?

ANSWER: Yes. I learned to wire appliances in the manpower program at the institution. This related to my job as an electrician at the mobile home construction firm.

QUESTION: What job skills did you possess prior to being incarcerated and what types of jobs did you hold?

ANSWER: Prior to being imprisoned, I worked on a farm, on

construction jobs and as a cook in a restaurant. My last job was as a brick laborer. None of these jobs really required any skills—just the willingness to work. They would hire any flunkie.

QUESTION: Why did you have so many different jobs?

ANSWER: I really didn't want to stay at them for too long. I liked to experiment.

QUESTION: How much did you make on your last job as a brick laborer?

ANSWER: $7.00 per hour.

QUESTION: If you were making $7.00 per hour, why did you commit a burglary, a financially oriented crime?

ANSWER: It had nothing to do with money. It was a head trip— I didn't have my head together. It was really a way of getting back at society.

QUESTION: Would the job you had on work release been one which you would have personally chosen for yourself?

ANSWER: I really like the work, but I normally only worked four days per week. I guess this is because they have not been able to sell a lot of mobile homes. I really would prefer a five day per week job because of the money.

QUESTION: Do you think you will keep this job when you are released?

ANSWER: I don't intend to keep this job. I intend to go to Kansas City, Missouri when I am released. This is where my dad's side of the family lives. This is where I made my parole plan.

QUESTION: Do you have a job lined up?

ANSWER: No. You don't need a job as part of an out-of-state parole plan.

QUESTION: Won't the fact that you don't have a job lined up put you in a difficult financial position? Just how much money will you have saved from work release?

ANSWER: Not as much as I thought, less than $200.00. I only was on work release for about three months when I was approved for parole. I won't have as much money as expected because I had to use some of my earnings to buy clothes and tools. When I get out it will be tough but I will make it—I have got to make it. If I don't, this would be the second time I failed on parole and as far as I'm concerned I will have wasted my life. As soon as I get to Kansas City, I will take any job to support myself and meet necessary expenses. Then, I will try to join an electrical union and get the type of job I really want and like—that of an electrician. I want to remain in the electrical field. I know I have the potential in this field. I might even take more schooling in this area. I know what I want to do.

QUESTION: According to your work release supervisor, you had an excellent record on work release. Do you think this helped you get a favorable parole decision?

ANSWER: It might have helped some. But I really think my institutional record swayed the decision. Besides, I hadn't been on work release very long when my parole decision was made.

QUESTION: Is there anything you would change about the work release program?

ANSWER: In this particular work release program, work releasees live in the former director's house on prison grounds, but outside the main prison itself. This really bugs me. There shouldn't be such a close connection with the institution. The fact that there is a fence around the work release building really defeats the purpose of the program. This way the program is not really dealing with the community. Work release is supposed to be dealing with the community. Also, we hear that the other work release centers, which are not located on prison grounds, allow the participants to do more social things, like go to town on Saturday for a movie or go to church on Sunday. This is the way it should be on work release. A person should have more freedom to do things in the community. However, in this program it's like you're still incarcerated. You go to work and when you're done you come right back to the prison. You get outside the walls to work but then you're right back inside afterwards. I would rather have been in a work release program that was not situated on prison grounds. Here, because the program is on prison grounds and in the community in which the prison is located, they are too concerned that anything we do will reflect on the institution. Don't misunderstand me. As I said before, work release sure beats sitting behind the walls. Also, work release is a more relaxed atmosphere, there are less bullshit rules, you can have more contact with your family, and you get more "gate" money.

Summary

Work release is a correctional program under which certain selected inmates of a local county jail, or a state or federal correctional institution are allowed to be gainfully employed on a full-time basis in the community. They are returned to authorized custody during non-working hours.

The origin of work release is traced to the passage of the first work release law, the Huber Law, in Wisconsin in 1913. After a long period of inactivity, interest in work release appreciably increased following the successful experience of the North Carolina work release program, begun in 1957, and the passage of the Prisoner Rehabilitation Act of 1965 which extended the provisions for work release to prisoners incarcerated in federal correctional institutions.

Work release has several important benefits. It is a program of graduated release; participation in work release can be utilized by the paroling authority as an indicator of readiness for parole; it offers substantial savings to the taxpayer; it can enable inmates to develop a sense of self-esteem and self-respect; it may provide jobs for inmates upon release; and it can preserve family and community ties.

There are several important matters involved in the administration and process of work release programs. These include the establishment of eligibility requirements for selecting inmates for participation, the actual procedural steps in making an application for work release, identifying conditions for removal from work release status and the execution of work release plan agreements. In all of these areas, great concern should be exercised for the well-being and security of the community and for the safeguard of its property while at the same time attempting to make work release an optimally valuable experience for the inmate and preventing the possible exploitation of the inmate.

The implementation, administration and continuation of work release programs involves several peculiar problems. Included among them are: overcoming community resistance, appropriately relating the academic and vocational skills of the inmates to the supply-demand relationships in the local labor market, insuring that there will not be any exploitation of work releasees on the job because of their vulnerable status, arranging appropriate housing and transportation for participants, preventing the introduction of contraband into the institution by work releasees who may be pressured to do so by other inmates, helping inmates adjust to their "marginal status" experienced on work release, and preventing escapes and criminal violations by work releasees. Other problems include: handling additional administrative responsibilities due to program implementation and devising appropriate selection procedures.

There are definite demonstrable economic savings to the taxpayer offered by work release programs. Work releasees pay (1) federal and state taxes; (2) program maintenance (room and board) and transportation costs; (3) support to dependents who may be on welfare or public assistance rolls; and (4) acknowledged debts, court costs and/or restitution. Additionally, work release participants may accumulate savings for much needed use upon their release.

A principal concern in evaluating work release is its effectiveness in reducing recidivism. However, there is no clear-cut evidence regarding whether work release is effective in reducing recidivism. Studies conducted of work release programs in California, Pennsylvania, the Discrict of Columbia and North Carolina report conflicting findings.

Work release is almost exclusively an adult correctional program. This is understandable insofar as in juvenile corrections a premium is placed on academic instruction, vocational training and individual and/or group methods of therapy. Furthermore, education for youth is often mandated by law and work release programs for juveniles would be seriously hampered by child labor law restrictions.

Notes

1. David Duffee and Robert Fitch, *An Introduction to Corrections: A Policy and Systems Approach* (Pacific Palisades, California: Goodyear, 1976), p. 249.
2. Elmer H. Johnson, *Work Release: Factors in Selection and Results* (Carbondale, Illinois: Center for Study of Crime, Delinquency, and Corrections, Southern Illinois University, 1969), pp. 43-49.
3. Clemens Bartollas and Stuart J. Miller, *Correctional Administration* (New York: McGraw-Hill Book Company, 1978), p. 208.
4. American Bar Association Commission on Correctional Facilities and Services and Council of State Governments, *Compendium of Model Correctional Legislation and Standards* (Washington, D.C.: U.S. Government Printing Office, 1975), pp. X-180 - X-181.
5. Joan Potter "Will Work Release Ever Fulfill Its Promise?," *Corrections Magazine*, Volume 5 (June, 1979), p. 61.
6. Ibid., pp. 61-62.
7. Robin M. Williams, Jr., *American Society: A Sociological Interpretation*, 2nd ed. (New York: Knopf, 1960), pp. 415-468.
8. Lawrence S. Root, "State Work Release Programs: An Analysis of Operational Policies," *Federal Probation*, Volume 37 (December, 1973), p. 53.
9. Alvin Rudoff, *Work Furlough and the Jail* (Springfield, Illinois: Charles C. Thomas, 1975), p. 20.
10. Potter, "Work Release," p. 64.
11. William A. Ayer, "Work-Release Programs in the United States: Some Difficulties Encountered," *Federal Probation*, Volume 34 (March, 1970), p. 54.
12. Mason J. Sacks, "Making Work Release Work: Convincing the Employer," *Crime and Delinquency*, Volume 21 (July, 1975), pp. 255-265.

13. Elmer H. Johnson, "Work-Release: Conflicting Goals Within a Promising Innovation," in *Alternatives to Prison*, edited by Gary R. Perlstein and Thomas R. Phelps (Pacific Palisades, California: Goodyear, 1975), pp. 253-254.

14. Ayer, "Work Release Programs," p. 54.

15. Potter, "Work Release," pp. 62-63.

16. Ayer, "Work Release Programs," pp. 53-54.

17. Roul Tunley, "Making Prisons Pay," in *Criminal Justice 80/81*, edited by Donal E.J. MacNamara (Guilford, Connecticut: Dushkin Publishing Group, Inc., 1980), p. 198.

18. Duffee and Fitch, *Introduction to Corrections*, p. 252.

19. John D. Case and James F. Henderson, "Community Corrections in a County Jail," in *Corrections in the Community*, edited by E. Eugene Miller and M. Robert Montilla (Reston, Virginia: Reston Publishing Company, Inc. 1977), p. 197.

20. David R. McMillan, "Work Furlough for the Jailed Prisoner," *Federal Probation*, Volume 29 (March, 1965), p. 34.

21. Stuart Adams, *Evaluative Research in Corrections* (Washington, D.C.: U.S. Government Printing Office, 1975), pp. 79-80.

22. Ibid., pp. 79-80.

23. "Graduated Release," *Contemporary Corrections*, edited by Benjamin Frank (Reston, Virginia: Reston Publishing Company, 1973), p. 232.

24. Ibid., pp. 232-233.

25. Adams, *Evaluative Research in Corrections*, pp. 86-87.

26. Johnson, *Work Release: Factors in Selection*, p. 206.

27. Rudoff, *Work Furlough*, p. 22.

28. "Graduated Release," pp. 233-234.

29. Rudoff, *Work Furlough*, p. 22.

30. John P. Elder and Stanley H. Cohen, "Prediction of Work Release Success with Youthful, Nonviolent, Male Offenders," *Criminal Justice and Behavior*, Volume 5 (June, 1978), pp. 181-192.

31. H.M. Lebowitz, "Work Release Prediction Tables," in *Federal Work Release Evaluation, Fiscal Year 1967* (Washington, D.C.: U.S. Bureau of Prisons, 1972).

32. Fair, Isaac and Company, Inc., *A System to Predict In-Program and Community Success of Work Releasees. Technical Report* (San Rafael, California: Fair, Issac and Company, Inc., 1972).

33. Duane E. Brookhart, J.B. Ruark, and Douglas E. Scoven, "A Strategy for the Prediction of Work Release Success," *Criminal Justice and Behavior*, Volume 3 (December, 1976), pp. 321-334.

34. Gordon P. Waldo, Theodore G. Chiricos, and Leonard E. Dobrin, "Community Contact and Inmate Attitudes: An Experimental Assessment of Work Release," in *Community-Based Corrections: Theory, Practice and Research*, edited by Paul G. Boesen and Stanley E. Grupp (Santa Cruz, California: Davis Publishing Company, Inc., 1976), p. 337.

35. Ayer, "Work Release Programs," p. 56.

36. Daniel Katkin, Drew Hyman, and John Kramer, *Juvenile Delinquency and the Juvenile Justice System* (North Scituate, Massachusetts: Duxbury Press, 1976), p. 381.

Chapter 6
Study Release

Study release is a program in which an approved inmate leaves the correctional institution to attend some kind of school, i.e., college, vocational school, high school, business college, hair dressing school, etc. The study release programs vary from state to state. In the situation where the Southern Illinois University at Carbondale was only twelve miles away, inmates and officers from the United States Penitentiary at Marion, Illinois, went together to study. In situations where correctional institutions are more rural and located quite some distance from a college campus, a program similar to work release is developed to permit an inmate to leave the correctional institution and live in the community to attend the college, e.g., Ohio.[1] Like work release or furlough programs, state legislation sets the limits as to what can be accomplished, who is eligible and who is accountable to whom.

History

Smith et al., in 1971, conducted a national survey to determine the extent of study-release programs throughout the 50 states, the District of Columbia and the Federal Bureau of Prisons.[2] That survey was replicated in 1974 by Shichor and Allen.[3] In the 1971 survey, Connecticut stated that they had established a study release program in 1959 while the Federal Bureau of Prisons began theirs in 1965. Both the 1971 and the 1974 surveys show that nearly half of the states began their programs during 1966-1970.

The slow development of study release programs is, perhaps, understandable when one thinks about prisons. Originally, prisons were intended to isolate and punish. Rehabilitation, both as a concept and a reality, has only been an expectation of this century. With this attitude of punishment, few prisons offered educational systems to inmates inside the prison, let alone permitted inmates to participate in educational programs located outside the walls. Even though the first prison school was established in 1798, that school provided the "three R's" and was considered a leisure time occupation.

Real change in educational systems in prisons did not come until nearly a century later. At that time, in 1870, the American Prison Association proclaimed that academic learning was one step in the path to reform. Later, in the 1930's, as our country became more socially minded, recommendations of sociologists, economists and psychologists were being accepted in many areas of our society, including prisons and their educational programs. Programs were offered inside the walls for inmates to complete their high school education and/or business or vocational training. Still, at that time for the most part, higher education was available only through correspondence—if at all.

Between 1962 and 1967, a few pilot programs were initiated to test the feasibility of college level instruction in correctional institutions. The Upward Bound Oregon Prison Project, established in 1967, had several objectives. Besides the opportunity for higher education both in and out of the institution, the project provided additional follow-up support services in the post-release period. In 1968, after a successful evaluation of the project, the Oregon program became *Project New Gate* and served as a prototype for programs in Colorado, Kentucky, Minnesota, New Mexico and Pennsylvania by 1971.[4]

New Gate Programs, promoted by the National Council on Crime and Delinquency (NCCD), are located physically inside a correctional institution with its own full-time staff, thereby operating a residence program rather than an extension program. Outside the prison, the New Gate staff operates an education release housing facility, similar to a halfway house, for students on study release. Where such facilities are not available, New Gate personnel help the inmates find suitable housing, select educational programs and prepare the necessary forms for financial assistance or admission to a college or university. In addition, the New Gate program also espouses intensive personal counseling and/or group counseling.

The New Gate program has a strong commitment to follow-up services for paroled or otherwise released inmates. The program personnel work with parole officers, vocational rehabilitation agencies, community service organizations, colleges and universities, veterans' organizations and other interested groups. Even after graduation, the ex-offender may utilize job counseling and assistance in securing employment from New Gate staff.

No doubt, the success of this New Gate program has lead other prison officials to think about study release. In December of 1971, Chief Justice Warren Burger at a national conference on corrections, added more credence to such programs. He said that convicts should "learn their way out of prison."[5]

As the 1974 survey shows, an additional 20 states implemented a study release program from the years 1971 through 1974.[6] "All but three of the 41 states that have established study-release programs reported that they are open to male and female participants, with Oklahoma, Utah and West Virginia reporting that their programs are open only to male participants. (The other four agencies—District of Columbia, Federal Bureau of Prisons, Guam and Puerto Rico— noted that their programs are for both males and females").[7]

To summarize, through the exemplary efforts of New Gate and the assistance and support of the federal government, study release programs have been encouraged, implemented and maintained as one of the newer community-based alternatives.

Purpose

The purpose of study release programs is to allow the offender access to community academic and vocational programs. The hope is that the offender will be exposed to greater quality education, updated equipment and will, of course, be affected in a positive way from the socialization with fellow classmates and instructors. Secondly, by using community resources, the correctional institutions are spared the expenses of staffing and duplicating facilities within the correctional facility.[8]

Another salient purpose of study release programs is to reduce recidivism and build a bridge between the prison institution and the community via a college campus or some other educational facility.[9]

Administration/Process

According to the 1971 survey, "of the 40 states that were operating study-release, 20 indicated that their program was authorized by law, eight reported that their program was operated in accordance with an administrative policy, and 12 indicated that they operated under the provisions of both a law and administrative policy."[10]

Sponsors for a New Gate program may be a correctional institution or department of corrections, a college or university or an independent agency. Some critics advocate the sponsoring of such programs by colleges or universities because they have more manpower and influence which can be utilized in the project. Such a sponsor provides a necessary community advocate of the highest stature.

States that have not taken on a New Gate program generally administer their study release programs with the same criteria for inmates as they do their work release programs. Depending upon the state, the inmate is released into the community to attend a specific vocational training, or other educational programs. States which cannot provide such technical training as computer programs or conventional trades welcome the communities' efforts to provide these programs.

In 1968, the Department of Corrections for the State of Connecticut assumed authority for existing state prisons and all county jails. The

Department of Corrections also took over the administration of parole. Through this endeavor, the state was able to bring the county jails, now called community correctional centers, into conformance with the United Nations minimum standards of imprisonment. As part of their administration, Connecticut has developed an extensive community-release program. For example, offenders at all institutions have access to the home furlough program. Inmates at all but the maximum security prison may attend classes at nearby schools, or work at outside jobs.[11]

The process for study release is similar, if not the exact same, for those individuals applying for participation in a work release program, a home furlough or a halfway house.° Usually the inmate makes an application. That application has to be approved by several key persons in the prison. A record search is completed to make sure the prospective inmates have no warrant or detainer against them.

In the application process, a review of the inmate's records and files are conducted to assess the results of previous vocational or educational testing. Those test results need to be reviewed. Sometimes they will have to be retaken for circumstances may render the results invalid, such as a long period of time since the first testing.

A selection committee then screens the applicants. Since the committee looks to fill the number of vacancies in the program, some inmates are placed on the alternate list. Factors that are used to screen inmates include time served on sentence, custody grade and educational need. In the 1971 survey, 23 states indicated that applicants had to be in minimum custody grade before they were eligible.[12] For some study release programs, the primary factor in selection was length of time served while for others it was the nature of the offense and the educational needs of the applicant.

The final step in the process is the contractual agreement. At this point, the inmate is given a full explanation of the entire program and it's ensuing responsibilities. Failure to comply with the contract, needless to say, produces unwelcomed side effects for the inmate. The standards outlined for the New Gate program make it such that an inmate's academic standards should always be reflective of those of the educational host institution. That means that even though an inmate has not broken the contract, if he/she does not meet the university requirements, he/she is to be dropped from the New Gate program. Thereby, the inmate would either have to return to the prison institution or apply for a halfway house or work-release program.

An example of this contractual agreement comes from the state of Wisconsin. They call it the mutual agreement program (MAP). MAP

° At this point, the student might want to review the material on administration/process in the chapter on work release or preview the administration/process section in the chapters on furloughs and halfway houses.

involves the inmate, parole board, probation and parole agent, institution, state employment service and community correctional groups. All of these persons participate in the parole preparation and parole release decision. In areas of education, vocational training, discipline and treatment, specific objectives are identified and developed into a plan by the inmate and the MAP coordinator. Under the terms of a legally binding contract, the inmate agrees to the conditions in that plan, including improvement of vocational and educational skills. The correctional institutions provide the programs and the MAP coordinator monitors the adherence of all parties to the terms of the contract. Meanwhile, the parole board agrees to parole the inmate on a certain date upon successful completion of the negotiated plan.[13]

In the New Gate program in Oregon for example, once an inmate is accepted into the program, the individual remains in the inside phase of the program from six months to two years. Counseling, group therapy and academic work all continue during this period. As the inmates show their readiness for transfer to a campus, they are transferred to the outside phase, either by a school release channel, or by parole or discharge. At the college campus, the New Gate students remain in the school release facility from three to 18 months, depending on the dates of college graduation, parole or discharge. During that time, New Gate pays for initial clothing, room and board, books, tuition and a monthly stipend. When the inmate is discharged or paroled, however, the student moves out of the study release facilities and begins to receive decreased financial support for three college quarters. Discharged students or paroled students who come directly from prison to college also follow the same pattern of decreasing support.

Problems

The major problem with study release programs stems from two sources: state correctional systems and inmates. State correctional systems, heretofore, have given education a low priority. As discussed earlier, these attitudes and values may well be a reflection of past attitudes and values.

The second group that poses problems for study release programs are the inmates themselves, more specifically, their low educational attainment levels. The Federal Bureau of Prisons estimates that up to 50% of adults in federal and state facilities can neither read nor write.[14] Roberts found that 85% of inmates dropped out of school before their 16th birthday, and that the average inmate functions two to three grades below the actual number of school years he/she has completed.[15] In 1976, Roberts and Coffey found that two thirds of inmates have had no vocational training of any kind.[16] With that kind of clientele, characterized by low educational attainment levels, it would seem that most of the educational programs could be inside the prison. Some might also ask what would an inmate do with a college education? Often, they lack the proper motivation for college degrees. Remember though, study release programs are not necessarily for all inmates. Assessment of inmate needs might show which group could have their rehabilitation enhanced by college education. Others, with their attitudes, past experience and family background, might be more likely candidates for technical or training schools.

Another problem with the program has been cost. Denton and Gatz, in discussing the situation in Ohio, said one of the problems they saw involved finding an educational institution that was willing to house furloughees below the maximum cost allowable by the state.[17] (In some places, it is cheaper to retain a person in prison than it is to house him in a college dorm.) In addition, the inmate must pay for tuition, books and materials. Some programs financed through the federal government, such as New Gate discussed earlier in the chapter, have assisted in this cost. The necessity for finding financial resources serves to be a stumbling block for this program.

Another set of problems stems around the issue of adjustment for inmates. As one inmate related, it is like having one foot in and one foot out. The inmates no doubt, because of the tie to the penal institution, are held to a higher standard of behavior than the college students. Thus, inmates must deal with temptations by developing self-discipline and learning to budget their time and their money accordingly.

Cost and Effectiveness

Clendenen and others, in cooperation with the University of Minnesota, evaluated the educational program at the Minnesota Reformatory for Men. In it's first five years, the project New Gate was considered successful for the following reasons:

1. A large number of the offenders completed their educational plan—85 percent or 123 out of 145.
2. The program has a low reinstitutionalization rate for those offenders who enter the outside phase of the program—29 percent, or 20 out of 70.

According to the records tabulated during the first five years with 145 inmates, the cost per day per person inside the institution was $30.48, while the New Gate cost per person per day was $25.68.[18]

In a 1971 article by Murphy and Murphy, they cite the cost of maintaining a person in prison at $3,200, while "college as a parole plan" costs $2,600. Furthermore, they argued that additional savings came in the productivity rate of educated college parolees.[19]

Effectiveness measures seem to center around the issue of "abscondence rate" (the rate of skipping out) and the administrator's opinions concerning study release. According to the 1971 survey, slightly more that 2 percent of the more than 3,000 inmates who participated in all forms of study release absconded during the reporting period.[20] Since the abscondence rate is often tied to the screening process, states that have tightened restrictions also have fewer abscondents but may also have fewer people who could be eligible for participation.

In the 1974 survey, administrative officers in 37 agencies said they believed that study release was helpful to further rehabilitation efforts. Three agencies said they thought the program was helpful "in some cases." The Kansas Department of Corrections claimed the program did not help and they were discontinuing their program. The California Department of Corrections, although not discontinuing their program, thought the study release program did not help because it was not used often enough.[21]

Juvenile Program Application

Juvenile institutions, under mandates of state law, have always had to provide educational experiences for the youth. Only recently, however, have some states like Colorado and Florida developed alternatives within the community. The Florida program received national coverage in the mass media, due to their participants trying to save the lives of sea animals covered with oil from oil slicks. In 1967, in Deerfield Beach, the original Marine Institute called Florida Ocean Science Institutes, Inc. (FOSI), changed its emphasis from marine research to rehabilitation. Youth, 15-18, who are either committed or on probation, are selected by the state Youth Services counselor for a six-month plan of study in a marine environment. The Jacksonville Marine Institute, Inc. (JMI), located in Jacksonville, Florida, provides a curriculum of marine oriented subjects plus subjects needed for graduation requirements from high school. The marine oriented subjects are all approved for high school credit and involve a 50-50 ratio of classroom to field activity in Red Cross first aid, life saving, skin and scuba diving, seamanship and oceanography. Counseling includes reality therapy, behavior modification and perceptualism.* Due to the success of this program, expansion has occurred in cities such as St. Petersburg, Panama City, Miami and Key West.[22]

The program out of Denver, Colorado, is called Project New Pride. It is an exemplary project supported by LEAA funds to develop a community-based program to offer remedial education, vocational and individual counseling and cultural enrichment services. Their target population is 14-17 year old juveniles, some of whom have lengthy criminal records. In 1977, Blew and Bryant reported that during a 12 month period in the community, 32 percent of a control group were rearrested at least once while only 27 percent of the New Pride clients were. Following vocational training 70 percent of all clients were placed in full or part-time

---

*Perceptualism is based on the idea that young people are innately "good people" expected to act in responsible ways and to accept the consequences of their irresponsibility.

jobs. Forty percent of New Pride clients returned to school. In terms of cost, incarcerating a youth is estimated to be $12,000 per person per year. New Pride, because it has developed a unique blend of professionals and volunteers working in a high staff-to-client ratio, costs approximately $4,000 annually. Of the 161 youths who had completed the program, 89 percent have not been incarcerated. According to the authors, this amounts to a potential savings of slightly over $1.1 million, had all the youths been incarcerated for one year.[23]

Up Close and Personal

Jim Marriott is a male who at age 19 was convicted by a jury of burglary and one year later pleaded guilty to interstate transportation of firearms by a convicted felon. Now, some fifteen years later, he has successfully completed two correctional educational programs, one inside the walls and one outside on study release, and has risen to a top administrative position for the Division of Youth Services for a department of corrections in a southern state. Since he only had a GED high school diploma, the accomplishment of this person making good out of a bad situation is particularly noteworthy.

QUESTION: Why did you apply for the education programs offered through the institution, including the study release program in the community?

ANSWER: To gain a marketable talent (specialty) that would offset my criminal record and to also help reestablish my credibility and other personal attributes.

QUESTION: What were the general eligibility requirements for participating in the education programs?

ANSWER: To pass entry exams and to have a fairly clean disciplinary record. I also had to pass an interview by the institutional education coordinators (interview screening) and already possess a high school diploma or a general education diploma (GED).

QUESTION: Describe your educational experiences as an inmate. What schools did you attend?

ANSWER: I initially attended the Wright Junior College (Chicago, IL) Extension program which was brought into the institution. I obtained an Associate of Arts (A.A.) degree through the program. I later attended Northern Illinois University on study release or educational furlough in the community, pending parole for two months.

QUESTION: How long did you participate in the program?

ANSWER: Approximately 2½ years altogether.

QUESTION: What degree(s) were you pursuing in the educational program? What field of study?

ANSWER: I was initially studying for an Associate of Arts (A.A.) degree, then a Bachelor of Arts (B.A.) degree in Sociology.

QUESTION: While attending the program where did you live? (At the institution with the general population, at the institution but in separate housing facilities or some other arrangement?)

ANSWER: A complete A. A. (Associate of Arts) program sponsored by Wright Junior College was offered while I was confined in the institution. I did not even go to the campus itself. This program solely operated within the "walls." While attending Northern Illinois University (N.I.U.), I stayed in a campus dorm and later moved to a private dorm near the campus boundaries.

QUESTION: Were you supervised by a custodial person while participating in the program?

ANSWER: Yes, for the Wright Program — I was still in prison. No, for the program at N.I.U. which I attended in the community.

QUESTION: Did you receive a degree? If so, what degree in what academic area?

ANSWER: I received both A.A. and B.A. degrees in Sociology. I later obtained a Master of Science (M.S.) degree from a major university in the south after I was released from parole.

QUESTION: Did your professors and/or fellow students know you were an inmate? If so, how did they treat you?

ANSWER: Yes, of course, they knew while I was enrolled in the Wright Junior College Program at the prison. While attending N.I.U., only a couple of professors were aware of my status. No students knew. Treatment by professors was fair and almost sympathetic.

QUESTION: Was the study release aspect of the educational program valuable for you? If so, in what way(s)?

ANSWER: Yes! It provided an opportunity to me that I would have never pursued upon release. Also, it enabled me to assimilate a middle class lifestyle and it exposed me to so very many things that I was ignorant about. It also provided an opportunity for me to interact with an appropriate peer group that was not involved in deviant activities.

QUESTION: Is there anything about the educational program you participated in that you would have changed to make it a more valuable experience? If so, what?

ANSWER: Yes, especially with the program offered within the walls. Improvement was necessary in the area of educational counseling and guidance. That is, we did not have anyone assisting us in determining occupational fields. The program also lacked opportunities to use the newly acquired knowledge, thus it was often difficult to adequately retain or integrate information. Due to a lack of enrichment opportunities, there was a high failure (dropout) rate among fellow "students." A prison environment is also not the most conducive atmosphere for learning. It violates several education learning theories. That is why the opportunity to participate in the study release program in the community is so valuable.

QUESTION: Did your study release experience help you adjust once you were released from prison (for example, obtaining a job, easing the transition from institutionalization to freedom)?

ANSWER: Yes, definitely! It opened up employment opportunities and it, without any doubt, was the contributing factor for my not becoming a recidivist. It helped me significantly to know how to interact with people that were not associated with the criminal subculture.

QUESTION: Are correctional educational programs, including study release, a worthwhile rehabilitation tool, that is, are the costs of operating such programs worthy of the taxpayers' dollars?

ANSWER: Yes. However, the screening process needs to be much stricter. Furthermore, those programs operated as extension programs within the institution are somewhat limited as the inmate does not have the opportunity to fully integrate the knowledge due to the repressive environment. It also restricts the entire learning process.

QUESTION: Compare the study release program with other correctional programs.

ANSWER: Study release shifts the burden of responsibility entirely upon the inmate. It also brings havoc on personality theories of criminality.

Jim Marriott was sentenced 60 days to 6 years for the federal crime and 5 to 8 years for the state offense. During his serving of "a little over five years," he used his time to pursue his educational goals. After having been paroled, he continued to study and obtained a Masters of Science degree. Jim feels that had it not been for those early educational programs that lead into the study release programs outside the walls, he would not have been able to go on to complete the Master of Science degree he now holds nor the occupational position he has obtained.

Summary

Study release programs are a recent development in the history of community-based operations. Spurred on by federal government support and exemplary projects like *"New Gate,"* many states implemented their programs beginning in 1959 to 1974 — a period of 15 years. Study release programs are to aid the inmates' rehabilitation efforts and reduce recidivism by providing necessary education, e.g., high school or college or some type of vocational training.

Like work release and furlough programs, state legislation sets the limits as to what can be accomplished, who is eligible and who is accountable to whom. Factors that are used to screen inmates include time served on sentence, custody grade and educational need. Once an inmate is selected for the program, then the individual enters into a contract agreement requiring not only law-abiding behavior but also minimum grade requirements.

In some states, an academic career begins within the walls of a prison. Through counseling, group therapy and academic work, the individual gains greater control over behavior and mental activity. With this proven track record inmates show their readiness for transfer to a college campus and are transferred to the outside either as a participant in a study release program.

The major problem with study release programs stems from two sources: (1) state correctional systems and (2) inmates. State correctional systems, heretofore, have given education a low priority. Since many prisons were built to isolate and punish, few prisons had educational systems inside the prison. This attitude of punishment made it difficult, until very recently, to offer programs to complete high school education and/or business or vocational training. Survey research showed that inmates have low educational attainment levels. In fact, many inmates in federal and state facilities cannot read or write, with the result that study release programs seem to be most useful with a select group of inmates. In addition, those inmates who are selected for the program often feel the temptations of living on a college campus are extremely high. The financial costs involved in study release programs, such as tuition, books, materials and housing, also constitute a serious stumbling block for such programs.

Although juvenile institutions have always been mandated to provide educational programs for residents, juvenile correctional authorities are also seeking educational opportunities within the community. In Florida for example, youth 15-18 who are either committed or on probation, are selected by the state Youth Service counselor for a six-month plan of study in a marine environment. The marine oriented subjects are all approved for high school credit and involve a 50/50 ratio of classroom-to-field activity in Red Cross first aid, life saving, skin and scuba diving, seamanship and oceanography. In addition, counseling is given which includes reality therapy, behavior modification and perceptualism. Due to the success of this program, expansion has occurred in other major cities such as St. Petersburg, Miami and Key West.

Study release programs are not widely used programs for several reasons. First, the clientele for such a program requires certain skills and attitudes which are not prevalent among many prison inmates. Secondly, those inmates who might be eligible for such a program, because of the nature of their offense and/or the history of their behavior inside the walls, are also eligible for many other programs such as work release. Yet, as the example from the "Up-Close and Personal" section showed, Jim Marriott probably would not have eventually received his Masters of Science degree and/or the occupational position he now holds if it were not for his participation in and the benefits he derived from correctional education programs, including a community-based study release program.

Notes

1. Vernon Fox, *Community-Based Corrections* (Englewood Cliffs, N.J.: Prentice Hall, Inc., 1977), p. 91.
2. Robert R. Smith, John M. McKee, and Michael A. Milan, "Study Release Policies of American Correctional Agencies: A Survey," *Journal of Criminal Justice* 2 (1974), pp. 357-364.
3. David Shichor and Harry E. Allen, "Study-Release: A Correctional Alternative," *Offender Rehabilitation* 2 (1977), pp. 7-16.
4. National Council on Crime and Delinquency (NCCD), *New Gate: New Hope Through Education*. (Paramus, N.J.: Newgate Resource Center, NCCD).
5. John J. Marsh, "GED Testing in State Penal Institutions," *Correctional Education* 25 (Winter 1973), p. 13.
6. Shichor and Allen, "Study-release;" *op. cit.*, p. 10.
7. Ibid., p. 11.
8. Smith et al., "Study Release Policies," *op. cit.*, p. 358.
9. Shichor and Allen, "Study-Release," *op. cit.*, p. 11.

10. Smith et al., "Study-Release Policies," *op. cit.*, p. 359.
11. R. Conrad, "Profile/Connecticut," *Corrections Magazine* 1 (January, February 1975), pp. 63-72.
12. Smith et al., "Study-Release Policies," *op. cit.*, p. 362.
13. "Wisconsin-Mutual Agreement Program — Exemplary Project Screening and Validation Report," Washington, D.C.: LEAA, 1975.
14. M.V. Reagen et al., *School Behind Bars — A Descriptive Overview of Correctional Education in the American Prison System* (Abridged ed; Syracuse, NY: Syracuse University Research Corporation, Policy Institute, 1973).
15. A. R. Roberts, *Source Book on Prison Education: Past, Present, and Future,* (Springfield, Ill.: C. C. Thomas, 1971).
16. A. R. Roberts and O.D. Coffey, *A State of the Art Survey for a Correctional Education Network,* (College Park, Md.: American Correctional Association, September, 1976).
17. George J. Denton and N. Gatz, "Ohio Work Furlough: College for Felons," *American Journal of Corrections,* 35, No. 3. (1973), pp. 44-45.
18. Richard J. Clendenen, John R. Ellingston, and Ronald J. Severson, "Project Newgate: The First Five Years," *Crime and Delinquency* 25, No. 1 (January, 1979), p. 55-64.
19. Melvin L. Murphy and Maribeth Murphy, "College as a Parole Plan," *Federal Probation* 35 (March 1971) pp. 45-48.
20. Smith et al., "Study-Release Policies," *op. cit.*, p. 362.
21. Schichor and Allen, "Study-Release," *op. cit.*, p. 13.
22. R. Stephen Berry and Alan N. Learch, "Victory at Sea: A Marine Approach to Rehabilitation," *Federal Probation* 44 (March, 1980), pp. 44-47.
23. C. H. Blew and G. Bryant, *Denver-Project New Pride,* (Washington, D.C.: LEAA, 1977).

Resources

"Exemplary Projects," Washington, D.C.; L.E.A.A., 1977.

New Gate-New Hope through Education. Paramus, N.J.: National Council on Crime and Delinquency.

Smith, Robert R., John M. McKee, and Michael A. Milan. "Study release policies of American correctional agencies: a survey," *Journal of Criminal Justice* 2 (1974), pp. 357-364.

Schichor, David and Harry E. Allen, "Study-release: a correctional alternative," *Offender Rehabilitation* 2 (Fall 1977), pp. 7-17.

Chapter 7
Furloughs

A furlough is an authorized absence from a correctional institution in which the inmate is not normally escorted by a member of the institutional staff. Furloughs are oftentimes granted to allow inmates to make a home visit to strengthen family ties, seek employment, visit a sick or dying relative, obtain necessary medical care, attend a job or school interview or participate as a volunteer in an activity serving the general public. Furloughs are distinguished from "special leave." Inmates almost always have been able to leave the institution to attend the funerals of family members but they did so under an agreement of "special leave" and in the presence of an institutional officer.

Generally, there are two types of furloughs: day and overnight. The day furlough usually does not exceed 16 hours, and the inmate must return to the institution before 11:59 p.m. To facilitate the time limit, geographic limits are also placed on the inmate so that the individual is not to be in areas beyond the institution's commuting area (approximately 50-mile radius). The overnight furlough is obviously for longer periods of time and/or longer distances.[1]

History

Like many other programs developed in correctional institutions, furloughs were no doubt developed informally as an outgrowth of specific, local attitudes and values before there was any enabling legislation to validate the practice. Mississippi documents their program as beginning in 1918. Markley, in surveying furlough programs in adult correctional institutions in each of the 50 states, the District of Columbia and the Federal Bureau of Prisons, asked several questions including when the program was operationalized.[2] For example, Arkansas replied that its program began in 1922. From that detailed information, Table 7.1 was constructed showing selected states and summary data on their furlough programs. Notice how each state differs in its purpose of visits, criteria for selection of participants and restrictions on participants. These are not all of the states which authorize furloughs. At the time Markley published in 1973, he stated that 29 departments of corrections out of 51 had furlough programs.

Table 7.1 Selected Summary of States with Furlough Programs

STATE	DATE PROGRAM WAS INTRODUCED	PURPOSES OF VISIT	CRITERIA USED FOR SELECTION OF PARTICIPANTS	RESTRICTIONS ON PARTICIPANTS
Alaska	July, 1970	Home visits, job or school interview, medical care, attendance at civic or social functions in community.	Custody, time remaining to serve, program participation analysis of furlough situation, need for furlough.	Compliance with furlough agreement, no drugs, no alcohol, notify institution if any problems develop.
California	1969	Pre-release planning, emergency leaves, job or school interviews, finding residence, family visits, obtain auto license.	Individual need, no detainers, no life sentences or condemned prisoners, no serious custody risks.	Up to 72 hours and remain in the state.
Florida	Oct., 1971	Emergencies, e.g., funeral, sickness, etc. Employment, residence, other compelling reasons. Church, A.A., civic club, recreation, family other.	Minimum custody, good work record, program participation, no disciplinary problems.	NA
Idaho	July, 1971	Home visits, job or school interviews, sickness or funeral trips.	Minimum custody, must have a parole date, permitted two (2) leaves.	Remain within the state.
Illinois	1969	Family visits, medical trips, residence, job interview, family illness, panel discussions, television/radio programs.	Different criteria for different purposes of visits.	No alcohol, obey laws, no contracts without permission, use approved transportation, return on time, possibly have medical exam on return.

State	Date	Purpose	Eligibility	Restrictions
Mississippi	1918 (Approx.)	Home leaves for ten (10) days.	Good record in institution, two yrs. prior to release, must be serving three yr. sentence, half or full trusty status.	NA
Oregon	1967	Visit family, sickness, funeral trips, obtain medical care, job interview and other approved trips.	History of offenses, length of sentence, time served on present sentence, parole hearing date; detainers, self-control patterns, escape history, patterns of conduct, emotional stability, community factors.	Not to exceed 30 days.
Pennsylvania	1971	Home visits, job or school interviews, strengthen family ties.	Individual need, overall adjustment and behavior, participation in programs.	Same as parole.
South Carolina	May, 1967	Home visits.	Must have been in "A.A." trusty status for a minimum of 90 days prior to applying, clear conduct record, no community objections.	Remain at home, notify sheriff's office.
Vermont	1967	Home visits, job or school interview, work, funeral trips, Christmas visits and hospital appointments.	Attitude of community, attitude of family, general living conditions, overall effect on treatment.	Remain in general area.

Modified and adapted from C.W. Markley, "Furlough and conjugal visiting in adult correctional institutions," *Federal Probation*, 37 (March 1973), pp. 22-24.

According to McCarthy, practically every state was granting inmate furloughs on a routine basis by 1978.[3] Some of the rationale for the operationalization of this concept has come from the experience and scientific literature of nine European countries which authorize absences from their correctional institutions for reasons other than emergency purposes. Much of that information was utilized by the President's Commission on Law Enforcement and Administration of Justice (1967) which then recommended the following in our country: (1) expansion of graduated release and furlough programs; (2) integration of furlough programs with institutional treatment; and (3) coordination of inmates with community treatment services. It is of little wonder, then, that most of the furlough programs that have been developed in the United States occurred during the 1960's and 1970's.

While the concept of furloughs in this chapter will continue to be discussed in general terms, it is well to remember that there are as many differences as there are states with such programs. In one respect, however, virtually all furlough laws and programs are the same. That is, inmates failing to return from a furlough can be charged with escape. Also, all returning furlough inmates are subject to searches.

Purpose

Home furloughs have many purposes. First and foremost, furloughs provide an opportunity for an inmate to prepare for release by permitting a pre-release to visit families or to be interviewed by prospective employers. According to Markley, one of the most compelling reasons for granting furloughs is to reinforce family ties—where and if these exist.[4] Correctional workers can make "timely and judicious use of home furloughs" to advance the investments that the state has made in working with the offender with the work that also needs to be done with offenders' families. In addition, "furloughs for adults benefit the children by allowing the parent to appear in the home on occasion, before he is completely forgotten."[5]

According to Eugene Miller, furlough programs are equated as conjugal visits, although not advertised as such for political reasons. In essence, a furlough program is a sensitive and practical method of permitting conjugal visits. Instead of having the institution-based conjugal visiting which often seems degrading for all concerned, furloughs permit inmates to engage in sex in a normal environment as a natural part of the role as husband or wife. In this manner, then, furloughs help as a reintegration method.[6]

Since only a few states have conjugal visitation and there is some concern about their effectiveness, i.e., single inmates feel discriminated against, home furlough programs seem to be a more tactful approach to an awkward situation. In this manner then, the furlough's major purpose is to gradually reintegrate the offender into the community. The culture shock that has so often accompanied abrupt releases is minimized. Through the use of furloughs, the offender is enabled to become gradually accustomed to life in the community.

Administration/Process

In the Federal system, inmates are received into the custody of the U.S. Attorney General for a specific period of time. This is usually the result of a "judgment and commitment" order issued by one of the U.S. courts. The basic task of the Bureau of Prisons, therefore, is to carry out this custody order. That means that the Bureau of Prisons and agencies which contract with the Bureau are held accountable for the responsibility of the custody of committed persons. The U.S. Attorney General shares this authority under the Prisoner Rehabilitation Act of 1965 to extend the limits of confinement for committed persons. The authority from the Attorney General is the basis for community programs and furloughs.

In the Federal system, furloughs are viewed as a privilege, not as a right. Thus, inmates who are within six months of release and are assigned minimum or community custody may be granted a three to seven day furlough for a family emergency. Inmates serving terms of one year or more may be granted furloughs to seek employment and establish release plans, but only during the last phases of the sentence. In this manner, then, their furlough program is not part of a halfway house program, because residents of halfway houses are already in the home community and can accomplish their purposes without using a furlough program.[7]

In the formative stages, rigorous screening procedures for inmates is highly desirable to avoid failures which may be magnified out of proportion and result in the cancellation of the program. Secondly, by developing extremely tight restrictions, the staff develops a "track record" so to speak. As the staff develops confidence and a record of success, they may decide to exercise more discretion in the screening process.

Eugene Miller, who held the post of Correctional Facilities Administrator in Alaska, comments on the fact that some administrators, unfortunately, subvert the purposes of furloughs for more short-range goals in the institution. By this he means some administrators use furloughs to buy peace in the institution. Believing that a furloughed inmate is a docile inmate, some administrators make deals with inmate leaders and thereby give furloughs without regard to overall program goals or public safety. Needless to say, "such practices will inevitably lead to serious problems which will no doubt come to the attention of persons opposed to such reintegration attempts, and as a result, the very existence of that particular furlough program may well be jeopardized."[8]

Since many states that have furlough programs view furlough as part of the gradual release process, the selection procedure for furlough participation begins when the offender enters the institution. Through the classification process, a full battery of tests from psychologists, educational specialists and medical personnel are administered. The purpose, of course, is to gain insight into an inmate's abilities, personality, educational level, motivation and any other factors that could reasonably affect the individual's rehabilitation.

The correction counselors and other persons who might work in a unit or support team with inmates help explain a pre-release program like home furloughs. Their task is to make the inmates aware of the goals and modifications of behavior that must be achieved before an inmate is recommended for a status of pre-release that would later permit the inmate the opportunity to participate in a furlough program.

In the state of Kansas, for example, a furlough is granted to an inmate as part of a program, anticipating when that individual is in minimum custody security status and is eligible for parole. If, however, the inmate is not eligible for parole, the individual can still apply for a furlough if one has been incarcerated for at least two years, has a good behavior record and is classified in the minimum custody security status. If an individual becomes eligible for participation in a work release program, the inmate may have furlough privileges when he/she has served time to within one year of his/her parole eligibility date and has successfully participated in the work release program for a minimum of 30 days.

From this discussion, then, the student should realize that much care and concern is utilized in selecting persons for furlough programs. Caution is exercised to make sure that an inmate has maintained a good behavior record, is classified in minimum security custody classification and is considered a good risk by the correctional counselor and/or the principal administrator. Inmates must also be free of formal protests filed against the granting of the furlough. Inmates who do have a history of repeated violence are not rejected from the furlough program. Rather, they have to wait until 30 days prior to the release date for purposes of seeking employment or finalizing parole plans. Even then, those individuals are closely monitored due to the state's involvement.

Procedures for the actual processing of the furlough plan are as follows:

1. The inmate initiates the plan by filling out an application stating the name of a sponsor with whom the inmate will stay while on furlough. Needless to say, this has to be a responsible adult such as a family member, friend or volunteer sponsor who is willing to have the inmate for that specific time period. It is, understandably, the responsibility of the program to protect the participants and the public. Thus, some verification of the situation in the community is essential.

2. Upon receipt of an application for furlough, the counselor sends "staff recommendation forms" to the appropriate persons who have frequent contact with the applicant. These personnel then are required to state reasons for recommending or denying the request. The unit team or sponsor team, which includes the counselor, then carefully considers the recommendations and includes all of the materials in the inmate's permanent file.

3. Following approval by the sponsor team, the principal administrator may elect to request a field investigation. This is usually done through the cooperation of the local probation and parole office of the county in which the furlough will take place. If the unit team recommends denial, they must so state it as a written reason. The principal administrator can follow their recommendation, or request more information to resolve the impasse. In the end, however, the inmate's counselor must notify the sponsor and the inmate of the reason for the denial.

4. When the inmate receives approval of the furlough plan, appropriate notification is made to persons such as the inmate's sponsor, the parole officer in the county of the inmate's destination and even to law enforcement agencies in that particular area.

5. The inmate leaves the institution with a copy of the furlough order which is to be carried at all times, and an identification card with photographs that must be returned at the end of the furlough.

Figure 7.1

UNITED STATES DEPARTMENT OF JUSTICE FEDERAL PRISON SYSTEM	FURLOUGH APPLICATION APPROVAL AND RECORD	NAME REGISTER NUMBER INSTITUTION

APPLICATION

PURPOSE: _____

PERSON AND/OR PLACE TO BE VISITED: _____
ADDRESS: _____

TELEPHONE: _____   _____
                  Area Code   Number

POINT OF CONTACT FOR EMERGENCY: _____

METHOD OF TRANSPORTATION: _____

NOTE TO APPLICANT: You are reminded that should any unusual circumstances arise during the period of your visit, you should notify the institution immediately at telephone _____.

I understand that my furlough only extends the limits of my confinement and that I remain in the custody of the Attorney General of the United States. If I fail to remain within the extended limits of this confinement, it shall be deemed as escape from the custody of the Attorney General, punishable as provided in Section 751 of Title 18, United States Code. I understand that I may be thoroughly searched upon my return to the institution and that I will be held responsible for any item of contraband or illicit material that is found. I have read or had read to me, and I understand the foregoing conditions governing my furlough, and will abide by them.

_____   _____
              Witness   Signature of Applicant

_____   _____
               Title   Date Signed

ADMINISTRATIVE ACTION

INFORMATION VERIFIED BY: _____ TITLE: _____

USPO NOTIFIED: _____

DOES USPO HAVE ANY OBJECTIONS TO FURLOUGH? _____

Approval for the above named inmate to leave the institution on a furlough as outlined is hereby granted in accordance with P.L. 93-209 and the FPS Furlough Program Statement for the period _____ to _____.

                              APPROVED _____
                                                Chief Executive Officer

RECORD

DATE/TIME RELEASED _____ DATE/TIME RETURNED _____

TRAVEL SCHEDULE: _____

White—Original - Control Center - Use Original for Count Control. Complete Section under Record.
     Forward to Record Office at furlough termination for BP-1 and J & C File
Canary—Control Center - Enter Release Date/Time. Forward to Record Office. Record Office -
     Use for BP-2 and enter Date/Time Returned from Original and Forward to Central File

Figure 7.2

(Use Institution Letterhead)   Page 1

U. S. Probation Officer
*
*
                                        Re:

Dear

    The above named inmate has requested a furlough into your district.
Since this is the offender's first furlough into your district, we are
requesting that you complete the following questionnaire and return it
to us within two weeks. This questionnaire will remain on file, and it
will not be necessary on subsequent furloughs. We will not proceed with
the furlough request until you have returned the questionnaire.

The inmates' residence while on furlough will be: _____
_____
_____

The telephone number is: _____

The purpose of the furlough is: _____
_____
_____

Please indicate your response to the following questions:

1. Is the proposed residence acceptable to you?   _____YES _____NO
    Comments:

2. Do you believe the purpose for the furlough can be fulfilled?
        _____YES _____NO
    Comments:

3. Is there any objection in the community (including law enforcement and/or
    the court) to the inmate returning on furlough? _____YES _____NO
    Comments:

4. This is the first furlough for the inmate to your district. Do you
    wish contact with the inmate? _____YES _____NO
    If so, how? _____Telephone _____In Person

5. If subsequent furloughs are granted to your district do you wish to be
    notified by the institution? _____YES _____NO

BP-IS-132
May 1978
                                        Attachment B
                                        7300.12E
                                        5-26-78

Figure 7.2—Concluded

Page 2
Form BP-IS-132

6. If subsequent furloughs are granted to your district, do you wish
   contact with the inmate? _____ YES _____ NO
   If so, how? _____ Telephone _____ In Person

7. Do you wish a copy of the furlough order? _____ YES _____ NO

8. Is local felon registration required? _____ YES _____ NO

Please return this form to the undersigned.

_____
(Signature) Case Manager

_____
(Signature) U. S. Probation Officer

Attachment B
7300.12E
5-26-78

Figure 7.3

(Use Institution Letterhead)

DATE:_____

U. S. PROBATION OFFICER
*
*   RE:_____

Dear

The above named inmate has been sentenced from your district and is presently

incarcerated in _____.

This individual is requesting a furlough to the following district.

_____.

We have forwarded a questionnaire to the United States Probation Officer in
that district.

In compliance with Bureau of Prisons Policy Statement on Furloughs, we are
also forwarding this questionnaire to you for the needed responses. Please
return this form to this institution within two weeks from receipt.

The inmate's residence while on furlough will be:_____

_____Telephone #:_____

The purpose of the furlough is:_____

_____

                                    _____
                                    (Signature) Case Manager

Please indicate your response to the following questions:

1. Are there any objections from you, law enforcement agencies or the court
    to the inmate furloughing to the above named district? _____NO _____YES

2. If subsequent furloughs are granted, do you wish to be notified by this
    institution? _____NO _____YES

ADDITIONAL COMMENTS:

                                    _____
                                    (Signature) U. S. Probation Officer

                                    _____
BP-IS-131   (Date)
May 1978   Attachment A
                                                          7300.12E
                                                          5-26-78

In this section, the process has been simplified for discussion purposes. The actual detailed procedures with its appropriate time limits, accountability factors and necessary numbers of copies of specific forms is a matter of public record. Under the statutes of your state dealing with the department of corrections, you can see the actual procedures for your state.

Problems

Perhaps the greatest stumbling block to the furlough programs has been the notoriety of those inmates who have violated the conditions of the program by either escaping or by doing criminal acts that incite public hostility, i.e., murder or rape. The reality is that any success or failure of any correctional program, especially furloughs, is dependent upon community hospitality and the behavior of inmates themselves. In fact, the people with the most at stake in community corrections are correctional clients. Even those who are not yet eligible for furlough still have hope. So even they recognize that any failure threatens their chances. The end result when community alternatives fail is that the security-oriented penal facilities again become the dominant mode of handling all offenders.

Cost

Throughout the existing literature there seems to be no empirical study addressing the cost factor. In fact, it is a rather difficult factor to determine because of the nature of the program. In justifying the home furlough programs in the Pennsylvania Bureau of Corrections, Commissioner Werner said that such programs provided certain residents an opportunity to participate in many rehabilitation programs that cannot be provided within the institutional setting, i.e., psychiatric treatment, community treatment centers, or halfway houses, group homes or other independent agencies functioning in work release and study release. In so doing, offenders earn money to help support families, pay taxes, pay court costs and, in general, assume responsibility for their own lives.[9] The clear implication is that furlough programs do not actually cost more to operate for the departments of corrections, and they save money because inmates are less dependent upon the state at an earlier stage in their incarceration.

In terms of the actual cost of the furlough, i.e., transportation, the inmate or someone on behalf of the inmate usually pays the expense. Therefore, furloughs do not constitute an additional expenditure for the state.

Effectiveness

Since the widespread adoption of furlough programs beginning in the early 1960's, there have been several descriptive studies of the actual program operations of specific states.[10] In addition, several national surveys in the early 1970's have documented the number of correctional systems utilizing furloughs in the United States. One of the most noted has been Markley's work discussed earlier in this chapter. However, very little research material is available that concretely measures the effect of the program as a correctional device.

One reason is that furlough programs are usually viewed as a technique of reintegration. Since they do not seem to be discussed in treatment terms, there seems to be an absence of evaluation measures. When people talk about effectiveness of this program, they seem to mean the percentage of successfully completed furloughs. In other words, how many inmates came back to the institution on time?

For example, the state of Mississippi believes that their program is successful.

> Since 1933, Mississippi has permitted inmates with three years of good behavior and rated as trustworthy, to go home for a period of ten days. The data reported by Zemans and Cavan show that from 1944 to 1956, 3,204 prisoners were released for home furloughs under the program. Of this number, 15 failed to return, 12 of whom were accounted for, and 3 of whom were still at large. Hopper (1969), updating Zemans' and Cavan's data, reported that each year, between December 1 and March 1, approximately 300 inmates were granted home furloughs of ten days' duration. During 1967, only two of the 219 inmates granted furloughs, did not return voluntarily.[11]

Smith and Milan[12] surveyed home furlough policies by sending questionnaires to all 52 agencies (50 states, the District of Columbia and the Federal Bureau of Prisons). All 52 agencies responded. With eighteen agencies that reported sufficient data to determine rates of abscondence from home furlough programs during either 1968 or 1969, the reported rates were uniformly low, ranging from a low of zero in nine instances, to a high of .080 (eight per 100) in one instance. In developing a rank order correlation statistic, the authors determined that those agencies which allow the greatest number of furloughs and of maximum duration, are also those agencies which tend to experience the highest percentage of abscondences.

Miller, introduced earlier in the chapter, believes that from an operational perspective, a rate of 1.5 percent or less usually indicates that the screening process is too severe. Therefore, many other good applicants are being rejected, and that will lead to other institutional side effects, i.e., low morale. A rate of 5 percent or more, however, means that some aspect of the screening process, or of the program, needs to be monitored. He mentions that sometimes a period of extreme tension inside the prison will adversely affect the escape rate.[13]

Just recently, LeClair, working with the Massachusetts Department of Corrections, addressed this research question: Are inmates who experience one or more furloughs during the term of their incarceration less likely to be reincarcerated within one year of their eventual release from prison than are similar types of inmates who do not participate in the furlough program during the period of their incarceration? The expectation that inmates participating in the furlough program prior to release would have lower rates of recidivism were proven true. "The recidivism rate of 16% for the 610 individuals in the furlough group was significantly lower (X^2=13.9, df=1, p<.001) than the rate of 27% for the 268 individuals released without furlough in 1973."[14] Using a second sample (N=841) consisting of males released from the same institutions during the year 1974 and divided into a treatment subsample and a comparison subsample, significant differences were found with those individuals experiencing a furlough versus those who did not have a furlough in terms of rates of recidivism.[15] Stressing some of the limitations of the study, LeClair's research does provide tentative evidence of the positive effectiveness of the furlough program. In other words, the reduction in recidivism was due to the impact of the furlough program and not simply to the types of inmates selected for furloughs.[16]

Juvenile Program Application

Furlough programs with juveniles are not as formalized in their procedures as are programs with adults for several reasons. First, juveniles have shorter lengths of incarceration due to their age of majority, i.e., age 21. If a juvenile has committed a serious crime, depending upon the state statutes, the state has the right to either waive the juvenile rights and try as an adult or to try as an adult due to original jurisdiction. If that juvenile is sentenced as an adult, then that person would have the same right to furloughs as anyone else regardless of their age. Due to the time served on sentence, however, the juvenile would probably be an adult person in the legal sense. Thirdly, some states use furloughs as a part of their phasing-out process so that juveniles can anticipate a weekend home before their actual release.

At Valley View School for Boys, Illinois Department of Corrections, home furloughs are used to practice and learn desired behaviors. Based on social learning theory, delinquents, while in the institution, concentrate on scripts, rehearsals and assignments. That means before leaving for home furlough, young men participate in a series of role-plays designed to help them deal with the problems which they can expect when they return to the community, such as talking to the police, or applying for a job. In behavioral scripts, the young person first shows the counselor and fellow students how he usually handles the situation. Then, they show him how that behavior created problems for the student. So the group either develops a revised script or a model script which is offered to the individual for another attempt at role-playing or behavioral rehearsal. The thinking is that when a person is able to practice a specific behavioral pattern in a protected situation where there is less anxious feelings, that individual will be able to succeed in the real situation outside the protected environment. Secondly, the protected environment with feedback gives the person a chance to judge for himself the appropriateness or inappropriateness of his behavior. Thus, practice develops a specific behavior and increases the probability that the newly learned behavior will be maintained.[17]

> After the scripts have been performed and various individualized situations have been rehearsed, the students then try out some aspect of this new behavior on a furlough. For example, one student while at home in a situation with others who were drinking, had to refrain from drinking. He was allowed to do this only after he could demonstrate in role-playing that he was able to respond to the situation in several different ways, regardless of what his peers said. The boy was monitored at home by an older brother who did not have a delinquent history and who had expressed concern about his younger brother.[18]

Prior to going out on a home furlough, the student negotiates, in the form of a written contract, a specific assignment. This contract specifies conditions which the student must fulfill, and the extent of his privileges while on leave. For example, "I, _____, agree to spend one hour a day at home talking to my mother about furlough and the program here. I will keep my cool while talking to her, and I will have her put down the time and sign on the back of this paper." This behavioral assignment is hard for a student who has had little communication with his parents. Yet, it is typical of the beginning phase. In the event of unclear assignments or excessive or too limited demands, the contract may be returned to the counselor for renegotiation with the student.[19]

Parents are informed about furlough procedures through letters, telephone and visiting days. They are also prepared at a special parent's seminar for their monitoring role. These precautions are devised to avoid power struggles over the assignment and monitoring process. The following comments reflect the monitoring of a highly cooperative parent in response to a specific behavioral assignment:

> Friday Night
> David was driven to the youth center by his brother's girlfriend. He called twenty minutes later to say the youth center wasn't open, and that he and Larry Miller were going to just "drive around." On the advice of his dad, he came home instead. No trouble.
> Saturday Night
> David left Larry's phone number and went to Larry's house. At 12:15 we called Larry's house because it was fifteen minutes after

curfew and he wasn't home. Larry's parents gave us a phone number of a party they went to. The phone was answered by an adult, so the party was a supervised party. However, David failed to call us that he was there. He came home immediately, arriving at 12:22 — 22 minutes after curfew. He said he wasn't aware of the time.
Sunday
He spent at home with the family.

Mrs. R.K.

Note that in all cases, two requirements are universal: maintenance of curfew and knowledge of the student's whereabouts. Additional student assignments to be completed while on furlough depend upon the student and his particular problem.[20]

Up Close and Personal

John, a 31-year-old male, is serving a life sentence at Kansas State Penitentiary, Lansing, Kansas. Eleven years ago, John was found guilty of second degree murder in the death of a man in a barroom fight. At that time, he was sentenced to a life sentence. Counting the time he spent in the county jail, John had served 11 years and five months of this mandatory 15 years. At the end of 15 years, John will be given a parole hearing before the parole board. They may choose, at that time, to deny parole.

In the meantime, John has applied for a home furlough to reestablish family ties with his mother. His mother is the closest relative since John is not married, has been an only child and his father was deceased several years prior to his conviction. His furlough plan was to leave the institution 6 p.m. on Friday and return by 6 p.m. on Sunday. While he was out, John was to stay with his mother at her residence and to make one personal visit with his attorney to discuss an appeal.

The parole officer investigating the furlough plan interviewed the mother who lives in a middle-class home in a small community. She is self-employed and therefore has made arrangements to be free for John's visit. She was also willing to provide transportation to and from the institution since John did not have a valid driver's license. All in all, John's mother knew her responsibilities as a sponsor and was willing to abide by those rules.

The parole officer also interviewed persons in the criminal justice system. The county attorney had no objections to John's home furlough but he did want close supervision. The sheriff had no objections to the furlough. Five individuals in the community (mayor, post office clerk, tavern owner and two next door neighbors) were also interviewed. Although none of them were negative towards the home furlough plan, they wanted to make sure that John would not be permitted to drink or run around. The victim's family no longer lived in the state so the parole officer did not interview them.

From these interviews, the parole officer recommended that if John were to have his plan for home furlough approved, he should also agree to the following conditions:

1. No travel outside of county without permission of parole officer.
2. No travel outside of the city without being accompanied by his mother, nor outside of the residence after 7 p.m. without his mother.
3. No alcoholic beverages at any time including at the mother's residence.
4. Report to sheriff daily at 12 noon at the post office.
5. Call parole officer by phone when he arrives in the city and before he leaves to return to the state peniteniary.

This initial home furlough plan was denied because John had not spent enough time in minimum custody. Seven months later, however, John was granted his home furlough. No problems or difficulties were experienced by the parole officer, the community or John. According to the institution, John's furlough was successful because there was no trouble and John returned to the institution on time.

In terms of John's definition of success, the furlough left a lot to be desired. "There were a lot of silent moments. Heck! What can you expect after 11 years. Sure my mother visited me in the joint — but a lot of things change in 11 years even in a small town. In some ways, the furlough was too long and other times too short. The constant threat of making it back on time hangs on you. Yet, the weekend went so quick just doing the things you have to do. For example, my mom has a car. So, she drove up to get me and drove me to her place. A lot of the furlough time is taken up just in transportation. Friday night and Sunday afternoon are wasted just because of the distance. Then Saturday morning, I spent with my attorney. One word might express my weekend — frustration. So much newness — so much to do — so little time. Yet, I feel so lucky I had this chance that I am looking forward to trying for another."

He was asked, "Did you ever think of not returning?"

"I guess I wouldn't be honest if I said no. Sure the idea crosses a guy's mind but I don't have to act on that thought. In fact, I'm not sure which group would come after me: (1) the prison staff or (2) the other inmates whose chances I've spoiled. It's probably the other guys in the joint I fear most. I know what this program has meant to me. I don't want to let them down. Plus, I want to go again myself."

John did return to the institution to finish his sentence and to await his second furlough program.

Summary

By definition, a furlough is an authorized absence from a correctional institution in which the inmate is not normally escorted by a member of the institution staff. Furloughs are a leave of absence from the institution for the purpose of a home visit to strengthen family ties, seek employment, visit a sick or dying relative, obtain necessary medical care, attend a job or school interview or participate as a volunteer in an activity serving the general public.

In terms of the historical development of furloughs, some programs were developed informally as an outgrowth of specific, local attitudes and values, such as an early program in Mississippi in 1918. Many programs were developed during the 1960's and 1970's due to scientific literature documenting European success with these programs and encouragement by the President's Commission on Law Enforcement and Administration of Justice.

Furlough programs vary state by state. Yet the main purpose seems to be to permit an individual the chance to re-enter society on a conditional basis with, of course, a planned approach which has been checked out beforehand. The gradual exposure to the community before outright release has merit. People who are against these programs frequently lack awareness of the selection procedures and process for furlough participation. As indicated in the process section of this chapter, the procedures are clearly delineated by the departments of corrections to maintain and protect their responsibility for the inmate. Usually, an inmate, to qualify for furlough, must have maintained a good behavior record, be classified in minimum security custody and generally be considered a good risk by the correctional counselor and/or the principal administrator. In some states, inmates who do have a history of repeated violence have to wait until 30 days prior to the release date for a furlough to seek employment or finalize parole plans. Although the chapter discussed a simplified version of the process, students were advised to investigate the statutes of their particular state dealing with the department of corrections. The actual detailed procedures noting time limits and accountability factors are a matter of public record.

In terms of problems, the greatest stumbling block to the furlough programs has been the notoriety of a few inmates across the country who have violated the conditions of the program. In other words, that individual has either escaped or did some violent criminal act, such as murder or rape. That kind of behavior only incites public hostility.

In terms of cost, there seems to be no empirical study addressing the issue. Even if there were, furlough programs would be hard to financially assess. For example, furloughs permit inmates to participate in many rehabilitation programs that cannot be provided within the institutional setting. In addition, because of furloughs, inmates are less dependent upon the state at an earlier stage in their incarceration. Thus, furlough programs do not actually cost more to operate.

Furlough programs are also used with juvenile offenders. The Valley View School for Boys, Illinois Department of Corrections, uses home furloughs to practice and learn desired behaviors. Based on social learning theory, delinquents, while in the juvenile correctional institution, practice scripts so that in the real situation at home, for example, the individual can have more reassurance that their behavior will be in keeping with societal definitions. Parents are also involved so that juveniles can complete additional assignments while on the furlough. Furloughs with juvenile and adult offenders maximize an inmate's chances of rehabilitation while giving an administrator a much more valid measure of an inmate's readiness for release.

Notes

1. U.S. Dept. of Justice, Federal Prison System, "Policy Statement on Furloughs," #7300 12E, dated May 26, 1978.
2. Carson W. Markley, "Furlough Programs and Conjugal Visiting in Adult Correctional Institutions," *Federal Probation* 37 (March 1973), pp. 19-26.
3. B.R. McCarthy, *Easy Time—Female Inmates on Temporary Release* (Lexington, Massachusetts: D.C. Heath and Company, 1979), p. 1.
4. Markley, "Furlough Programs," p. 19.
5. Ibid., p. 20.
6. E. Eugene Miller, "Furloughs as a Technique of Reintegration," in *Corrections in the Community*, eds. E. Eugene Miller and M. Robert Montilla (Reston, Virginia: Reston Publishing Co., c. 1977), p. 202.
7. U.S. Dept. of Justice, *op. cit.*
8. Miller, *"Furloughs," op. cit.*, p. 203.

9. Steward Werner and J. Harvey Bell, "Pre-Release and Furloughs in Pennsylvania," *Prison Journal* 52 (Autumn/Winter, 1972), p. 38.
10. A.E. Reed, *Temporary Leaves for Felony Inmates: Oregon's Experience*, Salem, Oregon, 1972 (unpublished); N. Halt and D. Miller, *Explorations in Inmate-Family Relationships*, California Department of Correction Research Report No. 46 (Sacramento, California, 1972); F. Farrington, *The Massachusetts Furlough Assessment*, Massachusetts Department of Correction Research Report No. 115 (Boston, Mass., 1974).
11. Robert R. Smith and Michael A. Milan, "A Survey of the Home Furlough Policies of American Correctional Agencies," *Criminology II* (May 1973), p. 97.
12. Ibid., pp. 95-104.
13. Miller, "Furloughs," op. cit., p. 206.
14. Daniel P. LeClair, "Home Furlough Program Effects on Rates of Recidivism," *Criminal Justice and Behavior* 5 (September 1978), p. 234.
15. Ibid., p. 255.
16. Ibid., p. 256.
17. David Brierton, John Flanagan, and Sheldon D. Rose, "A Behavioral Approach to Corrections Counseling," *Law in American Society*, 4 (1975), pp. 10-16.
18. Ibid., p. 14.
19. Ibid., p. 14-15.
20. Ibid.

Resources

Brierton, David, John Flanagen, and Sheldon D. Rose. "A behavioral approach to corrections counseling," *Law in American Society* 4 (1975), pp. 10-16.

Markley, C.W., "Furlough programs and conjugal visiting in adult correctional institutions," *Federal Probation* 37 (March 1973), p. 19-26.

Miller, E. Eugene and M. Robert Montilla (eds.). *Corrections in the Community: Success Models in Correctional Reform* (Reston, Virginia: Reston Publishing Company, Inc., 1977).

Serrill, M.S. "Prison furloughs in America," *Corrections Magazine*, 1 (July/August 1975), p. 2-12, 53-56.

Smith, R.R. "Survey of the home furlough policies of American correctional agencies," *Criminology II* (May 1973), p. 95-104.

Werner, Stewart and J. Harvey Bell. "Pre-release and furloughs in Pennsylvania," *Prison Journal* 52 (Autumn/Winter, 1972), p. 36-43.

Chapter 8
Halfway Houses

All halfway houses are *not* alike. In fact, such words as diversity, variety and heterogeneity are those which best describe those programs generally subsumed under the heading of "halfway houses." The term is used to describe programs which are marked by substantial differences with respect to their size, target populations, organizational structure, funding sources, length of stay, physical location, services provided, admissions criteria, quantity and quality of staffing and goals which they attempt to achieve. This situation has compounded the confusion about halfway houses and makes it difficult to present any but the most general of definitions.

Generally, a correctional halfway house may be defined as a transitional community-based residential facility, either publicly or privately operated, that is designed to facilitate the offender's difficult transition from incarceration to community living or to serve as an alternative to incarceration. This definition alludes to the two principal types of halfway houses—"halfway-out houses" and "halfway-in houses." In the first instance, the facility is "halfway" between confinement in a penal institution and the resumption of freedom in the community, whereas in the latter instance the facility is "halfway" along the process of commitment to a penal institution. "Halfway-out houses" are designed specifically for such clients as mandatory releasees or parolees who require a transitional support system to re-adjust to the community after release from prison, or inmates who are released from correctional institutions prior to mandatory release or parole for whom halfway houses serve as pre-release, work release and educational release centers. "Halfway-in houses," on the other hand, are designed specifically for such clients as probationers as an alternative to incarceration and neglected juveniles or juveniles adjudged delinquent as alternatives to detention facilities or training schools. It should also be noted that many halfway houses restrict their clientele to criminal offenders with special problems, such as drug abusers, alcoholics and individuals with mental health problems. Halfway houses attempt to reintegrate their clients into community living through the provision of concentrated supportive services, such as a home, assistance in vocational counseling/training and finding employment, financial support, educational opportunities, psychological and emotional support/counseling, community activities and recreational opportunities, referral services and a supportive environment. Naturally, there are differences among halfway houses in terms of the amount and types of supportive services provided.

History

The extensive development and utilization of halfway houses for offenders is a relatively recent phenomenon. However, the halfway house concept and its adaptation and application to the field of corrections is not new, having originated in England and Ireland in the 1800's.

Shortly thereafter, the halfway house concept for offenders spread to the United States. Massachusetts, New York and Pennsylvania were the first states to establish such facilities. A Massachusetts Prison Commission, cognizant of the formidable barriers facing offenders upon their release from prison, such as being destitute, the natural prejudice against offenders, difficulty in obtaining employment and the need for shelter, recommended the establishment of such facilities in 1817 hoping that they might reduce the high recidivism rates of released offenders. However, the Massachusetts Legislature did not follow the suggestion. In fact, this suggestion was not implemented in Massachusetts until 1864 when a halfway house for women offenders released from prison opened in Boston. However, earlier in New York in 1845, a group of Quakers, concerned with the plight of the released offender, founded a halfway house in New York City. The Issac T. Hooper House, as it is known today, has remained continuously in operation from that date to the present. The Pennsylvania halfway house experience began in 1889 with the establishment of the House of Industry in Philadelphia. It continues to receive parolees from the Pennsylvania prison system today. In 1896, Maud Booth, together with her husband, co-leader of the Volunteers of America, opened a halfway house eventually called Hope Hall for ex-offenders in New York City. During the next three decades, the Volunteers of America founded Hope Halls in several cities across the country. The preceding examples underscore the pivotal role played by religious and private volunteer groups, such as the Salvation Army, the Quakers, and the Volunteers of America, in the historical development of halfway houses for offenders.

Despite the opposition, hostility and apathy encountered by these and other early programs, the halfway house concept spread. However, the introduction and expansion of parole, the requirement that offenders have a job before release and sentences of increasing length during the early 1900's effectively checked the growth of halfway houses.

The Depression made it extremely difficult for released prisoners to locate jobs and to raise the necessary finances for halfway house operations, which had been inadequately financed at best. Consequently, from the 1930's until the 1950's represented a period of relative inactivity for further halfway house development.

During the 1950's the halfway house concept experienced a substantial revival with the establishment of numerous programs, such as Crenshaw House in Los Angeles by the Society of Friends, Dismas House in St. Louis by Father Charles Dismas Clark (the "Hoodlum Priest"), St. Leonard's House in Chicago and 308 West Residence in Wilmington, Delaware by the Prisoner's Aid Society of Delaware. The beginning of this "national halfway house movement" is generally attributed to a growing dissatisfaction with the ineffectiveness of institutional corrections as an instrument of rehabilitation as evidenced by high recidivism rates, an appreciation of the problems confronting the offender released from prison and a recognition of the need to provide offenders released from prison with essential supportive services to assist them in making the transition from institutional living to community living.

Several key events occurred in the 1960's which added impetus to and provided legitimation for the national halfway house movement. In 1961, Robert Kennedy, then Attorney General of the United States, endorsed the utilization of halfway houses by recommending the establishment of the first federal pre-release centers or "halfway houses." Initially restricted to juvenile and youthful offenders, by 1964 Kennedy was satisfied that the programs were successful. The following year, in 1965, Congress authorized expansion to include adult offenders. To this end, the Federal Bureau of Prisons began to establish a network of state, county and private pre-release placements for adults. In 1968, the Omnibus Crime Control Act was passed by Congress. Among other things, it established the Law Enforcement Assistance Administration (LEAA) which served as the principal means for providing substantial amounts of federal assistance to state and local governments to initiate criminal justice programs, including halfway houses. This provided the modern halfway house movement with all the impetus it required. The decade of the 1970's witnessed the proliferation of halfway houses.

The remarkable growth of halfway houses can be appreciated through tracing the formation and development of the International Halfway House Association (IHHA). A meeting of concerned persons operating halfway house programs for ex-offenders convened in Chicago, Illinois in 1964. The purpose of the meeting was to assess the possibility and feasibility of establishing a professional organization related to the goals and objectives of community-based treatment programs. This was the beginning of the International Halfway House Association. A perusal of this organization's Directories gives credence to a halfway house "explosion." The first edition of the IHHA Directory, published in 1966, listed approximately 40 names and addresses of halfway houses in the United States and Canada. However, the 1971-72 IHHA Directory listed over 250 programs; the 1974 IHHA Directory listed approximately 1,300 programs; and the 1976 IHHA Directory listed more than 1,600 programs.

The private and public sectors are both deeply involved in the modern halfway house movement. In the private sector, halfway houses are sponsored by a diversity of groups, including nonprofit social agencies, churches, religious fellowships, fraternal orders, business associations and private practitioners. In the public sector, many cities and counties administer their own halfway house programs while most states operate halfway houses or contract with private agencies for such services. In addition, the Federal Bureau of Prisons operates several facilities and contracts with more than 250 other community treatment programs or halfway houses for the provision of residential care for Federal offenders.

Purpose

Persons leaving prison face several fundamental problems, such as finding employment, obtaining money to meet basic expenses for shelter, food, clothing and transportation, locating a place to live, establishing credit, repaying debts, gaining social acceptance, acquiring companionship and resolving other social and emotional problems related to their incarceration and return to the community. Despite the existence of such anticipated difficulties in the post-release social world, an offender's desire to succeed is strongest at the time of his release from prison. However, research clearly reveals that recidivism is highest during the period immediately after an offender is released from prison. The failure of many persons at this critical juncture, that is, the first days, weeks or months after release from prison, is certainly not a mystery. The reasons for such failures are well-known. According to Clendenen et al.:

> ... Traditionally, most (prisoners) come out handicapped by their inability to meet material needs—housing, clothing, meals, jobs, training—and by their lack of an interested family or friends who could help them meet these needs. Consequently, even those with good intentions sometimes have little choice but to return to ... criminal activity.[1]

The fundamental objective of the traditional halfway house is to provide a transitional support system for the offender during this critical readjustment period. The importance of such transitional support systems for offenders in their reintegration into society is underscored by Chamberlain. He states:

...The evidence indicates that if offenders are provided with supportive services in a structured environment for a reasonable period of time during this critical re-entry period, the probability of success will be enhanced.[2]

As a transitional support system, the traditional halfway house is specifically designed to provide offenders with the essential supportive services during this critical reentry period and thereby ease their transition from prison to the community. Halfway houses often provide the following body of core supportive services to their clients in order to afford them more advantages and opportunities in establishing themselves successfully in the community: a home, assistance in vocational counseling/training and finding employment, financial support, educational opportunities, psychological and emotional support/counseling, community activities and recreational opportunities, referral services and a supportive environment.

A Home

Persons released from prison are concerned with the immediate provision of their basic needs, such as shelter and food. A halfway house satisfies these basic needs by providing its clients with general living accommodations and meals. Insofar as many halfway houses are situated in residential settings in a center of population close to schools, employment, social and cultural activities and other major components of the community, it serves as a "base of operations" during this critical period of readjustment for the individual. Additionally, the halfway house provides a structured living environment through a system of house rules and regulations which afford a reasonable degree of supervision and provide safeguards for the community.

Assistance in Vocational Counseling/Training and Finding Employment

Another essential reintegrative need for the client is that of finding suitable employment. Some clients may possess the necessary job skills and simply require job placement assistance whereas others might require additional job training and job skills before they are marketable. Therefore, halfway houses, often in conjunction with other community social service agencies, provide the following specific services for clients if needed: vocational testing, vocational counseling, vocational training, job counseling, the teaching of job hunting and interview skills and job placement assistance.

Financial Support

If the person released from prison is to have a fair chance of making a successful adjustment in the community it is imperative that he have a sufficient amount of money upon release for basic living expenses until he becomes reestablished and financially self-reliant. However, he is often released with a paltry amount and is expected to succeed. Releasees are also frequently hampered by their inability to responsibly manage their finances. In recognition of these important needs, halfway houses attempt to make their clients more financially self-reliant by providing them with temporary financial assistance until employment has been obtained, informing them about how to get a loan, if needed, assisting them in setting up savings accounts and managing their expenditures and teaching them budgeting skills and consumer education.

Educational Opportunities

A person's successful reintegration into the community might be enhanced by further education insofar as it may be related to his employment potential and allow him to continue and complete his preparation for a career. To assist their clients with their educational pursuits, halfway houses often provide or arrange for educational testing, educational training and educational placement assistance, if needed.

Psychological and Emotional Support/Counseling

An offender's successful readjustment to the community is often dependent upon his ability to cope with readjustment problems related to his incarceration, release and return to the community. Consequently, halfway houses usually provide various kinds of counseling services to their clients, such as individual or group counseling, assisting them in discussing, identifying and responsibly dealing with potential problem areas, such as self-image, improving family and interpersonal relationships, coping with tension and meeting basic physical, material, social and psychological needs.

Community Activities and Recreational Opportunities

Participation in community social and cultural activities is an important ingredient in the gradual reintegration of the person into the community. Clients are, therefore, strongly encouraged to participate in social, cultural and recreational activities. Halfway houses may provide their clients with informal as well as structured social, cultural and recreational events to assist them in their gradual reintegration into society.

Referral Services

Oftentimes, halfway house clientele are in need of services that are inappropriate or impossible to provide within the halfway house itself, such as medical services, psychological evaluation, counseling or therapy, vocational training and academic upgrading. Therefore, halfway houses, if they do not provide such services themselves, usually see to it that their clients have ready access to such services by maintaining relationships with other community agencies, such as mental health agencies, medical agencies, welfare agencies, vocational training agencies and family service agencies, which possess the appropriate resources and provide the necessary services. In these instances, halfway houses serve as social service referral agencies by channeling their clients in the right direction and eliminating unnecessary confusion and "red tape."

Supportive Environment

The aforementioned services provided by halfway houses underline, perhaps, the most important overall service they provide—the provision of a much needed supportive environment for their clients. Faced with countless problems emanating from their incarceration and release into what can seem to be a changed and hostile environment, releasees may experience great anxiety from a sense of being totally on one's own. Oftentimes, persons released from prison lack the essential supportive relationships with family members, relatives and friends which are necessary for successful reintegration and reentry into society. Halfway houses attempt to fill this void by providing a place where clients can be given support and guidance to enable them to deal successfully with their problems. In effect, the halfway house serves as a concerned sponsor for releasees in introducing them gradually into the community until they become socially anchored. The halfway house helps prepare the individual for reintegration into society through a graduated step-by-step process and the provision of the previously identified essential services.

Administration Process

The viable operation of a halfway house is dependent upon several key administrative and procedural factors. Funding, organizational structure and staffing pattern are certainly among the most important of these factors.

Funding

Funding is a crucial function in the operation of a halfway house, whether it is privately or publicly operated. In fact, the ultimate success or failure experienced by the halfway house may well be related to the manner in which the administrator handles funding issues. Administrators must be concerned constantly with obtaining the resources necessary for both the immediate and long range operation of the halfway house program and facility.

An important variable in planning funding activity is whether the halfway house is primarily privately or publicly operated. A private halfway house is operated and funded entirely by a private profit or nonprofit organization or it may receive some financial assistance and support from public revenues, whereas a public halfway house is operated and funded by a federal, state, county or municipal agency.[3] Halfway houses which are primarily private operations are characterized by diverse funding patterns with multiple sources, while halfway houses which are primarily public operations are almost exclusively funded by State Criminal Justice Planning Agency grants or state and local monies.[4]

There are numerous potential funding sources available, both in the public and private sectors, from which the administrator of a private halfway house can seek funding for the operation of his or her halfway house. *Among the prominent potential funding sources located in the public sector are: the Law Enforcement Assistance Administration, the National Institute of Mental Health, the Office of Economic Opportunity, the U.S. Department of Health and Human Services, the U.S. Department of Labor, special titles under the Social Security Act and state and local governments.[5] Key funding sources located in the private sector are: Community/United Appeal organizations, private foundations, religious and service organizations, local contributions and fees for service.[6]

A recent National Evaluation Program study revealed that the most frequently mentioned funding sources currently being utilized by halfway house administrators to operate their programs were: state monies (64 percent), county and local monies (43 percent) and private donations (36 percent). Of course, multiple funding sources are utilized by many halfway houses. In addition to the aforementioned funding sources, the study also indicated that the following were also among the funding sources currently being utilized by halfway house administrators: U.S. Bureau of Prisons, Comprehensive Employment Training Act (CETA) funds, revenue sharing monies, fees from clients, donations from business and contributions from nonprofit organizations. Among the most frequently cited planned funding sources for replacing Law Enforcement Assistance Administration funds upon their expiration were state monies, private donations, county and local funds, fees from clients and Comprehensive Employment Training Act (CETA) money.[7]

There are several significant funding related issues which must be addressed by the halfway house administrator. These pertain to the issues of funding source, limitations and restrictions of funding sources, future funding security and funding continuity.

---

*Some of these agencies have since experienced major organizational restructuring and/or funding level cutbacks.

Although the halfway house administrator can exercise some funding flexibility given the array of potential funding sources, it is essential that he or she should carefully consider and assess the implications of utilizing any particular funding source. Funding sources may carry various limitations regarding their usage. The administrator must determine whether such restrictions and limitations can be "lived with" or whether they will be a detriment to the overall purpose and operation of the halfway house program.

Another critical funding matter pertains to the related issues of future funding security and funding continuity. Given the condition that most grants have definite funding time periods, it is imperative that the halfway house administrator be sensitive to the length of the grant, the probability of future year funding from a funding source and alternative potential funding sources which can be looked to when, and if, a funding source should decide to terminate its participation in a program.

Organizational Structure/Staffing Pattern

The principal executive body for most privately operated halfway houses is a board of directors. Frequently, the board of directors is composed of representatives from community groups, organizations and agencies, such as the courts, law enforcement agencies, universities, social service agencies, probation and parole departments, churches and various other responsible citizens of the community. Ideally, members of the board should possess expertise in resource development, program development and/or evaluation, finance, personnel or public relations, have the capability to represent the program with community groups that affect program operations, possess the ability to provide input to the program on community issues which affect the accomplishment of program operations, demonstrate a sincere interest in the work of the program and commitment to its goals, express a willingness to carry out assignments within some area of special talent and competency and to attend board and committee meetings.[8] In general, the board is responsible for policy administration, finance, personnel, public and community relations and evaluation.

Next in order in the formal organizational hierarchy of a halfway house is usually an executive director who operates under the general direction of the program's board of directors. Essentially, the executive director serves as the chief operations executive of the halfway house. Among the executive director's principal administrative responsibilities are: recommending appropriate policies to the board of directors for consideration; implementing policies adopted by the board of directors; preparing the budget and directing all financial operations of the halfway house; recruiting, developing, supervising and evaluating halfway house personnel; evaluating halfway house services and suggesting program developments and modifications when and where appropriate; establishing and maintaining good public and community relations; recommending to the board of directors both long and short term plans for the development of halfway house programs and services; and keeping the board of directors apprised of general agency operations and developments.[9]

Next in the halfway house formal organizational structure hierarchy, under the direction of the executive director, is the operating staff of the halfway house. There are several factors which will determine the amount and type of staff which will be required for the operation of a halfway house. Those of particular importance include the type of target population to be served by the program, the number of anticipated clients to be served at a given time, the goals and objectives of the program, the needs of the clients, the type and extent of services to be provided for the clients by the agency and the services to be provided by other agencies in the community.

Although staffing patterns will, of course, vary between individual halfway house programs, according to the aforementioned factors and their distinctive orientation and focus, there is a fairly consistent staffing pattern for the halfway house having a capacity of 25 residents. Though halfway houses range in size from six to 140 residents, the average house has a capacity of 25. Under the executive director is the house staff. A house director is responsible for actually administering house operations on a day-to-day basis. This involves supervising and evaluating all house staff; assisting the executive director in the development, coordination and implementation of house treatment, aftercare and out-client programs; approving applicants for residency as well as dismissing clients for program violations; assisting the executive director in liason with other community agencies used by the halfway house and assisting the executive director with public relations; extending casework and group work services to residents of the house; and approving cash disbursements and purchase requests for the house.[10] The principal treatment component on the staff is the counselor. The counselor's primary responsibility is providing formal counseling services, individual or group, to clients on a regular basis and making the necessary referrals for residents requiring more specialized psychological services in the community. In addition, the counselor oftentimes assists residents in locating jobs and functions as a social service referral agent for the house in obtaining specialized programming in the community for the residents, such as vocational training, academic education and mental health services. Additionally, the house staff usually consists of a secretary-bookkeeper, who performs clerical, secretarial and bookkeeping functions for the halfway house, and a cook-housekeeper, who is responsible for the planning, preparation and serving of meals to the residents and the performance of basic cleaning duties.

Larger houses are usually characterized by an even greater division of labor than previously described. It could include, in addition to a board of directors, an executive director, assistant executive director, clinical psychologist, house director, assistant house director, employment placement and vocational counselor, accountant, outclient counselor, night counselor, part-time counselor, secretary-bookkeeper, secretary, clerk-typist, cook-housekeeper and maintenance person.[11]

Publicly operated halfway houses are usually characterized by a somewhat different formal administrative hierarchy than that found in privately operated halfway houses. The administrative hierarchy developed in publicly operated halfway houses is oftentimes an extension of the formal organizational structure which characterizes the parent agency of which it is a part. The policy making function in a publicly operated halfway house is usually performed by an official in the parent agency rather than a board of directors as is the case in most privately operated halfway houses. Publicly operated halfway houses usually operate according to the administrative policies developed and handed down by the parent agency, that is, the agency of which the halfway house is a part, for example, a state department of corrections. The staffing patterns of publicly and privately operated halfway houses are normally organized in a similar manner.

Problems

There are a number of perennial problems involved in the establishment and operation of halfway houses. Among the most common types of problems are: community acceptance/hostility from the public, funding, fluctuations in the resident population, staff qualifications and high staff turnover.

As is the case with the implementation of most community-based correctional programs, halfway houses often face the problem of encountering varying amounts of community opposition and hostility. A Lou Harris poll discovered that although 77 percent of a representative U.S. sample favored the halfway house concept, 50 percent would not want a halfway house to be situated in their neighborhood, and only 22 percent thought that people in the neighborhood would favor a halfway house being located there.[12] The concerns, fears and anxieties of individual citizens and groups that unwanted criminal elements will invade the community, that a crime wave will arise and that property values will decline can generate strong negative public reaction. Community opposition and hostility may be expressed in several forms, including the staging of community protests by residential and civic associations, letter writing campaigns to elected officials, the passage of restrictive zoning regulations designed to prevent the establishment of halfway houses in specified areas and the filing of lawsuits.[13]

The success of a halfway house is dependent upon enlisting community support or, at least, the neutralization of this potential opposition and hostility. Rachin has identified the following steps which should be followed in sequence to establish the necessary community relations to promote community acceptance of halfway houses:

1. Important individuals and groups, such as local leaders of government, planning boards, private and public social, health and welfare agencies, fraternal, church and neighborhood improvement groups and local police should be met with individually to discuss the program and their reaction to it.

2. A steering committee comprised of community leaders should be established. It is desirable for the steering committee to meet on a regular basis to promote recognition and assurance of their mutual interest and support for the halfway house.

3. The halfway house program should be explained in a candid and straightforward manner. This should include a discussion of its potential difficulties and problems, as well as its purported benefits and advantages.

4. The help of neighborhood leaders, whose support has been enlisted earlier, will reduce or neutralize community hostility and opposition and help prevent the polarization of negative opposition groups.

5. Meetings scheduled on a regular basis should be convened both during the planning stages and after the program has been operationalized. Open houses should be held on an annual or semiannual basis to permit interested persons and groups to visit, become acquainted with staff and learn first hand of the progress, problems and needs of the halfway house.[14]

Adequate funding is another indispensable ingredient for the successful operation of a halfway house. However, funding constitutes, perhaps, the principal administrative problem for halfway houses.[15] Funding problems are experienced in a variety of forms. The operation of halfway houses is frequently hampered by the inability of halfway house operators to secure sufficient funds from funding sources. The operation of a halfway house at less than a sufficient funding level precludes the provision of necessary, desired or improved services for its clients. Another funding problem pertains to the uncertainty of funding by grants. Administrators are often uncertain that grants, upon which the operation of their halfway house depends, will be awarded or renewed. This tenuous type of existence is due to the availability of potential funding sources and the fierce competition for them. Furthermore, although a grant may be awarded or renewed, the level of funding received may be at a less than anticipated level. This necessitates difficult program cutbacks and modifications. Halfway house administrators also periodically encounter difficulties in maintaining cash flow. Delays may be experienced in receiving grant checks from the funding source, expenses incurred by the halfway house may not be reimbursed until the appropriate receipts are received by the funding sources or unanticipated expenses in certain program categories may exceed the projected budget for a specified period. Private halfway houses are particularly susceptible to such funding problems. In fact, private houses report such problems twice as often as halfway houses operated by state departments of corrections. Federally operated halfway houses report no funding problems.[16]

Halfway houses are also subjected to problems arising from fluctuations in the size of their resident populations. Periodically, halfway houses are faced with accommodating more residents than is dictated by their program's optimal operational size. This situation is often attributable to an attempt to compensate for the lack of a sufficient number of halfway houses by trying to place as many clients as possible in existent halfway houses and an attempt by prisons to reduce their problems of overcrowding by "dumping" their inmates into such community-based corrections residential programs. Excessive numbers of clients may seriously jeopardize the intended goals of the halfway house, generate strain, produce an undesirable staff/client ratio and result in the staff placing more emphasis upon security than initially intended. This could conceivably erode the supportive environment which the halfway house is designed to supply. On the other side of the coin is the problem faced by halfway houses when they function at a lower than anticipated occupancy rate. Generally, studies suggest that halfway houses are less costly to operate when at capacity utilization. Whereas prison costs are relatively unaffected by small changes in the inmate population, changes in the number of halfway house residents have greater impact. Therefore, unanticipated fluctuations in a halfway house resident population, whether more or less than an ideal occupancy level, can create problems for the operation of a halfway house program.

Another general category of problems concerns staff qualifications and staff turnover. A recent survey, conducted as part of the National Evaluation Program Halfway House Project, discovered that 71 percent of the administrators and only 54 percent of the treatment personnel possessed college degrees. This survey also indicated that the educational fields of specialization in which the administrators had received their degrees were more related to job assignment than the degrees earned by treatment personnel.[18] The International Halfway House Association (IHHA) has established four years of college plus two years of experience in social service or a Master's Degree as the recommended minimum qualifications for professionals in positions such as executive director or treatment personnel.[19] As a result of these conditions, the concern over educational attainment and the relevancy of received degrees to their positions, it has been suggested that there is an essential need for specialized training of all halfway house staff, including orientation of new staff, in-service training and increased academic training, to enable them to perform their duties in the most efficient manner.

High staff turnover is another serious problem frequently identified by halfway house administrators. This problem often results from low salaries, the lack of opportunities for job advancement and job "burnout" as a consequence of frequent and intensive personal interaction with house residents.[20] Possible remedies for this problem include careful staffing practices, establishing realistic staff levels and sufficient salary and fringe benefit categories when budgets are prepared for grants and utilizing volunteers to complement paid staff.

Cost

One of the justifications presented for the greater utilization of halfway houses is economic savings. It is argued that the cost of maintaining offenders in halfway houses is less than the cost of full institutionalization. However, a review of available findings reveals inconsistent conclusions and casts at least some doubts about the cost saving potential of halfway houses.

In 1975, Thalheimer reported that a cost analysis study of 22 representative halfway houses across the country revealed that, based on a capacity of 18 residents, the 11 least expensive halfway houses averaged $93,130 per year to operate. This represented a cost of $14.18 per resident per day. On the other hand, the 11 most expensive houses averaged $146,217 per year or $22.26 per resident per day to operate.[21]

Findings reported in Ohio and Michigan support the reputed cost-saving potential of halfway houses. They also point to other savings to be realized in the form of residents utilizing money they earned on jobs while employed and residing at the halfway house to pay for their own room and board in the program, family support, savings, taxes and restitution or payment of fines. According to Johnson, the cost of maintaining an offender in prison in Michigan during the 1976-77 fiscal year was $6,103 whereas it cost approximately $3,600 to supervise a parole-bound offender in a halfway house during the same period. Additionally, during 1977, halfway house residents earned $3.5 million. These earnings were utilized by halfway house residents to pay $490,771 in rent in the program; $876,618 for personal expenses, including transportation and clothing; $663,387 for taxes; $311,385 for family support; $477,232 for personal savings; and $565,232 for meals.[22]

In 1977, Gordon reported that in Ohio average institution costs per day were $16.33 while the cost per day in halfway houses was only $10.46 to Ohio taxpayers. Futhermore, offenders earned $240,000 while residing in Ohio halfway houses whereas they would have earned only $.40 per day if they had still been incarcerated in an Ohio correctional institution.[23]

Carlson and Seiter attempted to assess the premise that halfway houses could be operated at less cost than alternative placements through a review of twelve halfway house efficiency analysis studies, most of which employed cost analysis. Eight of the twelve studies compared the operational costs of halfway houses with state institutions, generally on a cost per person per day or per diem basis; six studies revealed that halfway houses were less costly to operate than comparable state institutions; one showed that it costs a comparable amount to operate halfway houses and state institutions; and one statewide study demonstrated that halfway houses in the state were more costly than state institutions to operate. Another study of several halfway houses estimated less cost at capacity utilization. The implication is suggested that present operating costs were higher at less than capacity utilization. The emphasis of the final three studies was on occupancy rate or capacity utilization of halfway houses. The majority of the cost analyses reported actual per diems followed by projected per diems at an ideal occupancy rate. It was determined that the ideal occupancy rate was approximately 85 percent. The overall assessment of Carlson and Seiter about the cost-saving potential of halfway houses, on the basis of their literature review, was that halfway houses usually operate at a lower daily cost than that of an institution but at a higher daily cost than parole and probation.[24]

There has also been considerable doubt cast about the supposed substantial economic savings of halfway houses. Miller, for example, maintains that halfway houses are expensive to operate. Unlike prisons where operational costs are spread over a large population of inmates and thus per capita costs are reduced, personnel are concentrated on a relatively small number of clients in halfway houses and thus per capita costs are increased. In fact, according to Miller, the daily per capita costs of a halfway house will, on the average, equal the daily per capita costs of a medium security prison. Miller notes, however, that the halfway house per capita cost will usually include the cost of room and board whereas the prison per capita cost will not include any amortization of prison construction costs. Additionally, halfway house residents who are employed pay taxes. This represents another redeeming economic advantage of halfway houses. Miller estimates that a halfway house with a capacity of 25 residents will normally cost from $50,000 to $175,000 per year to operate.[25]

Beha is also somewhat skeptical regarding the cost savings of halfway houses. He notes: "My own review of literature and experience with these programs leaves me unconvinced of... their cost-saving potential."[26] Beha maintains that the intrinsic "logic" of cost savings deteriorates in reality because whereas prison costs are relatively unaffected by small changes in the inmate population, changes in the number of halfway house residents have greater impact. In addition, operational cost increases can be anticipated in some halfway houses because they may provide services and personnel not normally found in institutions. Finally, substantial initial capital outlays are required to start a halfway house, such as start-up costs, the purchase or lease of a house, renovation of the facility and purchase of necessary equipment and furniture. Beha notes, however, that savings in the form of payments from residents may reduce costs and benefits may be realized from halfway house residents involved in income-producing employment.

Effectiveness

Several factors make it difficult to assess the effectiveness of halfway houses. First, despite the proliferation of halfway house programs, there is a paucity of evaluative research conducted on such programs. Second, much of the research which has been conducted is of questionable validity judged by social science standards. Third, due to the heterogenity of halfway houses, the diversity of research designs employed and the variety of definitions of outcomes utilized, it is extremely difficult to generalize from the results of available studies. Fourth, the findings reported are mixed and inconclusive thereby preventing the declaration of a final verdict on the effectiveness of halfway houses.

Carlson and Seiter, in a recent article, summarized the findings of current halfway house evaluations focusing on the effectiveness of such programs which were conducted by the Ohio State University Program for the Study of Crime and Delinquency as part of the National Evaluation Program of the Law Enforcement Assistance Administration.[27] Carlson and Seiter mention and discuss a total of 35 studies that were concerned with the post-release outcome of halfway house residents. According to the type of research design utilized, two studies employed experimental designs, 17 utilized quasi-experimental designs and 16 were non-experimental designs which were restricted to measuring the outcome of halfway house residents only.

The two studies which employed true experimental designs randomly assigned referrals to halfway houses (for one in lieu of jail, the other in lieu of honor camps). In the first study, persons who were serious escape risks, those likely to exhibit violent behavior and those deeply involved in selling and/or using hard narcotics were excluded. According to a one year follow-up, only 15 percent of the halfway house residents were unemployed versus 29 percent of the control group. Similar recidivism rates, operationally defined as any offense resulting in probation or a jail sentence, were experienced by the halfway house group (30 percent) and the control group (32 percent). There was not a statistically significant difference.[28]

In the second experimental design study, drug addicts, chronic alcoholics, active homosexuals, and violently assaultive offenders were excluded. Follow-ups were conducted at three-, nine- and 18-month intervals. For the experimental group (the halfway house group) 40 percent were rated as "failures," 45 percent were rated as "successes" (operationalized as no criminal behavior, control of drinking and self-supporting) and 15 percent were rated as "partial successes." For the control group, 40 percent were rated as "failures," 40 percent were rated as "successes," and 21 percent were rated as "partial successes." The differences between the experimental and control groups were not statistically significant.[29]

Of the seventeen quasi-experimental design studies, eleven indicated that the post-program recidivism rates or criminal behavior assessments of ex-halfway house residents were less than those of the comparison group which was usually comprised of institutional parolees. However, the differences between the halfway house and comparison groups were statistically significant in only three of these studies. There was no statistically significant difference in recidivism rates between halfway house and comparison groups in five of the 17 studies. Lastly, one study indicated that ex-halfway house residents had higher recidivism rates than probation and parole comparison groups. However, it was not possible to conclude that one program was superior to another because differences between groups could not be adequately controlled.[30]

A review of 16 non-experimental design studies indicated that recidivism rates for halfway house residents ranged from zero to 43 percent. The mean recidivism rate specified in the non-experimental studies was 20 percent. Caution should be exercised in comparing these figures since definitions of recidivism varied among the studies as did the follow-up study periods.[31]

On the basis of their review of the aforementioned evaluative studies, Carlson and Seiter concluded that:

> ...from these evaluations, it appears that community residential programs are as effective as their institutional alternatives, and there is fairly conclusive evidence that halfway houses are more effective than the traditional prison-parole cycle.[32]

Beha also conducted a fairly extensive review of those studies focusing on the effect of halfway houses on recidivism. However, he appears to be less convinced of their effect on recidivism. He concludes:

> Despite occasional indications of success, reports currently available on halfway houses generally fail to demonstrate the value of that experience in deterring subsequent criminal behavior.[33]

Martinson and Wilks have also addressed the issue of the effectiveness of halfway houses. They concluded that the mean recidivism rate for adults for partial physical custody in halfway houses is higher (24.82 percent) than imprisonment plus traditional parole (22.66 percent). In the case of juveniles, however, the mean recidivism rate for partial physical custody in a halfway house or group home following imprisonment is lower (28.84 percent) than training school plus traditional parole (30.08 percent)[34]

Lastly, a review of completed halfway house evaluations conducted by Sullivan, Seigel and Clear suggests that halfway houses are no more effective in reducing recidivism than other types of community supervision programs.[35]

The preceding discussion regarding the effectiveness of halfway houses points to the need for ongoing large-scale studies of halfway house programs.

Juvenile Program Application

McCartt and Mangogna note that halfway houses, or group homes as they are frequently called, are assuming an increasingly prominent role in the management and treatment of delinquents and dependent neglected children whose removal from their homes may be considered necessary or desirable for either a short-term or long-term basis.[36] Halfway houses for juveniles provide the court of jurisdiction with a much needed alternative to the incarceration of troubled youths.

Halfway houses for juveniles may be utilized as: (1) a viable alternative to incarceration of youths in detention facilities or training schools, which are oftentimes inadequately equipped to meet their special needs, or for the child who has not responded satisfactorily to probation and therefore may require a more intensive supervision than probation provides but who still does not require incarceration in the traditional institutional setting; (2) an alternative to institutionalization for the dependent neglected child whose behavior, which is usually minor in nature, is the product of an inadequate home experience; or (3) as a "halfway-out" facility for juveniles who have been incarcerated and do not have a suitable home plan.

Halfway houses for juveniles normally provide a supervised, structured homelike environment for troubled youths in which an attempt is undertaken to assist them in resolving individual, family and community social adjustment problems through the provision of concentrated supportive services. The juveniles usually attend school on a full-time basis or attend school and are employed and participate in community activities. Halfway houses for juveniles usually are designed for six to ten residents and are characterized by a high ratio of trained staff to clients.

Illustrative of this type of juvenile program is Residential Homes for Boys, Inc., a nonprofit corporation that operates two licensed group homes, Maple House and Lorraine House, in Wichita, Kansas. The purpose of Residential Homes for Boys, Inc., is to provide a comprehensive, community-based program for court adjudicated youths, 14 to 18 year old males, in order to prevent their unnecessary institutionalization. More specifically, it attempts to help youth with problem behavior patterns to recognize and make use of more positive behaviors. Youths served are those whose attitudes, development and functioning are identified to be inadequate for successful family living. Generally, this is determined by delinquent and pre-delinquent behavior, uncontrollable behavior such as runaways and chronic truancy or significant lack of social skills. Most often the above listed behaviors are accompanied by continual denial of responsibility for behavior and refusal to comply with requests of authority figures. The program does serve youth who have shown evidence of significant drug use with some serious delinquent background who have need of special educational programs and whose relationships with authority figures are very poor.

Maple House (capacity of ten) and Lorraine House (capacity of eight) provide structured, homelike environments for their residents. Residential Homes for Boys, Inc., provides the following services to its program clients: daily living services—room and board, transportation and academic advisement/supervision; situational training—personal hygiene, health care, consumer education, communication skills and home management; situational counseling; recreation; individual treatment planning; counseling services—individual and group counseling; educational and tutorial services—school/work supervision; and family services.[37]

Up Close And Personal

Jim Williams is a 29-year-old male from a small mid-western town of approximately 15,000 people. Jim claims to have grown up on the "wrong side of the tracks" in this community. Jim was born with a congenital heart problem which prevented him from going to community schools and participating in sports with his peers. He received his education at home through tutors and received a GED. Jim started drinking at approximately the age of 14. He began drinking to "become part of the group," something which his heart problem had prevented him from doing. He "hung around" with older kids and continued to drink heavily. He developed a lengthy juvenile record, usually for drinking.

However, this normally just resulted in fines. He claims that he was always let off easily because of his heart problem. Jim's drinking progressed and he also began to use drugs heavily. When he was 17 he started to write bad checks to support his alcohol and drug habits. About a year later he got caught for issuing bad checks. His first conviction resulted in probation. However, he continued to write bad checks and eventually spent nine months in the county jail. After his release from jail Jim continued to drink and use drugs. In fact, he developed what he called "one hell of a habit" on opium. He was employed in construction work, a job he really shouldn't have taken due to his heart problem. When the money he made from work was no longer sufficient to support his habit he started to "bounce" checks again and illegally use credit cards. He was convicted and received a sentence of from one to five years. However, he was granted probation and stayed in his hometown. He said this was a bad mistake because people don't let you forget. Jim maintains that nobody really cared about him and his problems. He never received any treatment for his alcoholism or drug addiction. One time he went to his scheduled meeting with his probation officer "crocked." However, his probation officer just made him fill out his report and said "see you later." Jim had heart surgery and was put on a supplemental security income of $165 per month. However, he had married and now had a wife and a son and the supplemental security income was simply insufficient to pay the rent, food bills and utility bills. Jim asserts that no state agencies would give him any kind of appropriate vocational training because they said he wasn't deserving due to his criminal record. Besides his own personal problems, Jim was trying to support his mother, who was a double amputee, and his son who was very ill and required costly medicine. Jim got a job and didn't report it. In March, 1980, Jim went to the largest city of his state with some of his friends. He started drinking and got very ill. He was taken to a local hospital. The staff discovered his serious drinking problem and he received beneficial treatment at the hospital's alcohol treatment unit. In fact, Jim claims the program had a tremendous impact upon his drinking behavior. Shortly thereafter, Jim was convicted for the false statements he had made to Social Security. He was given a sentence of one year at a state correctional institution located about 80 miles from his home. After serving two months of his sentence, he was returned to court because the institution couldn't provide the necessary medical care for him. The court, given his medical problem, placed him on probation as an alternative to continued incarceration. As a condition of his probation, he was placed in a halfway house in the state's largest city. This city was approximately 25 miles from his hometown. Placement in a halfway house enabled him to remain under more intensive supervision than normal probation and receive required medical services, such as biweekly blood tests, at one of the community's hospitals.

QUESTION: What was your experience like in prison?

ANSWER: In prison your life can be sold for a pack of cigarettes. You are your only friend. You don't dare show any emotion to anyone. For example, while I was there a guy's dad died. When he cried the other inmates made fun of him. When he objected they jumped him. The institution was segregated racially—whites stuck together with whites, blacks with blacks, and chicanos with chicanos. Guards accepted stuff for granting favors to inmates. Money slipped to guards could get you good food or a light work detail. Prison is a "buy off" system. You can even buy someone's life. In prison you don't take any shit off anyone or you'll be someone's old lady. Homosexuality is commonplace. The guards just turn their backs. You better believe it! Prison sure didn't help; it only made things worse.

QUESTION: How long have you been at the halfway house?

ANSWER: About six weeks.

QUESTION: How long must you stay here?

ANSWER: That depends on the discretion of the court. I have to stay at the halfway house for at least four months. However, it could be longer. It all depends on my ability to stay off alcohol and drugs and being able to handle society because I have hard feelings about society.

QUESTION: Why do you have hard feelings toward society?

ANSWER: Because I'm always made to feel that I'm not really part of the group. People just refuse to accept me as a person because of my physical handicap (heart condition), the fact that I've been an alcoholic and narcotics addict and now that I have a criminal record. Society just won't let you forget these things.

QUESTION: Do you think you needed to be placed in a halfway house?

ANSWER: Yes! I need help to deal with my problems and my hard feelings toward society. It also helps to be with other people who have done "time." Your problems are also their problems. When you experience problems you have the halfway house to come back to—a place where you can feel safe, a place where you can get help. If you have a problem, you have someone to talk to. The staff will listen to you. They want to work with you and want you to make it; they just don't condemn you. This produces trust in some people. The offenders help too. We are a close-knit family. If someone needs help, they get it. If you were to ask offenders why they do crime again after release from prison, most of them would give you an answer that would boil down to: "After I got out of prison I didn't receive any support from anyone. Nobody cared about what happened to me." If you want help, it's here. The staff will do what they can for you. However, you've got to make it yourself. You can make it rough or easy on yourself.

QUESTION: What types of services have you received at the halfway house to help you become reestablished in the community?

ANSWER: They are trying to get me into vocational school to acquire a worthwhile skill, realizing my physical disability (heart condition). Nobody ever tried to do this for me before. Acquiring a marketable job skill is important in getting back into society. If you don't get one you will most likely wind up "doing time" again. At the present time, they are arranging for me to take some vocational tests to determine what I would be good at. They teach you how to deal with problems. They know you are going to have problems—they teach you how to deal with them. They get you used to dealing with life. They make you open a savings account, teach you how to get an apartment, instruct you how to budget your money and provide you with other worthwhile skills for everyday living. They get you used to getting up, going to work, taking care of your room—things you'll have to do on your own. They also give you counseling to help you deal with day-to-day problems. I receive individual counseling at least once a week, or more, if needed. I tell the staff counselor what's going on. If I have any problems he works with me on resolving them. He helps me work them out. Due to the nature of my problems, the staff is also in the process of arranging to get me some additional professional psychological help through a mental health center in the community. I have a considerable amount of anger built up inside me for people on the outside in general. They find out that I've got a physical disability, a criminal record and past history of alcoholism and drug addiction and they hold it against you. They don't want you and they don't want you to succeed. I don't know how to safely release this anger. I have to learn how to or I know I'll wind up in trouble again. Also, periodically the staff takes us to events in the community. Sometimes they get us free tickets for such things as rodeos or the Ice Capades which are held at the Civic Center.

QUESTION: Do you have a job in the community?

ANSWER: Yes.

QUESTION: What do you do? How much do you get paid?

ANSWER: I work as a cook at the county courthouse. I cook for prisoners as well as for one of the cafeterias located there. I get paid $4.00 per hour but it's not worth it. I not only cook the food for the prisoners, I also have to serve it to them. They're always cussing at you. I don't look forward to it.

QUESTION: Did the halfway house assist you in getting this job?

ANSWER: I really got it on my own. I found out about it through the local employment office. However, the staff directed me to the appropriate places to check for jobs, including the employment office.

QUESTION: Are you going to school at the present time?

ANSWER: No, not right now. However, what I really want to be is an alcoholism and substance abuse counselor. Recently I went to the alcohol treatment unit at the hospital where I have received help in the past, and talked with the doctor in charge of the program and some of the counselors about the prospects of me becoming a counselor. They told me that, based upon their experiences with me, they thought that I would make a good one. They suggested that I acquire some additional training and take some counseling and psychology courses at the university. So, I'm thinking about enrolling in some of those classes.

QUESTION: What is your typical day like here at the halfway house?

ANSWER: I go to work at the courthouse at 3:00 a.m. and work until 12:30 p.m..When I get back to the halfway house things are pretty quiet because most of the other residents are either at work or at school. Usually, I'm here just with one other guy and the staff. I usually have house chores to do like vacuuming or cleaning the bathroom. I might watch my portable television or read for awhile. At 5:30 p.m. I eat supper at the house and talk to the rest of the residents who are coming back in. After supper I may watch some more television or, if I'm not on restrictions, I may walk downtown and look around. Normally I go to bed around 8:00 p.m. except when I go downtown to A.A. (Alcoholics Anonymous) or N.A. (Narcotics Anonymous) meetings.

QUESTION: Do you pay for your own room and board here at the halfway house?

ANSWER: Yes. I pay $21.00 per week. That's really reasonable for having a place to live and having good meals to eat.

QUESTION: In your opinion, is there anything which could be done to improve this halfway house?

ANSWER: First of all, I have a positive feeling about the halfway house. As I said before, the staff wants to work with you; they want you to make it. They give you help, if you need it. However, some things could be done to improve this halfway house. For one thing, we need more counselors— we've only got one! What we need very badly is an alcohol/drug counselor. Most everyone here has the need for such as person. I would also like to see the A.A. and N.A. people get more involved here at the house. Presently, we have to go to them. It would be much easier for most of the residents if they could come here. We also need more recreational equipment at the house. Most of the equipment we have is broken down. We need something like a pool table or a ping pong table. We could also use a better selection of reading materials. At the present time we do not have any chaplain service at the house. I know that many of the residents would like to have a chaplain to talk to.

QUESTION: Do you have a family to go back to after your release from the halfway house?

ANSWER: No.

QUESTION: What about your wife and son?

ANSWER: My wife and son were killed in an automobile wreck while I was in prison. They were hit by a drunken driver—a 16-year-old drunk (visibly shaken).

QUESTION: Do you have any other family to turn to for support?

ANSWER: No. I am one of eight children. However, I am the only surviving child. My youngest brother died at age 12, three

of my brothers were killed in the Korean War, two of my
brothers were killed in the Vietnam War and my sister was
killed in a car wreck.

QUESTION: With all of the traumatic experiences you have had,
do you think you will succeed when you leave the halfway
house? Will you go straight?

ANSWER: Yes. This time I am getting the help I need! I am
willing to work hard to make it. When I leave I will get an
affordable apartment and get some schooling. I want to
make it. If something goes wrong, I can't blame anyone.
I've got to make it. If I do experience some trouble I've got
the A.A. or N.A. program to go to for help. I'll also have a
probation/parole officer.

Summary

Generally, a correctional halfway house may be defined as a transitional
community-based residential facility, either publicly or privately
operated, that is designed to facilitate the offender's difficult transition
from incarceration to community living or to serve as an alternative to
incarceration. Halfway houses attempt to reintegrate their clients into
community living through the provision of concentrated supportive
services, such as a home, assistance in vocational counseling/training and
finding employment, financial support, educational opportunities,
psychological and emotional support/counseling, community activities
and recreational opportunities, referral services and a supportive
environment.

The extensive development and utilization of halfway houses for
offenders is a relatively recent phenomenon. However, the halfway house
concept and its adaptation and application to the field of corrections is not
new, having originated in England and Ireland in the 1800's. Shortly
thereafter, the halfway house concept for offenders spread to the United
States. Massachusetts (1864), New York (1845) and Pennsylvania (1889)
were the first states to establish such facilities. Despite the opposition,
hostility and apathy encountered by these and other early programs, the
halfway house concept spread. However, the halfway house movement
did not experience much growth until the 1950's. The beginning of this
"national halfway house movement" is generally attributed to a growing
dissatisfaction with the ineffectiveness of institutional corrections as an
instrument of rehabilitation (as evidenced by high recidivism rates), an
appreciation of the problems confronting the offender released from
prison and a recognition of the need to provide offenders released from

correctional institutions with essential supportive services to assist them in making the difficult transition from institutional to community living. Additional impetus and legitimation for the national halfway house movement occurred in the 1960's through the occurrence of several key events, including the recommendation of the utilization of halfway houses by Robert Kennedy, then Attorney General of the United States, and the passage of the Omnibus Crime Control and Safe Streets Act by Congress which among other things established the Law Enforcement Assistance Administration. The decade of the 1970's witnessed the proliferation of halfway houses.

Halfway houses provide their clients with a body of core supporitve services to afford them more advantages and opportunities in establishing themselves successfully in the community. Normally, these services include: a home, assistance in vocational counseling/training and finding employment, financial support, educational opportunities, psychological and emotional support/counseling, community activities and recreational opportunities, referral services and a supportive environment.

The viable operation of a halfway house is dependent upon several key administrative and procedural factors. Funding, organizational structure and staffing pattern are among the most important of these factors. Funding is a crucial function in the operation of a halfway house, whether it is privately or publicly operated. In fact, the ultimate success or failure experienced by the halfway house may well be related to the manner in which the administrator handles funding issues. The organizational structure/staffing pattern for most privately operated halfway houses usually is headed by a board of directors which constitutes the halfway house's principal executive body. Next in order in the formal organizational hierarchy is an executive director who operates under the general direction of the program's board of directors. Essentially, the executive director serves as the chief operations executive of the halfway house. Next in the halfway house formal organizational hierarchy, under the direction of the executive director, is the operating staff of the halfway house. The house staff for the halfway house with a capacity of 25 clients normally consists of a house director, who is responsible for actually administering house operations on a day-to-day basis, a counselor, who constitutes the principal treatment component of the staff, a secretary-bookkeeper and a cook-housekeeper. Larger houses are usually characterized by an even greater division of labor.

There are a number of perennial problems involved in the establishment and operation of halfway houses. Among the most common types of problems are: community acceptance/hostility from the public, funding, fluctuations in resident population, attracting a staff with the appropriate qualifications and high staff turnover.

One of the justifications presented for the greater utilization of halfway houses is economic savings. However, a review of available findings reveals inconsistent conclusions and casts at least some doubts about the cost-saving potential of halfway houses. Carlson and Seiter, for example, concluded that halfway houses usually operate at a lower daily cost than that of an institution but at a higher daily cost than parole and probation. However, other researchers, like Beha, remain unconvinced of their cost-saving potential.

Several factors make it difficult to assess the effectiveness of halfway houses. First, despite the proliferation of halfway house programs, there is a paucity of evaluative research conducted on such programs. Second, much of the research which has been conducted is of questionable validity judged by social science standards. Third, due to the heterogeneity of halfway houses, the diversity of research designs employed and the variety of definitions of outcomes utilized, it is extremely difficult to generalize from the results of available studies. Fourth, the findings reported are mixed and inconclusive, thus preventing the declaration of a final verdict on the effectiveness of halfway houses. A review of the findings of halfway house evaluations led Carlson and Seiter to conclude that "community residential programs are as effective as their institutional alternatives, and there is fairly conclusive evidence that halfway houses are more effective than the traditional prison-parole cycle."[38] However, a fairly extensive review of those studies focusing on the effect of halfway houses on recidivism by Beha led them to conclude that: "Despite occasional indications of success, reports currently available on halfway houses generally fail to demonstrate the value of that experience in deterring subsequent criminal behavior."[39]

Notes

1. Richard J. Clendenen, John R. Ellingston, and Ronald J. Severson, "Project Newgate: The First Five Years," *Crime and Delinquency*, Volume 25 (January, 1979), p. 59.
2. Norman F. Chamberlain, "Halfway Houses for Non-Dangerous Offenders," *Vital Issues*, Volume 26, Number 6 (February, 1977), p.3.
3. Harry E. Allen, Eric W. Carlson, Evalyn C. Parks, and Richard P. Seiter, *Halfway Houses* (Washington, D.C.: Office of Development, Testing, and Dissemination, National Institute of Law Enforcement and Criminal Justice, U.S. Department of Justice, November, 1978), p.5.
4. Ibid., p. 11.
5. Ibid.
6. Ibid.
7. See: Richard P. Seiter, et al., *Residential Inmate Aftercare: The State of the Art*—Supplement A—Survey of Residential Inmate Aftercare Facilities. National Evaluation Program Phase I (Columbus, Ohio: Ohio State University, Program for the Study of Crime and Delinquency, 1976).

8. Kellogg Foundation and United Way, *Functions and Responsibilities of Board and Staff in Non-Profit Organizations* (Alexandria, Virginia: National Academy for Voluntarism, United Way of America, 1980), p. 53.

9. Ibid., p. 40.

10. John M. McCartt and Thomas J. Mangogna, *Guidelines and Standards for Halfway Houses and Community Treatment Centers* (Washington, D.C.: U.S. Government Printing Office, May 1973), pp. 183-184.

11. Ibid., pp. 174-208.

12. Yitzhak Bakal, *Closing Correctional Institutions* (Lexington, Massachusetts: D.C. Heath and Co., 1974), p. 67.

13. E. Eugene Miller, "The Halfway House: Correctional Decompression of the Offender," in *Corrections in the Community*, edited by E. Eugene Miller and M. Robert Montilla (Reston, Virginia: Reston Publishing Company, 1977), p. 223.

14. Richard L. Rachin, "So You Want To Open a Halfway House," *Federal Probation*, Volume 36, Number 1 (March, 1972), p. 34.

15. See: Richard P. Seiter, et al., *Residential Inmate Aftercare: The State of the Art*—Supplement A—Survey of Residential Inmate Aftercare Facilities. National Evaluation Program Phase I (Columbus, Ohio: Ohio State University, Program for the Study of Crime and Delinquency, 1976).

16. Ibid.

17. Ibid.

18. Ibid.

19. Joint Commission on Correctional Manpower and Training, *Perspectives on Correctional Manpower and Training* (College Park, Maryland: American Correctional Association, 1970), p. 92.

20. Allen, Carlson, Parks and Seiter, *Halfway Houses*, p. 17.

21. Donald J. Thalheimer, *Cost Analysis of Correctional Standards: Halfway Houses*, Volume I, prepared for the American Bar Association under a grant awarded by the National Institute of Law Enforcement and Criminal Justice, Law Enforcement Assistance Administration, U.S. Department of Justice, U.S. Government Printing Office, Washington, D.C. (November, 1975), p.9.

22. Perry Johnson, "Halfway House Program 'A Truly Bright Spot' in State Adult Correctional System," *Corrections Digest*, February 24, 1978, p. 10.

23. Haralson Gordon, "Ohio's Halfway Houses Show Phenomenal Growth," *American Journal of Corrections*, March-April, 1977, p. 18.

24. Eric W. Carlson and Richard P. Seiter, "Residential Inmate Aftercare: The State of the Art," *Offender Rehabilitation*, Volume 1, Number 4 (Summer 1977), p. 389.

25. Miller, "The Halfway House: Correctional Decompression of the Offender," pp. 222-223.

26. James A. Beha, II, "Halfway Houses in Adult Corrections: The Law, Practice, and Results," *Criminal Law Bulletin*, Volume 11, Number 4 (July-August, 1975), p. 457.

27. Carlson and Seiter, "Residential Inmate Aftercare," pp. 387-389.

28. Ibid., p. 388.

29. Ibid.

30. Ibid.

31. Ibid.
32. Ibid., pp. 388-389.
33. Beha, "Halfway Houses in Adult Corrections," p.473.
34. Robert Martinson and Judith Wilks, *Knowledge in Criminal Justice Planning, A Preliminary Report* (New York: The Center for Knowledge in Criminal Justice Planning, October, 1976), pp. 2-4.
35. Dennis C. Sullivan, Larry J. Seigel, and Todd Clear, "The Halfway House, Ten Years Later: Reappraisal of Correctional Innovation," *Canadian Journal of Criminology and Corrections*, Volume 16 (April, 1974), pp. 188-197.
36. McCartt and Mangogna, *Guidelines and Standards for Halfway Houses*, pp. 25-26.
37. Information obtained from interview with Michael Lawson, Agency Administrator, Residential Homes for Boys, Inc., April 27, 1981.
38. Carlson and Seiter, "Residential Inmate Aftercare," pp. 388-389.
39. Beha, "Halfway Houses in Adult Corrections," p. 473.

Chapter 9
Program Implementation

There are several critical managerial and organizational issues that must be addressed in establishing and operating an effective and efficient community-based correctional program. The following are among the most important of these issues which must be carefully and skillfully addressed to maximize the chances for ultimate program success: the establishment of program goals and objectives, the selection of a program target population or clientele, the identification and solicitation of funding sources, the determination of the most appropriate strategy for introducing a program into the community, the selection of the appropriate type of community in which to situate a program, the selection of a specific program site and name, the enlistment of community support for the program and the neutralization of community resistance, the utilization and coordination of existent community resources and staffing considerations.*

Planning and Assessing
Community-Based Programs

Planning is a process of outlining the steps or actions that must be accomplished in order to reach a specific goal. The steps in the planning process, depending on the source, can be as few in number as four or as many as nine. Generally speaking, the process begins by identifying the goals, exploring the alternatives with their natural consequences, implementing the program and evaluating the results. The evaluation stage becomes a continuous flow of information about the successes or failures that serves as feedback and begins the process of planning and changing to adapt to the new situation.

---

*Several detailed community-based program models have been developed. For example, the Office of Development, Testing and Dissemination of the National Institute of Law Enforcement and Criminal Justice, U.S. Department of Justice, has prepared an excellent program model which deals extensively with these issues as they relate to halfway houses. Similarly, the U.S. Department of Justice, Law Enforcement Assistance Administration, Technical Assistance Division, has prepared an excellent technical assistance publication concerning the guidelines and standards for halfway houses and community treatment centers. These references are listed in the "Resources" section at the end of this chapter.

Planning may be as simple as a grocery list of items needed for the preparation for the family's meals. Or, planning may be as complex as some of the defense projects or programs to land men on the moon. For these complex plans, a critical path analysis might be required. A critical path analysis uses networks which clarify the relationship of each task to another task for determining the length of time needed to complete one part of the project before moving on to the next. For example, before ex-offenders can move into a halfway house, a house must be selected and renovated for that purpose. Before that can occur, monies have to be available and legislators have to give necessary permission by enacting specific legislation. Therefore, it becomes necessary in the planning stage to give priorities to tasks. Without getting the student lost in the vocabulary of planning and planning charts, it is important to realize that the purpose of planning is to identify the risks involved in each opportunity and to relate these opportunities and risks to the basic goals of an organization. As with classifying horses at the race track as favorites, possible winners and long shots, planners dealing with community-based programs can also speculate on their risks.

Assessment is part of the cyclical process of administration. A manager of an agency should know where he/she is, what he/she is expected to be doing, how it is to be done and why. Assessment is the process of evaluating how well an agency met those planned goals. In the past, many programs used offenders' performance, such as ratio of graduates to drop-outs and offense data, as a measure of effectiveness and assessment. Unfortunately, many programs do not have enough control over all of the variables in a person's life to claim that kind of success. Neither should the program be stuck with all the blame when individuals are viewed as having failed. Thus, accountability to the funding agency is now done in more realistic terms, such as the number of offenders admitted, number of offenders seen, number of referrals made, etc.

The point is that planning, implementing that plan and evaluating that plan is a continuous, circular process. Assessment is no longer viewed as if it were the last chapter in a mystery story—something to only be done at the very last to see whether the butler really did kill the victim. Assessment needs to be built into the planning so that a manager can always check on what is happening.

Type of Community

Before replicating or duplicating a pre-existing "exemplary project" (a title given to programs funded by the government which are proven effective by governmental standards and are deemed worthy to be reproduced elsewhere) in your community, one needs to assess the type of community. Pettibone has identified the following three different kinds of geographic areas which have different needs, strengths and weaknesses in regards to operationalization of community-based programs: (1) affluent suburban areas; (2) rural small town areas; and (3) inner city urban areas.[1] Affluent suburban communities are excellent supportive settings for innovative treatment programming of all kinds for the development of small community-based correctional centers and alternatives to incarceration. This is due in large part to the community persons who are educated, sophisticated and have a strong interest in public affairs. These geographic areas of "bedroom" suburbs of urban centers usually have many universities in the area with a number of progressive, public-spirited citizen groups interested in correctional problems and social reform. The local criminal justice systems—police, courts, corrections—are usually comparatively well financed, functionally adequate and liberal in outlook.

Rural small town areas, however, seem to foster only traditional parole and probation casework and reintegration programs. Many of these geographic areas possess a conservative and individualistic social philosophy, a philosophy that fits the agricultural, fishing and basic service occupations. Family cohensiveness in such areas tends to be comparatively strong. Thus, programs that would utilize the "traditional family strength and mutual support between relatives in such areas presents real opportunities for effective reintegration."[2] Needless to say, the local government backing for elaborate treatment programming is usually weak and criminal justice systems tend to be minimally staffed, thinly spread and conservative in orientation.

The last geographic area to be discussed is the inner-city urban area wherein the problems far exceed the resources. "Community resources available for offender treatment are elaborately proliferated and easily identified but the quality of services available is not equal to the need. Everything is in short supply."[3] In this heterogeneous population, there are more differences between groups. That means that some of the groups possess extremely conservative attitudes towards convicted offenders while a predominately black neighborhood might be more liberal. The reality is that few correctional treatment approaches are popular or even acceptable to all local communities and citizens within our cities. These statements of reality are not meant to scare you; they are meant to acquaint you with the challenge.

Other factors that might be of assistance in analyzing a community are the following:

1. remoteness from other large urban concentrations which inhibit people released from confinement from disappearing
2. population stability—few changes in size or demographic composition from year to year may be reflective of the prospects of the development of a sense of community

3. type and kind of support from local newspapers, television stations and leading businessmen
4. number and types of active, well supported social service agencies
5. rate and kinds of unemployment—will there be jobs for the clients of your program?

In summarizing, when analyzing any community, look at its geographic area and demographic factors so that you are better able to plan for a more successful community-based program. Since the offender population is far from homogeneous, correctional persons planning programs in the community need not look for treatment programs that are equally applicable nor that are meeting the needs of all offenders in all geographic areas. Different approaches will be called for. Therefore, these concerns about selecting a community are crucial in this planning stage.

Needs Assessment, Goal Setting and Funding

These two tasks, i.e., assessment of need and the setting of goals and objectives, are possibly the most important preoperation tasks. Once the goals of a program are established, then administrators can determine the type of management style and funding necessary to accomplish those goals.

Simplifying funding matters, community-based operations may be primarily private or public agencies. A public facility is operated and funded by a federal, state, county or municipal agency whereas a private program receives funds from a private profit or nonprofit organization. The importance of the funding source in this discussion is the fact that either source places limitations and restrictions upon the program. It is not the intention to say that one type of funding is more preferred than another. Rather, in establishing a program, one needs to be aware of the consequences of that particular funding approach.

When the funds are given to an agency, those monies are given for specific programs or purposes. In this manner then, budgets are a special form of planning. Just as a person takes his or her specific income and plans and decides which specific items need to be paid and when, so does an agency. When an agency spends its money, its transactions are written on lines. On each line, a specific item is listed, e.g., rent, staff salaries, retirement, sick leave, utilities. This type of budget is called "line-item." When an agency chooses to list services or functions instead of items, the budget is called "line-function."

Budgets are an important tool in determining what services were received for the specific amount of money. Waste can be eliminated.

Perhaps one of the most acclaimed and newest ways of working with the two types of budgeting previously discussed is zero-base budget (ZBB). Used as a management tool, ZBB identifies certain levels of services at specific costs. The lowest budget for the next year would be to reduce services such that only 80 percent of the current levels of service would be provided for the future. The next level would be where an agency receives monies at 100 percent of current levels of service so that present activities could be continued in the future. If the agency wants to add a new dimension to their programs, such as psychological counseling, then in the future year the agency would have to be funded for more than 100 percent of current levels of service. In this manner then, funding agencies can determine if a specific program or agency should be allowed to exist. As an agency complies with the demands of budgeting through data collection and reporting, accountability can be controlled. Thus, planning, budgeting and evaluation are intrical parts of a continuous and important cycle.

In a needs assessment, planners identify a target population and then indicate the potential number of clients within that target population who may be available for referral to a particular program. So, as you establish a "need group," you are also determining the types of programs the potential clients may find useful. For example, types of programs offered by the halfway house concept can be broadly identified as intervention or supportive. Intervention strategies involve a process of diagnosis, classification and treatment by specialized, professional personnel. Supportive programs usually identify available resources in the community to assist in meeting the needs of residents. In reality, most programs fall at some point along a continuum of intervention/supportive. Likewise, with public/private funding, most programs fall between those ideal types. What becomes important is the fact that the nature of the program and who can be its clientele are determined in large measure upon whether the program is primarily a public supportive, a public intervention, a private supportive or a private intervention-oriented program.

In determining and selecting a target population, such demographic factors as age and sex should be considered. Prior residency is also an important factor. Only those offenders who were prior residents of a particular community or those who are willing to relocate in that vicinity should be identified. Length of sentence is another factor if you want the participants' sentencing period to fit the time frame of your program. Persons who have a minimum sentence of less than 90 days would not be a target population for a program that envisions a six month residency. Finally, the nature of the offender and his or her ability to be drug or alcohol free needs to be considered. That does not mean that all drug addicted or alcoholic offenders are omitted from programs. They may, in fact, be admitted but only if the program has adequate trained staff to help these individuals cope with these specific problem areas. Dangerous, hostile and emotionally disturbed offenders are usually excluded from such minimum security community-based programs for several reasons, i.e., undue burden on the staff, safety of the other participants, the community and/or the existence of the program.

Along with an assessment of the needs, one must conceptualize and articulate the goals, the subgoals and how the basic objectives will accomplish the aspired goal. By stating the goals and objectives, you will also be determining the content of the program and the criteria by which the performance of the program can be measured. For example, the main goal of a program might be "to assist in the reintegration of ex-offenders." A subgoal of that main goal might be to provide programs and treatment services aimed at reducing disadvantages and problems of returning to the community after a period of incarceration. Then, in a simplistic version, an objective to meet a subgoal might be to have an employment program. You should be able to state your reasons for your belief that certain activities will lead to the accomplishment of the goal.

Goal Setting Strategies

The process of establishing goals and objectives can be initiated by two sources: (1) individual and (2) committee.

The individual initiative method of goal setting means that all decisions are referred to one person who had determined the goals and objectives of the program and retains the power for such execution of the program. If the person who has both power and accountability for the program shares with the staff through participant management, then realistic and measurable goals and objectives are usually annunciated. If the decisionmaker, however, takes on an authoritarian management style, staff may lack a strong commitment to accomplish goals and objectives. The staff, feeling left out from the process of setting goals, may even successfully sabotage the program.

The committee planning approach, although sometimes lengthy and involved, includes a group of individuals who work together, read, consult with experts and then develop goals and objectives. The most ideal situation would be to have a committee comprised of representatives from the various groups concerned, i.e., staff of the opertions, department of corrections and community persons. Involving community leaders in the planning stages can only help to establish a positive program image.

Strategies for Entering the Community

Some programs come into a community with an extremely low profile. To avoid difficulties, some programs have moved into an area with little assistance and foreknowledge on the part of the residents. Some administrators realize that programs initiated "in the still of the night" are long shots. Therefore, more attention is given to selection of the site, of the program name and the program content.

Selection of a Site

As mentioned earlier, different geographic areas have different potential for different programs. The reason for that is the "community attitude." Some community persons favor programs for ex-offenders but not in their neighborhood. You have to realize that you are dealing with people's unwarranted fears, perhaps, but if those fears are real to those persons, they can and will organize to force your program to either close or relocate even before opening at a selected site. Since the type of neighborhood is such an important issue, program managers should carefully consider the demographic and physical attributes of any neighborhood. That means choosing a location for your purpose that meets local zoning regulations, health and safety regulations. Structural concerns, such as the physical condition of the house, occupancy limitations, and inability to maintain residential character of a community might, indeed, be legitimate concerns about the suitability of the site.

Other considerations for a site might include accessibility of public transportation so that program residents can travel to and from work, and the safety and comfort of the program participants. Residents of a program should be located in a site where they can go and come and mix with the neighborhood. For the safety of the residents, the site should not be in a disorganized or deteriorating community. When this process has been stabilized or reversed, such as in areas of commercial-residential areas or locations adjoining light industrial sections, then you may have found the ideal site. The literature shows that successful programs have emerged from every conceivable type of facility, from older houses and hotels to renting the fourth floor of the YMCA. So, it is not just the location but also the physical facility and its adequacy for the programmatic activities that also counts.

Location and site selection are not easy issues to deal with. There seems to be no tried principle that works for all programs. All that can be said is that one has to consider many issues and anticipate the manifest consequences. In Massachussets, for example, an extensive study into community resistance to group homes was conducted by investigating which private and public agencies had successes and failures in particular tasks.[4]

Selection of a Program Name

Program names are symbols. As symbols they communicate to both community and clients. Acronyms such as PACT (People and Courts

Together) can identify the program but not threaten or increase the anxiety of potential neighbors. Since the name of the program can be misleading to the public, it might be the factor that helps or breaks the program. "Names such as Burn, Scare, Smack, Blow-up or JD may simply cause more problems with community relations than they are worth."[5]

Harvard researchers, in analyzing the successes and failures in Massachusetts as that state moved to community-based facilities for youth, mentioned the necessity for identifying "the generic label." By that they mean how do you describe your program? Even though community residents referred to the program as a halfway house, preferred labels were group homes, childcare centers, schools or family. "Choice of a label has an effect not only on how the program will be perceived in the community, but also on whether a zoning variance will be required in residential areas."[6]

Presenting Program Content

In *National Evaluation Program—Assessment of Coeducational Corrections*, the authors suggest that an advisory board presents the content of a program by the following procedure: (1) Program operations such as eligibility requirements, assessment of correctional needs; (2) Program resources such as staff, funds and facilities; (3) Environment factors; and (4) Outcome.[7] Since there really is no handbook on how to present your program, you can still gain insight from the previous materials so that you can develop a well-planned, well-articulated program to present to the community for endorsement.

> The importance of this presentation of program content can best be illustrated by the experience in Hebron (a Massachusetts community). As the result of a news leak and because of the name of the program, many residents were ready to organize opposition to the proposed home. At the Taxpayers' Association meeting, convened to discuss the group home proposal, however, the program staff presented a very honest, straightforward appraisal of their program. While they could not guarantee the community's safety, they did present the safeguards built into the program. Most of the participants agreed that the presentation neutralized any further efforts to prevent the establishment of the group residence.[8]

Enlisting Community Support while Neutralizing Community Resistance

Community relations is enlisting community support while at the same time neutralizing community resistance. Meeting individually with community leaders as part of the planning stage is most ideal. By discussing the program and permitting people to air their questions and concerns, you begin to develop a two-way street of communication. Meeting privately and individually permits people to be more honest about their feelings and fears. Those who favor a proposal will not always readily acknowledge this at a large community meeting, so it is best to leave the public meetings till later. Those who do not favor the proposal can privately discuss their misgivings. Knowing the oppositions' rationale or motivation makes it easier on you. You can replace misinformation with accurate information more easily on a one-to-one basis than you can in a large group which may be emotionally charged. Count on the people who favor the program to draw your attention to other interested members in the community who might aid in the organization, planning and adoption of the program proposal.

Two approaches that have been useful in establishing community support have been (1) an advisory council and (2) a board of directors. Both groups contain influential community persons. The advisory council usually has no policymaking powers. Usually their implied task is to develop a feeling of commitment between the community at large and your program. The board of directors usually have policymaking powers and can hire or fire personnel or enter into contracts. The board of directors can be active and called a "working board" or be relatively inactive serving as a rubber stamp for the director of the program.

There really is no "right way" to befriend community persons. Many variables including the personalities of the individuals involved, the setting and the circumstances will determine the appropriate approach to be selected. However, several points can be mentioned: (1) Use personal contact. Until trust is established, the phone should be used only as a temporary conduit between personal contacts; (2) Find ways to reward or reinforce assistance received. Public relations in its essence is the establishment of goodwill; and (3) Educate the public and its representatives. Just because a person occupies a community leadership position does not mean that that person knows all about the task and techniques you want to employ. After you have identified some community supporters, you might invite them to a community breakfast or luncheon to further enlighten them. Later, they might invite you to speak before their social club or organization. Use all these activities as newsworthy items to further educate the public.

Another group that needs your attention is the multiple private and public agencies to whom you will refer ex-offenders. Begin to lay the groundwork for understanding their restrictions and restraints placed upon them. Begin to develop cooperative ventures that lessen the "red tape" and establish trust so that when an emergency occurs in the future, you have someone in a particular agency who will come to the rescue.

Other important groups to contact might be police, leaders of government, planning boards, churches, social groups and neighborhood improvement groups. If school age populations are a target population, then school administrators should also be contacted. This is not meant to be an inclusive list, only a suggestive list of many of the important groups which should be contacted.

Sometimes community groups have been educated and sensitized to a specific problem and their support lies dormant awaiting local action, i.e., the National Council of Jewish Women (NCJW) who became concerned about community-based corrections for juvenile offenders through the 1970 White House Conference on Children. The NCJW established a task force on "Justice for Children." Utilizing the 108 affiliates nationwide, NCJW took surveys, conducted interviews with children, evaluated present systems, held neighborhood meetings to increase receptivity of the group homes within residential areas and published and distributed posters, pamphlets, cards and other publications to further reach the community and educate the public.[9] Similar things can be said about Junior League of Women and YWCA who have throughout the years established task forces in their communities and can be a great asset in reestablishing a viable network for your purposes.

The main thing to remember is that working relationships with people and agencies in the community should be cherished and reinforced. Public relations with community persons is human understanding. The degree to which we can understand the position of others, their power and their concerns, permits us to focus the attention upon the realistic issues and avoid unnecessary conflict. To maintain this relationship means continual contacts plus annual or semiannual open houses so that people can meet the staff and learn of their progress, problems and needs.

Utilization and Coordination of Community Resources

As was previously mentioned, the director of any program needs to become familiar with the referral agencies in the community—those which the program might need for support. New referrals will mean an increase in the work load to all agencies. Some of those agencies will already feel overburdened. Thus, the more the director can minimize the procedures and consider the needs and conditions under which the supportive agency operates, the more a feeling of cooperation will exist.

A list of the criteria, services available and hours of operation for all social services in the community should be made and maintained for the program's use. Community resources are constantly in a state of flux. One agency may lose its federal funding for that special service whereas another agency may gain a program due to a private donation. Moreover, agencies move, acquire new phone numbers and new personnel who need to be enlightened to your cause. Also, agencies may themselves change their focus.

To develop such a comprehensive list, utilize information offices like libraries which maintain active lists of public services. Also note the key persons in responsible positions in those agencies so that you can befriend significant agency persons. Private agencies work closely with other agencies and they, too, can help with the building of resources. Religious groups have also been known to be willing to assist the offender. In fact, some religious groups have personnel identified to assist in such endeavors a˞ a part of their outreach.

By identifying all the community resources, or at least most of them, you will permit a more even distribution of referrals. Sometimes a staff person, when finding a responsive agency, "hoards" the resource and overdoes a good thing. So, a director of a program is looking for long-range, as well as short-range, support from other agencies. If long range support is desired, the director will initiate coordination of activities and simplification of procedures and forms between the community-based program and the agency. The follow-up process to referral agencies can aid the director in modifying the list of agencies as well as determining the effectiveness of particular referrals.

The Role of Community in Community-Based Corrections

Historically speaking, communities have always felt a sense of responsibility for their community's problems. Inherited from the English tithing systems, the early American colonists continued an active involvement in their communities. Granted, sometimes the only method they seemed to employ to alleviate the community problem was banishment or capital punishment; the fact remains that people felt concern. Concern for the futility of the old ways motivated the Quakers in Philadelphia in 1773 to develop their community-based corrections program. Today, we call their endeavors the Walnut Street Jail and the beginning of the American prison system. Yet, at that time, it was a community-based operation wherein the spirit of firmness and friendliness were to aid the reformation of the offender as he/she engaged in hard work and used the silence to contemplate their behavior and seek penitence.[10]

Besides concern for their problems, the early, good-hearted, religiously inspired community persons volunteered their services and visited offenders. As early as 1823 in Philadelphia, an organization known as the Society of Women Friends made it their objective to visit women in the segregated quarters in jails and workhouses.[11] John Augustus, in 1840, volunteered his services to the court in Boston, Massachusetts to help with misdemeanants. Yet, these people were few and far between. Even today, the "do-gooders" are not necessarily evenly distributed in our populations. Furthermore, sometimes even the best intentions of these do-gooders go astray. Then, it becomes important to identify why a society will permit a penitentiary or an insane asylum, for example, to be perpetuated long after the original promise has faded. Thus, this section will look at two aspects of the role of communities: (1) active involvement in devising or creating agencies to work with their own social problems; and (2) enlisting the support of citizens.

Community Involvement

The 1960's challenged the assumptions and generated a national concern with issues of race, poverty, violence and international responsibilities. The "grass roots approach" in solving poverty, such as community action councils, was only part of the increased public concern and acceptance of citizen participation and community programs.

Since the 1920's, research concerning crime and delinquency has continued to show communities the role they play in creating crime and, subsequently, what they might do to alleviate the problems. Sociologists showed how crime was linked more to social factors than to factors in the individual such as "free will" and "rationalism." Their emphasis upon the social factors did not ignore psychological, physical or other individual characteristics but considered them as they occurred in a particular setting. "If the social milieu to a substantial degree causes criminal behavior, the social milieu itself must be attacked and changed."[12]

Assuming more responsibilities for the problems they generate, communities have either developed new programs with new agencies or have used and coordinated existing community service agencies. Many of the programs cited throughout this book are the direct result of these two approaches.

Persons who can be instrumental in establishing these programs have been referred to as "gatekeepers." These individuals are the custodians of access to important social institutions—employers, school administrators and welfare directors. These individuals are not utilized as volunteers but, rather, they are asked to use the power which adheres to their status toward a community effort in corrections. As such, these individuals become social persuaders using their group membership to mobilize resources. "For example, the Washington State Citizen Council of the National Council on Crime and Delinquency (NCCD) became interested in creating employment opportunities for offenders. Because of their prestige they were able to enlist the active help of the governor and the cooperation of some of the largest employers in the state."[13]

Citizen Involvement

The maximum feasible participation concept operationalized in poverty programs of the 1960's has also been utilized in the criminal justice system. Citizenry are again being sought as policymakers, as reformers and deliverers of direct services.

Often at the request of criminal justice officials, lay citizens function in task forces or study groups to advise the government in policy decisions. Recently, these advisory boards include not only "leading citizens" but also representatives from minorities, ex-offenders and other special community interest groups. Sometimes policymaking citizens will emerge through voluntary associations such as state citizen councils on crime and delinquency affiliated with the National Council on Crime and Delinquency—a nongovernmental agency.[14]

> In the past few years, all states have created instrumentalities of one kind or another for developing and administering state plans for utilization of funds from the Law Enforcement Assistance Administration. These agencies have taken a variety of forms, but invariably involve citizen participation, often in concert with professionals from law enforcement, the judiciary and corrections. This involvement represents another model of citizens serving in advisory roles.[15]

Citizen groups have also emerged to act as reformers in response to specific societal situations. For example, in 1972, after the prison riot in Attica, New York, an informal group of persons created an organization to oppose correctional programs. Reform groups have developed out of religious and other social groups as well.

The role citizens are asked to play most often, however, is the one in which they help to deliver direct services. In 1959, Municipal Court Judge Keith J. Leenhouts of Royal Oak, Michigan revived the volunteer movement. The judge, faced with neither pre-sentence report nor probation services, enlisted other concerned citizens to find some alternatives to the needs of the court. The group volunteered their services to the "probationers" of the court. When individuals needed the expertise of a professional, the volunteers sought out professionals who, at reduced costs, rendered their services or joined in the collaborative rehabilitation effort. The one-on-one approach of volunteers with probationers was so successful that Judge Leenhouts was instrumental in the establishment of volunteer programs in over 2,000 locations. In 1972, the Volunteers in Probation (VIP), which had been formalized in 1969, affiliated with the National Council on Crime and Delinquency. Thus, it is known today as VIP-NCCD.

Today, the use of volunteers in corrections—both inside the institution and outside—is massive. According to estimates of the National Information Center on Volunteers, citizen volunteers outnumber professionals four or five to one.[16] Because of this fact, there is substantial material to assist persons desiring to maximize the citizen's involvement, such as research information, organization and management aids, training guides and audiovisual materials. The National Information Center on Volunteers in Courts (Boulder, Colorado), the National Council on Crime and Delinquency (Hackensack, New Jersey) and the Commission on Voluntary Service and Action (Washington, D.C.) are among the organizations that can be consulted for this information.

One criticism on the use of volunteers is contained in a "letter to the editor" to *Federal Probation*. The letter was written in response to an article (December, 1976) in which Florida's Division of Youth Services had begun a volunteer program for status offenders called Volunteer Homes. The idea was to place in volunteer homes individuals who were considered "status offenders" and thereby required temporary detention but were not security risks. The author of the letter, Dennis E. Hoffman, felt that the short run policy impact of the program seemed "laudable" on the surface. Yet, he raised three ideas that merit future attention. First, he argued that by employing volunteerism as a cure-all for all social ills, "energy is diverted and the search for meaningful solutions to minor forms of delinquency is delayed."[17] Secondly, by seeking unpaid services the state literally denies "the poor and unemployed an opportunity for important human service jobs that merit a decent wage."[18] Thirdly, in these cases of the volunteer homes, Hoffman was concerned as to how the labor of caring for these youths might be divided. He felt that in this program, as with most of the programs throughout the United States, most of the free labor would be provided by women.

Hoffman, like many others, is not totally against the use of volunteers. Rather, he advocates what some might call an "ethical use" of volunteers. Furthermore, realizing that volunteers along with agents in the system suffer from "burn out," it is well for communities to seek root causes and mobilize resources and power to effectively deal with these community problems.

Staffing a Community-Based Corrections Program

Legal Considerations

In recruiting and selecting staff for community-based correctional programs, guidelines established by the 1972 Amendment to the Civil Rights Act must be followed. Generally speaking, that means people cannot be discriminated against for employment due to their race, ethnic background, religion, sex and marital status. As *Griggs* v *Duke Power Company* (1972) held, people should be selected for a job based on criteria that evaluate future job performance.[19] The resultant buzz word is "job-related." A person may be asked questions or asked to perform on tests as long as an employer can show that those tests are related to job performance.

In community-based programs, directors are often faced with the challenge of servicing different clientele i.e., males and females. Would a director be in violation of civil rights legislation and therefore subject to law suits if he/she hired a specific number of male staff and a specific number of female staff? There is no case law that specifically addresses this issue. However, there are two rules that are helpful and might be used by a director to justify staffing on a sex dimension. In the 1964 Civil Rights Act, Title 7 said sex cannot be used as a distinction unless it is a bonafide occupational qualification (BFOQ). That BFOQ clause makes it such that men cannot be hired to be employees in women's saunas or rest rooms. Thus, if your operations demanded that a counselor be involved, for example, with female clients in their sleeping quarters, it would be reasonable to assume you could hire only female staff persons to do specific tasks with female offenders. If there were areas of work such as fixing meals, it might we wise to employ both men and women staff persons for that supervision task. Not only would that aid the residents in more realistic role models but it would also save your agency from charges of sex discrimination.

The second legal rule that addresses staffing patterns stems from the 1969 U.S. Court of Appeals decision—*Porcelli v Titus.*[20] The result of that case held that the color of a person's skin can explicitly be made a qualification for a public teaching position without a necessary inference of discrimination. That legal opinion relied on testimony in the record to the effect that the education of Newark's (New Jersey) largely black student body was suffering from the absence in the administration of the schools of black authority figures with whom the pupils could identify. In that case, the school board had actively recruited and hired a black superintendent. The white persons seeking the same job viewed the situation as a denial of equal protection or infringement of civil rights statutes. The Supreme Court argued that in certain instances the courts may accept such justifications as the need for role models of a specific ethnic or racial group to overcome arguments of denial of equal protection or discrimination. This is especially true in cases where there is a furtherance of a proper government objective.

Staff Resistance

Sometimes the greatest obstacle for staffing new community-based programs comes from the state employee unions that staff the state facilities. In the state of California, for example, the state government was desirous of implementing a policy of relying on noninstitutional controls and shutting down "superfluous" institutions that handled mentally ill persons.

By January, 1973, four state hospitals had already been closed, and in that month the Reagan administration announced plans to close all remaining state hospitals by 1977 (with the exception of two wings to be kept open for criminal offenders); and to shut down all hospitals for the mentally retarded in 1981. By way of response, this provoked a carefully orchestrated campaign on the part of the California State Employees' Association, involving intensive lobbying of the state legislature and clever use of the mass media to highlight the least salubrious aspects of the decarceration process. This had the desired effect. The legislature was persuaded to pass a bill making future hospital closures conditional on its prior approval; and when Reagan vetoed this measure, his veto was overriden—the first time a gubernatorial veto had been overridden in California in twenty-eight years. Since then, other states, too, have reported abandoning or postponing hospital closures in the wake of organized resistance from employee unions—opposition which can prove politically troublesome not least because it often relies on the technique of creating "moral panics" in the surrounding communities to which patients are being released.[21]

This example from California illustrates several points. First, state employee unions do possess considerable influence in state legislatures. Secondly, that influence can be escalated not only because closure threatens the livelihood of the workers but also the economic viability of the relatively isolated rural area where the state institution was located.

A possible solution to this resistance might be to provide additional training and permit state employees from other institutions the preferred right to positions in other community-based programs. Jerome Miller, as director of the Department of Youth Services between 1969 and 1973 in Massachusetts, initially handled this problem by a strategy of gradualism. That tactic, used also in California, provoked opposition from the local communities that feared the loss of revenue and thereby pressured the legislature. So, Miller moved into another area of affecting the staff by changing and rotating administrators between the various institutions and employing other staff persons to launch a massive public relations effort. All of that, actively including newspaper and television coverage, was designed to at least neutralize opposition from those working within and committed to the traditional system. Then, during the January 1972 legislative recess, when political counteraction is harder to mobilize, Miller used his discretionary powers as commissioner to empty and officially close all juvenile institutions. Only after taking this official action did the Department of Youth Services begin to create community-based alternatives. Under the pressure of sheer necessity, private entrepreneurs developed programs and alternatives. The 35-40 delinquents, who even the department considered too dangerous to release, were given to a private agency which housed its operations in one of the old detention buildings the state had just vacated.[22]

The point of this illustration is to note the power of public employee unions. People who were actively involved with this social experiment in Massachusetts contend that the public employee unions also effectively destroyed Miller's entire program for several years. For example, there were guards working at juvenile prisons for years after they were closed down. In this manner, then, they were soaking up money that could not go to community programs. This, no doubt, was one of the primary factors behind Miller leaving the state. The lesson to be learned from this situation in Massachusetts is that if state employee unions develop resistance to the hiring and staffing of community-based programs, it might be fruitful to threaten the employee unions with complete decarceration with the hope that they will settle and cooperate with only partial closing of state institutions.

Hiring Ex-Offenders

Some ex-offenders can do, as much if not better, sensitive, skillful work as compared to other professional staff. They understand the rhetoric. The pioneering work of Grant, McGee, Toch, Cressey and others with the New Careers strategy was designed to employ ex-offenders in long-range vocational tracks financed by "hard" money as opposed to "soft money" that ends in a few years when the grant is over. Some states like Illinois and New York accepted the challenge to employ ex-offenders as staff members. In New York state, for example, under the Division for Youth, Director Milton Luger used youth ex-offenders as staff in the following situations: (1) advance program participants; and (2) program graduates. Adults who were parolees under the New York State Division of Parole were also used. Each specific group because of their own personal and professional stage of development had strengths and weaknesses. The usefulness of these individuals as contributors are mentioned because, in a recent survey of agencies contracting for correctional services in the community, ex-offenders are still discriminated against. "Former offenders run organizations with smaller budgets, lower mean split and fail rates and different referral sources (courts and social workers rather than probation and parole). These are gross indicators but suggest a somewhat lower risk clientele."[23]

Summary

Community-based corrections is not just a concept. In practice it is also an organization that must be managed and administered in order for the goals to be accomplished. Perhaps, you will never have to develop such a community-based program. Even if you do not, you should be sensitized to the fact that community-based programs are businesses. As such, they need to be operationalized in accordance with some of the principles in business administration. When programs neglect to follow some of these principles, they often fail.

Planning, implementing and assessing are part of a continuous, circular process. The assessing or evaluation stage provides the information that acts as feedback and, thereby, begins the process of planning and changing to adapt to the successes or failures of the past.

Too often, concerned citizens or administrators become excited about a successful program operated elsewhere. Without realizing that different localities have different attitudes, one can cause more harm than good. The types of communities and their respective needs, strengths and weaknesses in regards to the operationalization of community-based programs were discussed as (1) affluent suburban areas; (2) rural small town areas; and (3) inner-city urban areas. In order to plan for a successful community-based program, attention has to be given to a community in terms of its geographic area and demographic and attitudinal factors.

In needs assessment, planners identify a target population and then indicate the potential number of clients within that target population who may be available for referrals to a particular program. By conducting needs assessment, planners are also setting goals and that, in turn, effects funding activities.

Once the program is planned, effectiveness studies are built into the program, needs assessed, goals established and funding obtained, then one can begin to think of the appropriate strategies for entering the community. In that general area of concern, three specific problems were discussed: (1) selection of a site; (2) selection of a program name; and (3) presentation of program content to the community. While those concerns are being addressed, planners also need to enlist community support and neutralize what community resistance there may be. Two of the ways discussed to enlist community support were an advisory council and a board of directors. Enlisting and utilizing community support to neutralize community resistance in order to help build a program is dependent upon planners' understanding of the community's interests and power structure. Besides developing an articulate program, planners have to mobilize and coordinate community resources, i.e., finances, equipment, people and develop communication links between and among groups of persons in the community who do not normally interact.

In terms of the role of the community in community-based corrections, communities have either developed new programs with new agencies or have used and coordinated existing community services. Another way has been to involve citizens as policy makers and as reformers and deliverers of direct services as an outgrowth of the maximum feasible participation concept operationalized in poverty programs of the 1960's.

Today, the use of volunteers in corrections - both inside the institution and outside - is massive.

Staffing a community-based corrections program involves three areas of concern: (1) legal considerations; (2) staff resistance; and (3) hiring ex-offenders. In legal considerations, staff members must be selected by tests that are job related. Minority persons should not be discriminated against. In fact, their presence usually is advantageous because they serve as role models to the clients.

Besides the resistance to programs by community persons, state employees' unions have also been known to prevent community-based programs. State employee unions possess influence in state legislatures. In addition, they can escalate the situation by appealing to citizens who live in the relatively isolated rural areas and their economic needs so that institutions in those areas will not be closed down. Finally, in terms of staffing, the chapter suggested that ex-offenders can perform the work as well as other professional staff. Granted, those individuals have to be trained and selected for specific positions. To be sure, each specific individual because of their own personal and professional stage of development has strengths and weaknesses. Because some people still do not believe ex-offenders can be reformed, many ex-offenders are still discriminated against even when they work in community-based corrections.

Notes

1. John M. Pettibone, "Community-Based Programs: Catching Up With Yesterday and Planning for Tomorrow," *Federal Probation* 37 (September 1973), pp. 3-8.
2. Ibid., pp. 5-6.
3. Ibid., p. 6.
4. Lloyd E. Ohlin, Alden D. Miller and Robert B. Coates, *Juvenile Correctional Reform in Massachusetts* (Washington, D.C.: U.S. Printing Office, 1977).
5. Ibid., p. 88.
6. Ibid., p.88.
7. J. Ross, G. Hefferman, J. R. Sevick and F. T. Johnson, *National Evaluation Program-Assessment of Coeducational Corrections* (Washington, D.C.: U.S. Printing Office, 1978), p. 6-15.
8. Ohlin et al., *Juvenile Correctional Reform in Massachusetts*, op. cit., p. 89.
9. National Council of Jewish Women, "Volunteers Interact with the Juvenile Justice System," *Federal Probation* 39 (March 1975), pp. 39-42.
10. Harry Elmer Barnes and Negley K. Teeters, *New Horizons in Criminology* (Englewood Cliffs, N.J.: Prentice-Hall, Inc., 1959), p. 336.
11. Ibid., p. 408.

12. National Advisory Commission on Criminal Justice Standards and Goals, "Corrections and the Community—National Standards and Goals". In Robert M. Carter and Leslie T. Wilkens (eds.), *Probation, Parole, and Community Corrections* (New York: John Wiley & Sons, Inc. 1976), p. 494.

13. Vincent O'Leary, "Some Directions for Citizen Involvement in Corrections," *The Annals of the American Academy of Political and Social Science*, 381 (January 1969): pp. 99-108.

14. National Advisory Commission on Criminal Justice Standards and Goals, *op. cit.*, p. 1.

15. Ibid.

16. Ivan H. Scheier et al., *Guidelines and Standards for the Use of Volunteers in Correctional Programs* (Washington, D.C.: Law Enforcement Assistance Administration 1972), p. iii.

17. Dennis E. Hoffman, "Letters to the Editor," *Federal Probation* (June 1977), p. 57.

18. Ibid.

19. 401 U.S. 424 (1971).

20. 302 F. Supp. 726, 431 F. 2d 1254 (1970).

21. Andrew T. Scull, Decarceration. *Community Treatment and the Deviant: A radical view* (Englewood Cliffs, N.J.: Prentice-Hall, Inc., 1977), p. 73.

22. Ibid., pp. 52-53.

23. Gene Kassebaum, Joseph Seldin, Peter Nelligan, David Takeuchi, Billy Wayson, Gail Monkman, and Peter Meyer, *Contracting for Correctional Services in the Community*, Volume 1 (Washington, D.C.: U.S. Printing Office, 1978), p. 13.

Resources

Allen, Harry E., Eric W. Carlson, Evalyn C. Parks, and Richard P. Seiter, "Halfway Houses," (Washington, D.C.: Office of Development, Testing and Dissemination, National Institute of Law Enforcement and Criminal Justice, U.S. Department of Justice, November, 1978).

Goetting, Victor L. "Some Pragmatic Aspects of Opening a Halfway House," *Federal Probation* 38 (Dec. 1974), pp.27-29.

McCartt, John M. and Thomas J. Mangogna, "Guidelines and Standards for Halfway Houses and Community Treatment Centers," (Washington, D.C.: U.S. Department of Justice, Law Enforcement Assistance Administration, Technical Assistance Division, May, 1973).

Pettibone, John M. "Community-based Programs; Catching Up with Yesterday and Planning for Tomorrow," *Federal Probation* 37 (September 1973), pp. 3-8.

Polisky, R. J. "A Model for Increasing the Use of the Community Supportive Services in Probation and Parole," *Federal Probation* 41 (December 1977), pp. 24-27.

Rachin, Richard L. "So You Want to Open a Halfway House," *Federal Probation* 36 (March 1972), pp. 30-37.

Wooten, Harold B. "The Community and Its Resources," *Federal Probation* 42 (December 1978), pp. 53-57.

Chapter 10
Treatment Modalities

Treatment modalities utilized in community-based corrections vary in their assumptions about human behavior and the subsequent antisocial behavior, in their therapeutic approaches, in their applications and in their outcomes. In the broader sense, some people consider religion, recreation and medical services as treatment. In the narrow sense though, treatment usually means some kind of group or individual psychotherapy. Thus, in this chapter particular attention will be devoted to the psychotherapies of reality therapy, behavior modification, guided group interaction and transactional analysis. This does not mean that these are the only treatment modalities used.

On the contrary, other approaches such as psychodrama, family therapy and counseling are also used and many times a specific community-based program will use several modalities in concert to reach and change a particular person's behavior. The modalities discussed in this chapter, however, were developed during and after World War II and, therefore, have a rich literature with applications in various types of programs.

Reality Therapy[1]

Late in his training as a psychiatric resident, William Glasser began to experiment with a very different approach which he eventually named Reality Therapy. Reality Therapy is not a variation of Freudian analysis. Most forms of professional psychotherapy based on Freudian psychology have the following presuppositions or postulates: (1) reconstructive exploration of the patient's past; (2) transference; (3) an "unconscious" that has to be brought to the forefront or to the conscious level; (4) interpretation rather than evaluation of behavior; and (5) change through insight. Needless to say, the nondirective approach espoused by Freudian psychologists was extremely lengthy (as much as five years in psychoanalysis) and costly. Glasser's Reality Therapy, in both theory and practice, challenges the validity of the Freudian postulates. As we shall see, the essence of this newer approach might be called a psychiatric version of the three R's, namely reality, responsibility and right-and-wrong.[2]

Assumptions

According to Glasser, when individuals have and do behaviors which are judged by others to be abnormal, those individuals are experiencing the absence of an essential need fulfillment. When one satisfies or fulfills a specific need, the irrational, erratic behavior which is only an outward symptom, disappears. The degree to which the individual is unable to fulfill his/her needs will determine the severity of the obnoxious behavior. A consequence or common characteristic Glasser found in his patients was the denial of the reality of the world around them. Thus, the solution or the task was to stimulate the individual to give up denying the real world and its natural laws of consequence and begin to fulfill one's needs within the framework of reality.

Need Fulfillment

For Glasser, the basic human needs are for relatedness and respect. The need that all of us have is for at least one person, hopefully more than one, who will care about us and whom we care for at every stage of life from birth to death. The basic need that we have as human beings that needs fulfillment is the need to love and be loved. Love in this sense is the emotional capacity to mourn when another mourns and rejoice with another when they rejoice. Love in this deeper sense of the word should not totally be equated with sexual experiences. Rather, love is the ability to form friendships and the need to be worthwhile to ourselves and to others. This need becomes fulfilled when individuals maintain a satisfactory standard of behavior with another such that a satisfactory relationship, not a superficial one, emerges.

Responsibility

The ability to fulfill one's needs in a way that does not deprive others of the ability to fulfill their needs is the concept of responsibility. Responsibility must be taught to and accepted by the individual. Dr. Glasser argues that people get into trouble because they act irresponsibly. A cycle usually occurs in which a person has practiced misinforming others (and thus being irresponsible) such that the individual begins to lie to oneself in the sense of rationalizing and excusing the deviant behavior. When this happens, the person begins to be unrealistic and begins to "lose contact" with reality. (Now, can you understand why many psychologists claim that honesty and openness are two key elements of good mental health?) Dr. Glasser makes it clear that people are not necessarily responsible for what has happened in the past. Instead, he is saying that they have not been and are not now living responsibly. Thus, a reality counselor might say to a delinquent child, "It makes no difference that your mother was a prostitute and your father a 'junkie.' It's your behavior that is getting you into trouble with the law!"

Reality

The goal of the therapist is to direct individuals into more responsible, more realistic behavior patterns. Understanding the past may be helpful, but in another approach it becomes an excuse to reject the reality of the present. So, Glasser becomes concerned with the present behavior and the individual fulfilling the needs of the present and future—not the past. In this sense then, the individual is taught to make immediate sacrifices for long-term satisfactions and gains.

Reality Therapy with Offenders

Reality Therapy is a training or teaching approach that attempts to accomplish in a relatively short, intense period what should have been established for many young people throughout their normal growing up. Ideally, each one of us "learn responsibility through involvements with fellow human beings, preferably loving parents who will love and discipline us properly, who are intelligent enough to allow us freedom to try our newly acquired responsibility as soon as we show readiness to do so."[3]

Involvement

The first step is for the therapist or counselor to develop and establish a firm emotional relationship with the offender. Oftentimes, this is difficult because these individuals have failed to establish such relationships in the past. An offender who has been "burnt" too many times in the past is going to resist involvement. Thus, the counselor through his or her responsible behavior—being interested, human, sensitive and discussing some of his/her own struggles—shows the offender that acting responsibly is possible though sometimes difficult. Reality Therapy uses a *client-centered therapy* espoused by Carl Rogers in which therapists take an active personal regard towards the clients instead of the passive, nondirective approach characterized by Freud and his followers.

In his book, Glasser illuminates this concept by showing the involvement between Helen Keller and her social worker. In that drama, *The Miracle Worker*, William Gibson's story shows how Annie Sullivan had to struggle with Helen before she was able to teach Helen sign language. As delinquents in community-based corrections often do, Helen fought the therapist and had to be restrained by force in the beginning. Later, as many of you know the happy ending, Annie became one of the most important persons in Helen Keller's life. The accomplishments of Helen can be contributed in part to a person who was a tough, highly responsible person and who saw Helen as an intelligent child with high potential even though she was irresponsible.

Thus, therapeutic involvement may take time dependng upon the control over the offenders, the resistance of the patient and, of course, the skill of the therapist. Once the relationship has developed, the counselor begins to reject unrealistic behavior while still maintaining involvement with the individuals.

Rejecting Unrealistic Behavior

Since the counselor is concerned only with behavior, not necessarily attitudes, praise and encouragement can be offered when the offender acts responsibly, and disapproval when the behavior is not responsible. In this manner, then, the counselor accepts the offender as a person and approves or disapproves of specific behavior in specific interactions. Counselors rarely ask why. Their usual question is, "What are you doing now?" This tactic is to avoid the "blaming game," or to find excuses from the past. Usually, the offender cannot change them. The offender can only learn better ways to live.

Relearning

The counselor must teach the offender better ways to fulfill his/her needs within the confines of reality. Relying on the counselor's experience, the offender experiences better ways of behavior and the accompanied "good" feelings that fulfill the needs. Needless to say, as an offender finds new relationships more satisfying, therapy is approaching an end for that individual. In short, Reality Therapy is a process identified by Glasser as consisting of the following steps:

1. Make friends with the individuals.
2. Ask: "What are you doing in your life NOW?" Emphasis is upon their behavior, i.e., "What are you doing in your behavior?"
3. Help the individual make a judgment about his behavior as revealed in the preceding question. In this manner, each person examines his or her own behavior in a nonthreatening environment to determine how the behavior is contributing to success or failure.
4. Help the clients make a plan to change their lives/behavior. For example, "What can you do to make the marriage better?" The therapist might have to negotiate by saying, "I'll go this far and what can you do?"
5. Make a specific plan to engage in behaviors that will be evaluated as "successful" and get commitment to the plan for follow-through by the clients.
6. Next time, be tough enough not to accept the excuses. "Look, we have to do it or make another plan." If a person fails in his or her pursuit of planned behaviors, excuses are not needed; rather, a new plan has to be developed.
7. Eliminate punishment. The therapist is not to be punitive for this personal reaction does not show the client how to solve human problems without anger and/or violence.

8. Never give up. "I don't know what to do with you. I don't know what to say to help you. But, this I know. I won't give up on you."

Application and Practice of Reality Therapy

In Glasser's book, *Reality Therapy*, successful application is shown with delinquent adolescent girls, psychotic veterans, disturbed children in the school classroom and chronic mental hospital patients. Whether with private patients or on an individual basis, such as a probation officer with an offender or with groups of individuals, the process is the same as described previously. Most the the work at the Ventura School for Girls was done by Glasser in group methods. Also, the work of Dr. G. L. Harrington at the Los Angeles Veterans' Administration Hospital and that of Dr. Willard A. Mainord at the Western State Hospital in Washington, was done in group settings. The advantage of the group approach is that it "encourages the development of rectitude, responsibility and realism so much more rapidly than do the conventional forms of individual treatment."[4]

Many community-based programs in New York State which utilize reality therapy do so in group settings, i.e., Camp Brace at Masonville, New York. That means a small group of offenders meet with one regular trained reality counselor either on a daily or some other regular basis. The counselor and the group try to make each other aware of unrealistic behavior and then teach better ways to fulfill the needs. The counselor's immediate task was to provide a warm atmosphere so that behavior of individuals would be accessible. In some agencies, videotape equipment was used to record the sessions. When an individual continued to deny behavior, videotape playbacks usually helped the individual to develop more honest human relationships as well as to help the individual realize that it is he/she who is responsible for his/her behavior. Once the individual became aware of the part he/she was playing in the misbehavior or the depression, the counselor could then ask, "What can *you do* to make the relationship better? If what you are now doing isn't good for you, what could you do?" Sometimes, the counselor had to negotiate by saying, "I'll go this far. What can you do?"

Then, the offender and counselor made a plan with the idea of getting a commitment from the offender that he/she would do a specific action. Sometimes the counselor had to be tough enough not to accept the excuses. "Look, we have to do it or make another plan."

Reality Therapy has also been used in crisis intervention centers with potential suicidal or depressed individuals and with individuals arrested for driving while under the influence of alcohol. Usually the alcoholic is diverted from the criminal justice system into counseling. Therefore, the reality therapist uses the "wedge of the court." "The court has sent you here for sessions. You agreed to this therapy as part of your diversion. If you are unwilling to cooperate, then you will have to go back to the court and suffer the natural consequences." The counselor is not to be punitive. Not take excuses. "You gave me your word you would attend these counseling sessions and A.A. meetings, and you have not." The more the counselor is friendly and involved the greater are the chances for a commitment to be made. This approach also helps the alcoholic to discuss with someone the natural consequences that flow from particular actions. "You could be sent to a penal institution, county jail or state penitentiary depending upon the feelings of the judge." In this manner, the offender stands the consequences of his/her behavior even when his/her decision is to do nothing.

Criticism of Reality Therapy

Despite the claims by Glasser that Reality Therapy is unique, it still has much in common with other therapies currently in use. In fact, some critics argue that all Glasser has identified is a consistent, common sense approach to dealing with people in trouble that has oversimplified the dynamics of the human personality. Some professionals feel that it is not always possible nor helpful to stay in the "here and now." In fact, these critics argue that exploration of the past is sometimes necessary to deal adequately with the present. By gaining some insight of the past, some offenders are better able to understand their antisocial behavior.

Some critics feel that this modality encourages paternalistic and authoritarian attitudes in therapeutic interaction. Other critics say it is not the modality per se, but rather that it attracts rigid and inflexible persons who use it as a shield to hide their own authoritarian attitudes.[5]

Because many practitioners subscribe either consciously or sub-conciously to Reality Therapy, evaluation studies on Reality Therapy are difficult to develop. Counselors in community-based corrections see the difference in their clients and can appreciate the change towards more responsible behavior. That seems to be enough proof for them.

Behavior Modificaion

Assumptions

Unlike the Freudian psychotherapists, a behavior modification therapist does not use terms like self-concept, unconscious needs and super ego. These terms are used to refer to what is going on inside the mind or particular psychological characteristics. Instead, the behavior modification therapist notices the behavior. In particular, the therapist tries to determine what is the stimuli (cause) of the behavior or what is reinforcing the behavior. To change the behavior, one must take control over the stimuli and/or the reinforcements in order to get the desired behavior.

In order to more fully understand the assumptions, it is necessary to discuss those areas of psychology that have contributed greatly to behavior modification: (1) experimental psychology and (2) social/cognitive psychology.

Experimental Psychology

The central area of this approach has been what is called classical conditioning. Classical conditioning is the conditioning of a reflexive response as a reaction to a stimulus when the former response had been neutral. Particularly noteworthy is the scientific investigation of Ivan Pavlov who concluded that the flow of saliva in the mouth of the dog was influenced not only by the food placed in the dog's mouth (an unconditioned response), but also by the sight of food (conditioned or learned response). To determine how conditioned responses are formed, Pavlov used lights and sounds of a bell to produce stimulus-response associations. Pavlov always followed the dog's response of salivation to the conditioned stimulus (bell, light, etc.) by the unconditioned stimulus (meat powder). This procedure is termed *reinforcement*. Repetition of the conditioned stimulus without reinforcement is called *extinction*.[6]

To promote a better understanding of classical conditioning, it is essential to discuss in greater detail stimulus generalization and extinction. Stimulus generalization can and often does occur with small children. As a child comes near a rabbit, for example, and a loud bang is sounded, the child experiences a sense of fear. The rabbit becomes the conditioned stimulus and the fear response becomes the conditioned response. Then, the child generalizes the fear response to any furry white thing, even the fur collar on people's coats. The collar on the coat becomes a stimulus similar to the rabbit. Thus, the collar on the coat becomes a stimulus generalized from the rabbit.

In the case of the child and the rabbit, if one wanted to eliminate the fear response in the presence of the rabbit, then a process of extinction would have to occur. Extinction would occur when the conditioned stimulus (the rabbit) is presented to the organism (the child) a number of times without pairing it with the unconditioned stimulus (the loud noise). After a time, the conditioned response will start dropping in frequency and intensity until, finally, the conditioned stimulus no longer brings on the response.

The pioneer of behavior modification with humans was B. F. Skinner who believed that good behavior should be rewarded more. Working with disobedient children, Skinner proved that despite the impact of one's environment on behavior, behavior could be modified. To provide a better model for modifying human behavior, Skinner employed the concept of *operant conditioning*—"the strengthening of a stimulus-response association by following the response with a reinforcing stimulus."[7]

Operant conditioning was given that name because certain behaviors "operate" on the environment to produce consequences. One of the differentiations between classical and operant conditioning is that in the former, the *stimulus* which brings on the behavior comes *before* the behavior, while in the latter conditioning, the *stimulus* which brings on the behavior comes *after* the behavior. In operant conditioning, consequences are called rewards and punishments. Both rewards and punishments have a negative and positive dimension such that there are positive and negative rewards and positive and negative punishments. Some people prefer to think of a positive punishment as something added, while a negative punishment is something subtracted.

A positive reward or reinforcement is one which increases the probability of the occurence of the behavior in order to gain or add the reinforcer. Giving a dog biscuit to a dog when the dog has been told to "sit" by the dog trainer would be such an example.

An example of a negative reinforcement is based on taking something away from the environment. Thus, if one is able to remove or avoid unpleasant or painful stimulus, then one will be able to engage in some activity and the activity will be reinforced. For example, a small child who has stolen a cookie from the cookie jar receives positive punishment for that behavior in the form of a scolding by the mother. If the mother were to no longer scold the child, the probability of the behavior will increase. The behavior might also increase if the cookies themselves are extra special for they would serve as a positive reward.

Positive punishment is brought on by adding punishers as consequences of behavior. Spanking and other so-called forms of discipline are usually positive punishment. Negative punishment, on the other hand, is removing a privilege or reward.

In this discussion, the student should notice that there are four general approaches to increasing or decreasing a behavior. All too often, the only approach that is used is to "add" punishment. Some people advocate adding punishment or prison to change a person's behavior without even attempting any of the other three dimensions.

Besides Pavlov's classical conditioning and Skinner's operant version, investigators such as Wolpe and Eypenck pioneered the respondent form of behavior therapy.[8] One technique often used is a form of counter conditioning or systematic desensitization. It is used to reduce or inhibit the client's response to an anxiety-provoking stimulus by pairing it with a neutral stimulus—the relaxed state of the client. More specifically, the client, through extensive interviews, lists what stimuli provoke the most and the least anxiety. Then, the client is induced to relax. When the client is relaxed, the least threatening stimulus is presented first and then up the stimuli hierarchy until the most threatening is presented. This technique is useful for individuals possessing real or imaged phobias, e.g., a rape victim who is afraid to be in her house where the crime occurred. In this particular case, the client's anxiety response is specifically lessened by this technique to the point where the stimulus no longer evokes the anxiety.

To summarize, behavior therapists believe that behaviors are determined by antecedent causes. Behavior is responses to stimuli and that behavior an individual exhibits is a pattern of responses from learning—not expressions of "free will." From these assumptions, four different types of strategies in behavior therapy are employed: omission training, punishment training, avoidance training and reward training.

To eliminate a response, a counselor might employ *omission training*. That means simply that an undesirable response is not followed by a positive reinforcer. Another approach is *punishment training* or *aversion therapy*. In this therapy, an undesirable response is followed by a negative reinforcer, such as pain. Aversion therapy has been widely used with alcoholics and homosexuals. The major task is to provide the client with an unpleasant reaction to the problem behavior. For example, an alcoholic may be given a drug to induce vomiting. Just before the onset of the nausea, the patient must look at, smell or taste alcohol. Then, the patient gets sick. After a number of situations in which the patient gets sick, the alcoholic learns to avoid alcohol to avoid nausea.[9]

To aid or increase the frequency of a response, a counselor employs *avoidance* or *reward* training. In avoidance training, a desired response is followed by an opportunity to avoid a negative reinforcer, i.e., electric shock. Reward training has also been called contingency management. In this program, a desired response is followed by a positive reinforcer. Usually based on a token economy system, programs both in correctional and community-based settings reward specific behavior and punish other undesirable behavior by taking away a reward of a token which could have been used to buy goodies or take trips.[10]

Social and Cognitive Psychology

In an attempt to enhance the usefulness of behavior modification in our society, social and cognitive psychologists have made several contributions. Those contributions which will be discussed are: (1) expectancy, (2) perception of progress, (3) self-control; and (4) modeling.[11]

Expectancy

Various studies have shown that patients who enter behavior modification with the expectancy of improvement will have more rapid and longer lasting improvement than those patients who enter the therapy with no expectation of improvement. It has also been shown that if the specific goals and expected behaviors are made clear to the patient from the onset of the therapy, then the overall effectiveness will be enhanced.

Perception of Progress

Once the therapy has been started and some data has been acquired, the recorded data can serve as informational "feedback." When the patient can see or monitor his/her own progress, the patient is reinforced to continue to improve.

Self Control

In helping an individual to monitor their own behavior, the therapist also permits the patient to take responsibility in rewarding oneself for the appropriate behavior. Granted, this will eventually do away with the need of the therapist. Yet, the withdrawal of the therapist is the goal of behavior modification. The idea is to enable patients to reward themselves and to learn to recognize and desire naturally occurring reinforcers such that they can function normally in the society.

Modeling

Bandura, who has done many studies in the area of modeling, has shown that modeling can be effective in changing behavior in humans. Modeling plays upon the human tendency to imitate models. For example, in treating children who feared dogs, the model would pet the dog and show the child that there was no reason to fear the dog. In time, the child would overcome the fear of dogs. If the therapist models the type of behavior, then the patient will know exactly what is expected and will be better able to imitate the behavior.

Through the applications of these two schools of thought in psychology, various principles of behavior modification and behavior modification therapy have become widely used. One of these areas has been in the area of corrections.

Behavior Modification with Offenders

In summarizing the numerous studies and demonstration projects using behavior modification, Brodsky shows that in all of them, at least some of the target behaviors were modified in the desired directions. For example, Phillips' work with pre-delinquent youths in a community-based, home style, rehabilitative environment is considered a classic example of token reinforcement procedures.[12]

Phillips developed a program with male youth who exhibited disruptive behavior in their home settings that caused the parents to fear the "child" would have trouble with the law in the future. The pre-delinquent youth were placed in a house setting with house parents who gave points for desired behavior in social, self-care and academic areas. The boys carried 3" x 5" index cards. The house parents immediately posted the earned or lost points on the cards after the behavior was observed. Thereby, a prompt reinforcement schedule was maintained. At the end of each week, the points were tallied to determine the privileges for the next week. Examples of earning points included such activities as washing dishes, cleaning and maintaining one's room, reading pages in a book. Examples of behavior in losing points were arguing, stealing, lying or cheating. Phillips reported that the frequency of aggressive statements and poor grammar decreased, while tidiness, punctuality and amount of homework completed increased![13]

In order for the token economy to be applied, three defining characteristics must be followed:

1. A number of objectives or target behaviors be established or defined.
2. A token be present.
3. A variety of desirable reinforcers.

Needless to say, the target behaviors are behaviors which will help the participant to reenter society and live accordingly. The tokens usually are presented following the desired behavior and are later exchanged for a desired reward. It stands to reason that if the backup reinforcers are not desired by the participants, then there will be little incentive to demonstrate the appropriate behavior. Therefore, backup reinforcers should include a large variety of special activities and commodities so that people can experience their positive reward. In addition, tokens have to be nontransferable to prevent stealing, extortion or loans. The balance of points earned and the expenditures have to be kept up-to-date.[14]

The most problematic experience in behavior modification is the maintenance of the new behavior without the reinforcers. The weaning process usually includes a process of delaying the reward. Instead of giving a token daily, a token is given for weekly acceptable behavior until such time that the individual can learn and recognize the desired naturally occurring reinforcers. The idea then is to give artificial reinforcers and then gradually withdraw them so that individuals will continue the desired behavior.

Application and Practice of Behavior Modification

Behavior modification can be realistically used with all kinds of offenders, not just the pre-delinquent or delinquent youth. As stated earlier, the techniques can be utilized inside correctional settings, in community settings or in interaction settings such as meetings with a probation officer. The behavior modification program for adult drug offenders in Los Angeles County shows how a probation officer might employ this treatment modality.

In Los Angeles County, the contingency management program involved three phases with 26 subjects (15 males and 11 females) who had served an average of 12.5 months on probation before entering the program.

> In phase *one*, the probationer was scheduled to meet with the probation officer weekly. The probationer received a credit for prompt attendance at these meetings, politeness and serious discussion with the officer. After earning eight credits (a minimum of eight weeks) he would advance to phase *two*, which offered the probationer considerably more freedom. In this phase, the probationer earned credit for attendance at group meetings with other probationers in the program on a once-a-week basis—the probationer received credits for attendance and constructive participation. Once he had earned ten credits, he was entitled to advance to phase *three*...In phase *three*, probationers negotiated a written contract..detailed specific new and positive behaviors the probationers felt they could achieve (such as employment, non-drug activity, improved living accommodation, etc...) looking for a new job would be associated with a certain number of weeks off the total probation time at a later date...violations of condition of probation served would mean demotion to the first level; but, otherwise, no forms of coercion or punishment were used."[15]

Significant effects were achieved on criteria such as new arrests, violations of probation, attendance and months of employment over traditional probationary contact. At that time, the authors argued that more pilot studies dealing with drug and criminal offenders should be employed. Mainly, they argued that in California it costs approximately $1,000 a year to maintain the same individual on probation. They also supported this modality as treatment because they found most of the subjects possessed excessive defects in social behavior. That is to say, the subjects were unreliable, undisciplined and self-critical. Unless these defects were corrected, efforts to eliminate just the use of drugs would not have helped to serve these subjects. By using behavior modification, new behavior could be shaped, established and maintained.[16]

Criticism

Some of the criticism and difficulties with the application of behavior modification rest with knowing what is considered rewards and punishments for an individual. What is someone's reward may be someone else's punishment. Because of this fact, it will take a very skillful counselor to fully understand the reinforcers for people's behavior. Most counselors fail to realize that there are positive and negative reinforcers and positive and negative punishment. "Knowledge of group history, social structure, and cultural values enables us to make some predictions about what are likely to be effective and available reinforcers for members of specific groups and collectivities."[17] Secondly, establishing a token economy may resolve short-term problems, but it does not necessarily mean that individuals internalize behavior enough to function in a law-abiding capacity in a free world without external control monitors. In fact, some critics argue that the behavior that leads to criminal justice intervention is not usually the behavior shaped through positive reinforcement techniques. "In addition, ethical questions can be raised when a program merely makes a subject easier to manage or ensures the smooth functioning of an institution."[18]

Probably the most serious criticism of behavior modification stems from who has the right to program or modify the behavior of others. Some groups fear "behavior mod" is really *Clockwork Orange* or *1984* gone awry.

Guided Group Interaction (GGI)

During World War II, many American soldiers experienced battle fatigue or some other psychological side effect which hampered effective combat duty. Due to the large numbers of soldiers needing psychological assistance, coupled with the shortage of trained personnel and time, psychologists like J. Abraham developed group psychotherapy sessions. One of his students was Lloyd W. McCorkle, who later adapted those techniques to a demonstration project with delinquent youths which was called the Highfields project. Using peer group dynamics in New Jersey on the estate of Charles Lindberg in 1949, McCorkle's efforts are now known as the "granddaddy" of group encounters or guided group interaction (GGI). This Highfields project was the first of its kind to deal with delinquent youth on probation. The success of that project has, of course, lead to many others. Before considering its application, let us first gain a better understanding of how this modality works.

Assumptions

GGI is primarily concerned with peer group dynamics. The basic assumption of juvenile delinquency is that all too often the illegal behavior of an individual is the result of a group experience. Thus, if the delinquent behavior is to be changed, focus should be on a group like the one within which the individual operates. By using group processes, a new peer group is restructured around more socially acceptable norms and values. Thus, these programs encourage the development of a group "subculture," whereby members help and control each other. As the group culture develops, the youth are able to take upon themselves more responsibility. As this occurs, the staff group leader permits the group a greater degree of decisionmaking power.

Simply stated, GGI assumes that the group will influence an individual's behavior and thinking such that the individual will be manipulated by the group into legitimate pro-social behavior. Secondly, the group will develop characteristics such as intimacy, interaction and feelings of sentiment between and among group members. Lastly, given the predisposition of the individuals, coupled with interaction, there will develop a "liking for each other" that will serve as an incentive for legal behavior and a fear of reincarceration. The negative self-concepts are thereby changed by interaction and awareness of problems, problem solving techniques and group support. Negative self-concepts are defeated and more positive self-images develop. In short, the GGI approach is characterized by a nonauthoritarian atmosphere, intensity of interaction, group homogeneity and an emphasis on group structure.[19]

Guided Group Interaction with Offenders

Originally, the clients in the Highfields project were delinquent youth on probation. They lived on the project site, the Lindberg estate, worked during the day at a mental institution immediately adjacent to their residence, and held their group sessions in the evening. The Highfields project restricted its population to 20 boys, aged 16 and 17, who had not previously been committed to correctional school, nor were deeply disturbed or mentally retarded.

GGI involved a group leader who was active in free, frank discussions with clients. By using reflective listening, and parroting skills, the leader restated and paraphrased provocative ideas which came from the group to specific participants for analysis of their personal involvement.

The process that emerged for the client was a five stage process. First, the individual was guarded until the leader and group member encouraged involvement. In the second stage, he began to talk about himself and to reevaluate his values. In the third stage, as he built trust with the leader and group members, he gave up the games and defenses he had used in the past to deal with the world. Thus, in the fourth stage, he was ready for reeducation. As he saw that his problems were not unique, and as he watched other people deal with their problems, he became less antagonistic and more open to other ways to handle future experience. In the final stage, the individual made a conscious decision about his future. This decision had grown out of his own and the group's reexamination of his behavior.

Application and Practice

Variations on the Highfields project developed at Essex Fields, New Jersey, and at Pinehills in Provo, Utah. Both of these programs centered around gainful employment in the community, school and daily group meetings. However, unlike the Highfields project, the offenders lived at home.

In the daily group sessions, all group members were responsible for defining problems and solutions. By making offenders and staff solve problems together, the offender could become more aware of the responsibility he had over his own life.

Other variations of GGI projects have been "developed in the Parkland project in Louisville, Kentucky, in the GUIDE (Girls Unit for Intensive Daytime Education) program in Richmond, California and in another girls' program in San Mateo, California.[20] Since 1969, the Florida Division of Youth Services has been using GGI in all of its institutions.[21]

Difficulties and Criticism

GGI is most appropriate with the type of delinquent who is open and able to reveal by talking about his problem.[22] Unfortunately, some, if not many, of the most serious offenders are bypassed. Some people wonder if GGI is really a technique trainable to ordinary individuals, or if it is a specific influence generated by specifically gifted leaders who possess a particular style or personality. Can strong friendships, camaraderie and healthy family-like relationships be created and continually renewed in the face of the rapid turnover of staff and inmates inherent in community-based corrections? Furthermore, concern is raised over its lasting effects. Will recidivism be reduced?[23]

Effectiveness

Several studies at first glance seem to confirm the value of the Highfields project. As a part of McCorkle's program, projective personality tests were given to the Highfields boys and to the inmates of Annandale Reformatory, a conventional state institution, at the time of admission and at a later point in their school stay. The test results showed the Highfields youth to move in the opposite direction of the reformatory boys who moved toward "bleaker, darker outlooks on life." The reformatory youth became resigned to further deviation as a life or career of crime, while the Highfield youth did not.[24]

In a second evaluation, Weeks compared a sample of Annandale parolees with released wards from Highfields. His results showed that a higher proportion of Highfields youth succeeded even when background variables related to success or failure were held constant. He found little difference in parole failure for white youth, regardless of the program, but black youth from Highfields had a success rate of 60 percent, compared to 33 percent for Annandale black parolees.[25]

Lerman reanalyzed Weeks' data and showed that the effectiveness of Highfields was not as convincing as once thought.[26] Thus, the efforts to evaluate the effects of the project are still the subject of academic dispute.

However, the GGI employed at Highfields was still viewed at least as effective as the reformatory in a shorter period of time (three to four months) at a greater reduced monthly cost.

In evaluating the Provo and Silverlake experiments that had group meetings patterned after GGI, Lamar T. Empey cited the following statistics to show cost effectiveness:

> In the Provo experiment, the appropriate cost per boy in each of the three programs was as follows: For probation, $200; for the intensive experiment program, $609; and for incarceration, $2,015. Today, costs would be greater. Nevertheless, it is the differentials that count. If probation were used in lieu of incarceration, the savings would amount to about $1,800 per boy; or, if daily non-residential programming were used, the savings per boy would be about $1,400. Translated into larger terms, the savings would be greater indeed, somewhere between $1.5 and $2 million per thousand boys. In the Silverlake experiment, the average cost per graduate in the experimental community home was $1,735, as contrasted to $4,594 in the rather expensive private institution. Again, if the differences were extended, a savings of nearly $3 million per thousand boys would be realized."[27]

Statistics like these show that large sums of money can be freed from enlarging correctional budgets to experiment with more practical and humanitarian modalities. As Empey's research showed, delinquents were spared the negative effects of incarceration while they received equal, if not better treatment in the community through use of GGI. Furthermore, when youth are asked their perceptions of getting out of the group treatment program, the youth say it depends on their ability to solve their own problems, or how other youth in the group feel they are able to handle themselves. Unlike institutional programs that get conformity without commitment to change, this modality seems to get both commitment and conformity to more law-abiding behavior.

Transactional Analysis

Transactional analysis (T.A.) is the analysis of actions that come back or *trans* to a person. T.A., as it is commonly called, is the analysis of what I do to you and you do back to me. By 1970, over 1,000 psychiatrists, psychologists, social workers and professionals in the criminal justice system have been trained in this newer therapeutic approach.[28] Its increasing popularity resulted in the training of countless others.

Assumptions[29]

The major assumption of this modality is that people's behavior and subsequent misbehavior is the result of their social interaction with others.

Consciously or subconsciously, some people get treated in particular ways by others because of the things they do to stimulate those responses. In order to teach the client or inmate to be aware of the different kinds of social interaction he/she uses to deal with others, T.A. analysts develop a working vocabulary of *ego states*, i.e., parent, adult and child, *transactions*, *life positions, scripts* and *games*.

Eric Berne, the originator and primary developer of T.A., was trained as a psychiatrist and psychoanalyst. Even though he was influenced by Freud, Berne felt psychoanalysis was slow, overly complex and rigid. Combining his ideas about psychoanalysis with those of Wilder Penfield, a brain surgeon, Berne developed a simple terminology and an approach called *transactional analysis* in 1949. It was not until 1958, however, that he was able to develop a T.A. seminar that has lead into the present-day movement.

Since most persons are familiar with Freud's id, ego and superego, students reading this particular section will be aware of that particular influence in this modality. Wilder Penfield is not as well-known; however, his research is important for the understanding of what T.A. analysts call *tapes*.

Tapes

Penfield, as a brain surgeon, placed stimulating electrodes into patients' brains. From his research, it became evident that the stimulating electrode could force recollections clearly from the patient's memory. Four conclusions were reached from that electrode evoking a single recollection:

1. *Not only past events are recorded in detail but also the feelings that were associated with these events.*

   In other words, an event and the feeling which was produced by the event are inextricably locked together in the brain so that one cannot be evoked without the other. Perhaps, this is why when you ask a victim or a witness to go back into their mind to get information concerning an assault, the individual also reexperiences the feelings produced by that event.

2. *The brain functions as a high fidelity recorder, putting on tape, as it were, every experience from the time of birth.*

   That means that the brain serves as storage for information. When a playback is desired, as in an examination situation or when a situation stimulates the play back, the tape is played in high fidelity.

3. *Persons can exist in two states at the same time.*

   Most of us have already discovered our unique ability to daydream or make plans while attending lectures or other functions.

4. *Recorded experiences and feelings associated with them are available for replay today in as vivid a form as when they happened.*

Thus, these replays determine the nature of today's transactions. Furthermore, these experiences not only can be recalled but also relived. Thus, I not only remember how I felt, I also feel the same now.

One of the basic tenets of T.A. is that your mind has recorded events with meanings and subsequent feelings attached to them. These recordings, or "tapes" as they are called, are available for replay, either at will or as the result of being in a similar situation that triggers replay by stimuli or cue responses.

Ego States

Another assumption of T.A. is that every human being consists of three ego states: (1) parent, (2) adult and (3) child. Regardless of our age, we all possess these ego states from which we initiate social relationships.

1. Parent. The parent ego state stems from recordings we as a child heard our mother and/or father tell us.

These statements are unquestioned. They are the admonitions, rules and laws we perceived between birth to at about the age of five. Statements that are on our tapes might include such things as "Pay your

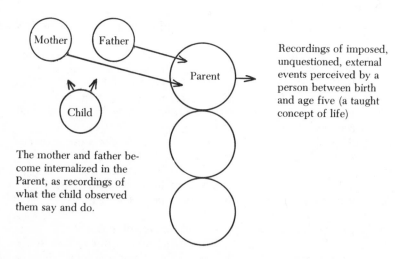

Recordings of imposed, unquestioned, external events perceived by a person between birth and age five (a taught concept of life)

The mother and father become internalized in the Parent, as recordings of what the child observed them say and do.

Source: Thomas A Harris, *I'm OK - You're OK* (New York: Avon Books, 1973), p. 41.

bills," "You can never trust a man," "Do unto others as you would have them do unto you."

Certain cues reflect this parent ego state, such as pursed lips, the pointing index finger, foot tapping, hands on hip, furrowed brow and perhaps, patting another on the head. "I can't for the life of me," "I'm going to put a stop to this once and for all" are statements coming from the parent ego state. Words like *always, never, should, ought*, "If I were you," stem from our recordings in our parent ego state.

The data, including these words and gestures, are taken into our nervous system and recorded straight—without editing. The reason this is done is because of the situation of a little child who has dependency and an inability to construct meanings with words. Thus, the condition of early development of children makes it impossible for any of them to modify, correct or explain these early recordings.

2. Adult. The adult ego state is the recordings of data acquired and computed through exploration and testings. The adult ego state is principally concerned with transforming stimuli into pieces of information and processing and assessing that information on the basis of previous experience. It is this ego state that examines data in the parent ego state to see whether or not it is true and still applicable today. If parental directions are grounded in reality, the child, through his own adult, will come to realize integrity or a sense of wholeness. "It really does feel better when my pants aren't wet," concludes the little girl who has learned to go to the bathroom by herself.

The adult checks out old data, validating or invalidating it and refiling it for future use. Words like "Why?", "What?", "Where?", "Who?", "When?" and "How?", help in this process. Cues that help one to identify the adult ego state are words like "In what way?", "I think", "I see", "In my opinion."

It is this adult ego state that can turn off the tape that plays the "not OK" feelings of the child ego state. If this "not OK" feeling repeats itself in adulthood, as when a person does poorly on an examination, the adult ego state can turn off the tape instead of letting it upset the person. As you can see, the adult ego state is extremely important to T.A. The goal or purpose of T.A. is to free this ego state so it can deal more objectively with the tapes of the parent and child ego states.

3. Child. The child ego state is the recordings of internal events or feelings in response to the external events between birth and about age five.

Since the little person has no vocabulary during the most critical of these early experiences, many of his or her reactions are feelings. Thus, a sour look turned in a small child's direction can only produce feelings that

Figure 10.2 - Child Ego State

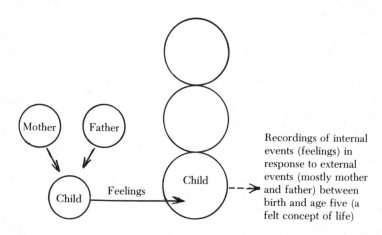

Recordings of internal events (feelings) in response to external events (mostly mother and father) between birth and age five (a felt concept of life)

Source: Thomas A. Harris, *I'm OK - You're OK* (New York: Avon Books, 1973), p. 47.

add to their reservoir of negative data (clumsy, inept, dependent). "It's my fault again. Always is. Always will be. World without end."

According to Harris, author of *I'm O.K., You're O.K.*, children who have not yet made any certain connection between cause and effect experience unhappy feelings recorded permanently in their brain that cannot be erased. This permanent recording is the residue of having been a child—any child. The feeling of "Not OK" can exist in children who were raised by kind, loving, well-meaning parents. It is the situation of childhood and not the intention of the parents which produces the problem. Can you then imagine the "Not OK" burden carried by children whose parents are guilty of neglect, child abuse or incest?

The cues that reflect the child ego state are: "I wish," "I want," "I don't care," "When I grow up." The child ego state in order to impress the parent ego state and to overcome the "Not O.K." child will play a "Mine is better" game. For example, "My daddy is bigger than yours," "My car is better than yours."

It is true that the child ego state also includes the desire to explore to know. The urges to touch and feel as well as the desire for creativity and curiosity stem from the child ego state. Thus, it is unrealistic and even unhealthy to rid oneself of this ego state. Rather, it is better to know which ego state you are in and for what reasons. For example, when anger dominates reason, the child is in command. The child can also demand certainty—wants to know if the sun will come up every morning. Will mother be there? Will the "bad guy" always get it in the end? The adult ego state, meanwhile, can accept the fact that there is not always certainty.

Transactions

In T.A. terms, the things people say and do to each other are called *transactions.* What we say and what we gain from the exchange depends upon the active ego state of each person involved in the interaction. T.A. is concerned with diagnosing the transactions between people in terms of the ego states which they employ in stimulus and response situations. There are numerous types of possible transactions, such as adult-adult, parent-parent, child-child, parent-child, adult-child, etc. Two types of transactions are of special importance in T.A.: complementary and crossed or uncomplementary. A complementary transaction is one in which the response to a stimulus is appropriate and expected. Transactions which are complementary facilitate communication. A crossed or uncomplementary transaction is the type of transaction which causes social difficulties and trouble. Communication stops when a crossed transaction occurs. A crossed transaction occurs when a person responds to a transactional stimulus in an ego state other than the one which is anticipated from the person who initiated the transaction.

Life Positions

Besides the three ego states and the subsequent transactions, T.A. analysts look at life positions people take. According to T.A., each one of us early in our lives has taken one of the four following emotional positions and used it as a backdrop for interactions throughout life[30]:

1. *I'm Not OK - You're OK*   This is the common, natural position of a small child who is often corrected by the mother or father and thereby feels "Not OK." But the person doing the correcting is also the one to whom the child counts on for attention, affection, food, etc. Therefore he/she must be OK.

2. *I'm Not OK - You're Not OK*   This is the position which is often taken when a very young child becomes mobile and is not "babied" as much as before. This leads the child to question the OK status of the parents. A person who remains in this position rejects stroking from everyone and, feeling no hope, withdraws from life. The resultant condition is that the child feels that nobody, including the child, is OK.

3. *I'm OK - You're Not OK*   This is the life position taken by many sociopaths, psychopaths and other violent offenders who believe that no one is basically good or OK. They, then, think that they can make it only if left to themselves.

4. *I'm OK - You're OK*   This life position is unlike the other three life positions which operate on the unconscious level and are based on feelings. This position is objective and must be sought. It desires to change to become active in this life position while interacting with other persons.

Games

People who are in certain life positions develop "games" to make life tolerable. A game is a series of transactions with a specific outcome in mind for the person initiating the interaction. This well-defined, predictable outcome Berne calls a "snare or gimmick." According to Berne, "games are a way of using time for people who cannot bear the stroking starvation of withdrawal, and yet whose Not O.K. position makes the ultimate form of relatedness, intimacy, impossible."[31] Games like "Ain't it Awful," "Look How Hard I've Tried" or "Blemish" are "defenses to protect individuals from greater or lesser degrees of pain growing from the Not O.K. position."[32] Blemish is the game we play when we try to find something wrong with a person in order to feel more secure about our own insecurity.[33] In the helping professionals, one of the games played most often is based on the therapist saying, "Why don't you - - -." The client hearing this idea and not really wanting help or desire to change responds, "Yes, but," and then proceeds to list a lot of reasons why the idea won't work. The end result is that the therapist stops giving advice and the client maintains the power.

Strokes

T.A. contends that sensory stimulation is very important to the development and survival of humans. Based on this premise of verbal and nonverbal stimulation, the word "stroke" was devised to describe this phenomena of feedback recognition. Needless to say, strokes may be positive or negative. The reality is, according to T.A., that the need for recognition is so great that some people will seek and accept negative strokes, i.e., child being beaten, as opposed to no strokes at all.

T.A. With Offenders

T.A. explores the "games" both treatment staff and offenders play that hinder personal growth and, thereby, rehabilitation. Martin Groder identified the game "K.I.U.D." (Keep It Up Doc). In this game, the therapist who has been taught to recognize and drop some of the games he/she plays, has taken on a new game in which he/she surrounds him/herself with clients who can be counted on to tell what a good job is being done, even if the work is actually ineffectual.[34]

At the Close Training School in California, residents identified the following games that they played by printing them on wall posters:

Try and Help Me

"My problems are 'out there,' not in here."

Stupid

"Nobody told me. How was I supposed to know?"

You Can't Trust Anybody
    "My parents turned me in."

I'm Just a Typical Teenager
    "Everybody my age gets into trouble sometime."[35]

The youth at Close Training School, felt their program encouraged autonomy, facilitated the learning of insight, helped solve personal problems and helped them to set practical goals. Furthermore, the data collected on the residents who were exposed to T.A. tended to show that they had higher morale, developed more positive attitudes toward staff members and became more hopeful and optimistic about the future as well as established greater feelings of self-esteem. Residents paroled from Close School did significantly better during the first 12 months following release than had offenders released in prior years. Most importantly, the parole violation rates were also significantly lower than those of comparable age groups released from other California juvenile institutions.[36]

In her work with delinquents, Lois Johnson has adapted the T.A. terminology for better results. So that they can understand the T.A. principles better, she uses "The Man" to explain the parent ego state, "The Cool Head" for the adult the "The Kid" for the child ego state.[37]

Other games that offenders, both juvenile and adult, have played include such games as "Bum Beef" and "I've Gotta Get Out." The "I've Gotta Get Out" game has variations such as "My Wife and Kids Need Me At Home," or "How Am I Going To Get Myself Together In a Place Like This?"

Application

According to Wicks, T.A. has "won considerable attention and acceptance in corrections and is being tried out in many facilities."[38] Under the direction of Martin Groder, the Synanon community in the U.S. Penitentiary in Marion, Illinois, used T.A. to teach inmates to recognize and understand the games they play and the ways they have been living.

T.A. is also used in the drug program in the Federal system at Leavenworth, Kansas. The work of Groder, coupled with the work of others such as Franklin Ernst,[39] have produced impressive results that suggest T.A. does have great potential for use both in closed institutions as well as open facilities.

Case Study[40]

The meeting commences with a brief discussion by the group leader on the four life positions. The desirability of striving for the position, "I'm

OK - You're OK" was stressed. Billy, a check writer recently re-paroled, attempted to maneuver the group into playing a game:

Billy: I can't buy this I'm OK, You're OK, because it's just brainwashing stuff, because nobody's OK. I just read where a probation officer was convicted of taking a bribe....

Leader: (interrupting): Of embezzlement.

Billy: So what! He's a crook! They're all crooks! A guy comes up on a check rap in front of a crooked judge and gets five years....

Judy: (interrupting): Are you saying you're OK and the rest of us are not? You're perfect?

Billy: You're right.

Don: Well, these federal probation officers haven't done me a bit of good. And those stupid bastards in the employment agencies! They're drawing their paychecks, and when you ask for help....what a runaround... .

Jerry: (referring to group leader): Mr. Nick's a probation officer and I think he's OK. He always played it straight with me....(I'm a good boy, aren't I papa?)

Billy: Oh yeah? What goodies are you getting out of this Mr. Nick?

Group Leader: My Adult gets a salary. My Parent is trying to do something about helping people free the Adult and making it the boss—and protecting society; and my Child is curious about what comes out of T.A.

Jerry: Don't you resent what Billy's saying? I would!

Group Leader: What's important for us to do is to analyze what part of us—Parent, Adult, Child—is doing the talking.

Judy: I think it was Billy's Parent talking just now—and, well, I guess it was my Parent telling him he thinks he's perfect (laughter).

Doug: Well, Billy, you're acting like a Parent, but I picked up a lot of Child in what you and Don said.

Don: Child!

Doug: Yeah, a Not OK Child and a scared Child.

The discussion went on with Billy protesting that he isn't afraid of anything. The noteworthy thing coming out of this session is Billy's confirmation of his life position of "I'm not OK, You're not OK," which actually represents his reversal of the position, "I'm not OK, You're OK." His unloved and frightened Child sought group support for his need to rehearse his defenses. An attempt was made to entice the group leader into playing games, but Billy's maneuver was diverted into the more productive activity of analyzing group transactions. Billy never returned.

Final Comments

Since all of these modalities involve an element of reeducation, it would seen reasonable to assume that the target population should have developed some level of rational thinking. Even though many of these modalities were developed with delinquent youth, reason would dictate that applications to younger population groups as well as older ones could be made. Serious offenders, those who are motivated more by fears than by reason, and those severely mentally handicapped do not seem to be, therefore, appropriate groups. That does not mean that these modalities in and of themselves or in concert with each other are completely ineffective with mentally retarded individuals. Rather, there is no extensive research to support such a program. The mature are the most likely to profit; the immature and sociopathic usually withdraw and the manipulator, such as in T.A., tries to "game" staff and other inmates.[41]

Secondly, one must remember that any new personal social skill takes time to develop and to mature. In others words, working with a person to bring about change towards more effective and less pain-producing social relationships takes time. Once a person is educated to these modalities and accepts them to be used in their life-style, then change is more readily apparent. Yet, it will take a conscious, organized effort to maintain those new skills.

Thirdly, none of these modalities, in and of themselves, have all the answers to the problems presented by persons in need of community-based corrections. Thus, some people who have tried one of these modalities, do not seem to profit by their participation. Yet, those who do use these approaches profitably have demonstrated remarkable improvement in their vocations and interpersonal relationships.

As mentioned at the beginning of the chapter, there are other approaches now being used in addition to the ones discussed in great detail in this chapter. For example, psychodrama is a form of group therapy. In this particular technique, the client dramatizes his or her conflicts with the assistance of trained or untrained personnel who take the other roles required for the dramatization. In the course of playing these various roles, the participants obtain insights into their own personalities, into some of their problems, into their own psychological workings and into their own feelings and those of others. In a theater specially designed to facilitate this technique, the participants release strong emotions. In the course of psychodrama, all persons involved including audience members and staff may gain insight. For this reason, psychodrama is not confined only to people with pathological problems. Rather, it is a training in acting out past and present problems, both realistically and symbolically, both alone and with others. Thus, it helps to develop spontaneity and awareness from which "normal" people can also benefit, because nobody is without fears, personality weaknesses and anxieties of some kind.[42]

For several years, psychodrama has been used with mentally ill patients.[43] Today, psychodrama is often coupled with the use of television videotape[44] so that the emotional involvement can be relived and discussed. As a therapy, it is used with marital counseling, incest and rape victims, delinquent groups, prisoners in some correctional institutions and potential offenders.[45]

Another treatment modality recently being utilized is family therapy. Family therapy is a modality in which the entire family is brought before the therapist to resolve family conflicts in a more healthy "problem-solving" manner. In addition, the goal of family therapy is to strengthen the individual member against destructive forces both within him/herself and within the family environment. This technique has been extremely useful in dealing with runaways, adolescents who act out their behavior as delinquents or those who withdraw from life through alcohol and/or drugs. Today, many therapists realize that youth are not running to something as much as they are running from something, e.g., a "bad" home life. In this technique, the phenomena of multiple interacting disturbances among the members of the same family group are dealt with. For example, father-daughter incest is usually the result of an aggressive father who is lacking appropriate and meaningful love supplies in his life coupled with a passive mother who lacks self-esteem and coupling styles which can protect the daughter. Thus, to take the daughter and counsel only with her does nothing to change the family situation. As more and more people realize that disturbed family relationships play a role in the genesis of what others call delinquency, more and more family therapy is being utilized as courts order this treatment as a condition of diversion, probation and as treatment in lieu of punishment in an institution.[46]

Summary

Many community-based operations realize that it is not enough to provide a room free from the prison environment. It is important to attempt to provide treatment that prisons have long espoused but have been unable to provide.

Although some mention was made of approaches such as psychodrama and family therapy, specific information was focused on these four modalities: (1) reality therapy; (2) behavior modification; (3) guided group interaction and (4) transactional analysis. Each of these modalities were discussed in terms of the underlying assumptions, the use of the modality with offenders and then the criticism of that modality. Examples continued to show that all of these modalities are widely accepted and utilized in community-based corrections.

According to Glasser who developed reality therapy, people's behavior is the direct result of need-fulfillment. If one is able to satisfy or fulfill a specific need, then one does not have irrational, erratic behavior. In addition, the more one is able to live in the "here and now" the more one can fulfill one's needs within the framework of realilty. Reality therapy uses such concepts as need fulfillment, responsibility and reality. The goal of the therapist is to direct individuals into more responsible, more realistic behavior patterns.

The trained therapist uses reality therapy by being involved with the client in a *client-centered therapy*. Rejecting unrealistic behavior, the therapist becomes a tough, highly responsible person who sees the client as an intelligent person with high potential even though irresponsible. The therapist then teaches the offender better ways to fulfill his/her needs within the confines of reality.

The behavioristic model of therapy is based upon and organized around the principles of learning theory and experimental psychology. The origins of the behavioristic model are generally traced to the work of Ivan Pavlov, with the credit for its elaboration and refinement attributed to such noted psychologists as John B. Watson, B.F. Skinner and others. Behavior modification therapists maintain that the study of directly observable behavior and the stimulus and reinforcing conditions that "control" it should serve as the basis for formulating scientific principles of human behavior. The principal underlying assumptions of behavior modification are:

1. Most behavior, both desirable and undesirable, is learned and most of the learning results from the process of reinforcement. In other words, people learn those behaviors for which they are reinforced.
2. Undesirable behavior is the problem that needs to be eliminated. The emphasis is placed upon the behavior itself rather than exploring "inner" conflicts and attempting cognitive change.
3. To change behavior it is necessary to systematically identify and control the variables which reinforce the behavior. Behavior modification therapists maintain that behavior is shaped and maintained by its consequences.
4. The major responsibility for the content of therapy rests with the therapist who is considered a "reinforcement engineer."

One of the major distinctions that is made by behaviorists is the difference between classical (respondent) conditioning and operant (instrumental) conditioning. Both classical and operant conditioning assume that there is a causal relationship between a stimulus (an environmental condition) and a response (a specific behavior). However, classical conditioning is different from operant conditioning in that it focuses upon the situation which precedes a specific behavior, whereas operant conditioning focuses upon the situation which follows it. Essential to both classical and operant conditioning is reinforcement. Reinforcement refers to the strengthening of a response by its repeated association with some stimulus. Such a stimulus is called a reinforcer; it may be either positive or negative. Omission training, punishment training or aversion therapy, avoidance training and reward training were identified in the chapter as examples of some of the strategies employed in behavior therapy.

Social and cognitive psychology have also made contributions to behavior modification by the use of (1) expectancy; (2) perception of progress; (3) self-control; and (4) modeling. Behavior is modified by what people *expect*. If people expect improvement, improvement usually occurs. As a patient is given feedback, the individual is able to reinforce the change through the *perception of progress*. In helping the individual to monitor their own behavior, the individual takes more responsibility in *self-control* and in rewarding one's behavior. In *modeling*, the therapist shows the client exactly what is expected by doing the behavior. In this manner, the client not only knows what is expected but also can imitate the behavior.

Guided Group Interaction (GGI) uses a group process to restructure a new peer group in which clients work to help and control each other so that more socially acceptable norms and values ensue. GGI assumes that the group will influence an individual's behavior and thinking such that the individual will be manipulated by the group into legitimate pro-social behavior. Then the group will develop characteristics such as intimacy, interaction and feelings of sentiment. In short, they begin to "like each other" and that serves as an incentive for legal behavior and a fear of reincarceration. The nonauthoritarian atmosphere coupled with intensity of interaction, group homogeneity and group structure aid in defeating negative self-concepts and developing more positive self-images.

The main assumption of transactional analysis (T.A.) is that people's behavior and subsequent misbehavior is the result of their social interactions. Through socialization, each one of us has developed a child, adult and parent ego state. Consciously or subconsciously, the way we treat others depends upon which of these ego states we are in. Transactions are the result of the things people say and do to each other while they are in a particular active ego state. In addition, early in our lives, due to certain situations we have taken upon ourselves, we acquire one of the following emotional positions or *life positions:* (1) I'm Not OK - You're OK, (2) I'm Not OK - You're Not OK, (3) I'm OK - You're Not OK and (4) I'm OK - You're OK. We use these positions as a backdrop for interactions throughout life.

T.A. also uses the vocabulary of games and strokes. A game is a series of transactions with a specific outcome in mind for the person initiating the interaction. Games are successfully used by people who do not want to feel their condition, whether it be pain or love. So, they develop games to pass the time away and to make their life tolerable. Strokes are feedback—positive and negative. According to T.A., the need for recognition is so great that some people will seek and accept negative strokes as opposed to no strokes at all.

Each one of these modalities has been found useful and effective with certain groups of persons. Sometimes, in an effort to change people, a number of community-based correctional programs will use many of these approaches in concert with each other.

Notes

1. Most of the material in this section comes from the book written by William Glasser, M.D., *Reality Therapy: A New Approach to Psychiatry* (New York: Harper and Row, 1965) and a two-day workshop under his direction.
2. Ibid., p. xii.
3. Ibid., p. 20.
4. Ibid., p. xvii.
5. Clemens Bartollas and Stuart J. Miller, *The Juvenile Offender: Control, Correction and Treatment* (Boston, Mass.: Holbrook Press, 1978), p. 293.
6. Ernest Hilgard and Richard C. Atkinson, *Introduction to Psychology* (New York: Harcourt, Brace & World, 1967), p. 273.
7. Ibid., p. 280.
8. Robert J. Wicks, *Correctional Psychology* (San Francisco: Canfield Press, 1974), p. 56.
9. Ibid., p. 57.
10. Ibid.
11. W. Steward Agras, M.D., *Behavior Modification: Principles and Clinical Applications* (Boston, Mass.: Little, Brown and Company, Inc., 1972), pp. 14-21.
12. Stanlye L. Brodsky, *Psychologists in the Criminal Justice System* (Chicago: University of Illinois Press, 1973).
13. E. L. Phillips, "Achievement Place: Token Reinforcement Procedures in a Home-Style Setting for 'Predelinquent' Boys," *Journal of Applied Behavior Analysis I* (1968), pp. 213-223.
14. Teodoro Ayllon and Michael A. Milan, *Correctional Rehabilitation and Management: A Psychological Approach* (New York, N.Y.: John Wiley and Sons, 1979), p. 90.
15. R. L. Polakow and R. M. Doctor, "A Behavioral Modification Program for Adult Drug Offenders," *Journal of Research in Crime and Delinquency* (January 1974), pp. 65-66.
16. Ibid., pp. 63-69.

17. Ronald L. Akers, *Deviant Behavior: A Social Learning Approach* (Belmont, California: Wadsworth Publishing Company, Inc., 1973), p. 51.
18. F. Hussey and D. Duffy, *Probation, Parole and Community Field Services* (New York: Harper & Row, 1980), p. 218.
19. Bartollas and Miller, *The Juvenile Offender, op.cit.*, p. 298.
20. *The President's Commission on Law Enforcement and Administration of Justice, Task Force Report: Corrections* (Washington, D.C.: U.S. Government Printing Office, 1967), p. 40.
21. Wicks, *Correctional Psychology, op.cit.*, p. 32.
22. Glen H. Joplin, "Self-Concept and the Highfields Program," *Criminology* (1972), pp. 491-495.
23. Wicks, *Correctional Psychology, op.cit.*, pp. 52-53.
24. Lloyd W. McCorkle, Albert Elias, and F. Lovell Bixby, *The Highfield Story* (New York: Holt, Rinehart & Winston, Inc., 1958).
25. H. Ashley Weeks, *Youthful Offenders at Highfields* (Ann Arbor: University of Michigan Press, 1958).
26. Paul Lerman, "Evaluative Studies for Delinquents: Implications for Research and Social Policy." *Social Work*, XIII (1968), pp. 55-64.
27. Lamar R. Empey, "The Provo and Silverlake Experiments" in E. Miller and M. R. Montilla (eds.), *Corrections in the Community: Success Models in Correctional Reform* (Reston, Virginia: Reston Publishing Company, Inc., 1977), pp. 112-113.
28. Richard C. Nicholson, "Transactional Analysis: A New Method for Helping the Offender," *Federal Probation* XXXIV (September 1970), p. 29.
29. Except where quoted, much of the material from this section comes from summarizing the work of Thomas A. Harris, *I'm O.K. - You're O.K.* (New York: Harper & Row Publishers, 1967).
30. Wicks, *Correctional Psychology*, op.cit., p. 26.
31. Eric Berne, *Games People Play* (New York: Grove Press, 1964), p. 48ff.
32. Ibid.
33. Ibid., pp. 111-113.
34. Martin G. Groder, "K.I.U.D.," *Transactional Analysis Journal* 1:2, April 1970, p. 19.
35. Carl F. Jesness, "The Fricot Ranch Study Outcomes with Small Versus Large Living Groups in the Rehabilitation of Delinquents," Research Report No. 4F (Sacramento, California: California Youth Authority, 1965), pp. 89-90.
36. Ibid., p. 313.
37. Lois M. Johnson, "T.A. with Juvenile Delinquents," *Transactional Analysis Bulletin* III, 30, p. 31.
38. Wicks, op.cit., p. 29.
39. Franklin H. Ernst and William C. Keating, "Phychiatric Treatment of the California Felon," *The American Journal of Psychiatry*, April, 1964.
40. Nicholson, "Transactional Analysis," *op.cit.*, pp. 38-39.
41. Bartollas and Miller, *The Juvenile Offender*, op.cit., p. 291.
42. For more detailed information see Samuel Kahn, *Psychodrama Explained* (New York: Philosophical Library, 1964). Also see James L. McCary and Daniel E. Sheer, eds., *Six Approaches to Psychotherapy* (New York: The Dryden Press, 1955).

43. R. L. Williams and J. M. Gasdick, "Practical Applications of Psychodrama: An Action Therapy for Chronic Patients," *Hospital and Community Psychiatry*, XXI (VI) June 1970, pp. 187-9.

44. M. D. Goldfield and P. Levy, "The Use of Television Video-Tape to Enhance Therapeutic Value of Psychodrama, *American Journal of Psychiatry* CXXV (V) 1968, pp. 690-2.

45. See Daniel Brower and Lawrence E. Abt, eds., *Progress in Clinical Psychology* (New York: Grune and Stratton, 1956).

46. See G. Zuk and I. Boszormenyi-Nagy, *Family Therapy and Distrubed Families* (California: Science and Behavior Books, Inc., 1967).

Resources

Akers, Ronald. *Deviant Behavior, A Social Learning Approach* (Belmont, California: Wadsworth Publishing Co., Inc. 1973).

Berne, Eric. *Games People Play* (New York: Grove Press, 1964).

Glasser, William. *Reality Therapy* (New York: Harper & Row, 1965).

Harris, Thomas A. *I'm O.K., You're O.K.* (New York: Harper & Row, 1959).

McCorkle, Lloyd, Albert Elias and Lowell Bixby. *The Highfields Story* (New York: Henry Holt & Co., 1958).

Wicks, Robert J. *Correctional Psychology* (San Francisco: Canfield Press, c. 1974.

Woollams, Stan and Michael Brown. *T.A.: The Total Handbook on Transactional Analysis* (Englewood Cliffs, N.J.: Prentice Hall, Inc., c. 1979).

Chapter 11
Social Service Agencies

In this chapter, you will learn that some offenders possess special problems which make it extremely difficult to place them in community-based correctional programs that have been operationalized for the so-called regular offender. The purpose of this chapter is to acquaint you with the necessity of making referrals to other social agencies in the community, or perhaps even creating new social service agencies to meet the needs of some of the clientele of the community-based programs. Some of the persons who argue against the entire philosophy of community-based corrections do so on the claim that community-based programs offer no treatment modality while abandoning institutional controls.[1] One of the ways of defusing this argument has been by referring clients to existing social agencies. Then the clients are more apt to get the specialized treatment that community-based corrections espouses.

The second reason referrals are made centers around the training, skills and time allocation of the staff of community-based programs. It is unrealistic and impractical to think that a staff person of a community-based correctional facility can meet all of the needs of all the clients. The diversity and expertise of specific key agencies in communities are actively sought and utilized to fill the gaps.

Thirdly, some jurisdictions are very reluctant to hospitalize or incarcerate any but the most severely disturbed or criminally active persons because of the cost. Private care or counseling is out of reach for all but the wealthy or the well insured. Thus, referrals to social agencies that have trained personnel who have more time to develop a meaningful human interaction and charge on a "sliding-scale"—geared to the client's ability to pay—are an asset to the community-based program.

Fourthly, many correctional institutions may not have the program budget and/or trained staff to deal with specific important prisoner problems "inside the walls." For example, some of the offenders when they committed the crime may have been under the influence of chemical substances, i.e., alcohol and/or hard drugs. When those individuals get "inside the walls" of the correctional facility they have already gone through withdrawal. So, the correctional institution could argue that such chemical abuse programs are unwarranted. Convicts play into that game by denying they are, for example, alcoholics. For many persons, including convicts, an alcoholic is exemplified by a New York City skid row bum. Since a convict can justify to him/herself that that particular degenerate level has not been reached, then the convict can further rationalize they have no need for any alcoholic program even though that person has a low level of tolerance for alcohol. By referring individuals with these specific problems that have not been met "inside the walls" to agencies in the community, greater chances for a released offender to "go straight" are afforded. Some of the programs discussed in this chapter will show how these programs reintegrate offenders into society despite their special problems.

Mental Health and Retardation Programs

"Ron, a 33-year-old man who functions at the level of a ten-year-old, is serving five years in Rhode Island's Adult Correctional Institution for holding up a bank. Police caught him because he signed his name to the holdup note."[2]

"Nuts!" "Crazy!" you say. "Who in their right mind would sign their real name on a note to a bank teller to rob a bank?" The criminal justice system is filled with people whose behavior caused others to wonder about their mental faculties. Granted, some offenders are caught because they are clumsy. Some, however, are caught because they ineptly commit crimes - they do not have the mental capacity to plan them or to follow through. They do dumb things like sign their real names to robbery notes. They are mentally retarded and, therefore, must be differentiated from those who have average intelligence and are also clumsy, inept or psychologically disturbed.

Identification Problems

There are many kinds and degrees of mental health or its counterpart, illness, as there are many different kinds and degrees of physical illness. While the cause of mental illness might be as diverse as those of physical diseases, they both entail some of the same components. In fact, it is not uncommon for a physical ailment to produce a mental problem or vice versa. The reality of the complexity of this phenomena produces a confusion when identifying and correctly labeling offenders. We often judge others by our own misconceptions and fears. Thus, a mentally retarded person might be diagnosed as mentally ill or a mentally ill person as mentally retarded and thus, not amenable to any community program.

The prevalency of this identification problem is not just inherent in agencies in the criminal justice system; it prevails in our entire society.

Statistics gathered on this topic are, therefore, suspect and underestimate the societal problem. Bruce De Silva, a medical reporter for the Providence (Rhode Island) Journal-Bulletin, writing on the retarded offender says:

> It is estimated that three percent of the American population - 6.5 million people - are retarded. Scattered studies indicate that at least five percent of the inmates in jails and prisons - about 25,000 people - are retarded. Some studies suggest the figure is far higher. Few jail or prison admimistrators even try to identify retarded inmates, much less provide them with any special programming. The same is true of police, courts, probation and parole agencies.[3]

Other experts like Miles B. Santamour, Coordinator of the President's Committee on Mental Retardation, believe that retarded persons are and will be disproportionately imprisoned because they are poor. Being poor and lacking adequate social skills, like knowing how to fill out job application forms, they commit crimes. Since they cannot think quickly or fully appreciate the natural consequences of their inappropriate behavior, they get caught more often. In addition, they often confess, seldom plea bargain and are considered poor risks for probation or parole due to poor job prospects. Thus, they are convicted more easily and tend to get more frequent and longer prison sentences than other lawbreakers.[4]

In terms of mental health in prison, the situation is even bleaker for it is estimated that between ten and 35 percent of the state and federal inmates have serious mental illnesses.[5] Granted, some of the mental illness was prior to institutionalization; for others, the prison experience helped to create the sickness. In an article entitled, "Who Will Care for the Mad and the Bad?", Rob Wilson shows the problems are created when prisons become dumping grounds and prison administrators are left to their own discretion, as opposed to guidelines and procedures based on empirical research, as to who would benefit from incarceration in a mental institution and who should be kept in the regular prison.

These introductory paragraphs, summarizing some of the problems of mental retardation and mental illness among offenders, do not adequately reflect the immensity of the problems. However, the purpose of the chapter is to show how referrals are made to social agencies. Because of that focus, attention will be directed from the problem to the specific programs that have attempted to deal with these problems.

Programs

Distinguishing prisoners having mental health problems from those mentally retarded is not easy. The South Carolina Department of Corrections has created a Special Learning Unit at Kirkland Correctional Facility in Columbia.[6] This program, begun in 1975, is one of the oldest of the special programs for retarded offenders. One of their main goals is to teach survival skills, i.e., money management, using the telephone, telling time, hygiene, sexuality, cooking meals, to the 17- to 25-year-olds serving indeterminate sentences as youthful offenders. In addition, the staff teach prison guards in the state system to identify and handle inmates who are retarded or have other developmental disabilities. Although not intensive training, the two hour course does give an overview of what retardation, autism, cerebral palsy and epilepsy actually entail. In giving useful clues to guards, the guards are able to lower their expectations and are less willing to force retarded persons to perform as average inmates. Needless to say, in the past, mentally retarded offenders were being written up or locked up more than the average inmate because they did not fully understand the rules or were unable to fully understand the subculture they were in.

Through the use of different kinds of intelligence tests administered to inmates under different conditions, South Carolina and North Carolina are in the forefront of identifying retarded inmates and providing special, appropriate programs. The American Association on Mental Deficiency and the agencies in the criminal justice system seem to be emerging upon a definition of retardation as an IQ of 70 or less.[7] Remember, the average IQ is 90 to 110. Granted, there are problems with cultural and educational factors in reaching a true IQ score. Yet, it is a method of identification.

Another method of identification was developed by Pima County Arizona Adult Probation Department.[8] The only apparently special probation program for retarded offenders, this program was begun in July, 1972. Funded through the Law Enforcement Assistance Administration (LEAA), this pilot project was to identify retarded probationers and develop services uniquely aimed at their problems. The staff found that even though they developed a list of numerous outward manifestations of retardation, many retardates failed to display any unusual manifestations. Furthermore, a fact that was given as an identifying factor in one case was totally inapplicable in another. So the Probation Department, in conjunction with the Court Clinic which does the psychometric testing and/or psychological evaluation, developed a test to screen all defendants so as to indicate the possibility of retardation. Those persons whose test scores suggested mental retardation were referred to the Court Clinic on a voluntary basis for further testing and evaluation. Then the more lengthy and costly tests were administered to confirm or to deny the mental retardation.

Through these tests, the Adult Probation Department became aware that the mentally retarded person was able to comprehend little, if any, verbal instruction. As some probation officers already suspected, mentally retarded persons cannot comprehend counseling instructions or probation conditions which are imparted in a verbal, conversational manner. (It is suspected that those persons, like children, might be inclined to say "yes" to things they do not fully understand.) To avoid this tendency of saying "yes," the retarded probationer is subjected to a verbal test to determine comprehension.

To counsel these persons, specific staff were trained in the "simple treatment modality which had been suggested by Elizabeth Nicholds. It embraces four techniques, as follows: (1) environmental manipulation; (2) supportive relationships; (3) clarification; and (4) interpretation."[9] Staff who were not previously trained in depth in either casework or problems of the mentally retarded were able to be effective with probationers.

In the previous example, referrals were made to another more highly skilled agency to determine the extent of mental retardation. Once that task was accomplished and the mentally retarded probationer identified, the Probation Department continued their services in a modified form.

In another community, Probation Officer William Breer, San Bernardino County, California, talked about supervising schizophrenic adolescents.[10] He mentioned that latent and incipient schizophrenics are often misdiagnosed. Because of their lack of interest in reality, schizophrenics score poorly on I.Q. tests and, therefore, are labeled as mentally retarded. When the mental condition has reached the state of catatonic stupor or there are florid hallucinations and delusions, the diagnosis is easy and the estimates of cure extremely low. The nature of Officer Breer's article, as exemplified by the following statement, is to identify when an adolescent suffers from this mental condition and how an officer can make proper referrals:

> The actual treatment and cure of schizophrenia, where it is possible at all, will take more time and training than most probation officers have. In many cases, medication will be necessary at least on a temporary basis. A probation agency is in no position to offer medication. Referral to an agency equipped to deal with schizophrenic problems is indicated whenever possible.[11]

As our society becomes more educated in mental health and retardation, more people will be willing to permit development of special programs to meet these specific needs. In the meantime, some departments of corrections are paving the way, such as the Morrison Youth Center, outside Pinehurst in North Carolina. The first half of the program for 18- to 21-year-olds who are first time prisoners and have not committed a violent crime is to teach the basic living skills. Usually, a retarded offender in the program spends four hours a day on academic subjects at their special education level, two hours in vocational instruction and one hour with their counselor who serves as a case manager. The second part of the program involves six social workers who work outside the institution "in the field" to help prepare the inmate and the family for the reintegration. Besides the obstacle of poverty, the social worker often finds retardation in other family members, sometimes even the mother or father. Due to their illiteracy and low social awareness, the family members need help to get through the maze of social services, job applications and food stamp questionnaires to get the benefits they need. In this program, the case worker, like a parole officer, helps to develop the inmate's home, job or school plan for parole. The social workers contact employers, schools or sheltered workshops. Sometimes, when the family is so disorganized that the parole board will not permit the youth to return home, the social worker locates for the retarded inmate a developmental center or state approved rooming house to live in.[12]

Whereas the state of North Carolina used social workers as the bridges to community agencies to service the needs of inmates, other programs which are community-based refer clients directly to any community mental health or retardation program just as any other citizen in the community might call up the agency for those services. On the other hand, instead of referring clients outside to a separate agency, some mental health programs feature counseling services as part or parcel of their program. An example of this approach has been the Community-based Adolescent Diversion Project, Champaign-Urbana, Illinois and Project CREST (Clinical Regional Support Team) of Gainesville, Florida.[13] Both programs have won the Exemplary Projects Program award as an outstanding criminal justice program by the National Institute of Law Enforcement and Criminal Justice, the research component of the Law Enforcement Assistance Administration (LEAA).

On the program in Illinois, undergraduates at the University of Illinois act as volunteer counselors with juveniles in a diversion project. That means the juveniles adjudicated have had police contact but have not been involved with the juvenile court. The volunteer counselors receive academic credit in psychology and training and supervision by experienced psychologists as an ongoing course activity. The program in Florida uses volunteer graduate students to counsel selected juvenile offenders on probation and to work with their families and schools. Guided by a small professional staff affiliated with the University of Florida, CREST volunteers help the juvenile probationers to "open up" and discuss their problems without fear of being judged. In this manner then, the counselors play a supportive role to complement the probation officer's role and approach. Both programs have proven themselves as being effective, less costly programs for dealing with individuals who are in need of psychological counseling.

Mental health and retardation programs can be parts of programs or be developed through referrals to outside and separate agencies. Obviously, referrals depend upon knowing the various agencies with their rules and regulations. Since much of that material on establishing and maintaining good working relationships with other agencies has been discussed in another chapter, no more will be said on how to get a referral program going. The examples of programs introduced in this section do show the variety of bases from which criminal justice agencies can build bridges to other social agencies to meet the particular needs of the offender.

Alcohol and Drug Treatment Programs

The special needs of persons who are addicted to drugs and other substances have long been recognized by our society. In fact, communities on a local level have long been plagued with the task of "what should we do?" Carrie Nation's tactic of using a hatchet to destroy barrooms never really became a national prototype. Instead, various programs like Alcoholics Anonymous (AA) were created to aid persons with alcohol problems. Alcohol and substance abuse is not only a problem in the society at large, it is also a problem within the prison as well. Statistics specifically gathered on federal prisoners show that 82 percent of the total inmate population has either been alcoholic or had committed alcoholic related crimes.[14] In cities like New York City, many officials assert that much of the crime committed is drug related. So, many of those offenders have need of drug treatment programs.

Today, there are innumerable alcohol and drug programs in this country. Some of the programs, like AA, have been permitted into the walls of prisons over the past 40 years. Other programs have been more recently organized as a diversion strategy and, thereby, operate outside the prison walls but with a similar high degree of control over participants.

In this particular section, specific approaches that are representative of the programs throughout the United States will be discussed. Alcohol treatment programs include discussion about AA, Luther Compass Center (a skid row mission in Seattle, Washington), behavioral conditioning and the newer megavitamin and mineral therapy. Drug treatment programs, such as Synanon, Daytop and Delancy Street will be illustrated. Then the newer programs representing a merger of different strategies in a concerted effort to alleviate both drug and alcohol abuse will be discussed.

Alcohol—Our Biggest Drug Problem

Alcoholism is the excessive use of alcohol to the point that one's health, social functioning or vocational objective is measurably impaired. (Alcohol is considered as a "mind changing" drug.) One does not have to be a "skid row" resident to be diagnosed as needing assistance with an alcohol tolerance problem. Since many authorities argue there is no single cause, there are many programs that represent physiological, psychological or sociological approaches or combinations thereof.

Decriminalization of Alcoholism

In 1970, President Nixon signed into law the "Comprehensive Alcohol Abuse and Alcoholism Prevention, Treatment and Rehabilitation Act." In 1971, the National Conference of Commissioners on State Laws adopted a Uniform Alcoholism and Intoxication Treatment Act which provided a model for states to decriminalize alcoholism and public intoxication. These acts gave the communities the legal framework within which to approach the problem.

The decriminalization of alcoholism from the criminal justice system had been recommended by courts, Presidential Commissions and professional organizations.

In 1974, Public Law 93-282 was signed and it renewed the national commitment to deal with alcohol abuse. It espoused the idea of direct federal assistance to community-based programs to develop methods to divert problem drinkers from criminal justice systems into prevention and treatment programs. This law amended the Alcoholism Act of 1971 to provide the first comprehensive approach to the issue of confidentiality and privacy for people with drinking problems.

To date, it is no longer a crime to be drunk and in public in most of the United States. If one is both drunk and in public, the person is taken by the police to the detoxification center where the individual can "dry out" and volunteer for the assistance the program has to offer. The alcoholic is not arrested and processed through the criminal justice system. The only time the criminal justice system comes into operation and imposes legal ramifications is when an individual is driving while intoxicated. Even in these cases, communities like Jefferson County, Missouri, have created an Alcohol Related Traffic Offenders Program (ARTOP).[15] Clients for the program come as (1) direct order of the court; (2) condition of probation; or (3) part of a suspended imposition of sentence. The participants are then subjected to lectures and films for five sessions to help break down the denial, projection and rationalization defense systems so well entrenched and to identify alcoholics who need more intensive treatment. ARTOP is viewed as an effective program to provide the initial stage of treatment. Then referrals to other treatment programs and aftercare are provided when necessary.

Alcohol Treatment Programs

Alcoholics Anonymous (AA)

There are many organizations which have been developed specifically to aid alcoholics and/or families of alcoholics. Most noted has been the efforts of Alcoholics Anonymous (AA). AA began in 1935, in Akron, Ohio, when a New York broker, Bill, an alcoholic, recovered through a spiritual experience. Bill assisted his alcoholic doctor-friend, Dr. Bob. Together they developed AA on the basic principles from the fields of religion and medicine plus their intuitive awareness of alcoholics and their defense and denial mechanisms. There were several years of trial and error as this society selected the most workable tenets. Three successful groups emerged, (1) at Akron, Ohio; (2) at New York City; and (3) at Cleveland, Ohio. In 1939, the infant society wrote the book *Alcoholics Anonymous* wherein the Twelve Steps and the application of these steps to the alcoholic's dilemma were made clear. Proof that alcoholics could recover brought national attention. Continuous publicity freely given by magazines and newspapers throughout the world brought an expansion of groups and membership. It was out of this explosive experience that AA's Twelve Traditions took form and were endorsed at AA's first International Conference held at Cleveland, Ohio, in 1950.[16]

Briefly, the program operates this way. A person who has an alcoholic problem is referred to AA. People who have volunteered to be AA sponsors meet with the referred person and invite him or her to the AA meeting. At the meeting, all the individuals present acknowledge the 12 steps and the 12 traditions. The following are the 12 steps:

1. We admitted we were powerless over alcohol - that our lives have become unmanageable.
2. Came to believe that a Power greater than ourselves could restore us to sanity.
3. Made a decision to turn our will and our lives over to the care of God as we understood Him.
4. Make a searching and fearless moral inventory of ourselves.
5. Admitted to God, to ourselves and to another human being, the exact nature of our wrongs.
6. Were entirely ready to have God remove all these defects of character.
7. Humbly asked Him to remove our shortcomings.
8. Make a list of all persons we had harmed, and became willing to make amends to them all.
9. Made direct amends to such people wherever possible except when to do so would injure them or others.
10. Continued to take personal inventory and when we were wrong promptly admitted it.
11. Sought through prayer and meditation to improve our conscious contact with God as we understood Him, praying only for knowledge of His will for us and the power to carry that out.

12. Having had a spiritual awakening as the result of these steps, we tried to carry this message to alcoholics, and to practice these principles in all our affairs.[17]

Sponsors help persons to work through each of the preceding steps on a step-by-step basis. When that has been accomplished and the referred person has reached step 12, then the referred individual becomes able to help others. This willingness to help others on a volunteer basis has been the only program that most local jails have been able to sponsor and are willing to permit inside the walls. Once inside the walls, like clergy, AA sponsors would hold weekly meetings for the prisoners. When the inmates had served their time and were released, the ex-offenders had at least one person in the community-at-large to whom they could turn for continued support—the AA sponsor.

Although AA is highly effective with most persons who attend the programs, AA has not had much success with such groups as upper-class persons and skid row alcoholics. The conceptual scheme of AA in which alcoholism is viewed as a physical, emotional and spiritual disease has meaning for many middle and upper-middle-class persons. This program provides an understanding for the individual and his/her disordered drinking. The opportunity to assist other alcoholics helps to alleviate the feelings of social guilt. For upper-class persons, however, AA has difficulty creating a social interaction model. Since upper-class persons often avoid public exposure or social interaction with other levels of society, they are more apt to refer themselves for treatment to a private hospital. Also, upper-class persons tend to reject the notion of abstinence from alcohol as a goal of treatment.

The skid row population, which often includes people from various social classes, finds AA programs less meaningful for them. The skid row alcoholic is often unable to respond to the demands for regular attendance at meetings. The verbal interchange about how he/she became an alcoholic does not hold great meaning or importance. Also, the AA program is not designed as a social and economic support system. Since these individuals have these special needs for their rehabilitation, some agencies have created a more encompassing program. One agency that has had some success with skid row alcoholics has been the street mission of Luther Compass Center.

Luther Compass Center

The Luther Compass Center was founded in 1920 by an erstwhile seaman-turned-minister in Seattle, Washington. In 1973 they experimented with a social delivery system to aid skid row alcoholics. Attributing high recidivism rates to the lack of a social reentry, this skid row mission developed five overlapping phases wherein the clients were able to rebuild effective social bonds: (1) recruitment and intake; (2) residential period; (3) transition period; (4) community reentry; and (5) follow-up. The intake phase was to collect pertinent background data and develop a strategy for rehabilitation. The residential period lasted from 30 to 60 days. This represented a drying out period in conjunction with formal and informal group and individual counseling sessions, development of reentry skills and meeting with the sponsor or advocate couple who as volunteers would aid in the reentry process and attendance at AA meetings. In the transition and reentry phases, the advocate couple would assist the individual in surveying prospective job opportunities, filling out job applications, etc. The advocate group did not find the man a place to live or a job, but, upon his request, assisted him in finding work and lodging.

In an evaluative study of this operation by Mauss and Fagan, they found that of the 97 enrolled in the reentry program, only 19% had been abstinent at least six months at the time of follow-up even though 32% were employed at follow-up and 48% have improved their income.[18] The implication is that even though some of the men may still be occasionally drinking, they are still able to be employed. The success of these figures rested with these major events: (1) favorable outcome of in-house experience; (2) length of stay in residence (abstinence was inversely related to length of stay, while employment was positively related to it); and (3) favorable experiences with the advocates or sponsors. As the evaluators also noted, the client success in terms of rehabilitation was also determined by personal traits, i.e., race, marital status, age, employment history, state of health and income. There are alot of programs that fail while others are only marginal. Perhaps the success of any program is determined by the clientele in that some clients bring more assets than liabilities into a program, i.e., job skills, younger ages. The reason this program was viewed as successful was the fact that a more comprehensive approach of counseling, finding employment and housing was utilized with AA as a component as opposed to it being the major and/or only treatment.

Behavioral Conditioning

There are two general behavioral conditioning techniques used in the treatment of alcoholism: (1) aversion therapy and (2) behavioral therapy. Since both techniques stem from the treatment modality of behavior modification discussed earlier in chapter 10, they have some similarities. They differ, however, on their goals. In aversion therapy, the ultimate goal is abstinence, while in the other model, the goal is control of drinking.

Aversion therapy, developed and used at the Washingtonian Hospital in Boston some 40 years ago, used emetine to establish a conditioned reflex of nausea and vomiting at the sight, smell and taste of alcoholic beverages. For the past 30 years, there has been another chemical treatment for alcoholism—disulfiram. Better known by one of its trade names, Antabuse, this chemical acts by interrupting the body's metabolism of alcohol, leading to the buildup of another chemical - acetaldehyde. Once Antabuse is introduced into a person's system, it takes a minimum of 96 hours to completely dissipate from the body. Meanwhile, if the individual with Antabuse in his system partakes of any alcohol, the individual experiences a reaction. The nature of the reaction varies with the individual. Usually, the individuals experience a headache, nausea and vomiting. In more severe cases, people can experience breathing difficulty, chest pain and dizziness. Even if a probationer with Antabuse in the body system puts on after-shave lotion which contains alcohol, he can expect to be sick.

Antabuse as a "pill for alcoholism" is most useful as a treatment method for people who do not plan to drink and are susceptible to impulse or spree drinking. Individuals with serious heart or liver disease cannot tolerate the potential reaction for medical reasons. While Antabuse may be strongly considered as one of many possible methods of helping an alcoholic return to a normal life, it is not an effective treatment method for all alcoholics. Thus, other methods have been devised.

To control the drinking behavior a fairly new approach has been designed to aid the alcoholic. Predicated by the beliefs and research of Lemere,[19] Davies,[20] Bolman,[21] Pattison[22] and Akers,[23] alcoholism is viewed as a learned behavior which can be unlearned and replaced with a newer, learned behavior. At the Alcohol Treatment Center at Washington State University (Pullman, Washington), in 1976, the therapy was accomplished through a three-part procedure. In the first procedure, the alcoholic was permitted to drink beer in the relocated bar room on the college campus. As he/she drank, he/she was periodically removed from the bar scene to a breathanalyzer. This was done to accomplish step one—teaching the alcoholic to discriminate their blood alcohol level (BAL). The level of the BAL was set at .06% since technically one could be arrested for DWI at such a level. As the alcoholic continued to drink, he/she was monitored. If the BAL is below .05%, the individuals experienced no adverse effects. If the level goes higher, they are punished by means of an electrical shock. This shock procedure is step two. In step three, the person tried to learn to sip the drink, set the glass down in between sips, choose less potent drinks, anything to keep the BAL below the shock level. Thus, this final procedure is called shock avoidance.

Procedures such as these which teach new drinking patterns are viewed by some as a more realistic treatment goal. Since our society is so drug oriented, and preoccupied with notions of food and drink, some individuals find it too hard and impractical to completely withdraw. When the court gives an offender an option to attend AA meetings or participate in this behavior therapy as either a part of the probation sentence or as a method of diversion for first-time offenders, many offenders choose this therapy. Obviously, some people would rather learn to keep their behavior within the societal limits than to completely abstain.

Megavitamin and Mineral Treatments
(Orthomolecular Treatment)

Numerous physiological, biochemical and hereditary causes for alcoholism have also been proposed based on research done on animals and severe alcoholics in hospital settings. Megavitamin therapy has proven successful with schizophrenics. Both alcoholics and schizophrenics have abnormal carbohydrate metabolism, hormone imbalance, nutrient deficiency, liver dysfunction, wheat-grain allergy, functional or metabolic disorder in the brain and, in extreme cases, similar hallucinations which have identical chemical origins.[24]

In scientific research directed by a famous biochemist, Dr. Roger Williams, wrong diet was found to be the cause of alcoholism. Williams and his colleagues, using rats, showed that diets deficient in essential nutrients encourage alcoholic consumption in animals and that their drinking habits could be reversed by adding the missing nutrients to their food.

The idea that malnutrition is a contributing factor to alcoholism has been tested by other leading scientists. In fact, replication of Williams research at Loma Linda University in California showed that cravings in rats for alcohol could be induced by feeding them a diet high in refined carbohydrates, low in vitamins, minerals and proteins.[25]

Orthomolecular treatment has been utilized with offenders in their respective institutions as well. To alleviate the effects of poor diet and malnutrition, Dr. Russell F. Smith, medical director of Michigan State Boys' Training School, used large doses of niacin (vitamin B_3). He noted 86 percent of the hard-core alcoholics as being effectively helped and niacin therapy to be more useful than other drugs used in other treatments of alcoholism due to alcoholics' high potential for abuse and for suicide.[26]

The Chrysalis Outpatient Treatment Program in Minneapolis, Minnesota, has incorporated nutritional counseling with its program for women and their children who are affected by alcohol or drug abuse. This center, funded by a grant by the National Institute of Alcohol Abuse and Alcoholism, is unique in that it offers nutrition education and counseling to a large population of native Americans. The word "outpatient" in this treatment program means that individuals/offenders do not live in or are not restricted to the confines of the institution. Rather, they are free to come on an appointment basis to receive the guidance they need.[27]

Additional confirmation of the megavitamin therapy approach to the treatment of alcoholism comes from North Nassau Mental Health Center and its director, Dr. David R. Hawkins. "In his program patients are given one gram of vitamin B_3, one gram of ascorbic acid, 200 International Units of vitamin E, all four times a day, and 50 milligrams of pyridoxine once a day."[28] In addition, patients are put on a diet of high protein and no refined carbohydrates to correct low blood sugar problems. Since 1966, Dr. Hawkins has documented a 71 percent success rate. In light of the fact that most drug and alcohol programs have operated with approximately 15 percent success rates, the success rate of Dr. Hawkins' program has been viewed very favorably.

Comprehensive Approach

The trend in alcoholic programs has been to use the detoxification units as umbrella agencies to develop and provide recovery services for persons both in and out of the criminal justice system. An example of such an umbrella agency that utilizes a comprehensive treatment strategy is the Recovery Services Council, Inc., in Wichita, Kansas. That agency operates the detoxification center to which police bring their worthy candidates. Participants of the program, though, do not have to be brought by the police; people can walk in from the street. During the detoxification stay wherein individuals go through withdrawal, the participants have a safe, protected place to sleep, meals, showers, clothing, individual and group counseling plus megavitamins. The idea of an umbrella agency means that an agency serves to sponsor or cover other programs. In this particular situation, besides the walk-in center and "detox" facilities which resemble a hospital ward, the agency sponsors reintegration facilities located in other buildings. These reintegration services are met by a halfway house specifically for men and one specifically for women. Then, the agency operates a "three-quarter" house for men who have completed the alcoholic treatment and still need a place to live until they are fully absorbed into the working and living life of the community.

This organization also works with the community, local courts and parole officers to aid in early identification and assistance with public education of alcoholism. Their family services section gives support and education to families while another section of the agency assists manufacturing, business and other agencies to provide help for alcoholic employees.

Drugs and Treatment Programs

We are a society preoccupied with food, drink and a great desire to reduce all pain. It really is not wonder we have a national problem with alcohol. It is also no surprise then that our country also has a drug abuse problem. Heroin, morphine, methadone, valium and librium are documented as the abused substances. Other abuse substances, especially for youth, are paint thinners, glue and metallic paints. Drug abuse stems from the idea that a person has developed an addiction or tolerance for a particular substance. That means that the body demands more of the drug to reach the previous physical or psychological levels of experience. So, the individual usually has to increase the dosages to feel a certain way whereas before, the person could feel that way with lesser amounts of the drug.

Treatment programs in the United States have included such programs as hospitalization, imprisonment, institutional group and individual counseling, community surveillance and testing as in methadone programs, case work programs in the community and self-help organizations composed of ex-addicts. The most celebrated of the ex-addicts mutual aid organizations have been Synanon, Daytop and Delancy Street which have served as community models for other ex-addicts in other cities.

Synanon House

Synanon House was opened in 1958 by an ex-alcoholic as a therapeutic community in which addicts could live and help each other to remain free of their addictions. Today, the organization provides a life-style for former drug abusers, juvenile delinquents, alcoholics, felons and other troubled and character-disordered people, as well as for people who have no history of self-destructive behavior. In short, this private community is for anyone who seeks a drug-free, integrated and nonviolent community. Communities are presently located in Santa Monica, San Francisco and Marin County, California with intake centers located in Detroit, Michigan and New York City. Associated communities have also opened in Berlin, Germany and Malaysia.[29]

The Synanon program provides a process of intellectual, vocational, physical and moral education through a process of a so-called Synanon Game. It is not a game in the conventional sense. Rather, it is a forum for conversation where people speak their subjective, uninhibited truths to each other in a controlled setting. Through encounter group sessions conducted by residents several times a week, rationalizations and deceptions of individuals are exposed. Synanon House got its name from a resident who was trying to pronounce the words he thought describe those group forums as "seminar" and "symposium."

Besides these group sessions of truth, another trademark of the Synanon House is the "haircut." Justified through the rhetoric of "attack therapy" in formal psychotherapy, a new resident is given a "haircut" and relentlessly, verbally attacked by the other residents until, theoretically, the person encounters their real self divested of the false fronts or masks.

Synanon has had many scholarly supporters. One such person has been Lewis Yablonsky who has written a definitive history of Synanon in his book, *The Tunnel Back*.[30] As the title suggests, the author favorably viewed this program as a help to persons who had few programs open to them save imprisonment. Synanon does have an exceptional in-house record of success. Yet, because Synanon has done little to prepare persons for adjustment to an outside world of frustration, the relapse rate for graduates who leave Synanon has been recorded at 90 percent by the director and founder himself, Chuck Dederich.[31]

In recent years, Synanon developed into a militaristic, religious cult which was forced to close down most of its centers after the conviction of most of its leaders, including Chuck Dederich, on charges ranging up to attempted murder. Since that conversion to a cult status and the jailing of its leaders, the group has lost most, if not all, of its respect as a treatment group. In addition, Synanon limited admission to only the most sincerely and deeply motivated to ending their addiction. This and the fact that they were not showing any particular signs of success were some of the other criticisms against the program.

Daytop[32]

Formerly known as Daytop Lodge, Daytop Village was established on Staten Island in New York City in 1963. Since that time, Daytop Village has expanded programs in houses to Swan Lake and on 14th Street in Manhattan. The founders of this enterprise were Joseph A. Shelby, chief probation officer of the Brooklyn Supreme Court, Dr. Daniel Casriel, a psychiatrist and Herbert Bloch, a professor-criminologist. These founders were disenchanted with past efforts to treat drug addiction. Yet, they were driven to do something about the problem due to the high cost of the drug problem. So, they made an on-site survey of detection and treatment programs throughout the United States. The foremost impressive program was Synanon, so they modeled their program accordingly.

"Daytop" is really an acronym for Drug Addicts Treated on Probation. As that full title reveals, the program was structured to accommodate addicts referred to them by the court on a probation status. Instead of being sent to prison, an offender would live in the halfway house with the idea of ultimately being reintegrated into the community-at-large. Chemical testing was also added to this program to provide research data and control over people. Thin-layer chromatography of urine samples acted as psychochemical deterrents to drug addiction.

Patterned on Synanon, Daytop uses the intensive group therapy. The resident is not permitted to project the blame for his/her addiction on anyone but him/herself. The theme of this program is that the reason a person is addicted is because of stupidity and the addict chose to act stupidly. Like Synanon, an individual initiates a request for admission and has to show the prerequisite sincerity before admission. If he/she is accepted, the person sits in a specific chair for several hours while the other, older residents ignore the new resident. As the hostility becomes filial affability, the new resident discovers the genuine concern and caring the residents have for one another.

Daytop's emphasis upon substituting a new value system and

reintegrating addicts into the outside community has made this program a model for many other communities.

Delancey Street[33]

Founded in 1971 by one of Synanon's "turned-off" disciples, John Maher, Delancey Street is located in the former Russian and Egyptian consulates in the exclusive Pacific Heights section of San Francisco. Similar to Synanon, Delancey Street uses the attack therapy. Yet it departs markably on the principle of the closed society. Realizing the reintegration into the larger society is the desired goal, the director has developed a program around communal family businesses such as a restaurant, a flower shop, a moving company, a garage and a maintenance service. The residents pledge themselves to a two-year commitment to either work in these businesses or to go to school. From the income derived from these businesses, the residents are fed, clothed, trained and sent to school.

Another unique feature of this program was the fact that it was created and nurtured without any federal government or endowed foundation's financial assistance. Maher, a reformed addict, thief, procurer and numbers runner, claims he financed the beginnings with a $1,000 donation from an underworld loan shark.

These three programs of the 1960's and 1970's have had numerous supporters—some of them eminent corrections scholars and practitioners. They have also had their critics and through those critics, newer approaches have emerged.

Newer Approaches

During the 1960's and 1970's, a vast array of innovative programs gradually unfolded for the treatment of drug addiction. Millions of dollars were generated and funneled into this national problem. The Drug Abuse Research and Training (DART) center was established. Yet, there has been no dramatic breakthrough. In fact, methadone, the treatment used most and acclaimed as the "cure," has now been attacked as part of the disease by advocates of drug-free therapy programs.[34] Because of the magnitude of the problem, innumerable drug programs have been developed. Yet, few have been successful or long-lived.[35] States that once advocated one approach have changed. For example, New York, California and Florida were the three states in which an addict received compulsory hospitalization for detoxification under civil commitment. In 1970, Florida repealed its civil commitment statute.[36] Recent articles on this topic suggest California is beginning to question its approach as well. Synanon, Daytop Village and Delancey Street, community-based, therapeutic communities that advocate intensive group therapy and the so-called "attack therapy" may become part of the past as well.[37]

The past history of despair with this problem and the recognition that there are increasing numbers of "poly-drug abusers" has caused some "realists" in the drug abuse treatment community to advocate "holistic" or "multimodality" approaches. From their arguments and support, programs in the future will offer many therapeutic and chemical techniques. In fact, since there are many similarities in alcohol and narcotic addiction, some people have argued for consolidation: "The physical plants, experienced staff and years of experience are available and could be utilized to eliminate costly duplication in many, if not all, of these areas."[38]

An example of such a consolidated effort has been Hospitality House (HH) in Albany, New York.[39] HH is a nonsectarian, nonprofit, co-educational therapeutic community incorporated under the New York State Department of Social Services. That program accepts drug abusers, alcoholics, criminals, etc., because of the belief that antisocial behavior in general can be attributed to the individual's inability to come to terms with his/her bad feelings about oneself in a positive way. Realizing that feelings may have been engendered by a myriad of causes: family, social environment, friends, bad self-image, this program serves as a vehicle for self-growth by confrontation and identification with others who have experienced the same emotional disability. In other words, this program does not consider drugs to be the problem as much as the people. People's problems seem to be centered around the lack of self-awareness, self-confidence and an understanding of social interaction. HH, by accepting referrals from New York State Parole and Albany County Probation, to only mention a few of the public agencies, is able to receive state financial support yet be able to maintain and control the agency as a private agency.

Perhaps, because of the successes of such programs as HH, federal regulations have recently been changed so that they require all methadone programs to design both short-term and long-term individualized treatment. The goal is to include therapeutic programs such as individual and group counseling and encounter groups so that methadone programs are not just "filling stations."[40]

Meanwhile, the search continues for a "cure" for drug abuse. The most promising research with drugs, like alcohol, comes with neurochemical research. It has been shown that the human nervous system produces naturally a morphine-like substance called "endorphins." The task has been to prove that the production of these naturally occurring substances may somehow be altered by long-term narcotics use. If it can be shown that there is a biochemical imbalance, then a direct chemical may be used to correct the imbalance.[41]

Alex Schauss, who has written a book called *Orthomolecular Treatment of Criminal Offenders* and continues to write and do research in this area, had firsthand experience working with heroin addicts in Harlem in 1968 using this newer approach of orthomolecular psychiatry. The combination of wholesome food, adequate in protein, with daily intense physical exercise turned pale skinny junkies into healthy, happy men and women.[42]

Further support for this approach comes from Barbara Reed, a probation officer in Cuyahoga Falls, Ohio, who has been treating all kinds of ex-convicts with diet for the past ten years. In her testimony before the Senate Select Committee on Nutrition and Human Needs in 1977, Barbara Reed said that 252 of the 318 probationers had serious dietary deficiencies. She convinced the group of 252 persons to reduce or eliminate red meat, eat more whole grains and vegetables, fish and poultry, and strike all refined sugar and flour products completely from their diets. Two and a half years later, of those who stuck with the diet change, not one had been in trouble with the law. In a more recent interview by a national health society, she stated that of the 1,000 ex-offenders who have gone through the dietary program and remained on the diet, 89 percent have not been rearrested over the past five years.[43]

Although this newer approach has been generating impressive results, there are critics who suggest that this approach is not the answer for all causes of crime or delinquency. The rebuttal among the researchers in this area is that once the addiction has taken place, the treatment for the addict, whether the addiction be to drugs or alcohol, must begin on a physiological level. Once the chemical imbalance has been corrected, then other psychological modalities can be used to address the personal and/or social factors which shaped the introduction to the addictive substance.

Structural Treatment Approaches

Persons who are addicted to drugs (including alcohol) differ in their abilities to independently support themselves and to maintain meaningful relationships with others. The differences in degrees of addiction are, therefore, considered in treatment programs. As was shown earlier, skid row alcoholics who experience severe difficulty in social and economic functioning need a rehabilitation program encompassing many support systems. They also need a program that permits them, at least initially, a chance to limit their functioning and suffering the consequences of their choices. Taking more control over some of these individuals is, indeed, a worthy goal. Some of these persons have never achieved adequate functioning because they had become addicted at a young age. By taking more control over their lives during the withdrawal stages, the program permits the individual a chance to know what it is like to be free of the chemical imbalance. It is really difficult to tell a sick person, he/she is sick until that person has experienced health. Having once experienced a more healthy state, the individual is more willing to remain in and seek treatment.

In order to take into account the differences in degrees of people's needs for rehabilitation, the general approaches to the effective treatment of addicted persons can be summarized as (1) crisis intervention; (2) semi-protected environments; and (3) rehabilitation services.

Crisis Intervention

Addicts that are in need of this type of program usually are functioning at a low level of independence. In fact, they are suffering from crises stemming from severe medical illnesses, lack of food, or shelter and/or legal action against them. Crisis intervention programs establish an immediate relationship to address the immediate crisis. Once that crisis is reduced where needed, referrals to other existing community agencies are made to attend to the underlying problems which precipitated the crisis. In this approach, the establishment of a trust relationship is extremely important. The addict usually wants to receive immediate and practical aid to a specific crisis, not necessarily a change in their lifestyle. Once that aid is rendered, however, the addicts are more willing to seek the advice and counsel of persons in that program. For some addicts, it is the crisis intervention programs in the community that are like glue—they hold them together.

Semiprotected Environment

The semiprotected environment is treatment in the first stage in what is often a long therapeutic process. The detoxification center of Wichita, Kansas, illustrated earlier in this section, exemplifies this approach of taking control over an addict's behavior for a period of time so that through experience, an addict can control his/her own body and mind and thereby function adequately.

One of the common fallacies in the design of this approach has been to conceive of the program as time-limited. The Luther Compass Center thought in terms of time and stages. Yet, even with the basic supports of food, shelter and sponsors, it is difficult for some individuals to utilize these supports and mobilize their resources as quickly as others. Just as parents soon learn that each of their children are different and grasp certain skills at differing times than the other children, program developers and administrators of alcoholic and drug abuse programs are recognizing the differing learning patterns among their residents. To facilitate more successful development and utilization of support systems, a graduated series of protected environments have been developed. Thus, programs in this approach will run the gamut of the continuum from high agency control in a totally protected living environment, to a halfway house requiring outside employment, to a three-quarter house with minimal supervision, to a boarding house or group living arrangements in the community with no formal agency control or supervision.

Rehabilitation Services

Once the addict has resolved the immediate crisis and/or the basic support systems have been mobilized in his/her life, attention can be directed toward rehabilitation services. Whether ordered by the court or sought for by the individual, the therapeutic task is to help the addict develop or redevelop social and job skills, find a place to live and work and to deal with other human beings in appropriate ways.

As mentioned in terms of crisis intervention, some programs incorporate rehabilitation services as a component of their services. Sometimes rehabilitation services are provided by other social service agencies in the community so that referrals have to be made to help the addicts be successfully reintegrated into the law-abiding community-at-large.

Ex-Offender Employment Programs

Think about yourself for a moment. Your job—especially the income it produces—determines to a great extent the kind of life you live. Now think about ex-offenders. Daniel Glaser, in his extensive study of prison and parole, concludes that "unemployment may be among the principal causal factors involved in recidivism of adult male offenders."[44] The problem, then, of unemployment among ex-offenders has been the major impetus for the development of private and public programs. Before a look is taken at selected programs, the obstacles of hiring ex-offenders will be examined.

Obstacles

Stigma

In 1946, a survey of businessmen was made by the Randen Foundation to ascertain the amount of discrimination against ex-offenders. Of the 475 prospective employers in most areas of business, 312 stated unequivocally that they would not hire an ex-offender while 101 stated they would, provided the men were qualified for the work. That stigma still exists in more recent times. "In a 1968 public opinion poll, 74 percent of those interviewed said that they would feel uneasy working alongside someone who had been convicted of a crime and would hesitate to hire an ex-offender for a job involving any degree of trust or responsibility."[45]

The hiring policies of many businesses, both private and public, restrict, if not totally refuse, admittance of ex-offenders. Some trade unions also deny membership to ex-offenders. So, if the ex-offender in applying for a job, tells the truth, he/she runs the risk of being disqualified for the job; if he/she lies, he/she runs the risk of being discovered at a later date and being fired for "falsification of application."

Lack of Work Habits and Skills

One of the greatest obstacles in working with ex-offenders has been their general unemployability. Although a few states have substantially increased their commitment to prisoners for vocational and higher education, for the most part much of the training inside prisons "are a sham, oriented more to institutional maintenance than to inmate's needs."[46] Even if a prisoner is trained in a marketable skill, the inmate often lacks good work habits, the necessary confidence and self-esteem and the knowledge of obtaining jobs. Yet, without employment, "the unemployed or underemployed parolee is four times more likely to be returned to prison than his fully employed counterpart."[47]

Bonding

A third major obstacle in the employment of ex-offenders has been the requirement in certain businesses that applicants be bonded. "Blanket bonds" protect the employer against dishonest losses caused by any of the employees in large retail and service businesses.

The Federal Bonding Program was designed to meet this need for ex-offenders. The Department of Labor would purchase a face schedule fidelity bond and provide it free to any ex-offender who had been refused bonding coverage by regular commercial sources and was seeking a job where bonding was a condition of employment. When an ex-offender has been bonded under this program and performs the job successfully for eighteen months, then he/she can be eligible for commercial bonding.

The obvious rationale behind the Department of Labor's efforts was to demonstrate "that hiring and bonding ex-offenders is not such a risky business and that when the ex-con is given a job with stable income, he is no more likely to pursue criminal activities than his unconvicted co-worker."[48] Yet, this program has not reached the majority of ex-offenders. Some reasons stem from lack of state employment offices' utilization and promotion of the program. Another reason stems from the commercial bonding's indifference or outright resistance to the program. Since they are able to use the past stigma and fears people have toward ex-offenders, commercial bonding companies lose the higher rates they could charge plus the actual business when the Federal Bonding Program insures an ex-offender. So, "many private sureties have threatened to cancel, or to refuse to renew, a company's coverage if it utilizes the Federal Bonding Program."[49]

The Law and Licensing

All states have some statutory and constitutional provisions that restrict entry into government employment and "licensed" occupations. Sometimes these restrictions are for anyone convicted of a felony. So, even if a person does not serve time an a penal institution, they can still suffer the consequences of the "civil death" which denies a whole host of civil rights, i.e., right to vote, serve on a jury, hold state or municipal office, etc.

Licensing of occupations serves several functions. The manifest function centers around the theme of "public protection." Yet, the reality is that licensing also restricts entry into the profession and thereby creates an economic advantage. In the penal institutions, many inmates are taught barbering. Yet, barbering is one of the most restricted of all regulated occupations. In 46 states and the District of Columbia, licenses are required. "Only in Alabama, Massachusetts, New Hampshire, and South Carolina can the ex-offender work as a barber without interference by the state licensing agency because of his criminal record."[50]

Summary

Any programs to help ex-offenders, especially with employment, will have difficulties. First, inside the penal institution we fail to train and educate. Then, members of our society, uninformed and misguided to be sure, refuse to hire the ex-offender. Then, the private bonding industry intimidates employers while restrictive occupational licensing requirements seem to serve their own self-interests. The irony of the situation is that we spend millions of dollars to rehabilitate the offender and then frustrate the reintegration of that individual by raising legal barriers against his full employment. The purpose, then, of ex-offender programs is to enhance the reintegration of the offender, especially in employment.

Programs

Programs to help in the employment of ex-offenders have been developed by self-help groups created by ex-offenders like Fortune Society and 7th Step. Businesses and departments of corrections in conjunction with other state agencies have recently developed impressive programs.

Self-Help Groups

The Fortune Society

Since 1967, this group of former offenders has been helping both men and women to restructure their lives so that they can be useful members of society. Fortune Society has developed a one-to-one counseling and tutoring program and career development, i.e., vocational training, job readiness workshops and job development.

This Society began in 1967 when David Rothenberg was producing a Broadway play, "Fortune and Men's Eyes." Since the play dealt with prison life and problems, the producer innovated a weekly forum which would permit audiences to interact with ex-cons. People in the audience invited panels of ex-cons to speak to their churches or school groups. When the demand was so large, the group formalized. Today the staff consists of 18 ex-cons, nine 'squares' and hundreds of volunteers. The Fortune News, once consisting of a one-page mimeographed letter sent to 37 people, is now a twelve-page printed newsletter sent to over 30,000 people in 50 states and 23 countries. Thirty-five ex-offenders comprise the speakers bureau to give presentations throughout the country. The Fortune Society offices are visited weekly by over 300 men, women and juveniles just released from institutions.[51]

7th Step Foundation

Founded in 1963 by an ex-convict, Bill Sands, this foundation of ex-convicts and other volunteers who have never been convicted of a felony unite to help rehabilitate inmates and former inmates of penal and/or correctional institutions. In his book, *My Shadow Ran Fast*, Bill Sands told of how he came to originate seven steps for convicts at the Kansas State Penitentiary, Lansing, Kansas. In the following seven steps, notice how each represents a short version of the 12 steps used in AA and how the first letters of each beginning word for each step spells FREEDOM:

1. Facing the truth about ourselves and the world around us, we decided we needed to change.
2. Realizing that there is a Power from which we can gain strength, we have decided to use that Power.
3. Evaluating ourselves by taking an honest self-appraisal, we examined both our strengths and our weaknesses.
4. Endeavoring to help ourselves overcome our weaknesses, we enlisted the aid of that Power.
5. Deciding that our freedom is worth more than our resentments, we are using that Power to help free us from those resentments.
6. Observing that daily progress is necessary, we set an attainable goal toward which we could work each day.
7. Maintaining our own freedom, we pledge ourselves to help others as we have been helped.[52]

This foundation works through its 85 local groups, mostly in the midwest, with referrals to professional and social agencies when necessary to offer a five part program:

1. Pre-release—to offer counseling and group meetings to people inside prison
2. Post-release—to hold meetings for released prisoners
3. Employment—to help ex-convicts find jobs
4. Juvenile—to work with the potential felon who is under 20 years old

5. Public information—to inform the public about crime and what is needed to prevent it and to reduce the tendency to return to criminal behavior.[53]

Business Groups—National Alliance of Business

There are many companies and corporations that recently have involved themselves in training offenders both inside and outside the prison walls. The National Alliance of Business is such a group. Founded in 1968, this organization is a coalition of executives from industry, U.S. Department of Labor and organized labor who work to solve the problems of unemployment in the nation's largest cities. In each of these cities, an Alliance team from their 4,000 staff persons, under the direction of a presidentially-appointed chairperson, conducts job pledge campaigns to locate meaningful employment for ex-offenders. This team also helps other groups to find employment, such as the disadvantaged, Vietnam veterans and needy youth.[54]

Formerly known as the National Association of Businessmen, this organization also developed a campaign to hire ex-offenders through the media. In one particular advertisement, there is a picture of a young, white male sitting on a jail bed. The title that captures the citizen's attention is, "When it costs up to $10,000 a year in taxes to keep a man in jail, he's not the only one who's paying for his crime."[55] The ad further says that if an ex-offender does not get a job, sooner or later he'll probably return to jail. That then, is not only a waste of money but also a waste of a man. What to do? Why, call the "National Alliance of Businessmen" if you can give ex-convicts a chance by giving them a job.

Department of Corrections

The Ex-Offender Program[56] in Kansas has been operating for five years and has served as a model for other departments of corrections that need and want to work in cooperation with multi-agencies in government to insure a former inmate a reasonable opportunity for success. Through the Governor's Special Grant and the Comprehensive Employment and Training Act (CETA),[57] the Ex-Offender Program was established under the supervising agency of the Kansas Department of Human Resources.

The staff of this program contact inmates at the correctional facilities throughout the state prior to release. The primary target group is state parolees. Yet, service and assistance is also given to federal parolees and county probationers. Through this program, the staff are committed to state parolees for the length of their parole.

The basic task of the Ex-Offender Program is to coordinate state and community resources such as the Department of Unemployment to attempt to place former inmates in a suitable job, commensurate with the offender's training experience and interests, as soon as possible before or after release. To accomplish this task, CETA sponsors vocational training programs at the respective institutions to broaden employment opportunities for inmates upon their release to the community. Secondly, a community awareness and acceptability of ex-offender programs has been created, especially with potential employers and business groups. For the fiscal year of 1979, this program had 835 active applicants of whom 811 were referred to specific job openings. Throughout that fiscal year, 514 individuals were placed through a total of 675 transactions. That means that some individuals left one job and went to another. Child molesters and rapists are the hardest offenders to place.

State parole officers welcome the services of the staff of the Ex-Offender Program. Parole officers, who often carry high case loads, lack the necessary time, skills and resources to find parolees jobs. If a parole officer did work on the job aspect of the parole, it would mean less time devoted to other aspects of the client's parole adjustment. So, the parole officers keep in touch with clients and available jobs and follow-up on individual cases. The job developers, staff of the Ex-Offender Program, take applications and interview inmates and assist inmates released from prison on work furloughs to find suitable work. In addition, the staff provides follow-up assistance for ex-offenders who want to better themselves through higher level employment and employment counseling for those individuals who find great difficulty in keeping a job.

Summary and Final Comments

An unprecedented effort has been made in the past ten years to expand job opportunities for ex-offenders. That task has included efforts to overcome the obstacles of stigma, lack of work habits and skills, bonding and legal issues. Some legal obstacles still remain to be resolved such as the potential liability incurred by an employer who hires a former offender. "Although many private businesses attest to the fact that the ex-offenders they have hired pose no greater risk as employees than persons hired 'off the street,' ... to what extent is an employer held accountable for the misdeeds of an employee with a prior criminal record?"[58]

To accomplish the goal of employment for offenders, more than 250 programs throughout the United States have been developed to offer a wide range of services such as counseling, work orientation, training, job development, job placement and follow-up assistance.[59]

As revealed by a national survey assessing community-based programs which provide employment services to prison releasees, there is a great variation in programs in the types of employment services offered and the ways in which these services are delivered.[60] Furthermore, little is known about the types of service which seem most effective or the organizational arrangement for delivering those services.

Some of the programs for employment for ex-offenders are initiated by self-help groups, business groups and/or departments of corrections. Many of the noted programs are prototypes from which programs of the future can be modified to develop a more comprehensive program with better linkages between staff of correctional facilities and community-based employment services programs.

Finding jobs is only part of the problem. The other part is keeping the job. Wildcat Service Corporation set up by the Vera Institute of Justice, Ford Foundation, has developed a unique experience to work with former drug addicts and ex-offenders in New York City to provide jobs. The jobs are real in that job holders are expected to show up on time, be at work every day and perform to high standards. What has been unique about this program to job creation is called "supported work." Supported work includes "an environment of low stress at the onset; with job demands increasing gradually as participants adapt to working conditions; and work with persons from the same background who can support and encourage each other. Wages are paid from a salary pool composed of existing public funds (welfare payments, job training grants and the like) and payments generated from jobs performed."[61] The supported work concept was funded in 1975 from the U.S. Department of Labor, five other federal agencies and the Ford Foundation to be applied to groups different from ex-offenders, i.e., welfare mothers, out-of-school youth and groups in different localities.

In the future, impact studies on employment programs might look to job quality, job stability and the severity and types of crimes committed. Certain ex-offenders because of their previous criminal activities are more difficult to place and, therefore, might be in need of even more assistance.

Legal Aid Programs

History

There is power in the knowledge of law and the ensuing complex institutional structure that utilizes law. This has been demonstrated by the success of legal services to the poor and to other groups historically denied such access. One of the last groups to whom these legal services have been granted has been incarcerated felons. That does not mean, however, that convicts never raised the issue until recently. In fact, as early as 1871 (*Ruffin v. Commonwealth*)[62] a convict raised a legal question and was told that he was a temporary slave of the state who had forfeited all his rights.

In terms of prisoners rights, the state and federal courts had taken a "hands-off policy." Their noninterference on the basis of separation of power meant that they viewed the administration of prisons as an executive function. In reality, their decision strengthened the status quo and continued to isolate penal systems from public scrutiny.

As the years went by, more and more cases were brought before state and federal courts. The rights to legal services for those incarcerated have been long in coming. What rights have been gained are only a frontier area. In a few states, a prisoner has regained the right to vote as well as a right to launch civil suits. In previous times, a prisoner could not launch a divorce case even though he/she could be sued by others.

Today, the rights gained by prisoners are numerous and lengthy and beyond the scope of this section. What is important is the fact that once the Courts affirmed the idea that there is an *affirmative responsibility* of the state to "insure that inmate access to the courts is adequate, effective and meaningful,"[63] then it became only a matter of time before several legal assistance programs showed the relevance of legal services to rehabilitation efforts.

In many states, the process of incarceration produces other legal consequences for the offender than just the obvious criminal sanctions and records. Stripped of civil rights, the inmate and ex-offender lack protection and knowledge and, therefore, become victims of others' criminal behavior. For example, if a prisoner orders some items through a mail-order house and never receives what he/she has paid for, what can he/she do? Many states permit the spouses of inmates to sue for a divorce based on their incarceration and, thereby, absence from the home. The inmate, however, cannot countersue. Right loses are different in every state, as are restoration procedures. So, legal programs both inside and outside the prison walls have been established to aid in the rehabilitation process of offenders. In ths section, four legal aid programs will be discussed which utilize the services of law students, jailhouse lawyers, resident attorneys and public defenders with expanded duties. Some legal aid programs for offenders in community-based corrections are primarily designed to refer offenders to existent legal aid societies, whereas others are programs in and of themselves which hire the services of attorneys on a part or full-time basis to address the legal problems of ex-offenders, reduce the hassles of those situations and facilitate the rehabilitation process. To gain a better understanding of the operations, a few of the programs will be discussed.

Programs—Inside the Walls

The Supreme Court in 1941 first ruled that inmates had a right to access to the courts.[64] But it was not until 1969 that the Court ruled in *Johnson* v. *Avery* that when there is no other available source of legal assistance, inmates may act as jailhouse lawyers and not be punished for their efforts.[65] A report from the American Bar Association's Resource Center on Correctional Law and Legal Services cites four specific groups which have emerged to provide ways of assuring meaningful access to the courts: (1) law students; (2) jailhouse lawyers; (3) resident attorneys; and (4) public defenders with expanded duties.[66]

Law Students

Prior to 1969 and the *Johnson* decision, there were few law programs to assist prisoners. Today nearly 100 exist, providing varying degrees of full legal service coverage to incarcerated individuals.[67] One such program is a program that utilizes law students.

Some states view law students working with inmates as a "reasonable alternative" to providing more expensive and legal services. Yet, there are shortcomings of law school programs. Law students are first and foremost students. Therefore, their time and resources are limited especially during examination periods and vacations. Their loyalty and commitment to becoming a lawyer, can, and often does, curtail the weekly trips to the institution for interviews and legal counseling. In general, commentators have identified the following five areas of deficiencies in services to prisoners by law students:

1. insufficient supervisory personnel
2. inability to respond promptly to requests for assistance
3. inability to follow through to litigation status
4. lack of continuity in handling cases
5. lack of effective preliminary screening.[68]

The critics do not mean that all law school clinical programs are a sham. Rather, the consensus seems to be that if law students are the *only* available source of legal aid, then the program could not possibly provide many prisoners with meaningful access to courts. Thus, recommendations include having the projects staffed with lawyers trained in the law of corrections and prisoners' rights. In this manner, the shorter, more straightforward cases can be handled by the law students and the more complex cases that will drag over a long period of time can be handled by the staff lawyer.

Jailhouse Lawyers

Prior to the growth of prisoners rights and more public awareness of prisons, jailhouse lawyers or writ writers were the only available source of legal aid to most prisoners. A jailhouse lawyer acted as his own lawyer in jail and for a fee would provide legal services to other prisoners. Since 1969, under the *Johnson* mandate, states have been required to provide adequate law libraries. As stated in the *Johnson* case, jailhouse lawyers or writ writers were given official sanction for their efforts in that they could no longer be punished for their efforts.

In some states, the administration of prisons have fostered the development of jailhouse lawyers as a source of legal assistance for other inmates. In Pennsylvania, for example, the institution provides work credit, supplies and office space to a group of writ writers who have banded together to provide free legal services to other prisoners. In Nebraska, writ writers are awarded good time credit for their work.

Jailhouse lawyers, however, are not necessarily adequately educated or trained or have sufficient legal materials. As a result, cases fail. The courts ask that a client exhaust all administrative procedures first. Another reason for failure is that in doing their own legal work, they apply the wrong remedy to the situation. An additional reason jailhouse lawyers are not as effective as regular attorneys centers around the issue of mootness. By the time a prisoner finds out how to prepare the case and brings the court's attention to that matter, the prison administration might have changed the policy. Thus, the courts will rule the challenge as "moot" when in fact, the injustice may exist simply in another form.

To counter some of these deficiencies, the American Bar Association granted the Michigan Bar Association permission to commence their program in which 20 inmates received intensive training as paralegals and were supervised by two staff attorneys. The results of their effectiveness study showed that paralegal trainees improved their legal knowledge and became a more visible legal resource for other inmates.[69] The positive results of this program will encourage others to develop similar programs and to enhance the status of writ writers as persons within the prison who through selection, training and supervision can be employed as meaningful legal assistance.

Resident Attorneys

Several states grant legal aid to prisoners by providing a program staffed by regular attorneys whose offices are at or close to the institution, i.e., Texas Staff Counsel for Inmates Program. These licensed attorneys and paralegals provide legal assistance that differs in scope and extent of services depending upon the state. For example, the Texas program handles all matters except criminal appeals and Section 1983* cases, while in Massachusetts, the project attorneys can handle all cases.[70]

The problems of using resident attorneys are mainly cost and allegiance. If the project is funded by the state, prisoners may not trust the attorney for fear he/she is working for the state. If the attorney is staff, how does he/she relate to correctional officials? The American Bar Association Center favors a resident counsel to be independent of correctional staff so as to win prisoners' confidence and be able to handle Civil Rights Act cases.[71]

One of the states that sponsors such a resident attorney program has been Washington state with their Washington Legal Services to Prisoners Project.[72] Established in 1972, the goal was to provide for the legal rights of prisoners and to reduce recidivism. At the time an effectiveness study was

---

*Section 1983 of the Civil Rights Act provides a good faith defense to shield the police from civil liability from an arrest that later turns out to be illegal. In addition, this section has been used by prisoners to challenge their condition of incarceration because inmates can present claims directly to the federal courts for review without first exhausting state remedies.

conducted by Alpert, et al., six attorneys, three paralegals and a supportive secretarial staff served more than 2,300 inmates incarcerated in the Washington state prison system.[73] Besides the normal civil legal assistance, the project staff taught in the pre-release classes on such topics as consumer protection, landlord-tenant law and other problem areas that ex-convicts and parolees might face. In short, the staff provide services for all kinds of situations except in those matters that generated a fee or that were strictly criminal matters. Most of the cases concerned civil cases, family problems and problems created by the incarceration.[74]

Using a longitudinal format of two time periods, 198 persons completed their interviews in February 1975. Of those 198 persons, 91 used the legal aid services and 107 did not. Controlling for the use of legal aid services, the researchers concluded that "participation in the legal aid project is a significant factor in producing positive changes in prisonization and in prisoners' attitudes toward police, lawyers, law and the judicial system.[75]

Public Defender—Expanded Duties

Some jurisdictions have statewide appellate defender services, some of which handle appeals, detainers and sentencing problems. Of the four groups offering access to the courts for inmates, this group is the least likely to provide the other needed services. "In several states, the public defender is not even authorized by state legislation to handle post-conviction relief cases, much less the more common civil law matters, such as divorce proceedings. A credible legal assistance office cannot, however, limit its representation to some types of legal matters, but not others."[76]

In conclusion, all four of these groups try to remove or at least satisfactorily settle the problems of inmates with the hope that by providing meaningful access to the courts, (1) the probability of criminal behavior will be reduced; and (2) faith in the legal system will be restored.

Programs—Outside the Walls

As programs to provide legal aid services developed inside the walls, programs have also emerged outside the walls usually as part of a total program to service the needs of ex-offenders. For example, *COSOAP* is a comprehensive one-stop offender aid program in Cincinnati, Ohio, to assist ex-offenders. Once the ex-offender is seen by intake workers, the area of needs are prioritized and together both caseworker and ex-offender plan to resolve the problems. If legal aid is needed, services are provided as well as vocational counseling and a workshop to learn the basic elements of seeking and keeping employment.[77]

Programs For Female Offenders

Programs for female offenders have had numerous problems closely parallel to the deep deficiencies of jails and prisons in general, i.e., limited financial resources and staff personnel for such a comparatively small population. In addition, this clientele has low economic and educational attainment levels which combine with their minority racial makeup and their status as mothers to produce problems that could be best resolved on a national level but are not.

One of the earliest programs created by a group of persons to give aid and succor to "that class of Unhappy Females who have Strayed from Virtue" was the Magdallen Society of Philadelphia, Pennsylvania in 1800.[78] Today, as in yesteryears, people on the outside of the prison walls have formed a number of organizations to respond to women prisoners' problems and to bring those problems into national view. Some of these organizations are funded by governmental agencies, particularly by the Law Enforcement Assistance Administration (LEAA) or the American Bar Association.[79] Some are service groups from the local communities who are inadequately aware of the political functions which the prison system serves. By providing literature, a sympathetic outside ear, caring for prisoners' personal affairs and helping to find employment and housing upon release, these service organizations provide services for which the prison should be responsible.[80] Some are support groups armed with political consciousness. The following names of some of the service and support groups reveal their purposes:

Buffalo Women's Prison Project (New York)

Women Out Now (Seattle, Washington)

Bay Area Committee for Women Offenders (California)

Women Against Prison (Ann Arbor, Michigan)

Action for Forgotten Women (Durham, North Carolina)

Coalition for Women in New York State Prisons

Chicago's Women's Prison Project (Illinois)

The Link Society (Alabama)

Help Our Prisoners Exist (Oklahoma)[81]

Some groups like Still Doing Time realizes that after release, a female offender has a record and, therefore, in essence is still doing time. So, these female ex-cons help women coming out of Cook County Jail to find employment, housing and other needed resources to deal with drug and personal problems.[82]

Some groups are not only geared to a woman's unique problems but also to her ethnic background. For example, the Puerto Rican Women's

Prison Project is aimed at helping largely neglected Hispanic women prisoners at Riker's Island facilities in New York City. Project Phoenix offers job, housing and educational counseling and referrals to Native American prisoners, probationers and ex-cons in Milwaukee, Wisconsin. Cor Azon y Sangre de los Mejicanos is a service group for women with Chicano heritage in the Arizona State Women's Prison.[83]

There are some model pre-release and work release programs for women. The Federal Reformatory for Women in Alderson, West Virginia has a pre-release program to aid the reentry into society.[84] The Nebraska State Reformatory for Women has a work release program which operates to meet the specific needs of the participants. Placement is viewed in terms of possible effects upon the citizens of the community, on the program, on the reformatory and on the inmates.[85]

Perhaps the most noted of the community outreach programs has been the one established by Purdy Institute for Women near Seattle, Washington. Outside the confines of the state prison (which looks more like a college campus than it does a prison) is a 22 two-person-unit apartment house. When the women have learned enough responsibility and control over their behavior such that they have moved from the maximum security unit to the medium, to the minimum, they are then placed in the apartment building. Then, they go to work for someone in the community and return to their apartment at night. This process is better able to meet the individual needs of women for it permits women to get job training in areas in which they are interested. As the inmate works, she also learns to care for herself and pay her bills. She is charged for rent and utilities, etc. When one visits the facilities, one is impressed with the play equipment purchased by community groups for the children who come to visit their mothers. As the authorities watched the interaction between mothers and children, they soon realized that they also needed to provide a program to help women develop more effective parenting skills. The essence of the Purdy program is to do all that is possible to teach a person responsibility for their own behavior by a series of steps and levels so that individuals will gain useful skills and higher self-esteem to avoid returning to a life of crime.

Before concluding this section, a few words need to be said about the efforts to develop other alternatives to prison. The YWCA in Seattle, Washington, has developed a community residence program in which selected women are sent from the court to this resident center where they are put into a work release program. In this residential setting, the residents are permitted to have their children with them. Thus, the program emphasizes teaching parenting skills and providing information about community resources so that women can better survive the multiple role demands.

Another example of a diversion program for women is Quest House,[86] located in a residential neighborhood in San Francisco, California. As of

1977, it was the only privately supported alternative to prison for women (or men) in the state of California. By recommendations of a probation officer or the court, women are referred to Quest House. Quest House will not accept those who have serious emotional problems or heavy drug habits. That means, the crimes of the women accepted by this facility have run the gamut from forgery to prostitution and manslaughter to bombing of government property.

The program at Quest House, like Purdy Institute, emphasizes independent living. In vocational counseling, the woman fantasizes about what she would like to be doing. Then discussions are held with a counselor to place the fantasies into realistic goals so that a woman can accomplish worthwhile desires. By a method of weekly contracts, the woman offender works on part of a long-term contract which will reach her vocational goals she set for herself. Besides vocational skills, women learn to plan menus, cook, clean the house and yard. All of this is done to help them be able to care for themselves. Before a woman can leave, she must have a source of income and a place to live. Usually, all of this is completed in six months because the average length of stay is six months.

In short, spurred on by the Law Enforcement Assistance Administration Task Force on Women and local feminist and community groups, more programs have been developed both inside and outside the prison walls. The purpose of these programs has been to mitigate the pains of imprisonment, address the unique problems of women and to develop a more total, comprehensive system of rehabilitation so that women stand a greater chance of being reintegrated into society and their families.

Summary

Although inmates may share the common experience of the "pains of imprisonment," their special needs or problems can greatly hamper the reintegration process.

The five specific problem areas center around programs developed for people with (1) mental health and/or retardation problems; (2) addiction to alcohol and/or drugs; (3) employment problems; (4) legal problems; and (5) being a female. In each of these five areas, programs are shown to either be developed especially for these groups or to utilize other community social service agencies through a referral system.

Mental health and retardation programs are one of the most neglected areas in the criminal justice system. Few jail or prison administrators even try to identify retarded inmates let alone provide them with any special programming. The pioneering work of the South Carolina Department of Corrections shows how prison administrators and guards can be trained to distinguish prisoners having mental health problems and those who are mentally retarded and can thereby develop programs to meet their needs.

The Adult Probation Department of Pima County, Arizona, is also an example of a program that identifies retarded probationers and develops services uniquely aimed at their problems. Examples of both juvenile and adult correctional systems show how some agencies use social workers as bridges to community agencies to service the needs of the inmates with these particular problems whereas other programs which are community-based refer that offender directly to a community mental health or retardation program just as any other citizen in the community might call upon that agency for services.

The need for alcohol and drug treatment programs reflects the fact that alcohol and drugs have long been a special problem with offenders. Alcoholic programs include the more successful programs like AA. Other treatment approaches available are a skid-row social reentry treatment program, the behavioral conditioning treatment of aversion therapy, behavioral therapy and the orthomolecular treatment which includes megavitamin and mineral treatment. Other treatment approaches are those that follow a comprehensive approach: the agency provides detoxification care and recovery services and may use many of the foregoing treatment approaches.

Treatment programs in the United States for drug addicts have included such programs as hospitalization, imprisonment, institutional group and individual counseling, community surveillance and testing as in methadone programs, case work programs in the community and self-help organizations composed of the ex-addicts. Because the ex-addicts' mutual aid organization had a substantial impact on the treatment of drug addicts in the 1960's and 1970's programs such as Synanon House, Daytop and Delancey Street were established. The newer approaches to drugs recognize the increasing number of "poly-drug abusers" and, therefore, have developed "holistic" or multimodality programs.

These three different approaches of structural drug and alcohol treatment take into account the differences in degrees of people's needs for rehabilitation: (1) crisis intervention, (2) semiprotected environments and (3) rehabilitation services.

An unprecedented effort was made in the past ten years to expand job opportunities for ex-offenders. That task included efforts to overcome the obstacles of stigma, lack of work habits and skills, bonding and legal issues. Some legal obstacles still need attention, such as the potential liability incurred by an employer who hires a former offender. Some of the programs for employment for ex-offenders were initiated by self-help groups like Fortune Society and 7th Step Foundation and by business groups like the National Alliance of Business and departments of corrections.

The loss of civil rights are different in every state and so are the restoration procedures. Yet, legal aid programs both inside and outside the prison walls have been established to aid in the rehabilitation process of offenders. Four legal aid programs established are: (1) law students; (2) jailhouse lawyers; (3) resident attorneys; and (4) public defenders with expanded duties.

Spurred on by the federal government and local feminist and community groups, programs have been developed for another group with special problems—female offenders. From inside and outside the prison walls, programs have been established by female support groups to help find employment and housing upon release and other needed resources to deal with drug and personal problems. Some groups, not of a national dimension but rather of a local area, are geared to a woman's unique problems and to her ethnic background. Some pre-release and work release programs for women have also been sponsored by the Federal Reformatory for Women in Alderson, West Virginia, and Purdy Institute for Women in the state of Washington. Diversion programs have also been sporadically developed.

One should be aware of the concerted effort to develop a more total, comprehensive system of rehabilitation. Through social services referrals, bridges are built from institutions into communities and vice versa to develop a more supportive system and to address some of the unique problems or special needs of inmates so that they will stand a greater chance of being reintegrated into a lawful society and meaningful relationships with their families.

Notes

1. Andrew T. Scull, *Decavation. Community Treatment and the Deviant: A Radical View* (Englewood Cliffs, New Jersey: Prentice-Hall, Inc., 1977).
2. Bruce DeSilva, "The Retarded Offender: A Problem Without a Program," *Corrections Magazine* 6, 4 (August 1980), p. 33.
3. Ibid., p. 25.
4. Ibid., p. 26.
5. Rob Wilson, "Who Will Care for the Mad and Bad," *Corrections Magazine* 6 (February 1980), pp. 12-17.
6. DeSilva, "The Retarded Offender" op. cit., pp. 30-31.
7. Ibid., p. 26.
8. Arnold Talent and Robert E. Keldgord, "The Mentally Retarded Probationer," *Federal Probation* 39 (September 1975), pp. 39-42.
9. Ibid., p. 40.
10. William Breer, "Probation Supervision of the Schizophrenic Adolescent," *Federal Probation* 40 (June 1976), pp. 21-28.

11. Ibid., p. 26.
12. DeSilva, "The Retarded Offender," op. cit., p. 26.
13. U.S. Dept. of Justice, *Exemplary Projects* (Washington, D.C.: National Institute of Law Enforcement and Criminal Justice, LEAA, 1974), pp. 22 and 25.
14. Douglas Haines, "Alcoholism in Prisons," *International Journal of Offender Therapy and Comparative Criminology* 22 (2), 1978.
15. Stephen F. Huss, "The Alcohol Related Traffic Offenders Program," *Federal Probation* 40 (September 1976), pp. 13-16.
16. *Twelve Steps and Twelve Traditions* (New York, N.Y.: Alcoholics Anonymous World Services, Inc., c. 1952).
17. Ibid., pp. 5-9.
18. Armand L. Mauss and Ronald W. Fagan, "An Evaluation of the Social Re-Entry Program of the Lutheran Compass Center in Seattle, Washington." Paper presented at the Society for the Study of Social Problems Meetings, Boston, Massachusetts, August 1979.
19. F. Lemere, "What Happens to Alcoholics?" *American Journal of Psychiatry* 109 (1953), pp. 674-676.
20. D. Davies, "Normal Drinking in Recovered Alcoholic Addicts," *Quarterly Journal of Studies on Alcohol* 23 (1962), pp. 94-104.
21. W. M. Bolman, "Abstinence versus Permissiveness in the Psychotherapy of Alcoholics," *Archives of General Psychiatry* 12 (1965), pp. 456-463.
22. E.M. Pattison, "A Critique of Abstinence Criteria in the Treatment of Alcoholism," *International Journal of Social Psychiatry* 14 (1968), p. 268-270.
23. R. Akers, *Deviant Behavior. A Social Learning Approach* (Belmont, California: Wadsworth Publishing Co., Inc., 1973).
24. E. Cheraskin, M.D., *Psychodietetics* (Briarcliff Manor, N.Y.: Stein and Day Publishers, 1974). pp. 43-56.
25. Ibid., p. 45.
26. Ibid., p. 49.
27. Alexander, G. Schauss, *Diet, Crime and Delinquency* (Berkeley, California: Parker House, 1980).
28. Cheraskin, *Psychodietetics*, op. cit., p. 51.
29. Nancy Yakes and Denise Akey (eds.), *Encyclopedia of Associations*, Vol. 1 (Detriot: Gale Research Co., 1980), p. 743.
30. Lewis Yablonsky, *Synanon: The Tunnel Back* (Baltimore, Md.: Penguin Books, 1967).
31. Louis P. Carney, *Corrections and the Community* (Englewood Cliffs, N.J.: Prentice Hall, Inc., 1977), pp. 162-163.
32. Joseph A. Shelby and Alexander Bassin, "Daytop Lodge: Halfway House for Drug Addicts," *Federal Probation* 28, 4 (December 1964), pp. 46-55.
33. Michael S. Serrill, "From 'Bums' to Businessmen: The Delancey Street Foundation," *Corrections Magazine*, 1, 1 (September 1974), pp. 3-13.
34. John Blackmore, "Prescription: Methadone," *Corrections Magazine*, 5 (December 1979), p. 24.
35. Edward W. Soden, "The Need for Realistic Treatment of Alcohol and Drug Addiction," *Federal Probation*, 37 (March 1973), pp. 40-42.
36. Carney, *Corrections and the Community*, op. cit., p. 171.

37. Ibid., p. 154-175.
38. Soden, "Realistic Treatment," op. cit., p. 42.
39. Personal visitation, 1972-1973.
40. Blackmore, "Prescription: Methadone," op. cit.
41. Ibid.
42. Schauss, *Diet, Crime and Delinquency,* op. cit.
43. Tom Monte, "Is America Going Crazy? A Nutritional Approach to Mental Health," *East-West Journal* 10, 9 (September 1980), p. 41.
44. Daniel Glaser, *The Effectiveness of a Prison and Parole System* (Indianapolis: Bobbs-Merrill, 1964), p. 329.
45. Mitchell W. Dale, "Barriers to the Rehabilitation of Ex-Offenders," in *Introduction to Corrections,* George G. Killinger and Paul F. Cromwell, Jr. (eds.) (St. Paul, Minn.: West Publishing, 1978), p. 354.
46. Ibid., p. 353.
47. Ibid.
48. Ibid., p. 357.
49. Ibid., p. 358.
50. Ibid., p. 361.
51. "The Fortune Society," pamphlet published by The Fortune Society, 229 Park Avenue So., New York, N.Y.
52. Bill Sands, *My Shadow Ran Fast* (Englewood Cliffs, N.J.: Prentice Hall, Inc., 1964), p. 205.
53. Yakes and Akey (eds.), *Encyclopedia of Associations,* op. cit., p. 698.
54. Ibid., p. 704.
55. The National Alliance of Businessmen, *Corrections Magazine* 3 (4), December 1977, p. 56.
56. Personal communication with state coordinator, Jim Huttenhoff, July 1980.
57. For more information regarding CETA programs for offenders, see Osa D. Coffey, "What's In It For Offenders? New CETA Legislation," *Corrections Today,* 41, 1 (Jan.-Feb. 1979), pp. 8-9.
58. Clearinghouse on Offender Employment Restrictions, *Employing the Ex-Offender: Some Legal Considerations* (Washington, D.C.: U.S. Government Printing Office, November 1976), p. 1.
59. U.S. Department of Justice, *The Transition from Prison to Employment: An Assessment of Community-Based Assistance Programs* (Washington, D.C.: U.S. Printing Office, July 1978). By Mary A. Toborg, Lawrence J. Center, Raymond H. Milkman and Dennis W. Davis.
60. Ibid.
61. Quote taken from the Ford Foundation's advertisement for their film *They Call It Wildcat.* Ford Foundation Films, New York, New York, 1980.
62. *Ruffin v. Commonwealth,* 62 Va (21 Gratt) 790, 796 (1871) as cited in Sheldon Krantz, *Corrections and Prisoners' Rights* (St. Paul, Minn.: West Publishing Co., 1976), p. 98.
63. *Bounds v. Smith,* 430 U.S. 817 (1977).
64. *Ex parte Hull,* 312 U.S. 546 (1941).
65. *Johnson v. Avery,* 393 U.S. 483 (1969); aff'd *Younger v. Gilmore,* 404 U.S. 15 (1974), footnote 10.

66. Geoffrey P. Alpert and Neal Miller, "Legal Delivery Systems to Prisoners: A Preliminary Evaluation," *The Justice System Journal: A Management Review* 4 (1), 1978, pp. 9-25.

67. Ibid., p. 10.

68. R.F. Conner, W. Davidson, and J. Emshoff, *Legal Aid and Legal Education for Prisoners: An Evaluation of the State Bar of Michigan's Prison Project* (Washington, D.C.: American Bar Association, 1978).

69. Alpert and Miller, "Legal Delivery Systems," op. cit., p. 12, footnote 22.

70. Ibid., p. 13.

71. Another state has been New York State. See *Corrections Digest* 7 (11), June 2, 1976, p. 4 for details.

72. Geoffrey P. Alpert, John M. Finney and James F. Short, Jr., "Legal Services, Prisoners' Attitudes and Rehabilitation," *The Journal of Criminal Law and Criminology* 69 (4), 1978, pp. 616-626.

73. Ibid., p. 624.

74. Alpert and Miller "Legal Delivery Systems," op. cit., p. 14.

75. Alpert, Finney and Short, "Legal Services," op. cit., p. 624.

76. Alpert and Miller, "Legal Delivery Systems," op. cit., p. 14.

77. Mike McCartt, "New Cincinnati Program Offers One-Stop Service," *American Journal of Correction* 40 (5), September 1978, pp. 22-23.

78. Negley K. Teeters, "The Early Days of the Magdallen Society of Philadelphia," *The Social Service Review* 30, No. 2 (June 1956), 158-167.

79. The American Bar Association and the Commission on Correctional Facilities and Services has developed a National Resource Center on Women Offenders. In bi-monthly reports, accurate information is gathered and disseminated on the woman offender. See also: Law Enforcement Assistance Administration (LEAA) Task Force on Women, *The Report of the LEAA Task Force on Women* (Washington, D.C.: LEAA, 1975).

80. *Women Behind Bars; An Organizing Tool* (Washington, D.C.: Resources for Community Change, 1975), p. 22.

81. Ibid.

82. Ibid., p. 24.

83. Ibid., pp. 27-28.

84. *Women Offenders* (Lincoln, Nebraska: CONtact, Inc., 1977), p. 14.

85. Ibid., p. 71.

86. Ibid., p. 112.

Subject Index

DATE DUE